Herman Melville
and the American Calling

Herman Melville and the American Calling

The Fiction after *Moby-Dick*, 1851–1857

WILLIAM V. SPANOS

Published by
State University of New York Press, Albany

© 2008 State University of New York

All rights reserved

Printed in the United States of America

No part of this book may be used or reproduced in any manner whatsoever without written permission. No part of this book may be stored in a retrieval system or transmitted in any form or by any means including electronic, electrostatic, magnetic tape, mechanical, photocopying, recording, or otherwise without the prior permission in writing of the publisher.

For information, contact State University of New York Press, Albany, NY
www.sunypress.edu

Production by Cathleen Collins
Marketing by Fran Keneston

Library of Congress Cataloging in Publication Data

Spanos, William V.
 Herman Melville and the American calling : fiction after Moby-Dick, 1851–1857 / William V. Spanos.
    p. cm.
 Includes bibliographical references and index.
 ISBN 978-0-7914-7563-8 (hardcover : alk. paper)
 ISBN 978-0-7914-7564-5 (pbk. : alk. paper)
 1. Melville, Herman, 1819–1891—Criticism and interpretation. 2. Melville, Herman, 1819–1891—Political and social views. 3. National characteristics, American, in literature. 4. Imperialism in literature. 5. Politics and literature—United States—History—19th century. 6. Political fiction, American—History and criticism. I. Title.

PS2388.P6S73 2008
813'.3—dc22   2007047987

10 9 8 7 6 5 4 3 2 1

For my son, Adam,
A New American,
with love and . . . alicrosity

If thou beest a man that lives without a calling, though thou hast two thousands to spend, yet if thou hast no calling tending to public good, thou art an unclean beast.

—John Cotton, "Christian Calling"

In the ordinary use of the term *subject* in fact means (1) a free subjectivity, a centre of initiatives, author of and responsible for its actions; (2) a subjected being, who submits to a higher authority, and is therefore stripped of all freedom except that of freely accepting his submission. This last note gives us the meaning of this ambiguity, which is merely a reflection of the effect which produces it; the individual *is interpellated as a free subject in order that he shall submit freely to the commandments of the Subject, i.e. in order that he shall (freely) accept his subjection*, i.e. in order that he shall make the gestures and actions of his subjection "all by himself." *There are no subjects except by and for their subjection.* That is why they "work by themselves."

—Louis Althusser, "Ideology and Ideological States Apparatuses"

It is therefore, a source of great virtue for the practiced mind to learn, bit by bit, first to change about in visible and transitory things, so that afterwards it may be able to leave them behind altogether. The person who finds his homeland sweet is still a tender beginner; he to whom every soil is as his native one is already strong; but he is perfect to whom the entire world is as a foreign place. The tender soul has fixed his love on one spot in the world; the strong person has extended his love to all places; the perfect man has extinguished his.

—Victor of St. Hugo, *Didascalicon*,
quoted by Edward W. Said in *Culture and Imperialism*

Contents

Acknowledgments	xi
Chapter 1. Melville's Specter: An Introduction	1
Chapter 2. Pierre's Extraordinary Emergency: Melville and the "Voice of Silence"	19
Chapter 3. Herman Melville's *Israel Potter*: Reflections on a Damaged Life	57
Chapter 4. "Benito Cereno" and "Bartleby, the Scrivener": Reflections on the American Calling	105
1. "Benito Cereno": The "Vision" of American Exceptionalism	105
2. "Bartleby, the Scrivener: A Wall-Street Story": Melville's Politics of Refusal	140
Chapter 5. Cavilers and Con Men: *The Confidence-Man: His Masquerade*	167
Chapter 6. American Confidence in the Age of Globalization: Melville's Witness	213
Notes	229
Index	271

Acknowledgments

Many years ago, in 1978 specifically, during a conference "On Problems of Reading in Contemporary American Criticism" sponsored by a then young *boundary 2* searching for an intellectual identity that would be commensurate to the polyvalent significance of the reference to cultural border-crossing in its title, I found myself in a conversation with Edward Said about the talk he had just delivered. This was the great, groundbreaking essay, "Reflections on American 'Left' Criticism," which, more than anything else, stalled the momentum of deconstruction, inaugurated at the conference on structuralism at Johns Hopkins (1966) that introduced Jacques Derrida to American literary criticism, and reoriented critical attention to the "worldliness" of the text and criticism to the sites of culture and politics. Somewhere along the line, he said to me in the playfully severe manner that was his style, "Bill, you're a pretty good critic, but why do you insist on contaminating your criticism with all that Heideggerian ontology?" I was taken aback, since I knew that he was referring not simply to the "worldlessness" of Heidegger's thinking, but also his complicity with Nazism. Having been deeply engaged by his powerful demonstration of the *"trahison des clercs"* of the American "Left," his remark momentarily obliterated from my mind the impression that what I had heard was not incompatible, despite the different registers of our concerns, with my own critical consciousness. But somehow, maybe out of self-defense or simply the pleasure of responding contrapuntally, I replied, "Edward, you're a pretty good critic, but why do you limit your criticism by avoiding all this Heideggerian ontology?" We both laughed and let it go at that. Curiously, however, on the rare occasions that our paths crossed over the ensuing years, it was that conversation that we recalled each time without fail.

I doubt very much that my response made any difference to Edward Said's thinking, but his criticism of my predilection for ontological representation, however playful, made a great impact on me. Hitherto, in the heady days of the late 1960s and early 1970s, when the disclosures of the repressiveness of Western logocentric thinking by poststructuralist theory—we used the phrase "the will to power" to refer to its operations—seemed to be affiliated with the social and political practices of the protest against the Vietnam War, the civil rights initiative, and the feminist movement, I all too easily assumed that the interrogation of the metaphysical philosophical tradition was a form of political practice and, thus, contributed to the promise of revolution. That conversation with Said disabused me of this assumption. I did not abandon my ontological perspective—or Heidegger, for that matter. But I did begin to think more intensely the relationship between ontology—and the question of thinking as such—and the spectrum of political practices. In the process I came to realize, rightly or wrongly, that we were both right and wrong: that insofar as I privileged the question of being in my interrogation of literary texts, I was, indeed, minimizing the importance of their worldly being in the operations of power; but also, that insofar as Said privileged the question of the worldliness of literary texts—their cultural and political being—he was minimizing the importance of ontological representation in the operations of power. Indeed, I will go so far as to say that the impasse in which the contemporary critical consciousness at large, but especially in America, finds itself at the present historical conjuncture—an impasse manifest in its impotence in the face of the resurgence of an American exceptionalism that, in its unilateral suspension of international law and human rights in the name of the state of exception, seems indifferent to the global cataclysm it is likely to produce—is largely the result not simply of the fateful dissociation of the ontological from the political sites on the continuum of being (gender, race, class, cultures, nations) but, under the aegis of fashion, of forcing these indissoluble related sites into a binary opposition.

I am not certain that Edward Said would approve of this diagnosis of the contemporary critical occasion. I am certain, sadly, that many of his ephebes in the academy would strongly disapprove. So be it. I have invoked this anecdote from a bygone time not for the sake of controversy, but to suggest that this book on Herman Melville's fiction after *Moby-Dick*, as I'm sure it will be seen by those who are familiar with Said's work, constitutes in some fundamental ways an *Auseinandersetzung* with him—a continuation of that apparently innocuous dialogic moment, so long ago, that inaugurated the supreme theme of my intellectual labors. Not least of these ways is my foregrounding of the American "isolato's" symptomatic struggle to expose the life-damaging yea-saying politics of the American exceptionalist interpretation of being—and the life-affirming nay-saying politics latent in that "non-being" of the American interpretation of being.

In the process of writing this book, I incurred far too many intellectual debts to be able to acknowledge them meaningfully here. Nevertheless, I would be remiss not to mention two Americanist scholars whose work is, in my mind, indispensable to anyone working in American literary studies. The first of these is Sacvan Bercovitch, who has demonstrated beyond doubt the Puritan origins of the American self. Without the benefit of his magisterial work on the Puritan legacy, I could not have perceived Melville's subversion of the American exceptionalist problematic as a proleptic subversion of contemporary America's "errand in the [global] wilderness," nor his subversion of the Puritan elect/preterite opposition as an anticipation of a yet to be fully articulated mode of warding off the otherwise irresistible contemporary American apparatuses of capture. The second is Donald E. Pease, my *boundary 2* colleague and dear friend, who, over the many years of our relationship, has not only undeviatingly encouraged me in my intellectual errancy, but also taught me, by the remarkable example of the sustained brilliance of his work, how to read American literature. Though I have explicitly and indirectly disagreed with Bercovitch and Pease about certain aspects of their reading of Melville and his American occasion, I have undertaken these out of admiration, not in the spirit of antagonism, but of collaboration. It goes without saying that I take responsibility for whatever distortions I have inflicted on the texts and ideas of those whom I have invoked in behalf of my argument in this revisionary book.

I also wish to thanks my student Taras Sak for proofreading the manuscript and for making valuable suggestions about style and content along the way; Ivy Wilson, of the English Department of Notre Dame, for allowing me to read his brilliant unpublished essays on *Israel Potter* and "The Paradise of Bachelors and the Tartarus of Maids"; and Joseph Buttigieg, whose invitation to speak at a conference on "Forms of Empire" at Notre Dame in May of 2005 enabled me to think more deeply the relationship between Melville's *Confidence-Man* and the neo-con-men in the current presidential administration who, contemptuous of history, are "creating [their] own reality," while we scholars, as one of them has been reported to have said, merely study it. Not least, I want to express my gratitude to Larin McLaughlin, my editor at SUNY Press, for her faith in my work, despite the controversial nature of its content, and for her graciousness all through the long process of seeing it into print. Thanks, as well, to Ruth Stanek, assistant to the chair of the Binghamton University English Department, and Anita Pisani, secretary to the chair, for all their generous help in preparing my manuscript for submission; and to the editorial and production staffs of SUNY Press, particularly Cathleen Collins, who saw the book through the process of publication.

Finally, it gives me great pleasure to acknowledge my gratitude to Charles Hewitt, a Melville enthusiast and extraordinary painter, for permission to use his untitled work from his great series of paintings "illustrating" Melville's *Moby-Dick* as the cover of this book, and to Geoffrey Gould for capturing its angry essence in his reproduction of Hewitt's painting.

On a more personal level, I wish to thank Susan Strehle for her deep and unwavering friendship in a trying time, for her kind encouragement of my work, and, not least, for reading the entire manuscript with inordinate care, editing my infelicities, and suggesting substantial revisions that have, in my mind, added scope and depth to my argument about Melville. Above all, I also want to express my gratitude to our son, Adam, to whom I dedicate this book. While I was working on the last chapters, he was writing an undergraduate honors thesis on Melville's "Benito Cereno" and Graham Greene's *The Quiet American*. It pleases me immensely to be able to say that this coincidence provided me, not with a sounding board for my thoughts, but an enthusiastic dialogic partner whose comments have contributed significantly to the deepening of my sense of Melville's contemporaneity. But it is not only for this that I am grateful to him. Not long ago, at a time I was beginning to think that intellectual work in America was futile, I was, by accident, rummaging through the drawers of a desk in my outer office that I had not opened in years. In one of them I came across a sheet of faded white paper that turned out to contain a message Adam, at the age of eleven, had scrawled out with a pencil to himself in his characteristically decisive yet errant hand. It read:

THE PLAN

FIRST, I must prove to Polly that I love the game of tennis.
SECOND, I must develop an endurance-riding course.
THIRD, I must read at least 20 books this summer.
FOURTH, I must learn to deal with life with fierce alacrosity.
    Then, I will
      be ready
        for
      seventh
       grade.

It was that message, bursting out of the distant past like a shoot of green grass out of concrete, not least the irrepressible force of the polyvalent word "alicrosity," that by a similar process of association of discordant temporal motifs convinced me of the viability and urgency of the new Americanist project.

An earlier version of chapter 1 was previously published as "Pierre's Extraordinary Emergency: Melville and the Voice of Silence, Part 1," *boundary 2*, 28, 2 (Summer 2001), 105–131 and "Pierre's Extraordinary Emergency: Melville and the Voice of Silence, Part 2," *boundary 2*, 28, 3 (Fall 2003), 133–155. I wish to thank the editor of *boundary 2*, Paul A. Bové, and Duke University Press for granting me permission to reprint.

Chapter 1

Melville's Specter

An Introduction

> It is common knowledge that nomads fare miserably under our kinds of regime: we will go to any lengths in order to settle them.
>
> —Gilles Deleuze, "Nomadic Thought"

In the last chapter of my book *The Errant Art of* Moby-Dick*: The Canon, the Cold War, and the Struggle for American Studies*, published a decade ago, I concluded that Melville's revolutionary novel

> speaks resonantly across the great divide of time not to (American) Man but to the present historical occasion. It is not, to extend a resonant motif in Michel Foucault, simply a genealogy, a "history of [Melville's] present": it is also a history of the American future of the present historical occasion that we precariously inhabit. This . . . is not only because Melville proleptically delegitimized the Cold War discourse of the founders of American literary studies—whom we can now call the Custodians of the American Cultural Memory. It is also and more importantly—if less discursively—because, in anticipating the self-destruction of the American episteme in the Vietnam War, it proleptically delegitimized the discourse of the New World Order.[1]

Since then, the world has borne witness to the systematic effort of the American political elite and the culture industry that reproduces its truth to recuperate the American exceptionalist national identity, to rehabilitate the reputation of the American military establishment, and to reaffirm America's missionary "errand in the [global] wilderness," all of which had been discredited by the arrogant incompetence of the Pentagon planners—"the best and the brightest"[2]—and the military command that executed their optimistic scenarios, the murderous excesses of violence perpetrated by the United States against a Southeast Asian colonial people struggling for self-determination, the vulgar prevarications of its leadership to the American public about the progress of the war, and, of course, its humiliating defeat at the hands of an infinitely less powerful army of insurgents. This massive recuperative effort at rewriting history was realized between the dubiously decided presidential election of 2000, which brought an intensely nationalist president, George W. Bush and a neoconservative executive leadership to power, and September 11, 2001, when the attacks by Al Qaeda on the World Trade Center buildings in New York and the Pentagon in Washington consolidated the media and the American public and enabled the new administration to launch its "war on terror." This initiative, it must not be overlooked, has also involved not simply the tacit, if unofficial, annunciation of a state of national emergency, but, given the indefiniteness of the "enemy" in a "war on terror," the making of the state of exception permanent, the fundamental purpose of which, to appropriate a phrase addressed by one of the custodians of American culture to the readers of Melville's novel *Pierre*, is to "freeze" dissent in the United States "into [perpetual] silence." So arrogantly confident has the history of forgetting made this neoconservative leadership that it can announce with the certitude of impunity—and in a dehumanized managerial language that resonates with what Hannah Arendt called "the banality of evil"—that they need not be accountable to history, since it is they who produce reality:

> The aide said that guys like me were "in what we call the reality-based community," which he defined as people who "believe that solutions emerge from your judicious study of discernible reality." I nodded and murmured something about enlightenment principles and empiricism. He cut me off. "That's not the way the world really works anymore," he continued. "We're an empire now, and when we act, we create our own reality. And while you're studying that reality—judiciously, as you will—we'll act again, creating other new realities, which you can study too, and that's how things will sort out. We're history's actors . . . and you, all of you, will be left to just study what we do."[3]

To this end, the Bush administration, in an awesome reduction of historical reality reminiscent of Captain Ahab's ontological reduction of "all that most maddens and torments . . . ; all that cracks the sinews and cakes the brain; all the subtle demonisms of life and thought" to Moby Dick, personified the complex and volatile history of the Middle East, in large part the result of the ravages of British and French imperialism, and, more recently, American Cold War policy, in the figure of Osama bin Laden to make "it" "practically assailable."[4] What ensued was, first, "the shock and awe" preemptive invasion of Afghanistan in the name of "civilization" (regime change) and then, following the willful and duplicitous substitution of Saddam Hussein for Osama bin Laden as the United States' Moby Dick, the invasion of Iraq and defeat of Hussein's army and an occupation that, in the process of willfully imposing an American-style (ventriloquized) democracy on a recalcitrant and highly diverse Islamic people, has precipitated a guerrilla war all too reminiscent of the "quagmire" that Vietnam became. Analogous in so many ways to the Viet Cong's strategy of resistance, the Iraqi's resistance to the United States' occupation seems to be characterized by an awareness and exploitation of the "strength" of the Western "imperialist" occupier: they refuse in their tactics to be answerable to the deeply backgrounded and polyvalent instrumentalist ("can do") comportment toward being of the occupying enemy, the beginning-middle-end narrative, the forwarding/progressive orientation this temporal structure enables, and the "decisive victory," which resolves the conflict of differences into the same.

In other words, the figure of Melville I drew from my reading of *Moby-Dick* in 1995, continues to speak significantly and in a fundamental way to the present American occasion, indeed, more so now, it seems, than then. This is one of the reasons why I decided, in the wake of the announcement of America's "war on terror" after 9/11/01 to undertake this second study of Melville's fiction, this time focusing on some of the texts Melville wrote between the publication of *Moby-Dick* and *The Confidence-Man*, the last work of fiction he published in his lifetime: *Pierre; or the Ambiguities* (1852); "Bartleby the Scrivener" (1853); *Israel Potter: His Fifty Years of Exile* (1855); "Benito Cereno" (1855); and *The Confidence-Man: His Masquerade* (1857). The other, equally important, reason is that recent "New Americanists," however attuned to Melville's relevance to the contemporary American sociopolitical occasion, have not adequately dissociated the revolutionary Melville from the Melville of the liberal humanists of the Revival in the 1920s and the Melville of the Cold War founders of American literary studies in the mid-1950s, nor have they adequately conveyed his powerful witness to the dark side of America's exceptionalist errand.

A telling symptom of this failure announced itself glaringly at the very moment I began writing this preface. In reading Bill Ayer's account of the 1968 Democratic National Convention in Chicago in *Fugitive Days* (2001), the moving memoir of one of the Weather Underground, who resisted American racism and the United States' arrogant and brutal intervention in Vietnam, not as a reformer but as a revolutionary, I came across this startlingly traditional liberal humanist reading of *Moby-Dick*:

> Mayor Richard Daley played a perfect Moby Dick for us. . . . After King was assassinated and Daly's cops buckled before the ensuing fury, he called out the National Guard and troops and tanks

rolled down Madison Avenue, up Austin Boulevard. Daly issued his famous "shoot to kill/shoot to maim" orders then.... We girded our loins and sharpened our spears, preparing for the monster.

Our Captain Ahab was Tom Hayden, former president of SDS, now leader of the National Mobilization to End the War, the coalition leading the convention protest.[5]

The differential being—the very (non)object of the Weather Underground's care—that Melville represents in his novel as the intended victim of Captain Ahab's monomania, becomes personified in the figure of Mayor Daly, and the paranoid American exceptionalist perpetrator of the violence against differential being, one of the heroes of the protest movement. This, it should not be overlooked, was not written in 1968, when Captain Ahab was still more or less universally read and taught either as the ideal humanist battling heroically against an indifferent and violent nature or as the essence of American democratic man in his struggle against all forms of totalitarianism. It was written in 2001, in the wake of the end of the Cold War and America's announcement of the end of history and the advent of a New World Order under the aegis of the United States on the eve of 9/11/01.

I

What precisely makes these texts written by a very young Melville (he was, we need constant reminding, only thirty-two years old in 1851 when he published *Moby-Dick*) in the brief six or seven years between the publication of *Pierre* and *The Confidence-Man* so relevant to the contemporary post-9/11 occasion? To proffer some semblance of an answer to this question it will be necessary to go by way of a brief detour into the erratic history of the reception by the custodians of American culture of Melville's fiction after *Moby-Dick*. Such a detour is necessary because, among other reasons, Melville's creative production was, perhaps more than that of any other writer in the history of American literature, absolutely tethered to the reception of his work. It was not only that he committed himself at the outset of his career to earn his living by writing, but also that he wrote in a transitional society that, however conscious of the need to break the stranglehold English culture had on American writing, was lacking in cultural sophistication. This condition was amply demonstrated long ago by Perry Miller in *The Raven and the Whale*, which chronicles the flailing, moralist-bound efforts of the "Young Americans" under Evert Duyckinck, Cornelius Matthews, Jedediah B. Auld, and William Alfred Jones, to wrest control over the American literary imagination from the New York

"Knickerbocker Set," under Louis Gaylord Clark, whose model remained English literature.[6]

I have addressed the question of the volatile history of the reception of Melville's books *in The Errant Art of Moby-Dick*, but here I want to underscore an aspect of my analysis of this biographical/authorship issue that, however central to my reading of the novel, I had not fully developed in that book: the curious *anxiety (Angst)*—I use this word in the Heideggerian sense appropriated by many poststructuralist theorists[7]—Melville's fiction from *Moby-Dick* to the *Confidence-Man* has consistently activated in those journalists and academic critics who have assumed the responsibility of articulating Melville's place in the American canon; since it has "no thing" as its object, this anxiety could be equally related to the notion of *spectrality*. Despite the mixed reviews of *Moby-Dick*, which had as much to do with the bafflement over the novel's elusive structure—Evert Dyckinck, for example, called it "an intellectual chowder of romance, philosophy, natural history, fine writing, good feeling, bad sayings"[8]—that, following the formal experimentation in *Mardi*, replaced the "simple" narrative structure of the earlier realistic novels of adventure, as with its "raving," Melville was still considered to be an American writer of considerable "promise." With the publication of *Pierre; or the Ambiguities*, however, things changed radically. The reviewers at large undeviatingly condemned it as an outrage against American writing and American sexual and social morality, and/or as the depraved raving of a madman, all ostensibly lamenting his "desertion of the forecastle and the virgin forest, for the drawing room and modest boarding-house chamber."[9] Of these reviews, one of the most self-righteously incensed was that of the influential critic of *The American Review* (later renamed *The American Whig Review*) George Washington Peck,[10] whose language in his vitriolic attack was to become prophetic. I quote this representative review at some length both to recall the ferocity of the self-righteous moralistic attack on Melville's *Pierre* mounted by the antebellum (often racist) custodians of American culture and to underscore the resonant historical irony—one this book will make much of—informing the intended consequence of this unrelentingly negative criticism:

> It is not much matter if South Sea savages are painted like the heroes of a penny theatre, and disport themselves amid pasteboard groves, and lakes of canvas. We can afford Mr. Melville full license to do what he likes with "Omoo" and its inhabitants; it is only when he presumes to thrust his tragic *Fantoccini* upon us, as representatives of our own race, *that we feel compelled to turn our critical Aegis upon him, and freeze him into silence.* . . . It is always an unpleasant . . . statement for a critic to make, that he can find nothing worthy of praise in a work under consideration;

but in the case of Pierre we feel bound to add to the assertion the sweeping conclusion, that there we find everything to condemn. If a repulsive unnatural and indecent plot, *a style disfigured by every paltry affectation of the worst German school*, and ideas perfectly unparalleled for earnest absurdity, are deserving of condemnation, we think that *our already expressed sentence upon Pierre will meet with the approval of every body who has sufficient strength of mind to read it through.* . . .

Now, in this matter [the ambiguity of Pierre's relationship with Isabel] has done a very serious thing, which not even unsoundness of intellect could excuse. He might have been mad to the very pinnacle of insanity; he might have torn our poor language into tatters, and made from the shreds a harlequin suit in which to play up word upon word, and adjective upon adjective, until he had built a pyramid of nonsense, which should last to the admiration of all men; he might have done all this and a great deal more, and we should not have complained. But when he dares to outrage every principle of virtue; when he strikes with an impious, though, happily, weak hand, at the very foundations of society, *we feel it our duty to tear off the veil with which he was thought to soften the hideous features of the idea, and warn the public against the reception of such atrocious doctrines.* If Mr. Melville had reflected at all . . . his better sense would perhaps have informed him that *there were certain ideas so repulsive to the general mind that they themselves are not alone kept out of sight, but, by a fit ordination of society, everything that might be supposed to even collaterally suggest them is carefully shrouded in a decorous darkness.* Nor has any man the right, in his morbid craving after originality, to strip these horrors of their decent mystery.[11] (My emphasis)

What needs to be stressed is that the point of view informing Peck's apparently astonishing judgment against Melville in the wake of the publication of *Pierre* is not unique. It is, in fact, characteristic of the perspective of the great majority of the reviewers, although he spells out the moral and social issues more fully than they do.[12] That is to say, Peck's outrage constitutes something like a synecdoche of antebellum American cultural identity, a dilettante elitist identity, as the underscored text clearly suggests, informed by an evangelical Christianity that is indissolubly related to a severely narrow sexual, familial, and national morality that resonates with vestiges of Puritanism; a racism associated with cultural, if not exactly political imperialism; an exceptionalist disdain for the decadent affectations of European culture; an absolute certainty of the rightness of the practical, simple, homely, ethos of the American way; a blindness, in the name of the "proper," to the hypocrisy of a comportment toward being that would at all costs "shroud" whatever threatens the truth, stability, and wholeness of this American world "in a decorous darkness"; and, not least, insofar as the American critic sees him- or herself as the custodian of the American cultural memory, a commitment to monumental history. The reviewers of Melville's book, whether those who referred to his writing as the "ravings" of a madman or, those, like Peck, who condemned its content and style as morally decadent, would, like Medusa's gaze, "freeze" Melville's daringly originative and differential voice—its unflinching acknowledgment of the "ambiguities" of being—"into silence" in the name of the exceptional status, the integrity, and the oneness of "America."

The impact of this sustained assault on Melville's will to write was clearly dislocating, given his commitment to making his living by writing. Despite the insistent advice from reviewers to return to the kind of adventurous seafaring fiction that had gained him a substantial readership, he nevertheless resisted the temptation, even as he notified his publishers, as he did Putnam, "that the story [of Israel Potter] shall contain nothing of any sort to shock the fastidious" and that, "there will be very little reflective writing in it; nothing weighty."[13] Indeed, in the process of the next six years, during which Melville published the transgressive texts I will address in this book, his resistance became increasingly affirmative until it culminated in the generically undecidable *The Confidence-Man* in 1857, the last fiction he would publish during his lifetime.

The consequence of this great refusal to be answerable to what I have referred to as "the American Calling" in my title—and to which I will return at length in chapter IV on "Benito Cereno" and "Bartleby, the Scrivener"—was, indeed, the "freez[ing] of [Melville] into silence." In the aftermath of the publication of *The Confidence-Man*, Melville, at the age of thirty-eight, was all too rapidly marginalized, if not entirely forgotten, both by American critics and the reading public in the United States until the so-called Melville Revival of the 1920s. But this exilic silence, as its verbal prominence in *Pierre* testifies, is a resonant silence. It is a silence, in other words, that, in Edward Said's words, *speaks* the truth to the power of the hegemonic discourse that had exiled and silenced Melville—the discourse I have provisionally identified above as the antebellum version of the American exceptionalist problematic[14]—in a "language" that is utterly *other* than or, rather, the other *of* this "totalizing" and "silencing" discourse.

The Melville Revival of the 1920s did not bring this national amnesia to its end; this long "sleep," to a "great awakening"; or, to use the metaphorics central to my book, this long interment of Melville's fiction to a decisive and joyous resurrection as it is now all to often asserted by his "liberal" exponents. On the contrary, the history of the reception of Melville's writing since then makes it forcefully evident that the Revival of the 1920s was in some fundamental way instigated by the unallayable force of Melville's subversive exilic imagination. Far more conversant with the complexities of the ontological, aesthetic, critical, cultural, and sociopolitical character of American life than their antebellum predecessors, the literary critics of the post–World War I Revival were also that much more attuned to the richness, the originality, the force, and the scope and depth—and in a subliminal way, the dangerous subversiveness—of his critical understanding of America. They were thus compelled by this haunting knowledge to reexamine the fiction beginning with *Moby-Dick* in the light of their contemporary postwar moment, which is to say, at a time when (1) the relationship between humanism and democracy had perforce become a major intellectual, cultural, and educational issue in the United States,[15] (2) the Puritan ethic was rapidly metamorphosing into the spirit of capitalism; and (3) this momentum toward the vulgarization and disintegration of American culture was envisioned as under threat from the influx of southern Europeans into the factory cities and towns of the Northeast. The result of this rethinking was not the rehabilitation of Melville's late fiction at large—*Pierre* and *The Confidence-Man*, for example, remained tainted by the stigma of insanity—but the apotheosis of *Moby-Dick* as the great American novel. However, this canonization or, to invoke an analogous term that has great symbolic prominence in Melville's post–*Moby-Dick* fiction, most notably, *Pierre* and *Israel Potter*, this *monumentalization* of Melville's elusive novel was not based on the subversive aspects of his fiction that had haunted his contemporary critics to the point of compelling them to silence him. On the contrary, these liberal humanist American critics, as I argued in *The Errant Art of* Moby-Dick, in a characteristically democratic ideological maneuver that rendered them (temporarily) immune to the charge of repression, domesticated by *accommodating* Melville's spectral subversions to the *logos* of a secularized elitist version of the American exceptionalist national identity:

> The Melville revival inaugurated by such biographers and critics as Raymond Weaver, John Freeman, Van Wyck Brooks, and Lewis Mumford . . . went far, if not the whole way (a project fulfilled by the next generation of Americanists), to reverse the judgment of the earlier critics, without, however, disturbing the *logos* informing the earlier representation of America's national identity and its canon. The critics of the revival apotheosized *Moby-Dick* as an American masterpiece because it intuited and expressed an essentially *human "spiritual"* Real that, in its integral and universal comprehensiveness, transcended the ideological partiality—the Hebraism, as it were—of American sociopolitical existence, an existence precipitated by the inevitable reduction of the Protestant prohibition of art and the vulgar materialism of post-civil War capitalism. This reversal, based on an "opposition" between the reductive and alienating (repressive) Puritan/capitalist ethos and the "emancipa-

tory" spirit of individual genius (the self-reliant... subject of an earlier American time) is, *mutatis mutandis,* a discursive regularity of the revival criticism of the 1920s. It is also... a reversal based on an opposition that derived as much from Matthew Arnold's "English" classical humanism (the "best self") as from Emerson's "American" transcendentalism.[16]

Melville's status as one of the great American writers was irreversibly established by the critics of the 1920s Revival. But as the turbulence of American literary criticism, particularly Melville studies, since then testifies, Melville's specter does not seem to have been finally laid to rest. Not long after the classical humanist appropriation, another resurgence—or, in the language of *Pierre,* another "extraordinary emergency"—of intense interest in his work occurred, this time in the context of World War II and the founding and institutionalization of American literary studies. But again the focus of this renewed interest was primarily on *Moby-Dick,* and its purpose, like that of its predecessor, was discreetly ideological. Instigated by a strong dissatisfaction with the earlier humanists' tendency to universalize an essentially American novel—the representation of Captain Ahab as tragic Man—these critics—F. O. Mathiessen, but especially Lionel Trilling, Henry Nash Smith, Richard Chase, Harry Levin, Leo Marx, Quentin Anderson, Walter Bezanson, among others, as Donald Pease has decisively shown[17]—appropriated the novel first in behalf of America's war against Nazism and Fascism and then, more decisively, in behalf of the Cold War against Stalinism: however nuanced the argument, Ishmael became the spirit of American democracy and Captain Ahab, the ominous threat of totalitarianism. Thus once again Melville's ontological, moral, and sociopolitical subversions of the American exceptionalist identity enacted in the fiction of the 1850s were reinterpreted coercively (or "overlooked") to enhance the authority of the very national identity Melville was interrogating.

It was not until the "New Americanists," the generation of critics that emerged from the rubble to which the self-destruction of the perennially confident American exceptionalist identity had been reduced during the decade of the Vietnam War, that the subversions of Melville's fiction—specifically its interrogation of the exceptionality of American exceptionalism and the prominence this interrogation gave to the rhetoric and thematics of spectrality—would come to be openly acknowledged. Unlike their predecessors, these New Americanists—precursors such as Richard Slotkin, Michael Paul Rogin, Richard Drinnon, and Sacvan Bercovitch, and practitioners such as Donald Pease, John Carlos Rowe, J. Hillis Miller, Amy Kaplan, Robyn Wiegman, and Eric Cheyfitz, among many others—became increasingly responsive in significant ways to the emergence in Europe of "poststructuralist" theory. This was the antimetaphysical (or -essentialist) theory that not only interrogated the canonical—"logocentric"—ontological, linguistic, psychic, and, to a lesser extent, social and political structures of the Western tradition, but also forced into "visibility" the *nothing* that, as the poststructuralists have shown, essentially *belongs to* the (metaphysical) Being of the West—the *specter* that has always haunted (the peace of) its House. Accordingly, these New Americanists began, if only in an unsystematic way, to take seriously the Melville texts that had been marginalized, above all *Pierre*, *Israel Potter*, and *The Confidence-Man*, in the wake of the retrieval and overdetermination of *Moby-Dick*; more important, they began to identify the ubiquitous ghosts that insistently haunt this uncanny fiction or, more accurately, that instigate anxiety in their American exceptionalist "protagonists," with the *nothing* that the Western tradition, especially in its post-Enlightenment phase, has systematically, which is to say anxiously, "wishe[d] to know nothing about."[18]

I am suggesting, in short, that the "narrative" of Melville's career as an American writer is a mirror image of the "narratives" he wrote after *Moby-Dick*, particularly in the wake of the representation of Melville's originative fiction as the ravings of a madman and/or the blasphemies of a jaded and nihilistic decadent that culminated in the will to "freeze him into silence" by the confident custodians of the American national identity. His biography and the stories he wrote immediately after *Moby-Dick* are, ironically, as I will show, stories of the obsessive effort of the custodians of the dominant (democratic) American culture to "contain," "enclose," "marginalize," "forget," "repress," "inter" (anti-)Americans who, in one way or another, simply *do not answer to* or *refuse to be answerable to* the *call* of the *American narrative*—to take their allotted or proper place in the larger whole whose "center elsewhere"[19] is the (transcendental) Word of the caller. They are, in other words, stories that disclose the American calling to be a willful gesture of summons enabled, indeed, demanded by a plenary philosophy of optimism that, because it is *all*-encompassing (and -embracing), cannot imagine an alternative comportment toward being, yet has always already been fraught with an anxiety that betrays a distrust of this trust. To put it in a way that is reflective of Melville's deepest intention, his stories after *Moby-Dick*, like his refusal to be accountable to his critics, *passively allow* the "can do" logical economy informing the American narrative—the attorney's deeply inscribed need to "do something" in "Bartleby," for example—to "self-destruct": to fulfill its imperatives in order to dis-close in this contradictory "*telos*" not simply the impotent violence latent in its welcoming embrace, but also, the positive possibilities for thinking the decentered, silent, unaccountable, and unnamable (no)thing which this logic would annul—render "accountable"—in the name of truth.

To appropriate the resonant term Giorgio Agamben, a new, "Old World" philosopher, invokes, no doubt against the received negative connotations of the *nothing*, to "identify" the passive copyist who "would prefer not to" in his provocative essay on "Bartleby, the Scrivener," what the always and recalcitrantly open-ended narrative of the history of the reception of Melville's fiction and the deliberately undecidable narratives he wrote between *Moby-Dick* and *The Confidence-Man* dis-close is pure "potentiality."[20] This, in an America that, in the name of the "New World" and its highly prized rhetoric of possibility, reduced the elusive, life-enhancing intensities of potentiality to the comprehensible, which is to say, the takeholdable or manipulable. To sharpen the focus on this thematic itinerary, I have, in this book, as an attentive reader will notice, slightly but pointedly rearranged the order of the publication of those fictions that were written between *Pierre* (1852) and *The Confidence-Man* (1857). "Bartleby" (1853) was published before *Israel Potter* (1854) and "Benito Cereno" (1855), after "Bartleby." It will be seen, however, that (1) I have placed my discussion of *Israel Potter* immediately after *Pierre* in order to highlight the fundamental importance and the continuity of Melville's severe criticism of the indissoluble relationality between American exceptionalism, the calling, monumental history, and nationalism; and (2) my discussion of "Benito Cereno"—its portrayal of Captain Delano as the victim of the American calling (a subjected subject)—before "Bartleby" to highlight the all too often missed positive resonance of Bartleby's—and Melville's—refusal to be answerable to the American calling.

It is this passively induced disclosure of the violence latent in the confidence of New World—exceptionalist—America and, even more important, this retrieval of the potentialities of the nothing from the oblivion to which they has been relegated by the custodians of the cultural memory of the nation, that renders Melville, both the tumultuous vagaries of his status as an American writer, and the recalcitrantly uncontainable fiction he wrote between 1850 and 1857—proleptic of the poststructuralist or postmodern occasion. By this last, I want to make it clear, I mean neither the unworlded world under the aegis of a highly refined unmethodological method diagnosed by Edward Said, nor the commodified world under the aegis of the "logic of late capitalism" diagnosed by Fredric Jameson. I mean, rather, the volatile literary and philosophical moment in Western history that has borne witness to the *symptomatic* self-de-struction or de-centering of the Western representation of being (aided and abetted by various internal and external constituencies of the West's *Others*) in all its manifestations—ontological, subjective, racial, social, political; the e-mergence of the countermemory and what Foucault aptly called "the philosophy of difference";[21] the demise of the self-reliant individual; the collapse of the disciplinarity of knowledge production; the waning of the nation state; the globalization of the hitherto local perspective; the rendering visible of the invisible *of* Western vision; and, not least, the releasement *for positive thought* of those indissolubly related "phenomena" of being—the nothing, temporality, historicity, potentiality, the various *others of* the West—that have been perennially represented as nonentities or nonbeings in the plenary truth discourse of the West. It is no accident that, unlike the fiction of virtually all the other premodern American writers, contemporary critics in the United States and abroad have come to identify Melville's, especially that following *Moby-Dick*, with such global counterclassics as Dostoyevsky's *The Idiot*, Kafka's *The Castle*, Robert Musil's *The Man without Qualities*, Samuel Beckett's *Watt*, and Joyce's *Ulysses*—late nineteenth century and modern European novels that are universally considered to be harbingers of the de-centered postmodern occasion—and are invoked by globally visible postmodern American writers such as Charles Olson, Thomas Pynchon, Robert Coover, Toni Morrison, and Don DeLillo, who identify themselves as his heirs. Nor is it an accident that a number of the revolutionary thinkers who have been identified with the origins and development of what I have been calling the antiphilosophical philosophy of poststructuralism—Jacques Derrida, Maurice Blanchot, Gilles Deleuze, and Giorgio Agamben[22]—have been compelled by the unaccountable force of Melville's philosophical imagination—and language—to perceive him, as they perceive Kierkegaard, Nietzsche, Freud, Heidegger, and a certain Marx, as what Foucault has called "initiators of discursive practices."[23]

But I have not undertaken to rehearse the analogy between the volatile history of the reception of Melville's fiction after *Moby-Dick* and the deliberately elusive thematics and "form" of these dislocating texts simply to suggest Melville's remarkable anticipation of the growing body of contemporary literature and philosophical thought that has had its raison d'être (1) in disclosing the debilitatingly repressive—on occasion annihilating—effects of the thought and the idea of literature that has been privileged by the Western tradition, especially by that optimistic "humanist" phase inaugurated in the Enlightenment, which masquerades as objective or disinterested and open, and, (2) in urging contemporary humanity to think the undecidability—the nothing—thus disclosed positively. My intention has also, and primarily, been to suggest the remarkably proleptic relevance of Melville's post–*Moby-Dick* fiction to the contemporary global sociopolitical occasion, specifically, that which has borne witness to America's declaration of a "war on terror" in the wake of Al Qaeda's attacks on America soil. I mean, more specifically, the occasion in which the American "elect"—empowered by a recuperated exceptionalist national identity, now informed by a rejuvenated and active Protestant evangelical church that overtly refers to America as "the redeemer nation"—has regained its ontological as well as historical confidence in the idea that it is America's manifest destiny to undertake its "benign," divinely or historically ordained, errand in the global wilderness in the "just" name of the *Pax Americana*. Under the aegis of what one of the most influential ideologues of this elect calls the "Anglo-Protestant core culture,"[24] the new American mission resonates with the significance of the title of Cotton Mather's history of the Massachusetts Bay colony, *Magnalia Christi Americana*: "The Great Deeds of Christ in America."

In suggesting the relevance of Melville's post–*Moby-Dick* fiction to the present post-9/11/01 occasion, I am not simply referring to this fiction's genealogical anticipation of the self-destruction of the American exceptionalist ethos during the twenty years of the United States' arrogant and ruthless intervention in Vietnam in the name of "the new frontier"[25]—the repressive violence to which, in the very process of monumentalizing itself, America has been willfully blind. Nor to Melville's anticipation of the poststructuralist exposure of those resilient mechanisms of forgetting and remembering that would enable the dominant culture to recuperate this most crucial ideological source of authority. I am also, and more urgently, referring to Melville's remarkable anticipation of both a mode of warding off or resisting oppression that is more adequate than direct confrontation to the power relations obtaining under the global dispensation of (capitalist) democracy, and, beyond resistance, to a way of comporting one's self toward being, in all its manifestations between thinking and acting, that is attuned to its radical contingency, a way of being "American" that manifests itself when the call to be American is refused.

II

In the chapter in *White-Jacket* (1850) condemning the brutality and "conscious imbecility" of the practice of flogging on board the ships of the American Navy, Melville famously—and problematically—wrote:

> Escaped from the house of bondage, Israel of old did not follow after the ways of the Egyptians. To her was given an express dispensation; to her were given new things under the sun. And we Americans are the peculiar, chosen people—the Israel of our time; we bear the ark of the liberties of the world. . . . We are the pioneers of the world; the advance-guard, sent on through the wilderness of untried things, to break a new path in the New World that is ours. And our youth is our strength; in our inexperience, our wisdom. At a period when other nations have but lisped, our deep voice is heard afar. Long enough have we been skeptical with regard to ourselves, and doubted whether, indeed, the political Messiah had come. But he has come in *us*, if we would but give utterance to his promotings. And let us always remember that with ourselves, almost for the first time in the history of earth, national selfishness is unbounded philanthropy; for we cannot do a good to America but we give alms to the world.[26]

And in the same "euphoric" vein in "Hawthorne and His Mosses":

> This, too, I mean, that if Shakespeare has not been equalled, he is sure to be surpassed, and surpassed by an American born now or yet to be born.... The world is as young today, as when it was created; and this Vermont mountain dew is as wet to my feet, as Eden's dew to Adam's. Nor has Nature been all over ransacked by our progenitors, so that no new charms and mysteries remain for this latter generation to find. Far from it. The trillionth part has not yet been said; and all that has been said, but multiplies the avenues to what remains to be said. It is not so much paucity, as superabundance of material that seems to incapacitate modern authors.[27]

In their seeming invocation of Puritan providential history in the figural mode, these encomia to exceptionalist young America have, no doubt, impeded critical recognition of the revolutionary character of *Moby-Dick* and the fiction that follows it. Indeed, it seems to have compelled even some New Americanists, who rightly identify the Puritans' divinely ordained errand in the wilderness with the origins of American imperialism, to tread gingerly around this issue as it pertains to Melville[28] or, in the case of Wei-chee Dimock, to indict Melville's fiction, most notably *Moby-Dick*, as a celebration of American individualistic liberty that conceals or justifies empire. There are two points about this matter I want to make in a preliminary way. The first is that the passage from *White-Jacket* and the one from the essay on Hawthorne have been taken far too literally by both traditional and revisionist Americanists or, more precisely, the America Melville exalts in them is assumed to be the America exalted by the traditionalists and criticized by the revisionists. Melville, I will claim, is indeed an *American*. It is his raison d'être as a writer. But his American is not and perhaps never was the divinely elected "*Nehemias Americanus*" imagined and institutionalized by the Massachusetts Bay Puritans[29] and then exalted by the post-Revolutionary American Jeremiahs, who secularized his return to Jerusalem out of the Babylonian captivity in the name of Manifest Destiny.[30] Rather, Melville's American is, like Ishmael, an orphan devoid of the burden of parentage, name, and identity, one of those "*no*"-sayers with whom Melville identifies Hawthorne, who, unlike "the *yes*-gentry" that are encumbered by "heaps of baggage," in their journey through the world, are "unencumbered travelers" that "cross frontiers into Eternity with nothing but a carpet bag."[31] He is, in other words, singular: the antithesis of the divinely or historically predestined redeemer. Even more radically, he is decreated man prior to his naming, to his subjection to a higher cause, or what is paradoxically the same thing, his election to lordship over being. He is, to use the language of my title, unaccommodated man prior to his or her *calling* (interpellation) by the transcendental (father's) voice of Europe: *Homo tantum*, as Gilles Deleuze puts it, who "has no other determination than that of being man,"³² or, as Giorgio Agamben characterizes Bartleby, "the extreme figure of the Nothing from which all creation derives; and at the same time . . . the most implacable vindication of this Nothing as pure, absolute potentiality."³³

To put this unencumbered and elusive, indeed, unpresentable figure of Melville's American in the stunningly suggestive, even prophetic, terms Deleuze uses in his great essay on "Bartleby"—they are, not incidentally, remarkably reminiscent of Vico and Said—he is the "pragmatic" American—and the America that never was:

> Pragmatism is misunderstood when it is seen as a summary philosophical theory fabricated by Americans. On the other hand, we understand the novelty of American thought when we see pragmatism as an attempt to transform the world, to think a new world or new men insofar as they *create themselves*. Western philosophy was the skull, or the paternal Spirit that realized itself in the world as totality, and in a knowing subject as proprietor. Is it against Western philosophy that Melville directs his insult, "metaphysical villain"? A contemporary of American transcendentalism (Emerson, Thoreau), Melville is already sketching out the traits of the pragmatism that will be its continuation. It is first of all the affirmation of a world in *process*, an *archipelago*. Not even a puzzle, whose pieces when fitted together would constitute a whole, but rather a wall of loose, uncemented stones, where every element has a value in itself but also in relation to others: isolated and floating relations, islands and straits, immobile points and sinuous lines—for Truth always has "jagged edges." . . . But to reach this point, it was also necessary for the knowing subject, the sole proprietor, to give way to a community of explorers, the brothers of the archipelago, *who replace knowledge with belief, or rather with "confidence"—not belief in another world, but confidence in this one, and in man as much as in God.*
>
> Pragmatism is this double principle of archipelago and hope. And what must the community of men consist of in order for truth to be possible? *Truth* and *Trust*. Like Melville's before it, pragmatism will fight ceaselessly on two fronts: against the particularities that pit man against man and nourish an irremediable mistrust; but also against the Universal or the Whole, the fusion of soul in the name of great love or charity. Yet, what remains of souls once they are no longer attached to particularities, what keeps them from melting into a whole? What remains is precisely their "originality," that is, a sound that each one *produces*, like a ritornello at the limits of language, but that it produces only when it takes to the open road (or to the open sea) with its body, when

it leads its life without seeking salvation, when it embarks upon its incarnate voyage, without any particular aim, and then encounters other voyagers, whom it recognizes by their sound.[34]

Whatever Melville felt about America prior to the publication of *Moby-Dick* in 1851—its founding, its national identity, its mission as a new nation among nations, and the role of the young American writer in this context—it became dramatically clear in the wake of the incredible indifference, if not hostility, of his contemporaries to this great novel, specifically, the general impatience, even resentment, against an imaginative excess that was crossing boundaries beyond which most American writers were unwilling to go, that Melville chose to pursue his de-structive or de-centering cultural/political project, knowing the likely economic consequences that would ensue in refusing to write the "charming" sea stories both his critics and friends were calling on him to write. And with the unequivocal and virtually universal condemnation of his next novel, *Pierre*, as a blasphemous outrage against the American way of life, Melville made a decisive turn. He did not say "NO! in thunder."[35] Rather, like the Bartleby he would imagine shortly after *Pierre*, he said, "I prefer not to"; he simply refused to be answerable to the call of an America that, he felt, had already been corrupted by the elect's will to render every thing and time in being, including the American writer, accountable.

The tension between the deeply backgrounded demand for accountability to the American exceptionalist narrative, on the one hand, and the passive refusal to be answerable to this American calling—a prefiguration, if not an overt manifestation of cultural guerrilla war, as it were—on the other, constitutes, in my mind, the supreme theme not simply of the history of Melville's reception as an American writer of fiction, but also of the fiction I will examine in this book: *Pierre; or the Ambiguities*, "Bartleby, the Scrivener," *Israel Potter: His Fifty Years of Exile*, "Benito Cereno," and *The Confidence-Man: His Masquerade*. It is also, not incidentally, the supreme theme of the exilic Melville's legacy to the present generation, which has borne witness to the annunciation of an unending "war on terror" and a permanent state of exception and is being called to a "Fifth Great Awakening" in the name of the "redeemer nation."

In a recent book rehearsing the history of the critical reception of *Moby-Dick* from the time of its publication to the current poststructuralist occasion, its editor, Nick Selby, insists on the continuous relevance of the novel for the various occasions of America's history:

> *Moby-Dick*'s power, it seems, is one of survival into a precarious future. As testimony to such powers of survival, the history of *Moby-Dick*'s reception is proof of its eloquent ability continuously to reinvent both itself and the culture which gave birth to it.

This pattern of survival seems set by Ishmael's final words, the *Epilogue* of *Moby-Dick*, where we see him as an orphan floating clear of Pequod's wreckage. But even earlier, in chapter 22, "The Doubloon," the survival of *Moby-Dick* in the hands of its readers and critics seems eerily anticipated by Stubb:

There's another rendering now; but still one text.[36]

But in the very process of this demonstration, the author paradoxically continues the tradition inaugurated by Melville's early critics: the tradition beginning with the call to "freeze him into silence" and culminating in the accommodations of the post–World War II critics, who incorporated Melville's heresies into the American exceptionalist problematic in behalf of the United States' global war against the "destabilizing" machinations of the Soviet Union: its extension of the "errand in the wilderness" to include the policing of the globe against "the Red menace." For in asserting cavalierly that the various generations of American (and English) critics have seen *Moby-Dick* as relevant to the particular concerns of their respective historical occasions, this recent author, like so many of his predecessors and contemporaries, is, in fact, universalizing the singularity of the novel and thus not only denying its dense "worldliness," as Said would say, but also, and more important, disarming its devastating historical insight into the exceptionalist American national identity: the perennially negative—and often appallingly inhumane—effects of its "benignity" *before*, *during*, and *after* Melville's time.

In sum, my book will show that Melville's fiction from *Moby-Dick* to *The Confidence-Man*—from his prophetic announcement of the self-destruction of the logical economy of the Adamic ship of state to his decisive de-realization of the antebellum American reality produced by the relay of optimistic philosophies that had their origin in the myth of Puritan election—constitutes a sustained haunting of the exceptionalist problematic, past, present, and future. It will not only reveal the above kind of celebratory commentary to be symptomatic damage-control, an indirect form of silencing that, consciously or not, is, as most of its predecessors, unwittingly complicitous with the discourse that has justified and enabled America's domestic and global depredations. More important, my intention in this book is also to retrieve the worldliness—indeed, the "postmodern" revolutionary force—of Melville's fiction after *Moby-Dick*. It is to show, in other words, that this fiction is, in its spectral "unaccountability," an exemplary mode of indirect resistance to the polyvalent imperialism that inheres in the myth of American exceptionalism, that, therefore, in the language of Edward Said, it speaks the "truth" to the power of American exceptionalism, now, in the wake of the America's annunciation of global "war on terror," which is to say, of a permanent state of exception, as it did in Melville's time.

Chapter 2

Pierre's Extraordinary Emergency

Melville and the "Voice of Silence"

In anxiety, we say, "one feels ill at ease [*es ist einem unheimlich*]." What is "it" that makes "one" feel ill at ease? We cannot say what it is before which one feels ill at ease. As a whole it is so for one. All things and we ourselves sink into indifference. This, however, not in the sense of mere disappearance. Rather in this very receding things turn toward us. The receding of beings as a whole that closes in on us in anxiety oppresses us. We can get no hold on things. In the slipping away of beings only this "no hold on things" comes over us and remains.

—Martin Heidegger, "What Is Metaphysics?"

We must articulate a philosophy of the phantasm that cannot be reduced to a primordial fact through the intermediary of perception or an image, but that arises between surfaces, where it assumes meaning, and in the reversal that causes every interior to pass to the outside and every exterior to the inside, in the temporal oscillation that always makes it precede and follow itself—in short what Deleuze would perhaps not allow us to call its "incorporeal materiality."

—Michel Foucault, "Theatrum Philosophicum"

American literary criticism has been and in some degree continues to be disabled by its parochialism, a limitation that is no doubt the consequence of the deep inscription of the myth of American exceptionalism in its discursive problematic. I am not only referring to the Old Americanists who established what Donald Pease, in opposition to traditionalist notions of disinterested inquiry, has aptly called the "field imaginary" that constructed the American canon around the grandiose exceptionalist idea of the American Renaissance.[1] I am also referring to the so-called New Americanists, who have rightly identified this field imaginary with Cold War ideology, but have not entirely extricated themselves from the exceptionalist net. This parochial perspective—this writing from the unexamined inside—has been especially disabling for Melville studies in that it has largely precluded recognition of the global scope of Melville's American fiction. More specifically and radically, it has blinded criticism to Melville's uncanny "un-American" American anticipation of the most liberating discursive insights of contemporary theory.[2] To read Melville's novels in terms of this exilic global perspective, and the postmodern theoretical insights it enables, is to realize that they constitute irreversibly decisive critiques of the myth of American exceptionalism. They bear witness to the fact that the idea of America that originates with the Puritans' *ontologically ordained* "errand in the ['New World'] wilderness" and reaches its secularized fulfillment in the ontologically ordained historical practice of Manifest Destiny in the antebellum period is essentially European and planetary in scope. By "European" I mean a comportment toward being that is simultaneously metaphysical and imperial, a comportment informed by a logical economy that pits the ontological principle of Identity in a binary opposition against difference, which in turn, elaborates itself in the sphere of sociopolitical practice as Us against them, Civilized against savage, White against black, Men against women, Captains of Industry against labor, Normality against social deviance, and so on. This is the thesis of my book *The Errant Art of Moby-Dick: The Canon, the Cold War, and the Struggle for American Literary Studies*.[3] Captain Ahab's monomaniac reduction of the anxiety-provoking differential temporal dynamics of being at large to One personified (named) object renders "it" "*practically* assailable."[4] This ontological/sociopolitical itinerary reflects the charted violent historical itinerary of America from the genocidal Puritan assault on the Pequots in the name of their divinely ordained "errand in the wilderness" to the virtual extermination of the native American "Other" and the aggressive war against Mexico in the name of Manifest Destiny (not to say the violence of slavery in the name of white supremacy in the antebellum period). I am referring to the process of what is called euphemistically Westward Expansion, but to be fully understood must be seen in the geographical trope informing that "frontier" discourse: that is, as a polyvalent imperial practice enabled and justified by the "theorization" of American space, which is to say, the "overseeing" civilizing project—inaugurated in and by the Enlightenment's invention of the panoptic classificatory table and brought to its logical fulfillment in America by Frederick Jackson Turner at the World's Columbian Exposition in Chicago in 1983)[5]—of mapping "unknown" or "unimproved" or, as in the case of Benjamin Franklin's map of the New World in *Israel Potter*, "desert" space: *terra incognita*.

In the following commentary on Melville's *Pierre; or the Ambiguities*, I want to suggest, partly against a critical tradition that continues to universalize the novel by reading it as an American tragedy or as a badly flawed psychological novel, and partly against a more recent American criticism that overdetermines "ideology" in its critique of American society,[6] that it is, in Edward Said's terms, like *Moby-Dick*, a "worldly text," which,

I would add, understands the social as a practice fundamentally informed by ontological representation. More specifically, I will suggest that what Melville's *Moby-Dick* is to the American global imperial project, *Pierre*, that apparently quite different novel, is to the American domestic project. And I intend to do this by invoking two *integrally related* postmodern motifs circulating around the concept of representation: the Gramscian notion of hegemony—that is, the coercive ideological discourse that represents itself as universal truth and finds its fulfillment in the "end of history"—and the still to be fully thought Heideggerian notion of *silence*—that "saying" that is rendered unsayable by the global triumph of the imperial logic of hegemony.

I

Before Pierre's discovery that he has, or may have, an illegitimate sister, the world of Saddle Meadows seems to him to be an Adamic Eden, a paradisiacal world of peace, harmony, order, certainty, and confidence presided over by the symbolic memorial portraits of his heroic grandfather and ideal father: an in-forming yet supervisory *logos* or principle of presence. Though everywhere there are signs that this ahistorical—and, in Leo Marx's term, "pastoral"—Edenic world is a historical re-presentation—an utterly charted and monumentalized space—that conceals a primal rupture, Pierre is oblivious to them. To invoke the metaphor that pervades the world of Saddle Meadows and that will become increasingly visible, the "face" he has seen earlier haunts Pierre and his Edenic environs, but the truth discourse of this post-Revolutionary moment of American history is so deeply inscribed in his consciousness that he can easily dismiss it as simply an irrational apparition, a nothing, in Heidegger's language, that the discourse of truth will have nothing to do with: "The nothing—what else can it be for science but an outrage and a phantasm? If science is right, then only one thing is sure: science wishes to know nothing of the nothing. Ultimately this is the scientifically rigorous conception of the nothing. We know it, the nothing, in that we wish to know nothing about it."[7]

When, however, Pierre comes to believe that Isabel is not a phantom but indeed his very real illegitimate sister, he experiences an "extraordinary emergency."[8] His world—the "world around him"—of which he was hitherto the (supplementary) center and in which he felt comfortably at home, disintegrates before his distanced or, more precisely, prospective eyes. The familiar world of Saddle Meadows undergoes a "change of terrain."[9] It suddenly becomes immediate and estranged—"the world," a mediated social space totally "colonized" by a privileged historical language—and he, a stranger in it (a-part): literally de-centered. In Heidegger's apt geographical trope, this occasion dis-locates Pierre (the Rock)—bereaves him of familiar reference points—and thus propels him into the domain of *die Unheimliche*, the uncanny or, as the etymology suggests, the not-at-home: an uncharted or unmapped space that precipitates ambiguity and anxiety, that which, according to Heidegger, has no thing (*das Nicht*) as its object[10]: "On all sides, the physical world of solid objects now slidingly displaced itself *from around him*, and he floated into an ether of visions" (*P*, 85; my emphasis).

As this quotation—and Pierre's later obsessive but futile search for the "Talismanic Secret" that would recuperate and make his disintegrated universe intelligible again—suggests, the decentering Pierre undergoes is ontological, a question of the being of being. But in so far as this ontological emergency also involves unnaming, that is, the disintegration of language, it is also and simultaneously sociopolitical. And it takes the form of his alienation not simply from the benign memorial representation of his father (as well as from his grandfather, the Revolutionary hero, "grand old Pierre," and his great grandfather, the heroic Indian fighter in the French and Indian Wars), but also from the formidable, present discursive authority of his patriarchal mother, who represents the far from exceptionalist post-Revolutionary American "world." Pierre's decentering is an emergency that takes the form of his estrangement from the social discourse which determines what is permissible to think and say and do in America:

> She was a noble creature, but formed chiefly for the gilded prosperities of life, and hitherto mostly used to its unruffled serenities; bred and expanded, in all developments, under the sole influence of hereditary forms and *world-usages*. Not his refined, courtly, loving, equable mother, Pierre felt, could unreservedly, and like a heaven's heroine, meet the shock of his extraordinary emergency, and applaud, to his heart's echo, a sublime resolve, whose execution should call down the astonishment and the jeers of *the world*. (*P*, 89; my emphasis)

In short, the crisis—the "extraordinary emergency"—Pierre experiences in the wake of Isabel's irruption into his Edenic world, is simultaneously an *e*-mergency: an expulsion from a merged—a de-differentiated or identical—ontological, discursive, domestic, and social fatherland informed by or presided over by a *logos*, a principle of presence, or in a phrase from Derrida that is applicable to antebellum America, a "Transcendental Signified." In Melville's rhetoric, he becomes, like Ishmael in *Moby-Dick*, an "orphan," not in the sense of self-authoring individual, as Wei-chee Dimock insists in her effort to implicate Melville's wish to be free from the father ("to be his own sire") with the panoptic spatializing imperial American project, but in the sense of a decentered subject:

Then Pierre felt that deep in him lurked a divine unidentifiableness, that owned no earthly kith or kin. Yet was this feeling entirely lonesome, and orphan-like. Fain, then, for one moment, would he have recalled the thousand sweet illusions of Life, tho' purchased at the price of Life's Truth; so that once more he might not feel himself driven out an infant Ishmael into the desert, with no maternal Hagar to accompany and comfort him. (*P*, 89)[11]

What exactly does Melville mean when he invokes the "world" as that domain from which Pierre is expelled as something foreign? The novel, not accidentally, begins with a light-hearted but also ominous conversation between young Pierre and his doting but devotion-yearning patrician mother, precipitated by a reference to Romeo's fatal disobedience to his parents. But it is not, as in Shakespeare, the psychological resonance of this disobedience that Melville emphasizes; it is the familial and social. In a way that anticipates Foucault's Gramscian analysis of the disciplinary society, this inaugural moment of Melville's text insinuates what the "world" demands from those who inhabit it. It is not obedience as such, which connotes the overt presence of a restrictive economy of constraining rules and regulations—and thus, in its visibility, is vulnerable to the possibility of insurrection. It is docility, a comportment toward the world, enabled by what Louis Althusser has called "the interpellation of the subject" and the related mechanisms of normalization, that assume its constraints to be natural, the way things actually are, and thus assure peace and confidence: "So be it!"[12] The word "docile"—in tension with a peace-threatening barbaric energy—reverberates throughout this self-consciously "pleasant" conversation like the ominous clanging of a bell, a process that culminates in the concluding anxious thoughts of Pierre's mother. These, not incidentally, are articulated beneath the supervising gaze of the memorial portrait of her father, "grand old Pierre," a "hero," we have been previously told, of the American Revolution, and a slave holder, albeit a benign one:

"A noble boy, and docile"—she murmured—"he has all the frolicsomeness of youth, with little of its giddiness. And he does not grow vain-glorious in sophomorean wisdom. I thank heaven I sent him not to college. A noble boy, and docile. A fine, proud, loving, docile, vigorous boy. Pray God, he never becomes otherwise to me. His little wife, that is to be, will not estrange him from me; for she too is docile,—beautiful, and reverential, and most docile.... How glad am I that Pierre loves her so, and not some dark-eyed haughtiness, with whom I could never live in peace." (*P*, 19–20)

The incantatory reiteration of the word "docile" (it recurs fourteen times in this scene) thus establishes the context for understanding the moral/linguistic crisis precipitated by Pierre's extraordinary e-mergency. For it assumes prominence precisely at the moment when the hitherto docile Pierre realizes that his mother could not possibly understand, let alone tolerate, his intention to acknowledge his illegitimate sister as anything but deviant, at the moment, in other words, when Pierre realizes that the moral/linguistic imperatives of the "world" are, far from being natural, an ideological construction of the dominant American culture: imperatives that say, with Emerson, "self-reliance," but mean subjection or, rather, the subjected subject. This tension between the charted identical world and the emergent—differential—world manifests itself all through the novel: for example, in his encounters with his mother (and the heritage she represents), the minister Falsgrave; Lucy's brother, the naval officer Fredric Tartan; and, not least, Pierre's cousin, Glendinning Stanley. And it is decisively underscored in the pamphlet on "Chronometricals & Horologicals," written by one Plotinus Plinlimmon, which Pierre finds in the coach on the way to exile in the city. For this pamphlet, which distinguishes between the discourse and practice of the "world" at large and the discourse and practice of one who cannot or refuses to accommodate his discourse and practice to the imperatives—the "call"—of the world, precisely theorizes the actual circumstances of Pierre's emergent occasion. And, in so doing, it goes far to explain Pierre's, Lucy's, and Isabel's deaths, not as self-inflicted, but as murders—an absolute silencing—committed by the truth discourse of America.

II

I am calling attention to the tension between the "world" and the emergent protagonist not only because I want to underscore, against the canonical tragic reading, that in a fundamental sense *Pierre* is a social text.[13] In so doing, I also want to suggest, against certain New Americanist readings, which overdetermine the social at the expense of the indissolubly related ontological site of the novel, that *Pierre* is simultaneously concerned with the question of *thinking* itself or rather with thinking *as praxis*. Almost unanimously, these recent Americanists all too easily identify the still "young Pierre" after his "extraordinary emergency" with the dominant discourse of Emersonian self-reliance, condemning him, therefore, as a self-deluded failure. Emory Eliot, for example, refers to Pierre's efforts to "gospelize the world anew" as "humorless" and "pathetic outbursts of his own narcissistic obsession with his fate."[14] They thus overlook the contradictory continuity that Melville, despite his ironic distance from Pierre, is thematizing between the dominant American cultural imperative to Identity—a logocentrically grounded mergence—and e-mergence, a decentered de-differentiation that can manifest itself only in a resonantly ambiguous silence. To put it alternatively, the New Americanists' overdetermination of Pierre's *failure* to break out of the individualism sanctioned by the dominant culture overlooks the positive content of the silence that is the necessary precipitate of the totalization of the "world's" discourse.

Those early American critics who condemned not only Melville's radical departure in *Pierre* from the intelligible "realism" of the earlier *Typee*, *Omoo*, *Redburn*, and *White Jacket*, but also its writing as the ravings of a madman and its morality as an unspeakable offense against American decency perfectly understood this relationship between the American world and silence. This is especially true of George Washington Peck, whose self-righteous, outraged "exposure" of Melville's moral corruption I referred to in the first chapter, but which deserves repeating at this juncture:

> But when he dares to outrage every principle of virtue [Peck is referring to the theme of incest]; when he strikes with an impious, though, happily, weak hand, at the foundations of society, we feel it our duty to tear off the veil with which he has thought to soften the hideous features of the idea, and warn the public against the reception of such atrocious doctrines. If Mr. Melville had reflected at all . . . his better sense would perhaps have informed him that there are certain ideas so repulsive to the general mind that they themselves are not alone kept out of sight, but, by fit ordination of society, everything that might be supposed to even collaterally suggest them is carefully shrouded in a decorous darkness.[15]

Only when *Pierre* is returned to the American cultural context that, as Peck's review testifies, self-evidently justified "turn[ing] our critical Aegis on [Melville], and "freez[ing] him "into silence,"[16] will the New Americanist reconstellation of the novel out of the aesthetic context in which it was hitherto embedded disclose its proleptic global import for the contemporary occasion. Indeed, I want to further suggest that *Pierre* is a "worldly" novel of social critique that, both in form and content, anticipates certain concerns about the politics of ontological representation that have become extremely important for late postmodernist theory and practice.

As I have already remarked in invoking Foucault, the "world" that Melville is articulating in the novel—the American world that in the end destroys Pierre, Lucy, and Isabel—is proleptic of Gramsci's concept of hegemony as that concept has been analyzed and extended by such early postmodern thinkers as Foucault, Althusser, and Raymond Williams in their respective interrogations of the truth discourse of post-Enlightenment modernity at large.[17] Melville, it is important to note, does not depict the social conditions characterizing Saddle Meadows in a historical vacuum.

That is made clear by the prominence he gives at the beginning of the novel to his satirical genealogy of the culture of Saddle Meadows presided over by the haughty Mrs. Glendinning, a genealogy which, like that informing the worlds of *Moby-Dick* and the fiction that follows it—"Benito Cereno," "Bartleby, the Scrivener," *The Confidence-Man*, and especially *Israel Potter*—traces the origins of the discourse of "the world" of Saddle Meadows back through the American Revolution (Pierre's grandfather) to the Indian wars (Pierre's great-grandfather), and the Puritan "errand in the wilderness." In the process Melville's genealogy discloses that this American discourse, far from being exceptionalist, turns out to be quite markedly "European," just as nationalist, traditionalist, patriarchal, class structured, racist, and expansionist, for example, as Ernest Renan's famous definition of the (French) nation, which has its condition of possibility in a people's will to monumentalize. I will amplify more fully on Renan's definition and its remarkable relevance to Melville in the next chapter on *Israel Potter*. Here, it will suffice to say that, for him, (1) the nation is "a soul, a spiritual principle," which is constituted by "two things, which in truth are one . . . the possession in common of a rich legacy of memories [and] present-day consent, the desire to live together, the will to perpetuate the value of the heritage that one has received in an undivided form;[18] and that (2) this monumentalizing—this metaphysically enabled remembering of "a heroic past, great men, glory" that reduces and binds a plurality of people into one organic nation—is not innocent. It is, as Renan admits, a rite of retrospective remembrance that functions *to forget* the violence that lies at the origin, and is an intrinsic imperative, of nation building: "Forgetting, I would even go so far as to say historical error, is a crucial factor in the creation of a nation, which is why progress in historical studies often constitutes a danger for [the principle of] nationality. Indeed, historical enquiry brings to light deeds of violence which took place at the origin of all political formations, even of those whose consequences have been altogether beneficial."[19] It is, to put it provisionally, precisely this "Old World" amnesiac remembering that Melville's genealogical solicitation of the monumentalist discourse that formed the "New World" of Saddle Meadows discloses:

> All the associations of Saddle-Meadows were full of pride to Pierre. The Glendinning deeds by which their estate had so long been held, bore cyphers of three Indian kings, the aboriginal and only conveyancers of those noble woods and plains. Thus loftily, in the days of his circumscribed youth, did Pierre glance along the background of his race; little recking of that maturer and larger interior development, which should forever deprive these things of their full power of pride in his soul. (*P*, 6)

Melville wants his contemporary American readers to realize that Mrs. Glendinning's insidiously benign moral discourse is the discourse of the contemporary American nation—including its canonical literature (that of "young America")—at large. It is a discourse that virtually everyone it affects (speaks for) assumes as a given: not simply those like Mrs. Glendinning, the young Pierre, Glendinning Stanly, Reverend Falsgrave, and the "unerring" writers of "young America," who capitalize on it, but also those such as Isabel, Lucy Tartan, the servant Dates, and Dellie Ulver (not to say the blacks who have been "freed" by their Glendinning owners since the time of the revolutionary hero, "grand old Pierre") who are its (blamed) victims. As such, it is the vehicle for the expression of the truth of the way things naturally are. What Melville is exposing by means of his genealogy is, of course, that this apparently natural American discourse is artificial. As the satirical pages the narrator devotes to "grand old Pierre" (and, as we shall see, *Israel Potter* at large) make clear, it is a discourse that has been fabricated by the dominant post-Revolutionary culture in America, which, far from being revolutionary, has become in the antebellum period, if it was not always, like "the Old World"—patriarchal, patrician, feudal, nationalist, class structured, and racist—in order to aggrandize its sociopolitical, moral, and economic authority. (Though this last appears to play only a marginal role in Melville's narrative, its marginality, like that of slavery, nevertheless constitutes a resonant shadowy presence in his genealogy of the truth discourse of antebellum America, one epitomized by the narrator's commentary on Pierre's response to Plinlimmon's pamphlet: "Sooner or later in this life, the earnest, or enthusiastic youth comes to know, and more or less appreciate this startling solecism:—That while, as the grand condition of acceptance to God, Christianity calls upon all men to renounce this world; yet by all odds the most Mammonish part of this world—Europe and America—are owned by none but professed Christian nations, who glory in the owning, and seem to have some reason therefor" (*P*, 207). Two things are worthy of note here: Melville's identification of America with Europe—his rejection of the myth of American exceptionalism—and his anticipation of Max Weber's identification of the Puritan ethic and the spirit of capitalism).[20] In other words, the "American" discourse Melville is interrogating is a "representational" discourse that has acquired hegemonic status (in the sense of becoming a truth discourse that has achieved universal legitimacy), and has thus coopted the language of dissent. The America this naturalized artificial discourse projects is, in Benedict Anderson's apt phrase, an "imaginary community."

It is precisely in this displacement of the focus of his interrogation of America from the site of politics as such to the related site of language—the representational discourse of the "world"—that renders Melville's disclosure proleptic of the kind of critique of modernity that Gramsci and those postmodern theorists who follow him have undertaken by way of the concept of hegemony. By "hegemony"—I rehearse its provenance because its sedimentation has obscured its essential meaning—these critics of modernity do not mean a discourse informed by a conscious ideology that is consciously organized to compel the differential constituencies of society into their proper place. Ideology, according to these adversarial thinkers, implies indoctrination: the conscious imposition of a totalized value system on the various constituencies of a society. And, in resorting to overt coercion, it becomes vulnerable to resistance and thus politically inefficient. Like ideology, hegemony constitutes the value system of the dominant social order. But, by way of the establishment of canons and monuments, periodic national rituals of remembrance (jeremiads), the insistent inscription of these historical "high" points in the national memory by educational institutions, literature, the media, the party system, churches, and so forth, this value system comes to seem to the multitude it works on as one they live. Hegemony, that is, is a democratic society's truth discourse. The ideology of the dominant culture is so deeply and pervasively saturated in the cultural body that it appears to its members to be natural, a matter of common sense, the way things are. It is thus total in its scope and yet more or less invisible, its center being a "center elsewhere," as it were, "*beyond* the reach of [free]play."[21] This is why resistance to it is ultimately *unspeakable* (in both senses of the word). As Raymond Williams puts it,

> The concept of hegemony often, in practice, resembles [usual definitions of ideology], but it is distinct in its refusal to equate consciousness with the articulate formal system which can be and ordinarily is abstracted as "ideology." ... Instead it sees the relations of domination and subordination, in their forms as practical consciousness, as in effect a saturation of the whole process of living—not only of political and economic activity, nor only of manifest social activity, but of the whole substance of lived identities and relationships, to such a depth that the pressures and limits of what can ultimately be seen as a specific economic, political, and cultural system seem to most of us the pressures and limits of simple experience and common sense. Hegemony is then not only the articulate upper level of "ideology," nor are its forms of control only those ordinarily seen as "manipulation" or "indoctrination." It is a whole body of practices and expectations, over the whole of living ... It is a lived system of meanings and values—constitutive and constituting—which as they are experienced as practices appear as reciprocally confirming. It thus constitutes a sense of reality for most people in the society, a sense of absolute because experienced reality *beyond which it is very difficult for most members of the society to move*, in most areas of their lives. It is, that

is to say, in the strongest sense a "culture," but a culture which has also to be seen as the lived dominance and subordination of particular classes.[22]

Hegemony, we might say, insofar as it is, as Williams observes, "a 'culture,' " is, as the etymological kinship of the two words suggest, the end of a process devoted to the *colonization* of the minds of a plurality of singular people. What needs to be added to Williams's otherwise definitive account of Gramsci's concept of hegemony is that its coercive center elsewhere remains invisible—beyond the reach of the free play of criticism, as it were—as long as those on whom it works offer their spontaneous consent to the "objective" and therefore "benign" truth of the discourse of hegemony. When, however, as in the case of Pierre after his emergency (and, as we shall see in chapter 4, in a different but analogous way, Bartleby), any individual or constituency of society refuses his or her or its spontaneous consent to its truth, the center elsewhere (unwillingly) *shows itself* in the *aporetic* form of violence perpetrated on the "deviant" by the policing agencies of the dominant culture (what Althusser, following Gramsci, calls the "repressive state apparatuses").

All this is precisely what Melville means when, in the context of the American "world" Mrs. Glendinning represents, he refers to the occasion of Pierre's discovery of Isabel's existence as an "extraordinary emergency." But we must not think of Melville's novel as simply proleptic of the postmodern counterhegemonic discourse, which is aware of the degree to which the benign truth discourse of America is in fact a social construction—a re-presentation—that invisibly identifies the "Other" as deviant or errant and thus the object of subjection. The novel, in fact, discloses something that, in some ways, is far more insightful about the nature and contemporary relevance of hegemony than Gramsci, Althusser, Williams, and all the postmodern thinkers who have made the analysis of the concept so prominent have said about it. Whereas these contemporary social critics tend to limit their accounts of the operations of hegemony to the site of cultural production in general, Melville shows that American cultural production is itself informed by—is indissolubly related to—*ontological representation*, that is, the *re*-presentation of being in terms of a "Talismanic Secret," a principle of presence. This intuition of the indissoluble relatedness of metaphysical and cultural representation explains (as it does the otherwise incommensurability of Ishmael's narrative and his disquisitions on cetology in *Moby-Dick*), the narrator's fluid movement back and forth between cultural, social, and philosophical criticism, not least his insistently satirical criticism of that Transcendentalist version of German idealist metaphysics that by his time had virtually colonized American thinking.

This fundamental affiliation between metaphysics and cultural production in *Pierre*, which has been entirely overlooked by the new as well as the old Americanists, is epitomized by Melville's commentary on Pierre's spiritual condition on the occasion of his and Isabel's departure from Saddle Meadows into exile, when he finds the Plinlimmon pamphlet. It follows the narrator's reference to Pierre's awakened suspicion that "the world seems to lie saturated and soaking with lies":

> Hereupon then in the soul of the enthusiast youth two armies come to the shock; and unless he prove recreant, or unless he prove gullible, or unless he can find the talismanic secret, to reconcile this world with his own soul, then there is no peace for him, no slightest truce for him in this life. Now without doubt this Talismanic Secret has never yet been found; and in the nature of human things it seems as though it never can be. Certain philosophers have time and again pretended to have found it; but if they do not in the end discover their own delusion, other people soon discover it for themselves, and so those philosophers and their vain philosophy are let glide away into practical oblivion. Plato and Spinoza, and Goethe, and many more belong to this guild of self-imposters, with a preposterous rabble of Muggletonian Scots and Yankees, whose vile brogue still the more bestreaks the stripedness of their Greek or German Neoplatonical originals. That profound Silence, that only Voice of our God, which I before spoke of; from that divine thing without a name, those imposter philosophers pretend somehow to have got an answer; which is absurd, as though they should say they had got water out of stone; for how can a man get a Voice out of Silence? (*P*, 208)

I will return shortly to Melville's reiterated reference to the "Silence" that the truth discourse of metaphysics not only runs up against, but indeed activates as a haunting force. Here I want to underscore his identification of the social question precipitated by Pierre's discovery that the world of Saddle Meadows/America is a construction of the dominant culture with the ontological question precipitated by "Chronologicals & Horologicals." Indeed, Melville is suggesting that the metaphysical representation of being characterizing contemporary American philosophical discourse informs the hegemonic discourse of Saddle Meadows/America at a deeper and more invisible ideological level, that they are manifestations of the same will to power over the differential "Other." In a way that remarkably anticipates Heidegger's destruction of the Western philosophical tradition, Melville suggests that the unexceptionalist American "Transcendentalists"[23] have resorted to the founding ontological fiction of European civilization—the Talismanic *Logos*—to compel the differential being of being (the nothingness of temporality) into intelligibility and order. In "pretending to have found [the Talismanic Secret]" informing or presiding over being, that is, this "preposterous rabble of Muggletonian . . . Yankees" ventriloquized European philosophy, which, according to Hannah Arendt, had perennially represented history as "acting behind the backs of real men—a personified force that we find . . . in Adam Smith's "invisible hand, in Kant's 'ruse of nature,' in Hegel's 'cunning of Reason,' and Marx's dialectical materialism."[24] In true Old World fashion, this New World philosophy would reduce the recalcitrant and aporetic force of history to "docility" in the name of achieving the *Pax Metaphysica*. (This metaphysically induced "docility" and "peace," as we shall see, is the calculated "end" of the optimistic philosophy that Melville mercilessly parodies in *The Confidence-Man*.) Melville, in other words, is suggesting here that this totalizing, coercive onto-logical economy constitutes the ground of the totalizing, coercive socio-logical economy of Saddle Meadows/America and the universal peace it would achieve at all costs. In the resonant terms of Heidegger's *Parmenides* lectures, Melville identifies the *Pax Metaphysica* of antebellum American philosophy with a domestic version of the *Pax Romana*.[25]

III

In *Pierre*, the indissoluble relationship between social/hegemonic and ontological representation manifests itself at various sites, including that of narrative, but, as I have been suggesting, they are indissolubly related by the "Talismanic Secret" presupposed by the metaphysical perspective. What each has in common is precisely *re-presentation*: the reduction of the unnameable, the ineffable, the unspeakable or unsayable force of the nothingness, of the temporality, of the difference, of the singularity of being to a totalized image or "world picture"—that can be grasped all at once by the mind's eye. Each, in short, ends in the reduction (domestication or pacification) of the errant force of the nothingness of temporal being to (narrative) structure or, to invoke the terms from geography I began with, to an inclusive, comprehensive, and intelligible map that finally precludes errancy. It is no accident, then, though their pervasive presence has been virtually overlooked, that Melville bestows inordinate importance on a spatiocultural relay associated with the *orienting* function of cartography wherever he refers to Pierre's emergency (the crisis of American culture) and to representation (of American time/history) as it is practiced by "young America": the portrait, the mausoleum, the sarcophagus, inscription, the canonical text, and, above all, the monument.[26]

As I will show in the next chapter, Melville's most sustained disclosure of the ideological—hegemony-producing—function of this privileged metaphorics of ritualized collective remembrance is enacted in *Israel Potter*, published in 1852, a mere two years after *Pierre*, which overdetermines the political implications of the monumentalizing impulse—above all, the *forgetting*—endemic to its remembering. This novel, it will be recalled, is the poignant life story of a preterited American veteran of the Battle of Bunker Hill retrieved by Melville in a remarkably Foucauldian gesture from the oblivion to which it had been interred by the American Cultural Memory in the very process of monumentalizing the battle in which he had fought so courageously. In that chapter on *Israel Potter*, I will develop at length Melville's brilliantly parodic de-monumentalization of the American Revolution by way of his ironic "dedication" of the novel "To His Highness, the Bunker-Hill Monument," a dedication that subtly but unmistakably evokes and parodies the canonical antebellum speeches of Daniel Webster, one of the most effective custodians of the exceptionalist American Memory, commemorating the Battle of Bunker Hill on June 17, 1825 (the laying of the cornerstone) and June 17, 1843 (the completion of the monument). Here, it will suffice to say that Melville's satire in *Israel Potter* of Webster's "lofty" patriarchal and nationalist/imperial jeremiads, so exemplary of Renan's Franco-centric analysis of the panoptic ideological function of national remembrance, leaves little doubt as to Melville's critical genealogical intention in *Pierre*.

Anticipating the postmodernists' refusal of the seductions of narrative closure, Melville understands this system of spatial tropes in *Pierre* not simply as a selective ritualized remembering that, by sanctifying tradition (the heritage of a community), legitimizes and enhances the power of the dominant American culture. He also reads it as the reification of the differential dynamics of being—the anxiety-provoking "*ambiguities*" that confront Pierre on the occasion of his emergence—and as endemic to the Western structure of consciousness. Examples of this totalizing, willfully forgetful tropic system circulating around remembrance are pervasive in *Pierre*, but two examples will suffice to suggest the degree to which it saturates the American "world" right down to its capillaries and becomes, paradoxically, the very means by which Melville precipitates the spectral absence that haunts the presence of this monumentalized world. The first is the well-known passage in which Melville, in a sustained rhetorical play on the metaphorics of ritualized memorialization, compares the young Pierre's highly mannered—baroque—representation of his idealized dead father to Prince Mausolus's tomb:

> There had long stood a shrine in the fresh-foliaged heart of Pierre, up to which he ascended by many tableted steps of remembrance; and around which annually he had hung fresh wreaths of a sweet and holy affection. Made one green bower of at last, by such successive votive offerings of his being; this shrine seemed, and was indeed, a place for the celebration of a chastened joy, rather than for any melancholy rites. But though thus mantled, and tangled with garlands, this shrine was of marble—a niched pillar, deemed solid and eternal, and from whose top radiated all those innumer-

able sculptured scrolls and branches, which supported the entire one-pillared temple of his moral life; as in some beautiful gothic oratories, one central pillar, trunk-like, upholds the roof. In this shrine, in this niche of this pillar, stood the perfect marble form of his departed father; without blemish, unclouded, snow-white, and serene; Pierre's fond personification of perfect human goodness and virtue.... Blessed and glorified in his tomb beyond Prince Mausolus is that mortal sire, who, after an honorable, pure course of life, dies, and is buried, as in a choice fountain, in the filial breast of a tender-hearted and intellectually appreciative child. For at that period, the Solomonic insights have not poured their turbid tributaries into the pure-flowing well of the childish life. Rare preservative virtue, too, have those heavenly waters. Thrown into that fountain, all sweet recollections become marbleized; so that things which in themselves were evanescent, thus became unchangeable and eternal.... (*P*, 68)

The second is the equally well known passage, following his extraordinary emergency, when Pierre retrieves and finally burns the "chair-portrait" of his father as lie. Aware now of the "turbid" "Solomonic insights" about "things which in themselves were evanescent," to which in his earlier innocence he was oblivious, Pierre, in remarkable anticipation of Nietzsche's (and Foucault's) genealogy of modernity to which I will return,[27] says:

Hitherto I have hoarded up mementoes and monuments of the past; been a worshiper of all heir-looms; a fond filer away of letters, locks of hair, bits of ribbon, flowers, and the thousand-and-one minutenesses which love and memory think they sanctify:—but it is forever over now! If to me any memory shall henceforth be dear, I will not mummy it in a visible memorial for every passing beggar's dust to gather on. Love's museum is vain and foolish as the Catacombs, where grinning apes and abject lizards are embalmed, as, forsooth, significant of some imagined charm. It speaks merely of decay and death; decay and death of endless innumerable generations; it makes of earth one mold. How can lifelessness be fit memorial of life?—So far, for mementoes of the sweetest. (*P*, 197)

By thus juxtaposing these two synecdochical passages referring to Pierre's representation of times before and after his emergency, I want to retrieve the motif of memorialization—the ideological work it does for the dominant social order—which has been marginalized by virtually all commentary on *Pierre*. These passages not only foreground Melville's proleptic recognition that this re-collective remembering of the cultural memory, like Renan's national "will to perpetuate the values of a heritage that one has received in an undivided form," is the dominant American culture's essential means of establishing hegemony: a total way of thinking/feeling that, in hailing them, accommodates or colonizes the differential or peripheral constituencies of society to its metaphysically ordained imperial center or, in Althusser's phrase, that render them "subjected subjects."[28] In thus exposing the constructedness—and global scope—of the present imperialist truth discourse, this constellation also, and more radically, suggests that Melville is symptomatically articulating a *positive* meaning in precisely those "phenomena" of being that an anxious memorialization inters and forgets, which is to say, that the binarist logic of the consensual discourse of hegemony represents negatively in order to accommodate them to its metaphysical center—or, as a last resort, to obliterate them by violence. I mean time, death, nothingness, singularity, errancy, ambiguity: all those peace- and confidence-"threatening" minority terms that Melville identifies with Pierre's extraordinary emergency and subsumes under the resonant word "Silence." To put it alternatively, this retrieval suggests that, in some decisive sense, Melville, the narrator, if not Pierre (for reasons I will invoke later), understands his protagonist's "extraordinary emergency," not simply as a crisis as such—the condition of utter and irreversible loss incumbent on the disintegration of his plenary Edenic world—but as *e*-mergency; as a crisis, that is, which paradoxically involves his breaking out—his liberation from—a totally leveled, totally in-different, totally mapped, totally colonized world, a world the movement toward which has all along been represented as dialectically evolving or, in Hegel's alternatively term, as "developmental." This intuition, as we shall see in the following chapters, which is hardly conceivable in such a globalized context, informs the novels and stories beginning with *Moby-Dick*. And it is one that virtually all who have commented on *Pierre*, New and Old Americanists alike, have overlooked at the expense of the relevance of Melville's fiction for the late postmodern, indeed, post-9/11, American occasion.

IV

In order to explain Melville's paradoxically positive understanding of the occasion of Pierre's "extraordinary emergency," it will be necessary first to consider another thematic trope that Melville, again proleptically, clearly affiliates with the trope of monumentalization in his cultural critique of the representational discourse privileged by antebellum America. I am referring to his pervasive references to canonical narrative, both in the context of Pierre's emergence from the narrativized world of Saddle Meadows and to his decision to "gospelize the world anew" (*P*, 273). In *Pierre*, Melville is not only acutely aware that antebellum American literary theory and practice, in its obsession to narrativize—to reduce to spatial form—the corrosive differences that time always already disseminates, is indissolubly related to Yankee metaphysics (its Transcendentalist assumption that the "Talismanic Secret" informs the apparent ineffability of differential time), cultural representation (its monumentalization of history), and morality (its reduction of human energy to docility, on which the consensus of nationhood relies). As such, he is also aware that American literary theory and practice are affiliated with the Europe with which America, under the aegis of Emerson's influential "exceptionalist" representation of the American national identity in "The Young American" (1844), decisively claims no kinship:

> America is newborn, free, healthful, strong, the land of the laborer, of the democrat, of the philanthropist, of the believer, of the saint, she should speak to the human race. American is the country of the Future. *From Washington, its capital city, proverbially "the city of magnificent distances," through all its cities, states, and territories, it is a country of beginnings, of projects, of vast designs, and expectations. It has no past: all has an outward and prospective look.* And herein is it fitted to receive more readily every generous feature which the wisdom or fortune of man has yet to impress.[29]

Melville makes this complicity between the "New World" and the "Old World" decisively clear in his sustained satire of Emerson's unexceptionalist "exceptionalism," which is foregrounded in the chapter "Young America in Literature," as he highlights the irony of Emerson's use of the essentially imperial metaphorics of the center and periphery to refer to the new worldliness of this "young America."

In the word that subsumes the various affiliated metaphorics that characterize the "centered" and "enlightened" American world before Pierre's extraordinary emergency, Melville knows that, like metaphysics, cultural monumentalization and the discourse of hegemony, the imposition of a beginning-middle-end on the errancy of being-in-the-world is informed by an imperial will to power, the end of which is the reduction of the living, singular force of being into stone (and saying into silence). It is no accident that the disintegration of Pierre's faith in metaphysics and monuments that ensues from his decentering and dislocating emergency is simultaneously accompanied by the unraveling of his faith not simply in the domestic novel as it is practiced in America, but also, as his elision of literary fiction and life story suggests, in (meta)narrative as such:

> In [Isabel's life] there was an unraveled plot; and he felt that unraveled it would eternally remain to him. No slightest hope or dream had he, that what was dark and mournful in her would ever be

> cleared up into some coming atmosphere of light and mirth. Like all youths, Pierre had conned his novel-lessons; had read more novels than most persons of his years; but their false, inverted attempts at systematizing eternally unsystemizable elements; their audacious, intermeddling impotency, in trying to unravel, and spread out, and classify, the more thin than gossamer threads which make up the complex web of life; these things over Pierre had no power now. Straight through their helpless miserableness he pierced; the one sensational truth in him, transfixed like beetles all the speculative lies in them. He saw that human life doth truly come from that, which all men are agreed to call the name of *God*; and that it partakes of the unravelable inscrutableness of God. By infallible presentiment he saw, that not always doth life's beginning gloom conclude in gladness; that wedding-bells peal not ever in the last scene of life's fifth act; that while the countless tribes of common novels laboriously spin veils of mystery, only to complacently clear them up at last; and while the countless tribes of common dramas do but repeat the same; yet profounder emanations of the human mind, intended to illustrate all that can be humanly known of human life; these never unravel their own intricacies, and have no proper endings; but in imperfect, unanticipated, and disappointing sequels (as mutilated stumps), hurry to abrupt intermergings with the eternal tides of time and fate. (*P*, 141)

In its focus on the willful reversal of the rhizomatic flow of events that is the *sine qua non* of that spatialization, systemization, classification, and territorialization—the mapping/colonization—of time and the differences time disseminates, this inaugural American critique of American narrative representation constitutes a remarkable anticipation of Jean-Paul Sartre's proto-postmodern distinction between living and telling a story about "it" (*la vie* and *l'aventure*) in *Nausea*:

> Things happen one way and we tell about them in the opposite sense. You seem to start at the beginning: "It was a fine evening in 1922. I was a notary clerk in Marommes." And in reality you have started at the end. It was there, invisible and present, it is the one which gives to words the pomp and value of a beginning.... This sentence, taken simply for what it is, means that the man was absorbed, morose, a hundred leagues from an adventure ... But the end is there, transforming everything. For us, the man is already the hero of the story. His moroseness, his money troubles are much more precious than ours, they are all gilded by the light of future passions. And the story goes on in the reverse....: "It was night, the street was deserted." The phrase is cast out negligently, it seems

superfluous; but we do not let ourselves be caught and we put it aside: this is a piece of information whose value we will subsequently appreciate. And we feel that the hero has lived all the details of this night like annunciations, promises, or even that he lived only those that were promises, blind and deaf to all that did not herald adventure. We forget that the future was not yet there.[30]

Equally telling, Melville's critique of narrative in *Pierre* also constitutes a remarkable anticipation of Jacques Derrida's postmodern deconstruction of the "Book"—the "unraveling" of the fabric of the traditional "text" that figuratively enacts the deferral of the being that its re-presentation would bring to presence. I will return to this relationship later. Here I want to emphasize—against a certain tendency of American deconstructionists to restrict their otherwise brilliant reading of *Pierre* to "the scene of writing" (and the outcome of this reading to a paralytic "undecidability")[31]—Melville's insistent exposure of the indissoluble relationship, indeed, complicity, between American philosophy, the practice of American cultural memorialization, and American literature.

The remarkable similarity of Melville's language in the two passages on Pierre's understanding of the metaphysics of memorialization quoted above, and in this passage on his understanding of narrative, bears persuasive witness to this complicity. Each practice involves a reversal of the immediate existential encounter with temporality. They begin from the end (*the logos, the cultural identity of the nation, the canonical model*) or, more precisely, from a privileged, plenary, and supervisory *telos* that is beyond the reach of free play. And they proceed retro-*spectively*, or, in the apt phrase Althusser employs to identify Hegel's disabling aesthetic comportment to history, from a "future anterior" perspective.[32] In short, they both are determined by an ideological gaze that, in its tendentious selection of what to include and exclude from its narrative, would re-present the differential phenomena it encounters in such a way as to confirm that *telos*, to render them, in Sartre's metaphors, prophetic "annunciations" or "promises" that the temporal process brings to plenary fulfillment. Each constitutes a derivative or mediating (as opposed to originative) perspective that compels discontinuities—the "grinning apes and abject lizards" of the second passage on monuments, the "imperfect, unanticipated and disappointing sequels (as mutilated stumps)" in the passage on narrative—into a *story*. Not any story, but a story that legitimizes the storyteller as the spokesperson of an original universal, transcendental, fatherly, authoritative,[33] and—if we recall the role that the prophesy/fulfillment structure (in *The Aeneid*, for example) has played in Europe's and America's nationalist/colonialist projects—imperial will: a luminous metanarrative, without a shadow, told as a "theogony," as Foucault puts it in his meditation on Nietzsche's genealogical carnivalization of monumental history:

> [Genealogical] History also teaches how to laugh at the solemnities of the origin. The lofty origin is no more than "a metaphysical extension which arises from the belief that things are most precious and essential at the moment of birth." We tend to think that this is the moment of their greatest perfection, when they emerged dazzling from the hands of a creator or in the shadowless light of a first morning. The origin always precedes the Fall. It comes before the body, before the world and time; it is associated with the gods, and its story is always sung as a theogony. But historical beginnings are lowly; . . . derisive and ironic, capable of undoing every infatuation. "We wished to awaken the feeling of man's sovereignty by showing his divine birth: this path is now forbidden, since a monkey stands at the entrance."[34]

Each of these "objective" practices—metaphysics, monumental history, and literary canon formation—is thus informed by the will to power, polyvalently imperial in essence, over all things and all times—every (shadowy) "Other"—that would contradict and threaten its luminous hegemony. Together as an indissoluble continuum, they constitute the "truth" as it is understood in and by Emerson's "Young American," who in fact, is hegemonic and has his origin in the Old World. To put this last in the terms that determine the terrible fate of Pierre, Isabel, and Lucy, this continuum constitutes that which *is permitted to be said* in "democratic" America. The alternative to this totalized imperial hegemonic discourse, which, as it were, has brought to brilliant light all that is darkly ambiguous and resistant to accommodation by thought—from temporal difference and deviant subject through the lowly servant to the female and the black slave—is *Silence*.[35] But what is remarkable, as I have been insinuating throughout this commentary, is how hauntingly *present* this silence increasingly becomes in the very truth discourse that has achieved hegemonic status. Addressing the issue of the planetary triumph of empirical science in modernity in his great but still to be thought essay, "What Is Metaphysics?," Heidegger puts the structure of its hegemonic language essentially:

> That to which the relation to the world refers are beings themselves
>   —and nothing besides.
> That from which every attitude takes its guidance are beings themselves
>   —and nothing further.
> That with which the scientific confrontation in the
>   irruption [of Man as the agent of knowledge
>   production] occurs are beings themselves—and
>   beyond that nothing.

Heidegger goes on to note the remarkable fact that "precisely in the way that [triumphant] scientific man secures to himself what is most properly his, he *speaks something different*. What should be examined are beings only, and besides that—nothing; beings alone, and further—nothing; solely beings, and beyond that—nothing." Then, in a gesture that anticipates the essential, but still to be adequately thought, disclosure of the various discourses of contemporary theory, he asks, "What about this nothing" that the triumphant discourse of science "will have nothing to do with"?[36] In a remarkably proleptic gesture, I want to suggest, this is also the question Melville's *Pierre* compels us to ask in thematizing silence as a presence that haunts the triumphant discourse of antebellum America. Following its directive, it will be the purpose of what remains to think this question. And it will take the form of wrenching *Pierre* by violence out of the sedimented Americanist matrix in which it has hitherto been embedded and reconstellating it into the late postmodern context, specifically that which has recently begun to attend not only to the neglected silent minority terms of the binary ontologic of Western metaphysics, as in the case of Heidegger, but also to the silent minority terms of the Western sociopolitical practices that this imperial ontology has enabled.

V

What, then, about "that profound Silence"—"that divine thing without a name" from which "those imposter philosophers pretend somehow to have got an answer"? As I have suggested, the passages on the metaphysics of monuments and on narrative quoted above are written by the narrator in the context of Pierre's "extraordinary emergency." They constitute *dis-closures* of the dark underside *of*—the shadow that belongs to—the luminously white truth discourse of America. I mean this not simply in the sense of the negative effects of a totalized thinking/saying that claims to be positively ameliorative, but also in the sense of precipitating into *visibility* the "ambiguities" which, in its will to power over difference, this thinking/saying finally—that is, essentially—cannot accommodate to its discourse of Presence: the spectral non-being, as it were, that haunts the dominant discourse of Being. As Pierre puts this resonant, if unspeakable, revelation in lines immediately following the second passage on the metaphysics of monumentalization quoted above—they are lines, not incidentally, that conflate the metaphorics of memorialization and narrative:

> As for the rest—now I know this, that in commonest memorials, the twilight fact of death first discloses in some secret way, all the ambiguities of that departed thing or person; obliquely it casts hints, and insinuates surmises base, and eternally incapable of being cleared. Decreed by God Omnipotent it is, that Death should be the last scene of the last act of man's play;—a play, which begin how it may, in farce or comedy, ever hath its tragic end; the

curtain inevitably falls on a corpse. Therefore, never more will I play the vile pygmy, and by small memorials after death, attempt to reverse the decree of death, by essaying the poor perpetuating of the image of the original. (*P*, 197–98)

What Pierre is intuiting in discovering the irreducible and thus dreadful ambiguities subsuming his father's portrait—the hitherto totally charted temporal and spatial world of Saddle Meadows—is precisely what Ishmael discloses in his narration of Ahab's pursuit of the white whale in *Moby-Dick*: the essential unnamability, the unpicturability, the unrepresentability, the unsayability of being itself.[37] In a way that uncannily anticipates the Derridean analysis of the nonconcept *differance*, the act of naming/picturing/monumentalizing/mapping is simply the substitution or supplementation of a sign for that which would be brought to presence.[38] The process of representation, whether it takes the form of a memorial portrait, a monument, a shrine, a narrative, a cultural model, or a structural "world," always already postpones or defers that which it would bring to presence, that which it would re-present. This motif of deferral, which is intrinsic to representation in general and to the American discourse of hegemony in particular, pervades Melville's novel. Indeed, it could be said provisionally that it constitutes the irreducible absence that haunts the *center* of Pierre's story. And its spectral force is underscored precisely because it is precipitated into "visibility" as a radically contradictory "Other" by the very fulfillment in violence of the imperial logic of the American discourse of hegemony.

A decisive example of this insistent motif of deferral occurs in Melville's commentary on Pierre's burning, but finally abortive, Titanic desire, in the face of the reigning "Olympian" gods, to write the "comprehensively compact" book that would "gospelize the world anew" (*P*, 273) after having "arrived" in the city and taken lodgings with Isabel in the "Church of the Apostles." Instigated by "the *unprecedented* situation in which [he] now found himself" (*P*, 283; my emphasis), Pierre, thus seemingly "disburdened" of the last vestiges of the patriarchal tradition, *envisions* this book as The Book, *lex naturae*: a spatial miniature that would include "digestively . . . the whole range of all that can be known or dreamed" (*P*, 283).[39] In this form, his "comprehensively compact" book would thus "deliver what he thought to be new, or at least miserably neglected Truth to the world" (*P*, 283). Invoking the contradictorily inclusive visualism of this heroic Titanism, Melville underscores the paradoxical blindness of Pierre's vestigial universalist (i.e.. metaphysical) narratological perspective to the things themselves: "He did not see [Melville foregrounds Pierre's visualism by repeating this locution three times in one paragraph] . . . that all the great books in the world are but the mutilated shadowings-forth of invisible and eternally unembodied images in the soul; so that they are but the mirrors, distortedly reflecting to us our own things; and never mind what the mirror may be, if we would see the object, we must look at the object itself, and not at its reflection" (*P*, 284). In its reliance on *mimesis*, that is, the "comprehensively compact" book Pierre, the rebellious Titan, would write reinscribes the dominant "Olympian" culture's essentially metaphysical/spatializing (Hegelian) notion of the work of art as a "microcosm" that *reflects* in miniaturized visible form the "macrocosm," which in its unmediated form is impossible to see and grasp.[40]

After thus disclosing the blindness of Pierre's over-sight, Melville then de-structures what we can call his structuralizing panoptic perspective. And he does this by invoking the sublime—that which Heidegger calls the "Nothing" and Lyotard, the "unpresentable"[41]—which it is the finally futile purpose of the "comprehensive" visualism of the dominant meta-physical perspective to re-present, map, and domesticate (make docile):

> But, as to the resolute traveler in Switzerland, the Alps do never in one wide and comprehensive sweep, instantaneously reveal their full awfulness of amplitude—their overawing extent of peak crowded on peak, and spur sloping on spur, and chain jammed behind chain, and all their wonderful battalionings of might; so hath heaven wisely ordained, that on first entering into the Switzerland of his soul, man shall not at once perceive its tremendous immensity, lest illy prepared for such an encounter, his spirit should sink and perish in the lowermost snows. Only by judicious degrees, appointed of God, does man come at last to gain his Mont Blanc and take an overtopping view of these Alps; and even then, the tithe is not shown; and far over the invisible Atlantic, the Rocky Mountains and the Andes are yet unbeheld. Appalling is the soul of a man! (*P*, 284)[42]

But Melville's destruction of Pierre's vestigial metaphysical vision does not culminate here. He goes on, in what might be called a Heideggerian repetition, to affiliate the vestigial subject-oriented panopticism of Pierre's "comprehensively compact" perspective with the tropes that he has insistently identified in the novel as the metaphors endemic to metaphysical/hegemonic perception and the agents of its imperial will to peace: the monument and inscription (writing as re-presentation):

> Ten million things were as yet uncovered to Pierre. The old mummy lies buried in cloth on cloth; it takes time to unwrap this Egyptian king. Yet now, forsooth, because Pierre began to see through the first superficiality of the world, he fondly weens he has come to the unlayered substance. But, far as any geologist has yet gone down into the world, it is found to consist of nothing but surface

stratified on surface. To its axis, the world being nothing but superinduced superficies. By vast pains we mine into the pyramid; by horrible gropings we come to the central room; with joy we espy the sarcophagus; but we lift the lid—and no body is there!—appallingly vacant as vast is the soul of a man! (*P*, 285)

The itinerary of the logical economy of naming, of representation, of monumentalizing, of mapping, whose end is to bring temporality and the differences that temporality always disseminates to stand, "ends" paradoxically in the deferral of the *end*, which is to say, in the precipitation of the absence of presence. The representational process claims as its narratological end a full totality, the perfection and beauty of the All. And this end is metaphorically represented as "arrival" and figured as the inclusive and plenary centered circle. But the fulfillment of its logical itinerary paradoxically discloses the evacuated circle, the zero: the nothing that precedes naming or the difference that is the condition for the possibility of Identity and that always already haunts the authority of the latter's imperial logic.

In the novel, Melville calls this absent presence—the shadowy "Other" of metaphysical representation—"Silence." And, it should be noted, this word or variants of it, resonates throughout *Pierre*, especially at junctures that refer to the epistemological perspectives that early Americanists have identified with the "American Renaissance." Thus, for example, in the passage where Melville mocks Plato, Spinoza, Goethe and the "preposterous rabble of Muggletonian Scots and Yankees, whose vile brogue still the more bestreaks the stripedness of their Greek or German Neoplatonical originals," Melville, we recall, writes, "The profound Silence, that only Voice of our God . . . ; from that divine thing without a name, those imposter philosophers pretend somehow to have got an answer; which is as absurd, as though they should say they had got water out of stone; for how can a man get a Voice out of Silence?" (*P*, 208).

Melville's reiterated invocation of God in these passages should not deflect us away from the philosophical, narrative, and social margins to which his deviant text *as such* compels our attention, back, that is, into our inscribed adherence to the concentering, self-present *logos*, and to the teleological structure, the narrative, the monument, the map that are endemic to its imperial project. His reference to God in this text should be understood, rather, as being within quotation marks, an ironic comment on the still powerful Puritan theology in antebellum America. The Silence is, in fact, the Nothing that this secularized Puritan spirit would pre*clude* or in*clude* or oc*clude* according to the reifying imperatives of theo-logical interpretation of being. More specifically, it is the ontological and sociopolitical condition vis-à-vis speech of having been bereft of the *logos* by emergency. It is for Melville, if not quite for young Pierre, the e-mergent unthinkable and unspeakable, the ex-orbitant—peripheral—unsayable, that *belongs to*—that returns as "visitant" to haunt—the central, monumental, and imperial Medusan voice of the dominant metaphysical/hegemonic culture that would have nothing to do with "it."

Understood in the context of the thematics of the thinkable and unthinkable, the sayable and unsayable, as the novel's overdetermination of the question of language demands, Melville's evocation of Silence as the "end" of the metaphysical/hegemonic thinking/saying of "America" constitutes another—indeed, the most important—insight that is remarkably proleptic of the postmodern occasion; namely, the recognition, first announced by Heidegger, that the "end" of philosophy in post-Enlightenment modernity constitutes not simply the fulfillment of its logical economy, but its demise.[43] I mean the recognition that, in fulfilling its spatializing logic, in coming to closure, as it were, Western metaphysical thinking—thinking from after or above (*meta*) the temporal process—has transformed the be-*ing*—the always already differential temporal dynamics—of being to a totalized "World Picture" (*Weltbild*),[44] and in so doing has exposed "to view" the temporality or, what is the same thing, the nothing that metaphysical thinking, in its optimism, will have nothing to do with. With the "triumph" of metaphysical thinking, which is to say, with its arrival at the limits of its logical economy, the Silence that metaphysical thinking cannot—indeed, will not—think "shows" itself as the shadowy contradiction—the finally irreducible excess—that delegitimizes its confident authority. Silence, as it were, *e-merges* from the saying that is permissible as the spectral presence that haunts metaphysical thinking's "triumphant" hegemony.

The language of spectrality I have all along insinuated into my text to suggest the affiliation of Pierre's "extraordinary emergency" with the postmodern occasion is not gratuitous. In a late essay on the poetry of Georg Trakl, for example, Heidegger refers to this occasion as *die Abgeschiedenheit*, "the place of apartness," and the poet who inhabits it, *der Abgeschiedene*, "the one who is apart," the "stranger" bereft of language—exiled from a discursive homeland—by the total mapping/colonization of saying intrinsic to the "Spirit" of metaphysical thinking, but who finds, precisely in that diasporic condition of bereavement, a "spiritual" language: the "ghostly" voice of silence:

> The apartness [*die Abgeschiedenheit*] is "ghostly." This word—what does it mean? . . . "Ghostly" means spiritual, *but not in the narrow sense that ties the world to "spirituality,"* . . . "[O]f the spirit" means the opposite of material. This opposition posits a differentiation of two separate realms and, in Platonic-Western terms, states the gulf between the supersensuous *noeton* and the sensuous *aistheton*. "Of the spirit" so understood—it meanwhile has come to mean rational, intellectual, ideological—together with its opposites belongs to the world view of the decaying kind of man. But the "dark journey"

> of the "blue soul" [of the *Abgeschiedene*] parts company with this kind.... Apartness is spiritual, determined by the spirit, and ghostly, but it is not "of the spirit" in the sense of the language of metaphysics....
>
> What, then, is the spirit? ... Trakl sees spirit not primarily as *pneuma*, something ethereal, but as a flame that inflames, startles, horrifies, and shatters us.... Trakl sees spirit in terms of that being which is indicated in the original meaning of the word "ghost"—a being terrified, beside himself, *ek-static*.[45]

There are, admittedly, problems in Heidegger's definition of the "ghostliness" of *die Abgeschiedene*. It could be said with Derrida that it remains vestigially metaphysical.[46] But I want to identify the spectral "one who is apart" with the *Dasein* of *Being and Time*. This is the being-in-the-world who, with a "break in the referential totality" (*Verweisungsganzheit*), e-merges from the world "as it is publicly interpreted"[47]—the individuated de-differentiated or charted and colonized world, as it were, reified by the privileged concentering *logos*. He or she is (now) the stranger, the orphan, the wanderer, the nomad whose dis-location from the homeland compels him or her into the de-centered and uncanny world of the not-at-homeness (*die unheimliche Welt*), where all the points of reference, as on a map, having dissolved, he or she comes face to face in anxiety with the unspeakable nothing.

It would be quixotically optimistic to identify this "changed terrain," as Althusser puts Heidgger's insight[48]—this dreadful condition of lack—in terms of the conventional understanding of the word "positive." And yet it is, precisely in its diasporic or dis-seminated status, a condition of positivity. This is because it discloses the lack of the *Abgeschiedene* not simply as lack but as the lack *of*—the lack that *belongs to*—the "plenary" totality of the imperial thinking that has driven him or her *out* of a homeland ("beside" him- or herself), because, that is, it reveals this lack as the *silence* that not only haunts what is permitted to be said by metaphysical thinking, but calls, precisely in its haunting, for the rethinking of (hegemonic) thinking itself. This defamiliarized terrain is a positive condition, in other words, not only because it opens up the reified and closed off realm of temporality and possibility—"potentiality," in the resonance term Giorgio Agamben's invokes to characterize Bartleby[49]—to a kind of "ec-static" thinking hitherto foreclosed by the achieved dominion of metaphysical thinking. In signaling an excess that is beyond the reach of the representational thought of metaphysics, it is a positive condition also because the occasion of silence *constitutes a directive to such a rethinking of thinking* that would render thinking adequate to the task of resisting the will to power informing what can now be called alternatively the spatial, monumental, cartographic, imperial imperatives of "the Truth."

Read in the context of this emergent, still to be adequately thought—I am tempted to say, inexplicably resisted—postmodern initiative, Pierre Glendinning is the *Abgeschiedene*. With the dis-integration of the "world" of Saddle Meadows, Pierre undergoes an "extraordinary emergency" that renders him, in Heidegger's terms, an "ec-static in-sistence."[50] He becomes acutely *aware*, that is, of a "reality" that hitherto, in his merged "Edenic" state has been foreclosed to him. In his e-mergency he not only comes to realize that the truth of the "world" of Saddle Meadows is a lie, a fabrication imposed on "it" by the dominant, imperial American culture. He also comes to the realization that his being-in-the-world is a condition of "thrownness," bereft of cartographic coordinates and thus of language. He becomes the one apart, the alienated or, more precisely, disaffiliated stranger or nomad who has been exiled from the "homeland" or, truer to Melville's text, the "Fatherland" of the American symbolic order into the uncanny not-at-home, where silence resonantly reigns.

The rhetoric Melville uses in *Pierre* to characterize the represented American homeland, as we have seen, circulates around the tropes of memorialization: the monument, the shrine, the relic (behind which lies the metaphor of the seed [*sporos*]), the portrait, the canon, the (meta)narrative. But if we read *Pierre* in the context of *Moby-Dick* (which, not incidentally, precedes *Pierre* by merely one year), as, that is, a domestic allotrope of the global scope of the earlier novel, in which the chart and the classificatory table predominate, it becomes clear that this metaphorical chain associated with memory and cultural formation also includes the trope of mapping, a trope which, as postcolonial critics have made decisively clear, is endemic to and the *sine qua non* of the colonialist project. In *Moby-Dick*, Melville overdetermines these geographical tropes in order to interrogate the geopolitical, imperial project of the United States in the antebellum period.[51] In *Pierre*, and, as we shall see, in *Israel Potter* (a novel, not incidentally, which also traces the genealogy of the American discourse of hegemony back through the American Revolution to its origins in the Puritans' providentially ordained "errand in the wilderness"), he overdetermines the metaphorics of monumentality in order to interrogate the American domestic or national hegemonic project. But these privileged metaphorical systems circulating around memorialization and mapping and the American practices to which they refer, are, as I have been suggesting, not incommensurate, but indissolubly continuous: they spatialize history and its singularities for the purpose of dominating it and them. "Culture" and "colonization" derive etymologically from the Latin "*colonus*," the planter/settler who domesticates—at-homes—the *agr(i)os* the wild and savage earth and its nomadic denizens.[52]

For Melville, in other words, the "mapping" and "colonization" of America inaugurated by the Puritans' "founding" of the "empty" and "unmapped" "New World" wilderness had been implicitly (theoretically) if not actually accomplished by the middle of the nineteenth century when he was writing *Moby-Dick* and *Pierre*. I put these affiliated key words—"founding," "mapping," "colonization"—in quotation marks not to indicate that they are simply metaphors drawn from the discourse of Western imperialism proper. Rather, in keeping with Melville's remarkably proleptic intention, I do it in order to suggest that they refer literally *both* to geographical space *and* to *knowledge production* itself, that is, to a Western thinking that, at least since the Romans and increasingly thereafter, is informed by a spatial metaphorics that represent the truth of being (knowledge) as a "territory," a "province," a "domain," a "field," an "area," a "realm," a "region" to be won and dominated.[53] In other words, the being of American thought in *Pierre*, even more than the being of American space, has been reduced by an epistemological comportment toward "it" that *sees* its "darkly" differential, ambiguous, and ineffable dynamics from the end (all at once) to a classified space, to an (enlightened) comprehensively compact map, as it were. By putting every detail in time and space in its *proper place* within the larger identical whole, to put it alternatively, this epistemological comportment toward being—this spatializing thinking/practice, epitomized later in the century by Frederick Jackson Turner's "frontier thesis"—facilitates imperial domination of the wild (nomadic) "Other." In short, the world of antebellum American thought in *Pierre* has been utterly colonized and domesticated (at-homed) under the aegis of the metaphysical/hegemonic discourse of Manifest Destiny. Even the emergent dissident who, like Pierre, would resist the domination enabled by this totally mapped/colonized American thinking is compelled to do so in the imperial metaphysical language of the American "world" that must render errancy "docile" even if, as a last, very reluctant, resort, it must kill him.

This, I think, against those New Americanist readings that interpret the narrator's distance from Pierre as a decisive condemnation of his protagonist's narcissistic subjectivity, is the testimony of Pierre's futile Titanic attempt, against the prevailing "Olympian" gods, to write a "comprehensively compact" book that would "gospelize the world anew."[54] It is not Pierre's *self-induced* failure to realize his Titanic project to "gospelize the world anew" in the form of a novel that brings Melville's novel to its "close." That "end" begins, rather—and this violence is the measure of Melville's agonized consciousness of the apartness of the *Abgeschiedene* in antebellum America—with the awesome Silence of the resounding suicidal pistol shots Pierre fires into the body of the relentless representative of the American "world" and its saying, a Silence, moreover, in which is also heard the outraged—and ominous—voices of those other constituencies of American society who have been denied speech: the Indian, the black slave or "freeman," the servant, the female, and the intellectual.[55] And it is that dreadful Silence—that possible consequence of the bereavement of language—much more than Pierre's ineluctable adherence to the principle of self-reliance that Melville intended his self-confident antebellum American audience to *think*.

VI

Pierre's silence—his failure to realize the indissoluble affiliation between the representation of being as such, of self, and of world, and thus to "say" what he has intuited about them—implies, just as Melville's later abandonment of writing fiction, in one sense his utter defeat by "the world." But, as I have tried to suggest by invoking Heidegger's exilic *Abgeschiedene*, Melville, as narrator of Pierre's "story," also suggests, paradoxically, something more positive, something that is only now, at the extreme limits of the late phase of the postmodern occasion, beginning, if all too tentatively, to be thought: when, that is, the domestication and forgetting of the original, potentially emancipatory force of the postmodern initiative by its own practitioners' inhibitions and its consequent reduction to a periodizing reference that equates it to the logic of late capitalism has become in some degree manifest.[56] Pierre's silence means that he has no language with which to resist the vengeful "world" that has closed in on him in his place of refuge. But for Melville, who, unlike Pierre, does "complete" his novel *without* succumbing to the disabling metaphysical imperatives of "comprehensively compact" completeness, it also implies "e-mergence," an incipient understanding of the indissoluble continuum of being that is totally foreign to the representation of being that informs the "world's" discourse. As the one a-part, as stranger, as exile, as outsider (*within* his homeland) Pierre, in Melville's view, is indeed the "barbarian" at the gates, not, however, in the negative sense given to this word by the imperial Romans, but in the positive sense, ultimately deriving from the ancient Greeks, given to it by the e-mergent discourse of contemporary postcolonialism: one who does not speak "Greek," that is, does not think/say in terms of—*refuses to be answerable to*—the accommodational imperatives of the truth discourse of the dominant order. As such, Pierre's death, which is to say, his silencing by the hegemonic American culture precipitates his spectral return. Pierre fails to think his occasion to its radically emergent end; Melville, however, does not. For Melville, dead Pierre becomes the "ghost" that, according to Heidegger, haunts the reified and reifying thought of American modernity which will have nothing to do with "ghosts," or, in Derrida's version (which, in politicizing the "trace," thematizes the imperial visualism that informs Western logocentric thinking), the *revenant*, the "dead" who returns to *visit* the (colonial) *visitor*.[57]

It is this resonant contradiction, this spectral silence, that e-merges with the fulfillment—the violent narrative end—of the "benign" circular logic of the "world" of antebellum America. The last spoken words of the novel, which Isabel pointedly addresses to the "world" that has murdered Pierre, are: "All's o'er now, and *ye know him not*" (*P*, 362; my emphasis). The dramatic narrative of Pierre's life has arrived at the denouement of its fifth act. But this "decisive" end does not bring the peace—the *catharsis*—of canonical tragedy, which, in rendering the catastrophic ontologically intelligible, reconciles "Man" to Being. This "denouement," that is, does not enable us—we inexorably "confident" Americans—to distance ourselves, as we want endings to, from the horror of this extreme American *event*. It does not allow us, as we, like the Panglossians in *The Confidence-Man*, would wish, to *see* Pierre's catastrophic fate as an essential detail in a larger and meaningful structural or aesthetic whole, a monument, as it were, that, not only obliterates the polyvalent violence at its core but vindicates its perpetrator. Instead, the "closure" of Pierre's story—his, Lucy's and Isabel's deaths—releases this differential "detail" as an ominous and disconcerting irregular force, a force that disrupts the will to harmonize and regulate. Isabel's last words, in other words, constitute a silent, irrepressibly phantasmic, accusation directed against the all-knowing and confident American "world's" truth—which would include representing Pierre's deadly assault on Glen Stanly as a murder—and against the American reader/auditor who would sublimate social violence against the shadowy "Other" of the enlightened "world" in the name of the universal (tragedy, for example): the "Talismanic Secret." "And you know him not": "Your knowing gaze," Isabel seems to say, "has silenced him, turned him into stone, compelled him into his 'proper' and intelligible place in the knowledge-producing discourse of the larger American whole. But he has escaped the petrifying gaze of your Medusan eye. And, despite his interment, you will *hear* from him again."

In his magisterial reading of *Pierre*, Sacvan Bercovitch notes Melville's use of the metaphorics of shadowing to evoke the return of the obliterated violence of the American past to haunt the hegemonic American present in all its social and political manifestations. But it is Isabel, not Pierre, whom he identifies with this ghostly visitation: "Isabel's shadow falls across all aspects of Saddle Meadows: across Indian mounds and traces of slave-quarters; across Mary Glendinning's abuse of Delly Ulver; across Falsgrave's abuse of religious principles; across the relations of master and servant, lady and tenant farmer; across the class hierarchy thriving 'in the heart of a republic.' "[58] Bercovitch's evocation of the metaphor of the shadow constitutes a significant insight into the essence of Melville's interrogation of "America" in *Pierre*. But because it is, I think, misplaced, it remains for Bercovitch nothing more than a disposable metaphor, a conclusion warranted by the fact that it vanishes from his text immediately after it appears. This is not to say that the terrible fate of Isabel at the hands of the "truth" of Saddle Meadows/America is irrelevant. It is to say, rather, that Bercovitch's dissociation of Isabel's fate from Pierre's forecloses the possibility of thinking what Melville's uncanny text wants us to think: the indissoluble affiliation between the metaphorics of the shadow and the theme of Silence. After all, it is not so much Isabel as it is Pierre who, in his extraordinary emergency, is given the task of thinking to the terrible and futile end the relation between Isabel's predicament and the world that has abandoned her: her "non-being" and the "world's" truth, the saying that hegemony permits. As a result of Bercovitch's dissociation of Isabel and Pierre—a dissociation, I would suggest, incumbent on an Americanist's continuing faith, despite his obvious suspicions about American exceptionalism, in the viability of American discourse—he fails to think Melville's insistent reference to the shadow adequately; fails, that is, to perceive that for Melville the shadow *is an ontological reality* that is at the dark heart of his novel, that, like the sun's shadow, *belongs to* the saying of the American world.[59]

This "dark" Other that *returns* to haunt the "world" in the form of Isabel's ominous accusation is not, as I have suggested, restricted to the type of Pierre. According to the anti-logical logic of *Pierre*, it also includes, as Bercovitch observes, women (the "dark" Isabel and the "deviant" Lucy Tartan), the working class (Delly), and, not least, if we are attuned to the historical (antebellum) context of the composition of *Pierre* and to the national (monumental) framework in which Melville places his domestic "romance," native Americans and black slaves (including those in the North who have been "freed" since the days of "grand old Pierre"). In *thinking* the occasion of Pierre's extraordinary emergency, Melville makes thinking the spectral nothing and its worldly manifestations possible. We might say, in keeping with the metaphor of the monument (and that which is inscribed in Pierre's name), he has in some latent sense gotten "water out of a stone," which is to say, "a Voice out of Silence." This "miracle," it should be emphasized, is not restricted to *Pierre*. It is, as I will show in the following chapters, also the resonant testimony of *Israel Potter* (the retrieved voice of the forgotten veteran of the American Revolution), of "Benito Cereno" (the ominous silence of Babo, whose severed head "met, unabashedly the gaze of the whites"), of "Bartleby, the Scrivener" (the echoing accusation of the law clerk's "I prefer not to"), of *The Confidence-Man* (the dia-bolic ironies of the many avatars of the confidence man), and, though it is outside the context of this book, of *Billy Budd* (the stutter that returns to haunt the official naval narrative that brings to a "decisive close" the terrible events on board the self-defeated HMS *Indomitable*). And if we understand Ishmael's errant garrulousness—its refusal to come to closure—as the obverse face of the white whale's silence, it is also the testimony of *Moby-Dick*.[60] I am referring, of course, to those "orphans" or, as Thomas Pynchon would say following his predecessor's interrogation of Puritanism, those aporetic "preterites" that the hegemonic discourse of a divinely or historically "elected" American Fatherland has passed over (in silence). Indeed, if we attend to the ghostly history of Melville's reception in America, as I have done in the introduction of this book, it might also be said that this is the resonant testimony of Melville's creative life itself, especially after the publication of *Pierre*, when the custodians of the confident, self-satisfied, arrogant, and lethal American Cultural Memory "turn[ed] their critical Aegis upon him" to "freeze him into silence."

It is, I submit, this voice of silence—this "saying" of what the thinking of the dominant American culture renders unsayable—that constitutes Melville's most revolutionary legacy to the postmodern American occasion. For in thus wrenching by violence a polyvalent positive content from Pierre's silence, Melville anticipates the postmodernist diagnosis of modernity as the "end" of philosophy. I mean, after Heidegger, its disclosure that the fulfillment of modernity's imperial spatializing logic in the "Age of the World Picture"—and, not incidentally, its ensuing confident pronouncement of the "end of history"—paradoxically precipitates into invisible visibility the nothing—the excess—that this reified and reifying, that is, stony, logic necessarily cannot finally accommodate. Melville, as we have seen, insistently identifies this unaccountable and uncontainable nothing with the emerged errant orphan. I, in order to identify "it" with the underdetermined question of thinking itself, have followed Heidegger in identifying it with the *Abgeschiedene*, the one a-part, the stranger, the exile, the wanderer. Whether "orphan" or "*Abgeschiedene*," or, for that matter, "pariah" (Arendt)[61] or "differend" or "jew" (Lyotard)[62] or "catachrestic remainder" (Spivak)[63] or the "singular event" (Foucault)[64] or "specter" (Derrida)[65] or "nomad" (Deleuze and Guattari),[66] or *homo tantum* (Negri and Hardt)[67] or "whatever being": *qualunque* (Agamben),[68] he or she is the spectral "non-being" who, at the extreme limit of the discursive empire, returns to haunt the Being of metaphysics and the totalized hegemonic world that has constructed itself on its imperial foundation: the "world" that, as it were, has buried him or her at its periphery in silence. And, as such, "it" thus calls for thinking.[69]

But the disclosure instigated by the reconstellation of Melville's *Pierre* from the Americanist context in which it has been imbedded into the contemporary context, opened up by recent continental theory and the achievement of global hegemony by the United States, is not limited to the urgency of the question of thinking/saying as such. If, as I think Melville intends, we read the domestic/national mise-en-scène of *Pierre* in the global geopolitical context of *Moby-Dick*, and if we attend to his insistent identification of his "defeated" preterites—social de-viants such as Pierre and Bartleby, authentic and spontaneous believers in the dignity of free humanity such as Israel Potter and Billy Budd, "mariners, renegades, and castaways" such as the crew of the Pequod, women, blacks, native Americans, servants, and ethnic migrants—with the one who has been orphaned (exiled) from the American Father(land) by the American symbolic order, we are enable—indeed, compelled—to project his proleptic thematization of the e-mergent specter into a wider social context. Specifically, such a reconstellation of the domestic site of *Pierre* will allow us to see that Melville's infusion of a latent positive content into Pierre's silence is also, however inaugurally, proleptic of that polyvalent strategy of resistance to global capitalist power that Gilles Deleuze and Félix Guattari, by way of positing a "smooth," "deterritorialized," "rhizomatic" thinking against the "striated" territorialized (mapped) thought of the late capitalist dispensation, have called "nomadology."[70] I am referring particularly to the late or post-postmodern theoretical initiative that, in infusing a positive emancipatory content into the minor—"errant"—terms of the "triumphant" binary logic of Western metaphysical thought, has precipitated a certain inaugural, polyvalent postcolonial discourse most suggestively, but far from adequately, exemplified by Edward Said's *Culture and Imperialism*, Gayatri Spivak's *The Postcolonial Subject*, Homi Bhabha's essays in *The Location of Culture*, and, in a more theoretical way, by Jacques Derrida's *Specters of Marx* and Antonio Negri and Michael Hardt's *Empire* and *Multitude*. This is the emancipatory postcolonial discourse that takes its point of departure precisely from the massive global demographic displacements that constitute the terrible legacy of modern Western imperialism (and, according to Hannah Arendt, from the anti-Semitism/racism that is endemic to it),[71] from, that is, the "extraordinary emergency" of a vast population of *emigrés*, exiles, displaced persons, migrants—nomads, as it were—who, as Edward Said has borne poignant witness, have been unhomed, both as subjectivities and as citizens, by the depredations of modern (post-Enlightenment) colonialism:

> [It] is no exaggeration to say that liberation as an intellectual mission, born in the resistance and opposition to the confinements and ravages of imperialism, has now shifted from the settled, established, and domesticated dynamics of culture to its unhoused, decentered, and exilic energies, energies whose incarnation today is the migrant, and whose consciousness is that of the intellectual and artist in exile, the political figure between domains, between forms, between homes, and between languages.[72]

Like Melville's in *Pierre*, this emergent postcolonial discourse is a "deterritorialized" or "diasporic" or "hybrid" discourse that, in intuiting the impotency of the power of the binarist spatial logic of Western representational thinking, is learning not simply to refuse to be answerable to the *saying* of the imperial First World, but to turn that refusal—that thunderous silence—into an effective emancipatory practice. It is, in short, an e-mergent discourse, that, like Melville's at the site of domestic America, is learning to get a "Voice out of Silence."

The reconstellation of Pierre I have attempted should by now have made clear the irony of Melville's emergent occasion. It is not simply that his sustained effort since *Moby-Dick*—and especially in *Pierre*—to think his estrangement from the American homeland in the context of the history of Old World philosophy culminates in the explosion of the myth of American exceptionalism. In thinking his emergency—his being inside/outside the American cultural machine—he anticipates the decentered and errant thought of the new Europeans and thus becomes truly American exceptionalist.

VII

It is, in other words, this resonantly proleptic Melvillean insight into the emancipatory possibilities inhering in the spectral "voice of silence" that the "Old Americanists"—whether those early critics who pronounced the Melville who wrote *Pierre* "mad" or branded him a moral monster to be "frozen into silence" or those much later revivalist critics of the 1920s who reified his fictions into monuments of the humanist American Spirit or those founders of American literary studies who, identifying his work with an "American Renaissance," harnessed Melville to the ideology of the Cold War—have tried to obliterate in the name of the truth of American exceptionalism. Nevertheless, these "Old Americanist" efforts have been futile. The obsessively recurrent historical projects to willfully accommodate Melville's late fiction—we can now call them spectral texts—to the central and, to appropriate the key word of *Moby-Dick*, "concentering" (nationalist) myth of American exceptionalism bear resonant witness to the anxiety their "silence" has always provoked. For the supplemental character (in Derrida's sense of the word) of these accommodational efforts has increasingly marked the deferral of the Melvillean "presence" they would bring to stand within the "space" of the nation, would, that is, turn into a marbleized monument of American exceptionalism. Like Pierre, Melville always already returns to haunt the American eye that would *know* and thus turn him into silent stone.

It is no doubt the visible recalcitrance of Melville's spectral texts—their silent excess that refuses to be accommodated to American saying—that has, in part, precipitated the so called New Americanist project to interrogate the Old Americanist problematic: the "field imaginary" that emanates radially and totally from the American exceptionalist center. But this initiative, however productive in exposing the reactionary, nationalist ideological agenda subsuming the abortive effort to monumentalize Melville's novels, remains vestigially blind to what I have called Melville's essential legacy. And this is because, with some significant exceptions, the "New Americanist" discourse, unlike Melville himself, remains too parochially *within* the American exceptionalist problematic it would call into question—too indifferent, therefore, to the critical imperatives of the voices of the exilic or outside "Others" silenced by the imperial American exceptionalist culture. As Paul Bové has put this disabling limitation in a telling critique of Sacvan Bercovitch's general New Americanist project that aptly appropriates Gayatri Spivak's (and, implicity, Edward Said's) version of the "postcolonial subject":

> While honoring the values of distance and the experience of exile that theorize it as a critical necessity, one must also wonder if the study of culture does not require an even more complex and difficult position: being in and of one's locale while understanding its needs and hence one's own projects in terms of a global or transnational set of interlocking perspectives. The best critical emblem for our time might be what Gayatri Spivak has taught us to call the "postcolonial subject," that is, the gendered intellectual engaged in agonistic analysis of global issues central to regional and national concerns and always motivated by an understanding of the complex position that any citizen of a postmodern cultural multiplicity must occupy.
> I want to suggest... that "American Studies" taken as a field in it "theoretical fullness"... has not yet reached the point of "exile" in relation to itself and its nationalist projects.[73]

In the specific case of Melville, the consequence of this vestigial parochialism has been a tendency to represent him as essentially an "American" writer, a writer, it seems, who eschews "theory"—by which I mean *the question of thinking*—as a decadent "European" penchant and therefore irrelevant or even detrimental to the good American life. Despite its interrogation of the myth of American exceptionalism, that is, the New Americanist literary discourse all too often fails to perceive that Melville's fiction, especially from *Moby-Dick* on, has its essential point of departure in his critical recognition that American exceptionalism is a myth that obscures America's affiliative relationship to a Europe that, in founding and historically reproducing its identity on metaphysics—the perception of temporality (and its disseminations) from the end—is *imperial in essence*. In thus failing to thematize this originative thrust of Melville's fiction, this New Americanist discourse also has failed to adequately recognize that its force (in the Nietzschean sense of this word, which is to say its proleptic relevance to the late postmodern occasion) derives precisely from his acute consciousness of being both inside and outside his culture (a part and apart): from, that is, having "reached the point of exile in relation to [himself] and [his] national projects." To put it in the terms that *Pierre* and, as I will show, the work that immediately follows, makes possible, what this vestigial parochialism of the New Americanist discourse misses in its revisionary readings of Melville's late texts is his proleptic announcement of the "*end*" of the kind of thinking that has mapped not simply American (and global) geographical space, but also, in its subjection of thinking to spatial categories, the "space" of thinking itself. By *end*, as I have suggested, I do not simply mean *fulfillment*: the establishment of a plenary condition that renders any other way of thinking/saying impossible. I also mean "limit": the e-mergence at the end—in the fifth act—of this enforced Silence as a *catachresis*: a spectral Voice that cannot finally be accommodated by and to the saying of (metaphysical) thinking and thus calls for thinking.

As I have suggested in thus reconstellating *Pierre* into the late postmodern context, it is precisely the now urgent question of *thinking* and its relationship to global sociopolitics that constitutes the supreme theme of Melville's writing from *Moby-Dick* on. Or, more precisely, it is his urgent sense of the need to rethink an American "democratic" thinking, a thinking that, far from exceptionalist, brought the deadly European metaphysical virus and its sense of an ending into the "new world wilderness." For this project the American Melville availed himself, perhaps more than any other American writer before or after him, with the exception of Henry Adams and Thomas Pynchon, of the entire history, or at least the primary monuments, of Western philosophical thought—of what Heidegger aptly calls the ontotheological tradition. And the knowledge he gained from his own reconstellation of this tradition allowed him not only to recognize the social and political violence its metaphysics enables, but also, however inaugurally, to think the Silence that the triumph of metaphysical thinking has precipitated as an emergent contradiction, as the specter that always already haunts the *Pax Metaphysica* and its optimistic/imperial end-of-history discourse.

As I will show more fully in the chapters that follow, it is Melville's reading of the ontological identity of America and Europe—his demythification of the American exceptionalist problematic—that affiliates the post–*Moby-Dick* Melville proleptically with a certain polyvalent, emancipatory strain of postmodern or post-European thought that begins with Heidegger and Arendt (*pace* her Habermasian disciples) and culminates in the late postmodern initiatives of the Bhabha of *The Location of Culture*, the Lyotard of *The Differend*, the Deleuze and Guatarri of *A Thousand Plateaus*, the Derrida of *Specters of Marx*, the Georgio Agamben of *The Coming Community*, and, on a more immediately *praxis*-oriented register, the Spivak of *Outside in the Teaching Machine*, the V. Y. Mudimbe of *The Idea of Africa*, the Said of *Culture and Imperialism*, The Ranajit Guha of *Elementary Aspects of Peasant Insurgency in Colonial India*, the Partha Chatterjee of *The Nation and Its Fragments*, the Dipesh Chakrabarty of *Provincializing Europe*, the Arjun Appadurai of *Modernity at Large*, and the Negri and Hardt of *Empire* and *The Multitude*. I am not simply referring to those ontological initiatives of postmodern thought that would think the *nothing*, or the *trace*, or the *aporia*, or the *differend*, or the *catachrestic remainder*, or the *hybrid* ("*the minus in the origin*") that the metaphysical thought of the West, especially its modern, instrumentalist allotrope, will, at all costs, have nothing to do with. I am also referring to those political initiatives of postmodern thought—indissolubly, if still only symptomatically, related to these ontological initiatives—that would think the massive and diverse constituency of the human community that the Western *polis*, especially in its modern, liberal democratic/capitalist manifestation, has had to reduce to non-being in its relentless effort to achieve hegemony over the planet: the *pariah*, the *migrant*, the *emigré*, the *stateless*, the *undocumented*, the *unhomed*, the *denizen*, the *multitude*. It is, in turn, Melville's critical reading of American "exceptionalism" that calls New Americanists to the task of availing themselves of this spectral post- "European" thinking to rethink American democratic thought and practice from an American point of view that is also beyond—outside—the American periphery. From, that is, an ec-static, in-sistent—ghostly—perspective that haunts the confidence of the *Pax Metaphysica* and the *Pax Americana* it enables and justifies. What, in short, I will suggest in the chapters that follow, the silent specter of Melville's post–*Moby-Dick* fiction calls for now, in the age that the arrogant intellectual deputies of the official culture of America first identified as "the end of history" and the advent of the "New World Order" presided over by the United States, and later, after the attack on American soil on 9/11/01, re-scripted as the perpetual "war on terror," is a spectral politics, a politics that puts into positive practice the dislocating refusal of Pierre, of Bartleby, of Israel Potter, of Babo, and of the Confidence-Man. Until that comes to pass, I will claim, resistance, no matter how vocal, will remain impotent or complicit with America's (exceptionalist) apparatuses of capture.

Chapter 3

Herman Melville's *Israel Potter*
Reflections on a Damaged Life

[Genealogical history] teaches how to laugh at the solemnities of the origin. The lofty origin is no more than "a metaphysical extension which arises from the belief that things are most precious and essential at the moment of birth." We tend to think that this is the moment of their greatest perfection, when they emerge dazzling from the hand of a creator or in the shadowless light of a first morning. The origin always precedes the Fall. It comes before the body, before the world and time: it is associated with the gods, and its story is always sung as a theogony. But historical beginnings are lowly.

—Michel Foucault, "Nietzsche, Genealogy, History"

Herman Melville's *Israel Potter: His Fifty-Years of Exile* begins with a "dedication": "To His Highness, the Bunker-hill Monument." In opposition to the traditional function of dedications in European literature—the apotheosis of an aristocratic patron—this one is ostensibly intended to bestow resonant grandeur to an American monument that celebrates the memory of the heroism of ordinary American soldiers who died in one of the first battles of a revolutionary war against the tyranny of British monarchical rule in behalf of the establishment of the experiment of American democracy. But this apparent intention is, of course, problematized by Melville's implicit genealogy of the Bunker Hill Monument, a genealogy, the general significance of which is embodied synecdochically by the *forgotten* "story" of the appropriately named "private," Israel Potter:

> Israel Potter well merits the present tribute—a private of Bunker Hill, who for his faithful services was years ago promoted to a still deeper privacy under the ground, with a posthumous pension, in default of any during life, annually paid him by the spring in ever-new mosses and sward.
>
> I am the more encouraged to lay this performance at the feet of your Highness, because, with a change in the grammatical person,

it preserves, almost as in a reprint, Israel Potter's autobiographical story. Shortly after his return in infirm old age to his native land, a little narrative of his adventures, forlornly published on sleazy gray paper, appeared among the peddlers, written, probably, not by himself, but taken down from his lips by another. But like the crutch-marks of the cripple by the Beautiful Gate, this blurred record is now out of print. From a tattered copy, rescued by the merest chance from the rag-pickers, the present account has been drawn, which, with the exception of some expansions and additions of historic and personal detail, and one or two shiftings of scene, may, perhaps, be not unfitly regarded something in the light of a dilapidated old tombstone retouched.[1]

There has been much scholarly commentary on this unusual ironic dedication, but most of it has been intended to demonstrate the (quite obvious) distinction between Melville's masterful "retouching" of this "dilapidated old tombstone" and the banal original, *Life and Remarkable Adventures of Israel R. Potter* (1824), universally thought to have been written and published by an opportunistic Yankee hack, one Henry Trumbull, at the dictation of Israel Potter.[2] As one Melvillian critic put it, "Melville had presumably set out in all good conscience simply to rewrite Henry Trumbull's *Life*.... After allowing himself the luxury of a lyric opening chapter, he had settled down into paraphrase.... But restlessness led to increasing invention, and then suddenly two things seemed to have happened at once. Melville discovered that at its midpoint his source itself fell apart, its simple narrative line giving way to a tangled recital of random disasters and bathetic appeals. His interest in it waned. He would come back to Potter's last years, but the four decades of bleak back-city deprivation and crime, of starvation, beggary, and domestic tragedy, *lost their powers of attraction, perhaps became repellent*. But as his source failed him, Melville's fictional urgencies began to assert themselves" (*IP*, 205; my emphasis). What I want to suggest in the following remarks is, in part, that Melville's "rescue" of this narrative "from the rag-pickers" was in fact a resurrection of Israel Potter's singularity from the oblivion into which it was interred by the custodians of the American cultural memory or, to put this intent more contemporaneously, a retrieval of his *being* that the emergent dominant middle-class culture and the American Archive had denied him in the necessarily forgetful remembering process of nation-building. In this symbolic act, which, in its critical phase echoes his genealogy of Saddle Meadows in *Pierre*, Melville was anticipating Friedrich Nietzsche's assault on "monumental history"—a history that, as Michel Foucault puts it, is "given to reestablishing the high points of historical development and their maintenance in a perpetual presence, given to the recovery of works, action, and creations through the monogram of their personal essence" as well as Foucault's own genealogical project.³ Foucault ransacked the European Archive to retrieve its discards for the double purpose of disclosing the relations of power concealed in the selective mnemonic process that produced the "benign" truths of Western modernity (the democratic subject, discourse, and polis) and of giving back a history to those "irrelevant" beings to whom History, which is to say, the intellectual deputies of the dominant Western culture, had denied a history. Similarly, though not methodologically, it was Melville's penchant to search for forgotten texts of the American Archive for the purpose not only of disclosing the ideology that led to their obliteration from the American cultural memory, but also of retrieving their singularity—that concrete and unaccommodatable aspect of their "stories" that threatened its hegemony—for positive thought. This "contrapuntal" interpretive process, to appropriate the apt language of Edward W. Said,⁴ is, for example, borne witness to by Melville's retrieval and rearticulation of the "stories" of Jack Chase (*White Jacket*), Colonel Moredock (*The Confidence-Man*), Captain Delano ("Benito Cereno"), Billy Budd (*Billy Budd*), and, most tellingly, Israel Potter, among others.

Understood from this genealogical perspective, then, Melville's "dedication" "To His Highness, the Bunker-Hill Monument," becomes a carnivalesque parody not only of the *monumentalism* of monarchical regimes, but also, and more important, of the democratic "regimes of truth"⁵ that emerged in the Age of the Enlightenment in the wake of the American and French Revolutions. Indeed, as his play on the physical height of the monument suggests—and as I will show at length—his "dedication" comes to be seen as an ironic revelation of the blindness or hypocrisy of the monumental histories of the custodians of the American cultural memory. I mean those selective histories, or, in Sacvan Bercovitch's more precise phrase, "American jeremiads," whose function in reality was and continues to be to archivalize *only* the *high* points—and, as in the case of the historian/biographer Jared Sparks, whom Melville identifies in the "dedication," the *exemplary* national leaders—of American history in behalf of the post-Revolutionary dominant Protestant middle-class/capitalist culture's effort to mobilize and secure or resecure the patriotism, national solidarity, and confidence of a diverse plurality of people in a state of social crisis.⁶ It is in defiance not simply of this indifference of the American monumentalist historians to the nameless and forgotten ordinary soldiers—the singularity of their being—who suffered the deaths and physical and psychological wounds of America's wars, but also, as in the case of *Pierre*, of the very ritual of monumentalizing that Melville "sponsors" the "lowly" and "irrelevant" story of "private" Israel Potter to "His ["lofty" and "exalted"] Highness"—the "Great Biographer"—who, finally, is nothing more than a towering structure composed of slabs of granite.

Such is the work, and such the man, that I have the honor to present to your Highness. That the name here noted should not have appeared in the volumes of Sparks, may or may not be a matter for astonishment; but Israel Potter seems purposely to have waited to make his popular advent under the present exalted patronage, seeing that your Highness, according to the definition above, may, in the loftiest sense, be deemed the *Great Biographer: the national commemorator* of such of the anonymous privates of June 17, 1775 [the date of the Battle of Bunker Hill], who may never have received other requital than the solid reward of your granite. (*IP*, viii; my emphasis)[7]

I have underscored Melville's acutely ironic personification of the Bunker Hill Monument as the authoritative "national commemorator" of the anonymous and forgotten lives of the "privates" who fought and died in the battle in his dedication on June 17, 1854 to mark two analogous and nationally significant ceremonial events that, reconstellated into the context of the novel, shed significant light on Melville's historical and theoretical intention in salvaging *The Life and Remarkable Adventures of Israel R. Potter* from the discards of the American Archive. I am referring to the two dedicatory speeches given by the renowned orator-statesman Daniel Webster on the anniversary of the battle and at the site of the Bunker Hill Monument, the first on June 17, 1825, at the laying of the cornerstone of the monument, and the second, on June 17, 1843, around five or six years before Melville found the original manuscript and decided to "retouch" this "dilapidated old tombstone."[8] As far as I can tell, this resonant connection has surprisingly gone unnoticed by the considerable number of recent critics who have written on *Israel Potter*, probably because the standard biographies of Melville and his published letters make only a few passing references to Webster and none to his Bunker Hill orations.[9] Whatever the reason for this remarkable oversight, the very fact that one of the most prominent "Americans" of that time, a New Englander of Puritan origins, a devout nationalist, and a powerful member of the dominant culture, gave two commemorative speeches, both of which immediately became American classics, on the anniversary and at the site of the Battle of Bunker Hill, speeches that, in addressing the monument, would suggest the possibility that Melville's "dedication" "To His Highness, the Bunker-Hill Monument" was intended as a carnivalesque commentary on Webster's lofty and orotund orations before this phallic "shaft." If, further, that history is not warrant enough, then the visible parallels in the rhetoric, tropes, and content between Melville's ironic "dedication" and the following lines of Webster's second oration should dispel any doubts:

The Bunker Hill Monument is finished. Here it stands. Fortunate in the high natural eminence on which it is placed, higher, infinitely higher in its objects and purpose, it rises over the land and over the sea; and, visible, at their homes, to three hundred thousand of the people of Massachusetts, it stands a memorial of the last, and a monitor to the present and to all succeeding generations. I have spoken of the loftiness of it purpose. If it had been without any other design than the creation of a work of art, the granite of which it is composed would have slept in its native bed. It has a purpose, and that purpose gives it its character. That purpose enrobes it with dignity and moral grandeur. That well-known purpose it is which causes us to look up to it with a feeling of awe. *It is itself the orator of this occasion. It is not from my lips, it could not be from any human lips, that that strain of eloquence is this day to flow most competent to move and excite the vast multitudes around me. The powerful speaker stands before us. It is a plain shaft. . . . To-day it speaks to us. Its future auditories will be the successive generations of men, as they rise up before it and gather around it. Its speech will be of patriotism and courage; of civil and religious liberty; of free government; of moral improvement and elevation of mankind; and of the immortal memory of those who, with heroic devotion, have sacrificed their lives for their country.* (*M*, 262–263; my emphasis)

In invoking the "parallel" between Webster's and Melville's dedication to the Bunker Hill Monument, my intention is not simply to restrict attention to a hitherto unnoticed "source" of *Israel Potter*. What I want to suggest, rather, is that, in alluding to Webster's renowned speeches in his inaugural dedication, Melville's intention is to render this American cultural and political "hero" an implicit "monumental" presence in his novel, a mock idealization, in other words, that will enable his readers to understand his larger parodic sociopolitical intention in pitting the lowly nobody Israel Potter against Benjamin Franklin, John Paul Jones, and Ethan Allen, three towering historical figures who, by Melville's time, had been canonized by the dominant culture in America, which is to say, had become assimilated into the American national identity. Despite his avowal to his publisher that "there will be very little reflective writing in it; nothing weighty. It is adventure,"[10] Melville is no less serious, however different in style, than he was in writing *Pierre*. His purpose, in other words, is genealogical in the Foucauldian sense: to disclose, for the *present antebellum occasion*, the dark underside of the nation-building tradition that had its "sacred" Origin in the Puritans' exceptionalist, divinely ordained "errand in the wilderness," its adolescence in the mythification of the singularity of the American Revolution, and it maturation in the imperial nationalism espoused by the symbolic figure of Daniel Webster—and, as Melville's ambivalent phrase, "nothing weighty," suggests, to hint, however, tentatively, at the positive sociopolitical possibilities inhering in the "ghostly" or "spectral" reality that the dominant culture's nation-building obsession would obliterate, forget, or accommodate to its *logos*.

To consider briefly the critical intention of his genealogy first, what Melville in his implicit allusion to Webster's Bunker Hill orations is pointing to is the latter's identification of Bunker Hill as "the sepulchre of our fathers" (*M*, 235) and the celebration of the Battle of Bunker Hill as the glorious *spiritual* birth (Origin) of the American nation. To Webster, this was the epochal event by which, through "their valor, their constancy, and the shedding of their blood" (*M*, 236) in behalf of the common cause of liberty from tyranny and their instigation of the patriotic and indissoluble filial unity of the diverse, linguistic, (white) racial, and ideological enclaves of the colonies, these "Fathers" not only brought the prefigurative Puritan past to fruition: "To us, their children, the story of their labors and sufferings can never be without interest. We shall not stand unmoved on the shore of Plymouth, while the sea continues to wash it" (*M*, 236).[11] In thus establishing a binding sacred Origin characterized by the apotheosis of liberty, Webster also celebrates its maturation in "a new spirit of enterprise and industry" (*M*, 252)—the Protestant work ethic in its capitalist manifestation[12]—and envisions an evolving global future under the aegis of an exceptionalist democratic/capitalist America:

> And now, let us indulge an honest exultation on the conviction of the benefit which the example of our country has produced, and is likely to produce, on human freedom and human happiness. Let us endeavor to comprehend in all its magnitude ... the part assigned to us in the great drama of human affairs. We are placed at the head of the system of representative and popular governments. Thus far our example shows that such governments are compatible, not only with respectability and power, but with repose, with peace, with security of personal rights, with good laws, and a just administration. (*M*, 252–253)

The triumphant last act of this "great drama of human affairs," to which "we" have been "assigned" (by Providence) to play the major (messianic) role, however, will, Webster warns his American audience, depend on "our" commitment to this sacred trust: our confidence in the principle of "liberty" for which the fathers died and the truth of America's exceptionalist errand and, not least, our filial (covenantal) fulfillment of the "sacred obligations which have devolved on this generation." Typical of the American jeremiad (and not unlike the confidence-man in Melville's last novel, though straightforwardly), Webster brings his "lofty" oration and its rolling periods to its resounding close with an appeal to this confidence by way of emphasizing, like his Puritan forebears (John Winthrop's sermon on board the *Arabella* comes especially to mind), America's global errand and the threat that would undermine it in the very process of disclaiming it:

Our history hitherto proves . . . that the popular form is practicable, and that with wisdom and knowledge men may govern themselves; and the duty incumbent on us is, to preserve the consistency of this cheering-example, and take care that nothing may weaken its authority with the world. If . . . the representative system ultimately fail, popular governments must be pronounced impossible. No combination of circumstances more favorable to the experiment can ever be expected to occur. The last hopes of mankind, therefore, rests with us; and if it should be proclaimed, that our example had become an argument against the experiment, the knell of popular liberty would be sounded throughout the earth. . . .

And let the sacred obligations which have devolved on this generation, and on us, sink deep into our hearts. Those who established our liberty and our government are daily dropping from among us. The great trust now descends to new hands. Let us apply ourselves to that which is presented to us, as our appropriate object. We can win no laurels in a war for independence. Earlier and worthier hands have gathered them all. Nor are there places for us by the side of Solon, and Alfred, and other founders of states. Our fathers have filled them. But there remains to us a great duty of defence and preservation, and there is opened to us, also, a noble pursuit, to which the spirit of the times strongly invites us. Our proper business is improvement. Let our age be the age of improvement. . . . Let us develop the resources of our land, call forth its powers, build up its institutions, promote all its great interests, and see whether we also, in our day and generation, may not perform something worthy to be remembered. Let us cultivate a true spirit of union and harmony. . . . Let us extend our ideas over the whole of the vast field in which we are called to act. Let our object be, OUR COUNTRY, OUR WHOLE COUNTRY, AND NOTHING BUT OUR COUNTRY. And, by the blessing of God, may that country itself become a vast and splendid monument, not of oppression and terror, but of Wisdom, Peace, and Liberty, upon which the world may gaze with admiration forever! (*M*, 253–254)[13]

In this first oration, Webster, from the perspective of this present ritualistic moment, envisions a glorious American future of national (and racial) unity—a various multitude transformed into a *people*[14]—that, like the monument symbolizing this transformation, will be the object of the eternal admiring gaze of all of humanity. This future is justified by the heroic and glorious American past that culminates in the sacrifice of the "fathers" epitomized by the (phallic) obelisk commemorating the Battle of Bunker Hill. And its permanence is dependent on the maintenance of the national covenant: the preservation of "the consistency of this cheering example." Informing and enabling this manifest destinarian (i.e., metaphysical) vision of history—and the jeremiadic call for unity in the face of the "daily dropping from us" of those heroes who "established our liberty"—is, as the references to God suggests, a more or less secularized version of the providential history on which Webster's American exceptionalism is founded. The incantatory repetitions of "Let us . . . " that bring the oration to its "dramatic" close underscore the unassailable finality of this.

In the second Bunker Hill oration in 1845, which, as I have noted above, is the one Melville seems to be referring to in his "Dedication," Webster mounts another jeremiad that reaffirms, this time with the triumphant finality of its completion, the symbolic significance of the monument—its embodiment of the exemplary heroism and patriotism of the fathers who died in the Battle of Bunker Hill; of the universality of their religious, moral, and political values; of the exceptionalist status of America; of the spirit of covenantal unity; and of the uncoerced commitment to the always threatened cause of liberty. "The mighty pyramid itself," Webster prophetically proclaims, echoing Shelley's "Ozymandias," "half buried in the sand of Africa, has nothing to bring down and report to us, but the power of kings and the servitude of the people. If it had any purpose beyond that of a mausoleum, such purpose has perished from history and from tradition." In contrast to its "silence" and that of "the millions which lie in the dust at its base," the Bunker Hill obelisk will always speak to humanity because it represents a "moral object." "And even if civilization should be subverted, and the truths of the Christian religion obscured by a new deluge of barbarism," Webster declaims, "the memory of Bunker Hill and the American Revolution will still be elements and parts of the knowledge which shall be possessed by the last man to whom the light of civilization and Christianity shall be extended" (*M*, 263). In this second oration, however, because of the divisions in the national consensus precipitated by the imperial Mexican War and the growing tension between the North and the South, Webster puts the threat to the confidence, patriotism, and national unity of the American people more forcefully. In a "moral majority" rhetoric that startlingly resembles the *exhortatio* of Father Mapple's prefigural sermon on and exegesis of the Jonah text, in *Moby-Dick*, Webster warns:

> Woe betide the man who brings to this day's worship feeling less than wholly American! Woe betide the man who can stand here with the fires of local resentments burning, or the purpose of fomenting local jealousies and strifes of local interests festering and rankling in his heart. Union, established in justice, in patriotism, and the most plain and obvious common interest,—union, founded on the same love of liberty, cemented by blood shed in the same common cause,—union has been the source of all our glory and

greatness thus far, and is the ground of all our highest hopes. This column stands on Union. (*M*, 265)[15]

In thus selecting the high points of American history to arrive at the universality and the unifying force of this American exceptionalist vision, what, according to Melville's satirical dedication of *Israel Potter* "To *His Highness, the Bunker-Hill Monument*," has Webster left out of his dramatic narrative on nation-building? Or, to pose the question more precisely, what has he relegated to non-being in order to achieve the (unified, filiative) Being of the American nation? In general, and provisionally, one can say that Webster's excessive emphasis on the threat to the "common cause" and the unity (the covenant) of the American people "betrays" to Melville not only the will to power that is concealed within the benignity of the "common cause" this monumental vision symbolizes, but also the contradictory *differences* it would repress. Specifically, this would consist of the savagery accompanying the "clearing, "settlement," and "improvement" of the "wilderness" of the "New World" (a pervasive motif of early American discourse that Melville will underscore in the chapters of *The Confidence-Man* devoted to "the metaphysics of Indian-hating"), the often unheroic and/or pedestrian and utilitarian motives of the leaders of the American Revolution (and their capitalist heirs), and the civilized barbarism of many of the warriors canonized in the aftermath of the war of independence. In *Israel Potter*, all these demystifying contradictions, as I will show, are subsumed under the remoteness of the physical and psychical suffering of the "patriot" Israel Potter—symbolized by Melville's overdetermination of the metaphorics of spectrality—to the consciousness of the dominant revolutionary and postrevolutionary culture in America, or, more precisely, under the relegation of Israel's rather visible singular "identity" to the status of non-entity or non-being. In short, his obliteration from the American national memory.

To further clarify the raison d'être of Melville's genealogical parody of Webster's encomiums to the Bunker Hill Monument, let me briefly (re)invoke a famous document that, though having no immediate bearing on the history in question, nevertheless can be interpreted without distorting its particular intent, as an acute theorization of Webster's monumentalizing historical project. I am referring to Ernest Renan's allegedly cultural (i.e., antiracial, antilinguistic, antireligious, and antigeographical—in short, antimetaphysical) answer to the question, "*Qu'est-ce qu'une nation?*" ("What is a nation?"), which he posed to his elite French audience at the Sorbonne on March 11, 1882:

> A nation is a soul, a spiritual principle. Two things, which in truth are but one, constitute this soul or spiritual principle. One lies in the past, one in the present. One is the possession in common

of a rich legacy of memories; the other is present-day consent, the desire to live together, the will to perpetuate the value of the heritage that one has received in an undivided form.... The nation, like the individual, is the culmination of a long past of endeavours, sacrifice, and devotion. To have common glories in the past and to have common will in the present; to have performed great deeds together, to wish to perform still more—these are the essential conditions for being a people.[16]

But to achieve this nation—the double *monos*—and to secure its permanence, Renan, unlike Webster, whose selective discourse is "legitimated" by a "theo-logy," is compelled by his nonmetaphysical problematic to admit that the nation is a cultural/political construction and that, therefore, the national memory must be a ruthless agency of forgetting: of overlooking all but the "high points" of the historical process of nation-building, indeed, the brutalities of the origin:

> Forgetting, I would even go so far as to say historical error, is a crucial factor in the creation of a nation, which is why progress in historical studies often constitutes a danger for [the principle of] nationality. Indeed, historical enquiry brings to light deeds of violence which took place at the origin of all political formations, even of those whose consequences have been altogether beneficial. Unity is always effected by means of brutality; the union of northern France with the Midi was the result of massacres and terrors lasting for the best of a century.... The nation which [the King of France] had formed has cursed him, and, nowadays, it is only men of culture who know something of his former value and of his achievements. (WN, 11)

Imbued by a tragic sense of history, the French Renan warns his audience of "Gentlemen"—the dominant culture of France—that paying too close attention to its singularities menaces the unity and stability of the *patrie*. A child of the "New World" and confident about America's *divinely ordained* exceptionalist errand, Webster, on the other hand, seems to be blind or indifferent to or disdainful of the delegitimizing, differential historical realities on which he builds his resonant image of the American nation. Despite this difference, however, both would repress the historical singularities that always threaten to disperse the "rich legacy of memories" and subvert "the present-day consent" on which the "soul" of the nation depends for its existence and sovereign authority. To put the disclosure of this unsaid of Webster's discourse, enabled by Renan's warning against a too inquisitive history to his elite audience, in the ironic terms Melville uses in *The Confidence-Man* in order to expose the fraudulence of the American philosophy of optimism, "[W]ith all sorts of cavilers, it was best, both for them and everybody, that whoever had the true light should stick behind the secure Malakoff of confidence, nor to be tempted forth to hazardous skirmishes on the open ground of reason."[17] It is Daniel Webster's synecdochical historical amnesia, the immensely consequential sticking behind the secure Malakoff of confidence by this influential custodian of the American national memory, that Melville intends to disclose by offering *Israel Potter*, this "dilapidated old tombstone," retrieved from the detritus of the American Archive and "retouched" to *underscore the singularity* of its living referent, "To His Highness, the Bunker-Hill Monument." In this genealogical disclosure—this "bringing to [present] light of the deeds of violence which took place at the origin of" the political formation named America—I suggest, *Israel* Potter, like *Pierre* before it, will be seen to be proleptic of the poststructuralists' and postcolonialists' theoretical delegitimation of the metanarrative of the nation-state.

I

As I have noted, most commentaries on Melville's revisions of the original *Life and Remarkable Adventures of Israel R. Potter* emphasize the obvious superiority of his writing, his opening out and deepening the more or less pedestrian account of some of the episodes (Israel's conversations with Sir John Miller and King George III, Squire Woodcock and Horne Tooke, Benjamin Franklin and John Paul Jones), and, not least, his highly wrought and imaginative fabrication, especially after the first few chapters, which follow the original rather closely, of characters and events not referred to in the ur-text, above all, the sea battle between the *Bon Homme Richard* and the *Serapis* (chapter 19), and his introduction and vivid portrayal of Ethan Allen. In the process of revising, Melville, as one authoritative commentator puts it, presumably to read his inventions as the endowment of mythic status to the self-reliant, lowly American, came to be repelled by what he considered to be Trumbull's public exploitation of the painful story of a long-forgotten, penurious patriot for the banal purpose of winning him a veteran's pension from the American government:

> Melville had presumably set out in all good conscience simply to rewrite Henry Trumbull's *Life and Remarkable Adventures of Israel R. Potter*. After allowing himself the luxury of a lyric opening chapter [the description of the Berkshire Mountains, where he relocated Potter's birth from Cranston, Rhode Island], he had settled down into paraphrase, touching up the prose toward felicity of expression, granting his narrator mild rights of commentary on the course of events. But restlessness led to increasing invention,

and then suddenly two things seem to have happened at once. Melville discovered that at its midpoint his source itself fell apart, its simple narrative line giving way to a tangled recital of random disasters and *bathetic appeals*. His interest waned. He would come back to Potter's last years, but the four decades of bleak backcity deprivation and crime, of starvation, beggary, and domestic tragedy, lost their powers of attraction, *perhaps became repellent*. But as his source failed him, Melville's fictional urgencies began to assert themselves. In the presence of the Franklin he invented, the narrator of *Israel Potter* came alive. From here on Melville filled his magazine installments with pages of comedy, melodrama, meditation, and adventure of his own devising, mixed half-and-half with pages of his own hurry-up brand of history. Melville, after all, was no scrivener. (*IP*, 205; my emphasis)

What I am suggesting by invoking Melville's dedication "To His Highness, the Bunker-Hill Monument," on the contrary, is that his revisions and augmentations of the original text are intended, above all, to expose the national amnesia incumbent on monumentalization and to make the case for Israel Potter's moral right to be remembered. More precisely, the process of revision was intended to underscore the inaugural, indifferent exploitation of the patriotism of this engaging ordinary American and the eventual forgetting of his being by the official culture of America. Put provisionally, Melville accomplishes this purpose in the text by five deliberate and brilliant revisionary gestures: (1) his symbolic identification, as the name suggests, of a latter-day Israel Potter with the Israelite/Puritan figural tradition, particularly the figure of exodus, exile, and return; (2) his deletion of Israel Potter's many Panglossian invocations to the "saving" intervention of Providence that are, in fact, deeply inscribed psychological compensations for the crushing pain he suffers throughout the many years of his dismal exile; (3) his enhancement of the original text's references to Potter's abandonment and forgetting by the American government; (4) his demystification of the canon of founding American heroes symbolized by Benjamin Franklin, John Paul Jones, and Ethan Allen; and, last but not least, (5) his representation of Potter's fate in the eyes of official America as an inexorably progressive process of de-substantialization, that is, the reduction of his body to nonbeing—ghostliness—*in the very process of its monumentalization of the hegemonic discourse of American exceptionalism*. In a language that takes us back to the beginning of Potter's exilic journey, this representation entails Melville's paradoxical portrayal of the American Revolutionary elect as relegating Israel Potter, the modern heir of the Puritans' "errand in the wilderness," to "preterition," a "passing over" that at the same time turns him into a specter (and *dia-bolos*) that haunts the very monumental historiography that reduced him to the status of a non-being

Melville begins his rewriting of Trumbull's *Life and Remarkable Adventures of Israel R. Potter* by infusing Israel Potter with a significance that is absent in the original text: he represents him as the symbolic heir of the early Puritans who settled America. He changes Israel's birth place from Cranston, Rhode Island, to the rugged, harsh, and resistant, but deeply attractive landscape of the Berkshire Mountains in Massachusetts. And in the process, he alludes to the larger-than-life, indeed, mythic, Puritans who, like "very Titans," built the now untenanted but still intact isolated houses that austerely dot the wild, forested mountainside, thus giving "us [the modern American] a significant hint of the temper of the men of the Revolutionary era"—and of "the devoted patriot, Israel Potter" (*IP*, 4–5). But Melville does this, not to give his protagonist heroic stature, but to instigate the reader's awareness of the oxymoronic resonance of his name. His intention, in other words, is to underscore the oblivion to which he has been relegated by the post-Revolutionary custodians of the American national memory—and, symbolically, as the reversal of the play on the exceptionalist binary metaphorics of the Old World and New World, promise and unfulfillment, confidence and bewilderment, purity and adulteration, clearly suggests, the "end" of the Puritan/American narrative of exile and return:

> Such, at this day, is the country which gave birth to our hero: prophetically styled Israel by the good Puritans, his parents, since for more than forty years, poor Potter wandered in the wild wilderness of the world's extremest hardships and ills.
>
> How little he thought, when, a boy, hunting after his father's stray cattle among these New England hills, he himself like a beast should be hunted through half of Old England, as a runaway rebel. Or, how could he ever have dreamed, when involved in the autumnal vapors of these mountains, that worse bewilderments awaited him . . . across the sea, wandering forlorn in the coal-fogs of London. But so it was destined to be. This little boy of the hills, born in sight of the sparkling Housatonic, was to linger out the best part of his life a prisoner or a pauper upon the grimy banks of Thames. (*IP*, 6)

At the outset of the novel, that is to say, Melville, fully conversant with the figural method of biblical exegesis that determined their exceptionalist discourse and practice,[18] invokes—and *reverses*—the New England Puritans' Providential interpretation of their exile from the Old World and "errand in the wilderness" ("settlement" and "improvement") of the New as the fulfillment of the promise prefigured in the Old Testament Israelites' exodus from Egypt into the Promised Land. Mocking this canonical promise/fulfillment narrative structure of Puritan biblical exegesis, Melville "prophesies," at the beginning, that the long and painful exile of this eighteenth-century American heir of the New England Puritan legacy, will not eventually end in his Providentially determined return to the Promised Land of milk and honey, but in the oblivion of a Potter's Field, which has been prepared for him by the dominant post-Revolutionary culture of America. To fully understand Melville's complex intent in this apparently simple novel of picaresque adventure, one must keep this symbolic identification of Israel Potter with the historical itinerary of American Puritanism always in mind.

Israel's "exodus," not incidentally, begins long before his capture by the British at sea. It commences, in fact, with his rebellion against the "tyranny" of his Puritan father (and, implicitly, the Providential Puritan theology that arbitrarily divided the elect from the preterite). "It appears," Melville tells us at the outset, that Israel "began his wanderings very early; moreover, that ere, on just principles throwing off the yoke of his king, Israel, on equally excusable grounds, emancipated himself from his [Puritan] sire" (*IP*, 7). It is this ferocious prodigal will to resist not simply political tyranny but also the tyranny of the filial and determinist theology of Puritanism that, in his adolescent "wanderings" at the edge of the English-speaking world, matures into the peculiar *secular* "freedom" and "patriotism" that will characterize Israel's thought and practice throughout his damaged life in exile. It is also to this *de-centered* or worldly freedom—the freedom of the estranged and *disaffiliated*, low-born prodigal—I suggest, that Melville, in opposition to the transcendental origins institutionalized and monumentalized in the post-Revolutionary period by Emerson, Parker, Webster, Sparks, Parkman, Bancroft, and other members of the American elect, is referring in identifying the young Israel's errant life in the wilderness as the breeding ground of "that fearless self-reliance and independence which conducted our forefathers to national freedom" (*IP*, 9).

Indeed, in using—and reversing—the promise/fulfillment structure intrinsic to the Puritan metanarrative and its secular post-Revolutionary allotrope, Melville intends to focalize the fundamental incompatibility between the singularity Israel Potter achieves in the process of his "adventurous" life and the universalizing imperatives of monumental history. Or, to put it alternatively, in putting the singularity of Israel Potter in a contrapuntal relationship with the monumentalist view of the history of the American Revolution, Melville demonstrates not only the ruthless amnesia inherent in the monumentalizing national memory, but also, in so doing, transforms the forgotten or passed over (the preterited) into a specter that haunts the monumentalizing memory. What we bear witness to in the aftermath of the Battle of Bunker Hill, in which Israel and his lowly compatriots bravely fought, were wounded, and died, first as marksmen and then, after their ammunition had been used up, in hand-to-hand combat, is a movement that brings this increasingly singular American nobody into a *contrapuntal* relationship with historical figures who have been monumentalized by the official American cultural memory: Benjamin Franklin, John Paul Jones, and Ethan Allen. It is a "relationship," that is, in which Melville, attuned to their spectrality, retrieves the singularities passed over by the American national memory in the nation-building process and, from this countermnemonic or genealogical perspective, transforms their latent into an active haunting that demonumentalizes these not simply fallible, but even dangerous, national monuments, renders them, in anticipation of his next and last novel, in some significant sense "confidence-men."

Israel's exilic journey in the aftermath of his estrangement from his Puritan home and family, takes him errantly and, in terms of the narrative perspective, rapidly from the wilderness of the Housatonic and of the oceans of the whale fisheries, through the Battle of Bunker Hill, to his brief time as a sailor aboard a brigantine intended to intercept British supplies, the capture of his vessel by an English ship, his failed mutinous attempt, as ringleader, to take the ship on which he was being transported to England as a prisoner of war, his escape from the hulk in which he is confined, and his several other captures and escapes in the British countryside in his effort to find sanctuary in the labyrinth of London, which culminate in his encounters with the kind Sir John Millet, the King of England himself, and finally, with Squire Woodcock and Horne Tooke, friends of America, who persuade Israel into assuming the role of a courier to the American ambassador to France, Benjamin Franklin. This accelerated picaresque itinerary up to Israel's encounter with Sir John Millett, where the narrative begins to slow down (following the original text more or less faithfully, it is accomplished in nineteen pages), has been represented by most commentators as Melville's lack of interest in the early pages of Trumbull's original text.[19] Understood from the dislocating perspective of the counter-memory, however, these early chapters in fact trace a contrapuntal movement that culminates in and enables us to understand Israel's encounter with Benjamin Franklin. Instigated by Israel's disaffiliation from his Puritan family—his decentering, as it were—and constantly renewed by his many experiences of adversity on his errant way, this contrapuntal movement, more precisely, involves an increasingly visible dialectical play of contradictory motifs: a gradual subjective process promising Israel's achievement of singularity that is simultaneously shadowed by a gradual social process that promises the annulment of this singularity.

The first voice—and the feint but ominous echo of the second—of this contrapuntal structural movement achieves definitive visibility in the comic but poignant episode depicting this hunted young man's inaugural encounter with Sir John Millet:

> Having heard the rich man of England charged with all sorts of domineering qualities, Israel felt no little misgiving in approaching to an audience with so imposing a stranger. But screwing up

his courage, he advanced; while seeing him coming all rags and tatters, the group of gentlemen stood in some wonder awaiting what so singular a phantom might want.

"Mr. Millet," said Israel, bowing towards the bareheaded gentleman.

"Ha,—who are you, pray?"

"A poor fellow, sir, in want of work."

"A wardrobe too, I should say," smiled one of the guests, of a very youthful, prosperous, and dandified air.

"Where's your hoe?" said Sir John.

"I have none."

"Any money to buy one?"

"Only four English pennies, sir."

"*English* pennies. What other sort would you have?"

"Why China pennies to be sure," laughed the youthful gentleman. "See his long, yellow hair behind; he looks like a Chinaman. . . ."

"Will you hire me, Mr. Millet?" said Israel.

"Ha! that's queer again," cried the knight.

"Hark ye Fellow," said a brisk servant, approaching from the porch, "this is Sir John Millet." (*IP*, 24)

This dialogue and that which a little later brings the encounter to it denouement in the disclosure of Israel's American identity has been interpreted as Melville's symbolic identification of Israel with the American national identity. But such an interpretation is an oversimplification. It is not Israel who identifies himself as American; it is, rather, the English knight (and his youthful friend and, not incidentally, the "brisk servant"), who, unlike Israel, wears his social distinction on his sleeve. Israel, on the contrary, spontaneously discards the received American view of the English gentleman—his "domineering qualities." He is innocent of ideological resonance; he addresses the English knight, not from an American exceptionalist perspective, but with the respect due to a fellow human being. When his dignity is degraded, as it is by the knight's young supercilious friend, Israel simply disregards him. Of course, the characteristics Israel manifests in his dialogues with the Sir John Millet are "democratic" and thus easily appropriatable to the American national identity. But Israel, here and throughout his exilic life—as is hinted at by the English gentlemen's first impression, "so singular a phantom"—is not an ideologue in the way, say, the Leatherstocking figure in Cooper's novels, the frontiersman in Francis Parkman's histories, or the veterans of the Battle of Bunker Hill in Daniel Webster's orations are.

This singularity is further suggested in Israel's second encounter with the good Sir John, when the latter, while offering Israel a glass of wine, confirms his suspicion that Israel is an American and an escaped prisoner of war:

> "Mr. Millet," exclaimed Israel aghast, the untasted wine trembling in his hand. "Mr. Millet, I—"
> "*Mr.* Millet—there it is again. Why don't you say *Sir John* like the rest?"
> "Why, sir—pardon me—but somehow, I can't. I've tried; but I can't. You won't betray me for that?"
> "Betray—poor fellow! Hark ye, your history is doubtless secret which you would not wish to divulge to a stranger; but whatever happens to you, I pledge you my honor I will never betray you."
> "God bless you for that, Mr. Millet."
> "Come, come, call me by my right name. I am not Mr. Millet. *You* have said *Sir* to me; no doubt you have a thousand times said *John* to other people. Now can't you couple the two? Try once. Come. Only *Sir* and then *John*—*Sir John*—that's all."
> "John—I can't—Sir, sir!—your pardon. I didn't mean that."
> "My good fellow," said the knight looking sharply upon Israel, "tell me, are all your countrymen like you? If so, it's no use fighting them. To that effect, I must write to his majesty myself. (*IP*, 26)

As in the first colloquy, Israel's inability to address his aristocratic interlocutor in the language of class distinctions is not determined by an "American" ideology. As his fear of being exposed to the authorities and his deference to the knight—his gratitude for the latter's kindness and his genuine, but unsuccessful, effort to comply to his request—makes clear, it is a matter, rather, of Israel's human singularity. As in the first colloquy, too, it is not Israel who reconstellates this singular event into the larger conflict of ideologies, the American Revolution; it is, again and as virtually always, the dislocated knight.

This reversal of traditional roles, in which the vagabond in tatters, by way of his simple humanity, emerges as a singularity starkly out of proportion to that of his socially superior interlocutor is repeated in the episode in which Israel encounters the King of England strolling in his garden. It is a singularity that accrues a particular acuteness at the stunning moment between Israel's qualification of his invocation of God's blessing in behalf of the King and the King's knowing non sequitur invitation to Israel to join his army:

> "You are rumored to be a spy—a spy, or something of that sort—aint you? But I know you are not—no, no. You are a runaway

prisoner-of-war, eh? You have sought this place to be safe from pursuit, eh? eh? Is it no so?—eh? eh? eh?"

"Sir, it is."

"Well, ye're an honest rebel—rebel, yes, rebel. Hark ye, hark. Say nothing of this talk to any one. And hark again. So long as ye remain here at Kew, I shall see that you are safe—safe."

God bless your majesty!"

"Eh?"

"God bless your noble majesty!"

"Come—come—come," smiled the king in delight. "I thought I could conquer ye—conquer ye."

"Not the king, but the king's kindness, your majesty."

"Join my army—army."

Sadly looking down, Israel silently shook his head.

"You won't? Well, gravel the walk then—gravel away. Very stubborn race—very stubborn race indeed—very—very—very." . . .

Following this conversion, the narrator concludes, "Without any impeachment of Israel's fealty to his country, it must still be narrated, that from this his familiar audience with George the Third, he went away with very favorable views of that monarch." It was not "the warm heart of the king, but the cold heads of his lords in council, that persuaded him so tyrannically to persecute America. Yet hitherto the precise contrary of this had been Israel's opinion, agreeably to the popular prejudice throughout New England (*IP*, 31–32).

Given the deliberateness of these reversals of status, it would seem, therefore, that Israel's "extraordinary emergency" into singularity, to borrow a crucial term from Melville's *Pierre*,[20] constitutes a prelude to the quite different relationship Israel will have with the American national idols he is about to meet. That is to say, Melville at the outset of his novel is inaugurating a fictional process that will eventually distinguish between two kinds of American: what I will call for temporary convenience the centered and the decentered, the sedentary and the nomadic, American.

If we call this process of "e-mergency" a heightening of Israel's singularity, then the contrapuntal motif that shadows its structural movement might be called a diminishment of this singularity. Unlike the first motif, which is activated by Israel's courageous and resourceful engagement with adversarial events, this second one is articulated by the narrator, who knows that Israel's sad fate is the consequence of his forced alienation from his Puritan/American homeland and the untethered nomadic existence this estrangement, exacerbated by contingencies, compelled. This contrapuntal motif of diminution, then, circulates around the notion of exile (which Melville at the outset identifies with the figural Puritan/Israelite exodus)—an unhoming that at the same time threatens the negation of identity—and it manifests itself initially at the rhetorical margins of Israel's story in the form of a number of seemingly unrelated and purely descriptive terms. I am referring above all to Melville's repeated description of Israel as an "exile" or a hunted "refugee" or a "wanderer" (a pejorative term in the hegemonic discourse of America), his various imprisonments as interments, his multiple changes of clothing to escape detection as metamorphoses of his identity, and not least, his exilic status as "ghost" or "phantom." But, as I will show, these various tropes will, in the process of the narrative, come to cohere and to accumulate a resonant double and paradoxical symbolic significance—let me call it in a prologomenal way, *disembodied body*—that, in a repetition, will bring our attention back to Melville's dedication "To His Majesty, the Bunker Hill Monument."

II

Following a period of time as one of the King's gardeners, Israel Potter once again becomes the object of a search for runaway prisoners, but is temporarily delivered from his fugitive state by English "friends to America," Squire Woodcock of Brentford and Horne Tooke, who employ Israel as a courier between them and the renowned American ambassador to France, Benjamin Franklin, in Paris. This turn in the exilic history of Israel Potter, which is where Melville slows the narrative of the original text down—elaborating and deepening the paradoxical symbolic content to which I have briefly alluded—inaugurates the process of demythologizing post-Revolutionary American history, the history synecdochically represented by Daniel Webster's Bunker Hill orations, by parodying the lifestyles of three exemplary monumental figures of that historical narrative: Benjamin Franklin, John Paul Jones, and Ethan Allen. In each of these episodes, Melville, fully conscious of the temporal distance between his contemporary occasion and that of the protagonist and his celebrated interlocutors, pits the American nobody, Israel Potter, against an American legend, but in such a cannily articulated way that, in the mind of the reader, the marginalized takes center stage and the centralized, the margins. In these encounters, in other words, Melville gives back Israel Potter the history that the official American culture has denied him.

This reversal is most effectively enacted by Melville in his representation of Israel's encounter with the American "sage" Benjamin Franklin. And it takes the form of a parodic genealogy of the instrumentalist logic, celebrated by the American Cultural Memory, that drives Franklin (as it will drive Egbert in *The Confidence-Man*). That is, it pushes the single-mindedness or, in one of Melville's favorite locutions to express this reductive single-mindedness, the "unerring" directionality of this rationalist logic "to its limit" and its "unrealization" through the "excessive choice of identities."[21] It is thus no accident that, on introducing Franklin to Potter's story, Melville characterizes this most disciplined, unrelentingly practical, and confident of American men—one who, as his *Autobiography* demonstrates, spent a life wilfully purging his self of the "errata" that deflected his thought and practice from his always utilitarian end[22]—as akin to his absolute antithesis, a conjuror—or, to invoke Don Quixote, one of Franklin's ancestors, "an enchanter."[23] I quote at length not simply to call attention to this particular resonant irony, but also to Melville's awareness of the polyvalency of Franklin's grave instrumentalist logic:

> Wrapped in a rich dressing-gown—a fanciful present from an admiring Marchesa—curiously embroidered with algebraic figures like a conjuror's robe, and with a skull-cap of black satin on his hive of a head, the man of gravity was seated at a huge claw-footed old table, round as the zodiac. It was covered with printed papers; files of documents; rolls of MSS.; stray bits of strange models in wood and metal; odd-looking pamphlets in various languages; and all sort of books; including many presentation-copies; embracing history, mechanics, diplomacy, agriculture, political economy, metaphysics, meteorology, and geometry. The walls had a necromantic look; hung round with barometers of different kinds; drawings of surprising inventions; wide maps of far off countries in the New World, containing vast empty spaces in the middle, with the word DESERT diffusely printed there, so as to span five-and-twenty degrees of longitude with only two syllables, which printed word however bore a vigorous pen-mark, in the Doctor's hand, drawn straight through it, as if in summary repeal of it.... (*IP*, 38–39)

This brilliantly articulated passage, whose carnivalesque parody of Franklin's "gravity" (he is referred to as "the man of gravity" several times in this chapter)[24] is, not incidentally, reminiscent of Laurence Sterne's sustained mockery of this undeviating, economy-driven perspective of inquiry in *Tristram Shandy*,[25] at the duplicitous heart of Melville's demonumentalizing project. It not only discloses the deeply inscribed American penchant to think practically to be informed by an optimistic metaphysics that, not unlike Don Quixote's and Dr. Pangloss's, enables a mode of interpretation that is justified in going to all lengths—even to invoking magic in the last instance[26]—to reduce the recalcitrant differential play of the world (represented by the multitude of apparently unrelated representative objects in his room) to the intelligible and explicable same, that is, geometrical figures. As the "summarily" annulling straight line Franklin has drawn through the word "DESERT," itself an astoundingly confident and peremptory reduction of "vast empty spaces in the middle [of the map of the New World]," to "only two syllables," suggests, the passage also discloses the indissolubly related American penchant, hidden beneath the rhetoric of practicality and liberty, to interpret a massive and complex geographical and demographic space inhabited by "alien" peoples as a *terra nullius* and, thus, to exterminate them and colonize it.[27]

Franklin's reductive (imperial) interpretation of being is not a consciously held ideology. As Melville's parodic commentary makes clear in the next chapter, it is a deeply inscribed and naturalized system of beliefs, a polyvalent "lived hegemony," in Raymond William's Gramscian formulation, that, as I noted in the previous chapter, "sees the relations of domination and subordination, in their forms as practical consciousness, as in effect a saturation of the whole process of living—not only of political and economic activity, nor only of manifest social activity, but the whole substance of lived identities and relationships, to such a depth that the pressures and limits of what can ultimately be seen as a specific economic, political, and cultural system seem to most of us the pressures and limits of simple experience and common sense. . . . "[28] For the peripatetic "Franklin," Melville observes after identifying him first with the worldly wise "patriarch Jacob" and then as "a tanned Machiavelli in tents," "all over is of a piece." His paratactic style is the man, and that style has it origins in a metaphysical (optimistic) philosophy and is characterized, necessarily, by a disciplined and calculative economy:

> He dressed his person as his periods [oral and written sentences]; *neat, trim, nothing superfluous, nothing deficient.* In some of his works his style is only surpassed by the unimprovable sentences of Hobbes of Malmsbury, the paragon of perspicuity. The mental habits of Hobbes and Franklin in several points, especially in one of some moment, assimilated. Indeed, making due allowance for soil and era, history presents few trios more akin, upon the whole, than Jacob, Hobbes, and Franklin; three labyrinth-minded but plain-spoken Broadbrims, at once politicians and philosophers; *keen observers of the main chance; prudent courtiers; practical magians in linsey woolsey.* (*IP*, 46–47; my emphasis)

As the italicized phrases suggest, what Melville is satirizing in his demonumentalization of Benjamin Franklin—the "unrealization" of the mystified truth of his optimistic utilitarian reason—is, of course, the Puritan work ethic, epitomized by the omniscient sententiae of *Poor Richard's Almanac*, that by the time of the antebellum period of American history had become, as Max Weber has shown—and the Bunker Hill orations of Webster inadvertently confirmed—the "spirit of capitalism."[29] I mean, specifically, its overdetermination of the binary that privileges *economy* over *waste*. For just as the optimistic logic of utilitarian reason necessarily reduces difference to identity, so economy, whether political or economic, as Foucault, following Weber, has shown, enables, indeed, demands the disciplining of waste, the transformation of the superfluous energy of the undisciplined masses into useful and docile bodies.

Though Foucault's formulation of the new power relations that were emerging in the West, including Jacksonian America, under the aegis of the triumphant bourgeoisie in the post-Revolutionary period is generally known, his deep insight into its restricted economy has not, as far as I know, been applied to Melville's fiction, not least to *Israel Potter*, which ironically has its mise en scène in the American Revolution and its immediate aftermath, and, by way of the fate of Israel Potter, interrogates in a fundamental way the relationship between democracy, especially in its disciplinary Franklinian mode, and (capitalist) economy. To put this more precisely, Melville's commentators (especially those modernists who invoked him in behalf of American democracy's Cold War against Soviet Communism) have failed to perceive in Melville's brilliant parody of Benjamin Franklin's "perspicuous" practical logic[30] his remarkable anticipation of Weber's analysis of the relation between the Protestant "calling" and capitalism and Foucault's genealogy of the disciplinary economy of post-Revolutionary Western societies: that historical moment "when an art of the human body was born, which was directed not only at the growth of its skills, nor at the intensification of its subjection, but at the formation of a relation that in the mechanism itself makes it more obedient as it becomes more useful, and conversely," that historical moment, that is, when this new mechanism, in harnessing knowledge and power, produced "subjected and practised bodies, 'docile' bodies."[31]

In the process of glossing Melville's parody of Franklin's *confidence* in the benignity of his work ethic, I have emphasized its origin in a philosophy of optimism (the Providential history of his Puritan ancestry) akin to Leibnitz's "best of all possible worlds" and Pope's "Whatever is, is right." This is because Melville, anticipating his devastating genealogy of American optimism in *The Confidence-Man*, represents Franklin as something of a conman, as one, more specifically, who, certain of his naive American victim's deeply inscribed confidence in the ultimate benignity of the world, dupes the latter by way of invoking a threat to his well-being the more to reenergize his confidence. This is suggested at the very outset of Israel's encounter with Franklin, when he tells his host about his being accosted on a bridge of the Seine by "a suspicious looking man, who, under pretense of seeking to polish my boots, wanted slyly to unscrew their heels, and so to steal all these precious papers I've brought you." In what follows, Melville makes Franklin sound like a sententious American Pangloss:

"My good friend," said the man of gravity, glancing scrutinizingly upon his guest, "have you not in your time, undergone what they call hard times? Been set upon, and persecuted, and very ill entreated by some of your fellow-creatures?"

"That I have, Doctor; yes indeed."

"I thought so. Sad usage has made you sadly suspicious, my honest friend. An indiscriminate distrust of human nature is the worst consequence of a miserable condition, whether brought about by innocence or guilt. And though want of suspicion more than want of sense, sometimes leads a man into harm: yet too much suspicion is as bad as too little sense." (*IP*, 40–41)

Indeed, like the confidence-man in the novel of the same name, Franklin, we are informed, conceals his real purposes behind a variety of masks that are calculated to be appropriate for each specific occasion of his con game. And in this, he epitomizes the calculative and economically rewarding prosaicness of the American national identity. "Having carefully weighed the world," the ironic narrator says, "Franklin could act any part in it. By nature turned to knowledge, his mind was often grave, but never serious. . . . Tranquillity was to him instead of it. This philosophical levity of tranquillity, so to speak, is shown in his easy variety of pursuits. Printer, postmaster, almanac maker, essayist, chemist, orator, tinker, statesman, humorist, philosopher, parlor-man, political economist, professor of housewifery, ambassador, projector, maxim-monger, herb doctor [one of the avatars of the confidence-man], wit:—Jack of all trades, master of each and mastered by none—*the type and genius of his land*. Franklin was everything but a poet" (*IP*, 48; my emphasis).

The contrast between the prosaic and the poetic in this culminating judgment should not be taken literally. Melville's text compels us rather to interpret these terms as symbolic of the distinction between a centered or restrictive economy: a "play based on a fundamental ground, a play constituted on the basis of a fundamental immobility and a reassuring certitude, which itself is beyond the reach of play," on the one hand, and a decentered, unrestricted economy—the play of difference,[32] on the other. I am not only referring to the narrator's commentaries on Franklin's character; I am also referring to his monologic dialogues with Israel Potter. In these, the "man of gravity," not unlike Pangloss to Candide, though on a materialist (anthropological), not a theological register, speaks to Israel undeviatingly in the manner of the sayings of *Poor Richard's Almanac*, in a patronizing discourse which is intended to teach his innocent ephebe the virtue—and material rewards—of plainness, gravity, industry, economy; that is, to "interpellate" and "normalize" him, render him, in Althusser's terms, a "subjected subject." But Israel refuses to be interpellated by Franklin's hailing. After the latter systematically strips him of all but the most necessary toiletry left on the marble mantel in his room by the concierge, including a seductive chambermaid, in the name of "frugality," Israel indicates his awareness of the duplicity of his "sage" tutor's "gifts": " 'Every time he comes in he robs me,' soliloquized Israel, dolefully; 'with an air all the time, too, as if he were making me presents' " (*IP*, 53). Left at the end of his "conversation" with *Poor Richard's Almanac*, which Franklin had given him at the close of his first sage disquisition on the economic and moral value of "plainness" (*IP*, 45)—this fundamental characteristic of the American exceptionalist ethos[33]—Israel opens the pamphlet at random and reads aloud: " '*So what signifies wishing and hoping for better times? We may make these times better, if we bestir ourselves. Industry need not wish, and he that lives upon hope will die fasting, as Poor Richard says. There are no gains, without pains. Then help, hands, for I have no lands, as Poor Richard says*' " (*IP*, 53; Melville's emphasis). Responding to the unwarranted optimism of this fastidious example of the Protestant work ethic, Israel exclaims (prophetically), " 'Oh confound this wisdom! It's a sort of insulting to talk wisdom to a man like me. It's wisdom that's cheap, and it's fortune that's dear. That ain't in Poor Richard, but it ought to be,' concluded Israel, suddenly slamming down the pamphlet" (*IP*, 54). In keeping with his earlier resistance to American authorities, Israel, this young and free American, feels "somehow," that is, symptomatically, "bound to be a prisoner one way or another" (*IP*, 52; see also 43 and 53) in the home of the grand symbol of American freedom. This is not simply an admission of defeat; it is also a manifestation of what I have been calling Israel's singularity, an absent presence that, despite Franklin's implicit but remarkable blindness to its differential play, haunts the unerring instrumentalist and disciplinary discourse and practice of the optimistic America this monumental figure symbolizes. To put it alternatively, though Melville puts Franklin at center stage to Israel's marginality in these chapters, he does so ironically: in a way, that is, that the marginalized Israel begins to assume center stage to Franklin's marginality in the consciousness of the reader. Melville will continue to pursue the resonant cultural and sociopolitical meaning of this aesthetic reversal in his account of Israel's encounters with John Paul Jones and Ethan Allen.

Melville portrays the legendary John Paul Jones, sea hero of the American Revolution, as the absolute antithesis of Benjamin Franklin. This is how he characterizes him on his arrival at Franklin's quarters:

> He was a rather small, elastic, swarthy man, with an aspect as of a disinherited Indian chief in European clothes. An unvanquishable enthusiasm, intensified to perfect sobriety, couched in his savage, self-possessed eye. He was elegantly and somewhat extravagantly dressed as a civilian; he carried himself with a rustic, barbaric jauntiness, strangely dashed with a superinduced touch of the Parisian *salon*. His tawny cheek, like a date, spoke of the tropic. A wonderful atmosphere of proud friendlessness and scornful isolation invested

him. Yet was there a bit of the poet as well as the outlaw in him, too. A cool solemnity of intrepidity sat on his lip. He looked like one who of purpose sought out harm's way. He looked like one who never had been, and never would be, a subordinate.

To Israel, Jones, "[t]hough dressed a-la-mode . . . did not seem to be altogether civilized" (*IP*, 56).

If Franklin represents the prosaic surface of the American national identity—its stifling instrumentalist logic of economy, its penchant for plainness, its disdain for waste, and its reductive disciplinary ethos—Jones represents what this logic represses: not the poetic as such, but that aspect of the American national identity, barely hidden by civility, that is undisciplined and extravagant, a flamboyant "poetic" side that is tethered to nothing other than an arrogant, certain, and self-admiring ego. He avoids the debilitating company of (civilized) men when he can, preferring solitude, indeed, the status of a predatory outlaw. In other words, he is, in some significant sense, an extremist, that is, self-parodic, avatar of the American exceptionalist or, to invoke Melville's characterization of "the Indian-hater par excellence" in *The Confidence-Man*, a virtual "Leather-stocking Nemesis"[34] of the ocean wilderness. The difference is that the exceptionalist Leatherstocking figure mutes his exceptionalist ego in favor of the murderous task at hand, whereas Jean Paul Jones broadcasts it at every opportunity.

Indeed, this excessively demonstrative penchant is Melville's primary means of demonumentalizing Jones. I am referring specifically to Jones's tendency to slip out of the first person into the third to represent himself. Taking up with Franklin the issue of the ship he will command in bringing the war to British shores, for example, he exclaims: "Congress gave me to understand that . . . I should be given immediate command of the *Indien*; and now, for no earthly reason that I can see, you Commissioners have presented her, fresh from the stocks of Amsterdam, to the King of France, and not to me. What does the King of France with such a frigate? And what can I *not* do with her? Give me back the 'Indien,' and in less than a month, you shall *hear glorious or fatal news of Paul Jones* (*IP*, 56; my emphasis). When Franklin asks what he would do with her, Jones continues: "I would teach the British *that Paul Jones . . . is no subject of the British King, but an untrammelled citizen and sailor of the universe*" (*IP*, 56; my emphasis). Following Franklin's ameliorative suggestion that Jones would serve the American cause better if he commanded a smaller ship, one able to draw out British privateers that were intercepting supplies going to America, he replies "in a fiery rage":

> Decoy-duck to French frigates!—Very dignified office, truly! *Doctor Franklin, whatever Paul Jones does for the cause of America, it must be done through unlimited orders: a separate supreme command; no*

leader and no counsellor but himself. Have I not already by my services on the American coast shown that I am well worthy all this? Why then do you seek to degrade me below my previous level? I will mount, not sink. I live for honor and glory. . . . Give me then something honorable and glorious to do, and something famous to do it with. Give me the *Indien.*" (*IP*, 57; my emphasis)

This self-destructive projective process culminates in the dialogue following Franklin's introduction of Israel as an escaped prisoner of war to Jones:

"Ah, captured in a ship?" asked Paul eagerly;—"what ship? None of mine! *Paul Jones never was captured.*"

"No, sir, in the brigantine Washington, out of Boston," replied Israel; "We were cruising to cut off supplies to the English."

"Did your shipmates talk much of me?" demanded Paul, with a look of a parading Sioux demanding homage to his gew-gaws; "*what did they say of Paul Jones?*"

"I never heard of the name before this evening. (*IP*, 58; my emphasis)

In thus habitually speaking about himself in the third person, Jones is objectifying his worldly being, which is to say, with Kierkegaard,[35] projecting himself *aeterno modo*, into an aesthetic structure, specifically, a (melo)drama, in which he is the heroic protagonist of an epochal struggle *that has already been won*. This aestheticized posture, which generates a boredom that ends in paralysis or violence for its own sake, not only suggests that, for Melville, Jones's primary motive in seeking a renowned frigate to harass the English shipping lanes has less to do with fighting in behalf of the freedom of the American people from the tyrannical rule of the British than with a monomaniacal self-aggrandizement, not unlike Odysseus boasting to the blinded Polyphemus, that puts his fellows at extreme risk. But to expose Jones's monstrous will to self-aggrandizement is only one dimension of Melville's intent. His other, and more important, purpose is to show that, in taking center stage in a drama of epochal struggle, Jones becomes the very *savage* Word that shapes the world picture, thus enacting symbolically the monomaniacal exceptionalist vision of America's errand in the global wilderness.

This larger meaning of Jones's self-dramatization is prefigured at the end of the chapter, when Franklin retires, leaving Potter and Jones alone. After going to bed, Israel, feigning sleep, observes the following scene:

He paced the room as if advancing upon a fortification . . . Presently, passing the large mirror over the mantel, Paul caught a glimpse of his person. He paused, grimly regarding it, while a dash of pleased coxcombry seemed to mingle with the otherwise savage satisfaction expressed in his face. But the latter predominated. Soon, rolling up his sleeve, with a queer smile, Paul lifted his right arm, and stood thus for an interval, eyeing its image in the glass. From where he lay, Israel could not see the side of the arm presented to the mirror, but he saw its reflection, and started at perceiving there, framed in the carved and gilded wood, certain large intertwisted cyphers covering the whole inside of the arm, so far as exposed, with mysterious tatooings. The design was wholly unlike the fanciful figures of anchors, hearts, and cables, sometimes decorating small portions of seamen's bodies. It was a sort of tattooing such as is seen only on thorough-bred savages—deep blue, elaborate, labyrinthine, cabalistic. (*IP*, 62)

What Israel sees and is struck by in the mirror, which is the physical counterpart of speaking in the third person, reinforces his earlier intuition about John Paul Jones: that pulsing just below the surface of his extravagantly civilized attire and speech lies, not so much an American patriot, as a frightening caged beast. To put this in terms of Melville's demonumentalizing intention—it is one, not incidentally, that anticipates Conrad's portrayal of the civilized European, Kurtz, in *The Heart of Darkness*—Israel, the patriot, senses the fragility of a civilizational cause in time of war, even that cause of liberty celebrated by America in the aftermath of the Revolution. And this savagery latent in Jones—and the myth of American exceptionalism he embodies—is enacted, following Israel's impressment by the English navy, his coincidental reunion with Jones aboard the *Ranger*, and, after its raids on the shores of Scotland, his reassignment to Jones's new command, in the brilliantly executed account of the famous battle of the *Serapis* and the *Bon Homme Richard* off the coast of England. This is what Melville says about this celebrated event of American history at the beginning of the chapter:

> The Battle between the Bon Homme Richard and the Serapis stands in history as the first signal collision on the sea between the Englishman and the American. For obstinacy, mutual hatred, and courage, it is without precedent or subsequent in the story of ocean. The strife long hung undetermined, but the English flag struck in the end.
>
> There would seem to be something singularly indicatory in this engagement. It may involve at once a type, a parallel, and a prophecy. Sharing the same blood with England, and yet her proved foe in two wars; not wholly inclined at bottom to forget an old

> grudge: intrepid, unprincipled, reckless, predatory, with boundless ambition, civilized in externals but a savage at heart, America is, or may yet be, the Paul Jones of nations.
>
> Regarded in this indicatory light, the battle between the Bon Homme Richard and the Serapis—in itself so curious—may well enlist our interest. (*IP*, 120)

And this, following Melville's account of the horrific—and utterly pointless—sea battle, is how the chapter concludes:

> In view of this battle one may well ask—What separates the enlightened man from the savage? Is civilization a thing distinct, or is it an advanced stage of barbarism? (*IP*, 130)

In a way that should by now be familiar, Melville creative tactic is to *allows* the "logic" informing Jones's (and America's) civilized identity to "fulfill" itself, to achieve its end, and that end turns out to be sheer barbarism, the very state the logical economy of American civilization would overcome. In other words, under the aegis of John Paul Jones, America, the "Paul Jones of nations," suffers its demise or, more precisely, becomes "indicatory," "at once a type, a parallel, and a prophecy" in the manner of the figural method of Puritan exegesis, *not* of a monumental high-point of the itinerary of American history, but of this self-destructive violence.

As in the case of his sojourn with Benjamin Franklin, Israel appears to be marginal to Jones, who remains at center stage throughout their encounters. But like his indifferent status under the aegis of Franklin, this marginalization, this apparent reduction of Israel to a non-entity—a reduction that is consistent with his recurrent awareness of himself as one who has been imprisoned or interred or rendered a homeless wanderer—is what, coupled with his acutely ironic awareness of the disabling limitations of the "great man" and the spontaneity of his commitment to liberty, endows this "nobody" with a paradoxical and resonant visibility. It is this *invisible visibility*—this "singularity," as I have been calling it—that Melville inaugurates in the wonderfully comic, but thematically important chapters recounting Israel's return to England bearing a message from Franklin to America's English sympathizers and his "interment" and escape ("resurrection") from the deceased Squire Woodcock's house:

> Slipping off his own clothing, he deliberately arrayed himself in the borrowed raiment; silk small-clothes and all; then put on the cocked hat, grasped the silver-headed cane in his right hand, and . . . felt convinced that he would well pass for Squire Woodcock's genuine phantom. But after the first feeling of self-satisfaction with his anticipated success had left him, it was not without some supersti-

tious embarrassment that Israel felt himself encased in a dead man's broadcloth; nay, in the very coat in which the deceased had no doubt fallen down in his fit. By degrees he began to feel almost as unreal and shadowy as the shade whose part he intended to enact. (*IP*, 75)[36]

I will return to this metaphorics of ghostliness later in this chapter. Suffice it to say at this juncture that Melville will increasingly identify Israel with this ghostly imagery and, in the process, transform its negativity into a positive aura: a haunting spectrality.

Unlike his encounters with Benjamin Franklin and John Paul Jones, Israel's encounter with Ethan Allen, the third monumentalized figure of the American Revolution to appear as a character in the novel, occurs as a spectator. Sailing back to America with Jones, the ship the latter commands is engaged by a British vessel and during the skirmish, Israel accidentally boards it and is separated from Jones. Subjected to a number of interrogations concerning his identity, which he manages to survive by insistently invoking the positive potential of his unnaming (I will return to this strategy), Israel, or rather "Peter Perkins," as he calls himself, is finally accepted as a member of the crew. On the ship's entering the Falmouth roadstead, he bears witness to the disembarking from a large man-of-war of a number of armed British soldiers between whom walked a "martial man of Patagonian stature, their ragged and handcuffed captive, whose defiant head overshadowed theirs, as St. Paul's dome its inferior steeples" (*IP*, 142). This "colossal stranger" turns out to be Ethan Allen, the hero of Fort Ticonderoga, who has been brought to England by his British captors to be put on public display at Pendennis Castle. In comparison to his devastating characterization of Franklin and John Paul Jones, Melville's portrayal of Allen (who does not appear in the original Trumbull narrative) seems to be mild. Indeed, in invoking the revolutionary discourse of liberty in the face of tyranny, both Allen's speeches and the narrator's commentary could be interpreted, as one critic has, as signifying Melville's identification of Allen as the ideal American.[37] But this rhetoric should not deflect attention to the manner of its articulation, which, as the brief passage quoted above suggests, involves rendering Ethan Allen larger than life, that is, according to the imperatives of monumentalization. Read in this way, Allen's speeches come to be heard as *larger* than the larger-than-life that is the prerequisite of the monumental. It becomes, as the combination of references to "Old England" and New England/biblical fire and brimstone prophecy—and to the *miles gloriosus*—makes clear, American exceptionalist rant or diatribe:

"Brag no more, Old England; consider you are but an island! Order back your broken battalions! home, and repent in ashes!

Long enough have your hired tories across the sea forgotten the Lord their God, and bowed down to Howe and Knyphausen—the Hessian!—Hands off, red-skinned jackall! Wearing the king's plate, as I do, I have treasures of wrath for you British. . . . Ye brought me out here, from my dungeon to this green—affronting yon Sabbath sun—to see how a rebel looks. But I show ye how a true gentleman and Christian can conduct in adversity. Back dogs! Respect a gentleman and a Christian, though he be in rags and smell of bilge-water." (*IP*, 143)

Or, as Allen's repartee with one of the ladies who have come to gawk at him suggest—he projects the situation in the hyperbolic terms of the biblical story of Samson and Delilah—ludicrously quixotic in its invocation of the protocols of courtly love:

"Why, he talks like a beau in a parlor; this wild, mossed American from the woods," sighed another fair lady to her mate; "but can this be he we came to see? I must have a lock of his hair."

"It is he, adorable Delilah, and fear not, even though incited by the foe, by clipping my locks, to dwindle my strength. Give me your sword, man," turning to an officer;—"Ah! I'm fettered. Clip it yourself, lady."

"No, no—I am"—

"Afraid, would you say? Afraid of the vowed friend and champion of all ladies all round the world? Nay, nay: come hither."

The lady advanced; and soon, overcoming her timidity, her white hand shone like whipped foam amid the matted waves of flaxen hair.

"Ah, this is like clipping tangled tags of gold-lace," cried she; "but see, it is half straw."

"But the wearer is no man-of-straw, lady; were I free, and you had ten thousand foes—horse, foot, and dragoons—how like a friend I could fight for you! Come, you have robbed me of my hair; let me rob your dainty hand of its price. . . ." (*IP*, 145–146)

In the following chapter, the narrator of Israel Potter's story offers the reader a brief summary account of Ethan Allen, the man, his exploits in the American Revolution, and, above all, his "wild" behavior as a prisoner in England, in what appears on the surface to be a defense of the "Titanic Vermonter's singular demeanor abroad"—his "boisterousness": "True," he writes,

he stood upon no punctilios with his jailers; for where modest gentlemanhood is all upon one side, it is a losing affair; as if my

> Lord Chesterfield should take off his hat, and smile, and bow, to a mad bull, in hopes of a reciprocation of politeness. When among wild beasts, if they menace you, be a wild beast. Neither is it unlikely that this was the view taken by Allen. For, besides the exasperating tendency to self-assertion which such treatment as his must have bred on a man like him, his experience must have taught him, that by assuming the part of a jocular, reckless, and even braggart barbarian, he would better sustain himself against bullying turnkeys than by submissive quietude. (*IP*, 150)

Read, however, in the context of Allen's words (in adapting his autobiographical narrative, Melville simply highlighted "several ranting passages" from the original),[38] it becomes quite difficult not to conclude that this summary, in keeping with the demonumentalizing excessiveness of Melville's portraits of Franklin and Jones, is parodic, a deflation of an American exceptionalist windbag intended to direct attention to an other, radically different and marginalized kind of American, the lowly "nonentity" Israel Potter.

III

Following the demythologizing portrait of Ethan Allen, in which Israel's role is tellingly diminished to observing the captivity of his fellow American, Melville, in a daring structural move, brings his symbolic biography of Israel Potter to its "close" by telescoping the last forty years of his exilic and miserably impoverished life in England into four very brief, but profoundly resonant chapters that, as the title of the first—"Israel in Egypt"—makes clear, reestablish or, rather, underscore the inaugural identification of Israel and the New England Puritan tradition and its figural promise/fulfillment narrative. But before addressing these, I want to return to Melville's demonumentalizing intention, though now in terms of its effects on those, like Israel, whose sacrificial bodies enable the production of monuments and the unified nation they symbolize, and yet, because of the very logical economy of monumental memory, must be relegated to utter oblivion. Earlier in this chapter I said that Melville's paradoxical intention in expanding the original roles of Franklin and John Paul Jones, and adding Ethan Allen, giving all three monumental figures center-stage status in the episodes in which they appear, is not simply to point to the gradual but inexorable diminution of the significance of Israel's being by the dominant American culture, but, in so doing, to enhance his singularity: to render a sociopolitical non-entity an "entity," a nobody a "somebody," precisely by way of underscoring his sociopolitical status *as nobody*. This gradual paradoxical movement, which, as I have also noted, is articulated in a metaphorics that relates images of imprisonment, interment, marginalization, exile, wandering, disguise (the numerous changes of clothing he makes), immateriality, ghostliness, spectrality, and so on, reaches its penultimate moment in the episode, immediately before his encounter with Ethan Allen, in which Israel, on his way home to America on Jones's ship, *Ariel*, inadvertently ends up, without being seen by friend or foe, on an English letter of marque in the process of a brief skirmish with, and sudden withdrawal of, the enemy ship. Melville's representation of the ensuing events is comedy of the highest order, but this should not deflect attention from the deliberate commonality of tropes of presence/absence informing them and thus from their quite deliberate symbolic significance.

In this episode Israel imaginatively and boldly attempts to conceal his American identity by insinuating himself as a member of one of the various companies of the ship's crew. As the narrator puts it to underscore the question of Israel's reality—identity, visibility, presence, that is, the status of his physical being—"to escape final detection, Israel must some way get himself recognized as belonging to some one of those bands; otherwise, as an isolated nondescript, discovery ere long would be certain; especially upon the next general muster" (*IP*, 133–34). Eventually the news of these visitations of "a vagabond claiming fraternity" makes its way to the master-at-arms of the ship, who brings him before the officer of the deck for the first of several cross-examinations, all of which, as the repetition of the question concerning Israel's identity suggests, resonate with ontological significance:

> "Who the deuce *are* you?" at last said the officer of the deck, in added bewilderment. "Where did you come from? What's your business? Where are you stationed? What's your name? Who are you, anyway? How did you get here? and where are you going?"
>
> "Sir," replied Israel humbly, "I am going to my regular duty, if you will but let me. I belong to the main top, and ought to be by now engaged in preparing the top-gallant stu'n'-sail for hoisting."
>
> "Belong to the main-top? Why, these men here say you have been trying to belong to the fore-top, and the mizen-top, and the forecastle, and the hold, and the waist, and every other part of the ship. This is extraordinary," he added, turning upon the junior officers.
>
> "He must be out of his mind," replied one of them, the sailing master.
>
> "Out of his mind?" rejoined the officer of the deck. "He's out of all reason; out of all men's knowledge and memories! Why, no one knows him; no one has ever seen him before; no imagination, in the wildest flight of a morbid nightmare, has ever so much as dreamed of him. Who *are* you? he again added, fierce with amaze-

ment. "What's your name? Are you down in the ship's books, or at all in the records of nature?" (*IP*, 137; Melville's emphasis)

Bewildered by Israel's deliberately ambiguous answers, the deck officer finally, in exasperation, orders the master-at-arms to "take him away!" But this visitor cannot be so easily relocated:

> "But where am I to take him, sir?" said the master-at-arms. "He don't seem to belong anywhere, sir. Where—where am I to take him?"
> "Take him out of sight," said the officer, now incensed with his own perplexity. "Take him out of sight, I say."
> "Come along, then, my ghost," said the master-at-arms. And collaring the phantom, he led it hither and thither, not knowing exactly what to do with it. (*IP*, 139)

As the master-at-arms is leading "Israel about in this indefinite style" (he is an Israel who, not incidentally, has become a ghostly "it"), the captain of the ship observes this unusual behavior and, thinking that it might be a new, unauthorized and degrading form of punishment, summons him, and the following exchange ensues:

> "To what end do you lead that man about?"
> "To no end in the world, sir. I keep leading him about because he has no final destination."
> "Mr. officer of the deck, what does this mean?" Who is this strange man? I don't know that I remember him. Who is he? And what is signified by his being led about?"
> Hereupon, the officer of the deck, throwing himself into a tragical posture, set forth the entire mystery; much to the captain's astonishment, who at once indignantly turned upon the phantom.
> "You rascal—don't try to deceive me. Who are you? And where did you come from last?"
> "Sir, my name is Peter Perkins, and I last came from the forecastle where the master-at-arms last led me, before coming here."
> "No joking, sir, no joking."
> "Sir, I'm sure it's too serious a business to joke about."
> (*IP*, 140)

What follows is another extended interrogation in which Israel's responses to the captain's questions about his identity, like his responses to this first one, always already defer their referent, deconstructs them, as it were.

Eventually, the bewildered captain, like the deck officer before him, orders the master-at-arms to "take him away." In the end, after "further devious wanderings," Israel gains his "liberty." Indeed, he is allowed to join the sailors of the maintop, where he had first applied. This brilliant and resonant chapter concludes, when, happening one day "to glance upwards towards the main-top," the officer of the deck sees Israel and admits to him that he did "belong to the main-top, after all"; to this Israel replies: "I always told you so, sir, though, at first, you remember, sir, you wouldn't believe it" (*IP*, 141).

What is especially noteworthy in this series of examinations is that they enact a peculiar reversal of normal power relations, which, not incidentally, prefigures the reversal in "Bartleby, the Scrivener." Though Israel Potter is ostensibly at the mercy of the British authorities, whose ship he has accidentally boarded—they "lead" him (as the lawyer "leads" Bartleby)—in reality, they are, in a certain sense, if not at his mercy, at least dependent on him—he "leads" them (as Bartleby "leads" the lawyer). And this is because he, like Bartleby, "accepts" the identity-less identity he has been assigned by the "world" (those who determine what constitutes its truth and rule it)—his exilic condition, his not belonging, his disaffiliation, his invisibility, his wandering, his status as ghost or phantom or *Homo tantum*—and, in so doing, is enabled to refuse to play by the received rules of the game of power. He refuses, that is, his spontaneous assent to the prevailing truth discourse, to be *answerable* to its imperatives. The consequence of this refusal is to subvert the authority of the regime of truth and to dis-locate the located, de-stabilize the stable, baffle the answerers—that is, to render power impotent: " 'Come along, then, my ghost,' said the master-at-arms. And collaring the phantom, he led it hither and thither, not knowing exactly what to do with it."

Of course, this "liberation" is temporary. And, insofar as it is a liberation from the authority of the British navy—does not manifestly help Israel's cause as an exilic American—the episode could be, as it has been, appreciated simply for its comedic *élan* at the expense of its crucial larger purpose. If, on the other hand, this episode is perceived as not only bringing the binarist metaphorics of visibility/invisibility, presence/absence, being/non-being, sedentary/nomadic, incarceration/freedom associated with Israel throughout the novel, but also the dialectical action by which this "non-entity" achieves a resonant singularity, to a culminating visible and dense unity, then it will also be seen that it prefigures Melville's highly telescoped, ironic "conclusion." I am not simply referring to Israel's damaged life: his forty-five year exile; his irredeemably miserable pauper's existence in London, "the City of Dis," as a brick maker, a porter in a riverside warehouse, an itinerant chair bottomer, a matchmaker, a rag collector, and a worker in the sewers; his eventual return in old age to America through the efforts of his remaining son; his futile visit to his New England birthplace; and, after his failed attempt to receive a pension from—which is to say, to be recognized/remembered by—the American government, his unnoticed death and pauper's burial: "He was repulsed in efforts, after a pension, by certain caprices of law. His scars proved his only medals. He dictated a little book, the record of his fortunes. But long ago it faded out of print—himself out of being—his name out of memory. He died the same day that the oldest oak on his native hills was blown down" (*IP*, 169). I am also referring to Melville's subversive genealogical project: his giving back to the non-entity, Israel Potter, a history that the monumental History of the United States, including that of jeremiadic orators like Daniel Webster, has denied him in the very process of nation-building. To put this "circular" itinerary—this "repetition" (*Wiederholung*)[39]—in a way that is consistent with the proleptic terms of his text, Melville *retrieves* the *specter* of Israel Potter's forgotten singular being, a retrieval that appropriates Israel's symptomatic liberatory refusal to be interpellated—*to be somebody*, which is to say, to be answerable to the American calling—for the purpose of subverting and delegitimizing the invisible repressive nationalist hegemonic discourse of American exceptionalism.

In thus resurrecting Israel or, rather, conjuring his ghost, Melville is, as we shall see, not far from Bartleby the scrivener's haunting "I prefer not to," by which he dislocates the certain, complacent, benign, and patronizing discourse of the Wall Street lawyer; that is, the dominant capitalist culture of antebellum America. Nor, for that matter, is Melville far from a certain defining postmodern or poststructuralist strategy for warding off what Deleuze and Guattari have called the life-damaging modern (as opposed to monarchical) "apparatuses of capture."[40] I will amplify at length on the remarkable affinity between Melville's exilic/passive/spectral strategy of resistance to the hegemonic antebellum discourse of American exceptionalism and the poststructuralists' strategy of refusal in my commentary on "Bartleby, the Scrivener" in the next chapter. Here, it will suffice to quote the passage from Theodor Adorno's *Minima Moralia: Reflections from a Damaged Life* that constitutes the point of departure of one of the most provocative and all-encompassing articulations of the liberatory potential inhering in the refusal to be answerable to the hegemonic call: Edward Said's in *Culture and Imperialism*:

> In an intellectual hierarchy which constantly makes everyone answerable, unanswerability alone can call the hierarchy directly by its name. The circulation sphere, whose stigmata are borne by intellectual outsiders, opens a last refuge to the mind that barters it away, at the very moment when refuge no longer exists. He who offers for sale something unique that no one wants to buy, represents, even against his will, freedom from exchange."[41]

IV

That it is, indeed, the myth of American exceptionalism that Melville is primarily subverting is made abundantly clear not simply by his return in the end to his identification of Israel Potter with the Puritan tradition at the beginning of the novel, but, more tellingly, by his insertion of Israel, *as synecdoche of the collective Puritan self*, into the founding myth of America; that is, the myth (still accepted as the truth of History by an astonishingly large number of Americans), grounded in a prefigurative Providential understanding of history, that interpreted the Puritans as God's chosen people, and their exile from the tyrannical and decadent Old World and settlement of the New World (their "errand in the wilderness") as the fulfillment *in history* of a divine promise that was inaugurated with the Old Testament Israelites' exodus from Egyptian captivity and its settlement in the "promised land." In so doing, however, Melville's purpose is not, like that of Webster (and the custodians of the American Cultural Memory) in his Bunker Hill jeremiads, to celebrate the myth—its universal (essentialist) truth and its filial continuity with the American Revolution and the (not-so-revolutionary) antebellum historical occasion—and to invoke its hallowed aura in behalf of nation-building and/or sustaining the self-identical and patriotic American Self in the face of the crisis it was undergoing. Rather, Melville's intent in invoking and identifying Israel Potter—his ghost—with the founding Puritan myth of the American national identity is to undermine and delegitimize its pernicious authority over the contemporary, antebellum, American occasion.

This deconstructive process, as I have suggested, begins in the first chapter, in which Melville (the narrator), while describing his protagonist's birthplace in the Berkshires of Massachusetts (from the perspective of his present, it should be noted) overtly invokes and ironizes the Puritan/Old Testament origins of his name (*P*, 6). From then, it takes the form of Melville's demonumentalizing of the august, larger-than-life prophetic figures of Benjamin Franklin, John Paul Jones, and Ethan Allen, which at the same time retrieves Israel's singularity. But it is especially the burden of the last four chapters of the novel, which telescope the many years of Israel's horrific nomadic exile in London into a few intensely suggestive pages, to bring this deconstruction of the founding myth of America to its dis-closive end.

The first of these chapters, appropriately entitled "Israel in Egypt," describes his first slave-like employment as a wretched brick maker and is fraught with the metaphorics of interment—pits, graves, dungeons—that renders his "home" in exile a living hell equal to Dante's lowest circles: "For thirteen weary weeks, lorded over by taskmasters, Israel toiled in his pit. . . . The yard was encamped, with all its endless rows of tented sheds, and kilns, and mills, upon a wild waste moor, belted round by bogs and fens. The blank horizon, like a rope, coiled round the whole" (*IP*,155–56). The prefigurative analogy with the Puritans under the authority of the Anglican Church, the American revolutionaries under the British monarchy, and the Israelites under the Egyptian pharaohs is manifest. But what needs to be underscored in attending to this reference to the providential history of the Puritans is the glaring omission of any reference to the (grave) optimism that was intrinsic to its (teleo)logic. Instead, Melville represents Israel's slavery in "Egypt" as an utter dead-end. Meditating on his fate as he lades out his dough, he invokes this Puritan/American figural interpretation of history, bitterly underscoring the terrible irony that its promise is not simply unfulfilled, but that it has culminated in its utter opposite: "He whom love of country made a hater of her foes . . . here he was at last, serving that very people as a slave, better succeeding in making their bricks than firing their ships. To think that he should be thus helping, with all his strength, to extend the walls of the Thebes of the oppressor, made him half mad." Extending the reference to the biblical Israelites' captivity (Thebes), Melville underscores his American "protagonist's" bitter irony by commenting: "Poor Israel! Well-named—bondsman in the English Egypt," and then, to mark the depths of this nobody's hopelessness, adds: "But he drowned the thought by still more recklessly spattering with his ladle: 'What signifies who we be, or where we are, or what we do?' Slap-dash! 'Kings as clowns are codgers—who ain't a nobody?' Splash! 'All is vanity and clay' " (*IP*, 157).

Melville sustains the prefigural structure identifying Israel's degrading itinerary with that of the American Puritans and the latter's with that of the Old Testament Israelites throughout the remaining chapters. "The City of Dis" (the Roman god of the underworld) extends the dismal hell of the "Egyptian" brickyard to include London and its denizens at large, deepening their funereal aura—"as in eclipses, the sun was hidden; the air darkened; the whole dull, dismayed aspect of things, as if some neighboring volcano, belching its premonitory smoke, were about to whelm the great town, as Herculaneum and Pompeii, or the Cities of the Plain" (*PI*, 159–60)—and accelerating the process of Israel's disappearance into the obscurity of a sepulchral Dantesque crowd, which is to say, intensifying his premonition of the metamorphosis of his singularity into a ghost among ghosts:

> On they passed; two-and-two, along the packed footpaths of the bridge; long-drawn, methodic, as funerals: some of the faces settled in dry apathy, content with their doom; others seemed mutely raving against it; while still others, like spirits of Milton and Shelley in the prelatical Hinnom, seemed undeserving their fates, and despising their torture.
>
> As retired at length, midway, in a recess of the bridge, Israel surveyed them, various individual aspects all but frighted him.

Knowing not who they were; never destined, it may be, to behold them again; one after the other, they drifted by, uninvoked ghosts in Hades. . . .

Arrived . . . on the Middlesex side, Israel's heart was prophetically heavy; foreknowing, that being of this race, felicity could never be his lot. (*IP*, 160)

In the penultimate chapter, "Forty-five Years," Melville summarizes the remainder of Israel's itinerant life of destitution in London, sustaining, in the process the prefigural providential narrative structure: "For the most part, what befell Israel during his forty years' wanderings in the London deserts, surpassed the forty years in the natural wilderness of the outcast Hebrews under Moses" (*IP*, 161). In this highly condensed summary, which recounts Israel's marriage, his various and increasingly dehumanizing employments, the squalor of his family's many habitations, the deaths of ten of his eleven children, and eventually of his wife, in the volatile economic contexts of the end of the American Revolution and then of the war with France, Melville further underscores Israel's inexorable drift into penurious obscurity and augments the poignancy of his "captivity" by reminiscing nostalgically—indeed, hallucinating—about his youth in New England. What is especially revealing about Melville's revision of the original text's account of this relentless and undeviating slide into miserable oblivion is that it ruthlessly deletes Israel's numerous encomiums to God's benign Providence—so prominent in the autobiographies of the Puritans—on occasions when the new disaster that befalls him is not as great as the previous one, a habitual quiescence that culminates in the final astonishing Panglossian paragraph of his memoir:

> To conclude—although I may be again unfortunate in a renewal of my application to government . . .—yet I feel thankful that I am privileged (after enduring so much) to spend the remainder of my days, among those who I am confident are possessed of too much humanity, to see me suffer; and which I am sensible I owe to the divine goodness, which graciously condescended to support me under my numerous afflictions, and finally enabled me to return to my native country in the 79th year of my age—for this I return unfeigned thanks to the Almighty; and hope to give during the remainder of my life, convincing testimonies of the strong impression which those afflictions made on my mind, by devoting myself sincerely to the duties of religion.[42]

Significantly, the prefigural historical narrative surfaces once more at the end of this summary, when, Melville tells us, Israel's remaining son ("the poor enslaved boy"), instigated by the fabulous stories about the

New World he has heard from his old father, arranges with the American consul for a return voyage to the United States. This time, however, it is pointedly the prophesied *fulfillment* of the narrative that Melville invokes: "In his Moorfield's garret, over a handful of re-ignited cinders . . . raked up from the streets, he would drive away dolor, by talking with his only surviving, and now motherless child—the spared Benjamin of his old age—of the far Canaan beyond the sea; rehearsing to the lad those well-remembered adventures among New-England hills, and painting scenes of nestling happiness and plenty, in which the lowliest shared." These stories about an Edenic, exceptionalist America, Melville says, "sowed the seeds of [Israel's] eventual return." For they instilled in this "spared Benjamin" an intense "longing to escape his entailed misery, by compassing for his father and himself, a voyage to the Promised Land." And he pointedly adds at the end of the chapter, this emancipatory voyage occurred in "the year 1826; half a century since Israel, in early manhood, had sailed a prisoner in the Tartar frigate from the same port to which he now was bound" (*IP*, 166).

Israel's story, like the Hebrew and Puritan narratives, comes full circle. But the end—the fulfillment of the inaugural promise—is far from cathartic; it manifests itself, rather, as a bitterly ironic and disturbing difference. In the brief last chapter, entitled "*Requiescat in Pace*," Melville tells us with rapid and brutal finality that Israel, and his son, arrived in Boston on the Fourth of July, was almost run over by a "patriotic triumphal car . . . flying a broidered banner, inscribed with gilt letters: "BUNKER-HILL, 1775. GLORY TO THE HEROES THAT FOUGHT!," gazed at the site of the "incipient monument" across the Charles River from a mound in the graveyard on Copp's Hill, traveled by stage to "the country of the Housatonic," where he is not recognized, and then to his father's homestead in the Berkshires, where, on asking a man plowing a field "whose house stood there," is answered: "Don't know; forget the name; gone West, though, I believe" (*IP*, 169). With this poignant recognition of the irreversible passing of Puritan New England into the past and the emergence of the secular hegemony of the Jacksonian West, the inexorable reduction of Israel's being—his preterition—has been completed. He tells the ploughman: "The ends meet. Plough away, friend." Israel, the American "patriot," has been relegated to oblivion, buried, not in a "Promised Land," but a "true Potters' Field" (*IP*, 168)—and the Puritan tradition along with the exceptionalist American national identity it constructed have been delegitimized. In the last paragraph of his narrative, Melville's judgment against exceptionalist America is brutal in its unerring finality: "He was repulsed in efforts, after a pension, by certain caprices of law. . . . He dictated a little book, the record of his fortunes. But long ago it faded out of print—himself out of being—his name out of memory. He died the same day that the oldest oak on his native hills was blown over (*IP*, 169).

And so is his judgment of the custodians of the exceptionalist America's memory. In circling back to its beginning, Melville retrieves, or, in the metaphorics that pervade its pages, "resurrects" this forgotten "little book, the record of [Israel's] fortunes": the name, indeed, the very singular being, of its author. In so doing, his intention is to remind the reader not simply of his inaugural ironic dedication "To His Highness, The Bunker-Hill Monument," in which he offers his "retouched" version of this "tattered copy, rescued by the merest chance from the ragpickers," to "His Highness." It is also, I submit, to recall the figure of Daniel Webster, the epitome of the canonical American nation-builders, whose orotund, ideologically laden memorials—they are secularized versions of the Puritan jeremiad and the providential history it assumes—proclaimed in the monogrammatic name of the *unity* of the "American people," must, as Ernest Renan admitted, in the very act of re-membering, forget not only the violence at the origin of the American national identity, but also the "lowly" singularities—the Israel Potters—who made the Revolution. It is no accident that Melville dates his acutely ironic dedication June 17, 1854, the anniversary of the battle *and* of both Daniel Webster's Bunker Hill Monument orations (1825 and 1843),[43] and changes the original date of Israel Potter's return to the United States—forty-two days after departure from England on April 5, 1823—to July 4, 1826, approximately one year after Webster delivered the first of these at the time of the laying of its cornerstone. In thus reinvoking Webster's Bunker Hill nationalist orations and their turgid periods in this paradoxical end, Melville's text cannot help but also instigate the memory of one of his great contemporaries, Emily Dickinson, who, in a way, was also "frozen into silence" by the dominant culture that had come to prefer answers to questions, certain directionality to creative errancy, providential design to improvisation, public visibility to the invisibility of privacy, the unity of abstract collectivity to plurality, that is, the accommodating one to singularity:

> I'm nobody! Who are you?
> Are you nobody, too?
> Then there's a pair of us—don't tell
> They'd banish us, you know.
> How dreary to be somebody!
> How public, like a frog
> To tell your name the livelong day
> To an admiring bog![44]

But the brutal last paragraph of Melville's novel, which returns the reader to its beginning, is, finally, more than a judgment It is also, however, tentatively, a de-structive *pro-jective* gesture that, in revealing the optimistic logic of the American exceptionalist self to be self-contradictory, points futurally to a different understanding of what it means to be an American from that of the custodians of the American national identity such as Daniel Webster. That is to say, in following the latter's circular logic to its end—the identitarian and nationalistic logic that monumentalized Franklin, Jones, and Allen in the name of the future generations of exceptionalist "America" and necessarily forgot or obliterated the singular being of Israel Potter—Melville's novel bears witness to a "repetition," a self-de-struction of the exceptionalist American national identity that precipitates and pro-jects a singular (unaccommodatable) difference, the very difference this collective identity was intended to annul. In that last paragraph, we recall, Melville writes: "But long ago it [Israel's autobiographical book] faded out of print—himself out of being—his name out of memory." This rhetoric, of course, echoes, indeed, brings to culmination, the metaphorics of interment, imprisonment, obliteration, and not least ghostliness that increasingly comes to haunt Israel's being from the moment of his departure from his Puritan New England home. But, as I have shown, Melville *retrieves* Potter's book (his "being," and his "memory") by way of rescuing it "from the rag-pickers"; rewriting it both to disclose the bankruptcy of the American national identity—the filiative national Self sponsored by Webster—and to remember Israel's unrepeatable and irreducible singular "self"; and offering it to "His Highness, the Bunker-Hill Monument, who "may be deemed the Great Biographer: the national commemorator of such of the anonymous privates of June 17, 1775, who may never have received other requital than the solid reward of your granite." And this retrieval transforms the negative connotations of ghostliness imposed on it by a culture that privileges matter over spirit (beings over being) into a resonant positive. Like Ishmael, Pierre, Bartleby, Babo, and the confidence-man, indeed, like Melville himself in the aftermath of the reception of *Pierre*, Israel, under Melville's sponsorship becomes a *specter*—the very *other* of an ontologically materialist culture—who haunts the (unexceptionalist) exceptionalist American national identity. In Jacques Derrida's resonant terms, he becomes a *revenant*, or, to foreground the visual metaphorics that, as Webster's exemplary orations testify, inhere in the metaphysical binary logic of national identity, the *visited* (the singular Israel reduced to non-being by the gaze of the custodians of American cultural identity) becomes the visitor.[45]

What would this Melvillian spectrality mean translated into the language of cultural identity? As I have shown, the exceptionalist American national Self privileged by its custodians, especially in the aftermath of the American Revolution—most notably the invisible but very much present "center elsewhere," Daniel Webster[46]—is an essentialist and ideological identity, one that either demonizes and excludes what it represents as its *others* or, more basically, accommodates its *others* to its privileged inclusive and self-present self: the American nation. But insofar as the nation is a collective abstract "ideal"—an integral whole—and the people who inhabit it are singularities, it can never be embodied. There will, as William Connolly puts it, always be a "lack" or a "hole" at its "center." Nevertheless, the idealization of the idea of the nation, in the manner of, say, Ernest Renan or Daniel Webster, will always already encourage the coercive filling of the lack, the centering of the uncentered center. It will, that is, make "the [plurally oriented] state practically vulnerable to takeover attempts by constituencies who claim to embody in themselves the unity that is necessary to the nation but so far absent from it."[47] This is, to recall the passage from his second Bunker Hill oration quoted earlier in this chapter, remarkably—and prophetically—evident in the restricted economy of Webster's nationalist discourse:

> Woe betide the man who brings to this day's worship feeling less than wholly American! Woe betide the man who can stand here with the fires of local resentments burning, or the purpose of fomenting local jealousies and strife of local interests festering and rankling in his heart. Union, established in justice, in patriotism, and the most plain and obvious common interest,—union, founded on the same love of liberty, cemented by blood shed in the same common cause,—union has been the source of all our glory and greatness thus far, and is the ground of all our highest hopes. This column stands on Union.

It is, I suggest, this threat to the singular plurality inhabiting the geographical and cultural space of America, which is inherent in Webster's ferociously pure—one is prompted by the ferocity of his warning to say "terrorist"—idea of the American nation, that Melville discloses and underscores in demonumentalizing the American exceptionalist national identity in the name of Israel Potter's irreducible singularity, that is, in identifying it with the spectrality to which his being is reduced by the monumentalist historian.[48] In thus revealing the nationalism that Webster espouses to be inimical to real democracy, Melville also anticipates the poststructuralist interrogation of nationhood, including its inevitable appeal to the state of exception. Israel, Melville everywhere insists, *is* an "American," indeed a patriot, but not in the reductive ideological (nationalist) sense of "Americanus" that Webster understands and brandishes the term; that is, as a totalized filial entity that is identical with itself, a member of "the people." This American is essentially no different from the "European," whom this exceptionalist American claimed to have superseded. He is, rather, as Melville's revisions of the original text everywhere demonstrate, an American precisely in the sense of being, like the "*orphaned*" Ishmael and Pierre, devoid of a filial identity, of being, as it were, an *un*-American American As I have shown, he leaves his plow to fight at Bunker Hill and at sea with John Paul Jones; he asserts his dignity as a human being in his relations with Sir John Millet, the King of England, and his American compatriots; he becomes a courier for Benjamin Franklin; he outwits the British officers on board the letter-of-marque; he survives the erosive degradations of poverty in the "City of Dis" not because he is an (exceptionalist) American, but because of his *singular will to be free* from *all* tyrannies, including his Puritan father's. Anticipating the anti-identitarian insight of Connolly and the poststructuralists on whom Connolly relies, Melville, that is, knows (as Renan does, and Webster may not), that the nation is a transcendental idea that cannot possibly be embodied in the secular world, that the attempt to do so by one constituency necessarily involves violence against other, less powerful ones or, to use Melville's own rhetoric vis-à-vis Israel Potter, manifests itself in the transformation of these others into unfilial specters. This damage inflicted on Israel's singular life by the futile effort to embody the covenantal nation, needless to say, is cause for anger and mourning, but it is also, as Theodor Adorno and Edward Said bear witness in their respective postmodern contexts, cause to think this damaged life—this spectrality—*positively*. Melville, in the context of antebellum America, does not explicitly, no doubt because such an effort might have been (mis)interpreted as a justification of secession from the "Union." But his sustained witness to the violence inhering in the exceptionalist American national identity—to his protagonists' damaged lives—in the fiction after *Moby-Dick*, not least in *Israel Potter*, provides resonant directives for such an undertaking. One is the recognition that the specter that has always haunted the "truth" of the idea of the (exceptionalist) nation is, in fact, the irreducible singularity of human being. The other, emerging from the first, is the recognition that democracy must be thought, not, as it is in exceptionalist America, in terms of a totalizing essence that, at best, reduces the singular to the individual and accommodates him or her to a dominant center elsewhere, but a pluralist community of irreducible singularities living together in care—or, to invoke Edward Said's moving revision of T. S. Eliot, " 'the complete concert dancing together,' *contrapuntally*."[49]

V

Melville's insight in *Israel Potter* into the complicity of monuments, whether histories, arts, literary canons, or biographies, and the damage nation-building inflicts on the lives of the nation's others, as I have been suggesting, is proleptic of the various postmodern or postcolonial interrogations of the nation-state. But what makes his novel especially relevant to the contemporary occasion is the light it sheds on the ominous turn the United States has undergone under the leadership of a coalition of neoconservatives and evangelical Christians in the wake of the attacks on the World Trade Center and the Pentagon on 9/11/01 by Al Qaeda.

During the turbulent 1960s, Americans bore witness to the self-destruction of the very idea of American exceptionalism—and the national consensus—by way of the excessive, indeed, barbaric "civilized" violence perpetrated by the American government in Vietnam in the name of "the free world." This was a period in American history which also rendered visible the racist, patriarchal, and imperialist tendencies deeply inscribed in the American national identity and thus the emergence to some degree of prominence of a number of discourses, variously called deconstruction, poststructuralist, postmodern, that interrogated not only the "truth" discourse of America, but also its cultural canons, a polyvalent momentum that inaugurated a transformation of the traditional, nation-state oriented "core curriculum" of American colleges and universities into multicultural curricula and contributed to the emergence of vocal ethnic and racial minorities demanding hitherto withheld rights and the beginnings of a dialogue on the multicultural community. This momentum, which the dominant culture in America resisted all along the way, was brought to a standstill in the aftermath of the Al Qaeda attacks on 9/11. They have enabled the contemporary custodians of the American national identity to recuperate the exceptionalist national identity that was shaken to its foundations in the 1960s.

During this time, Americans have borne witness not only to the annunciation by the American government of a global "war on terror" that justifies "preemptive" invasions and occupations of states that are deemed threats to global democracy. They have also borne witness to the tacit declaration of a permanent state of exception and the *orchestration* of public opinion for the purpose of re-achieving a religio-patriotic unity adequate enough to reoccupy the absent center of the nation and thus to enable the vilification and silencing of those constituencies of American society that, since the Vietnam War, the civil rights movement, and the feminist initiative of the 1960s, have, however tentatively and imperfectly, been engaged in a process of rethinking what it means to be an American in light of the plurality disclosed and empowered by the self-destruction of the American national identity in that decade. This orchestration of American public opinion in behalf of the recuperation of a patriotic national consensus in the "war on terror" is not simply a matter of government policy. It also involves a massive cultural initiative sponsored by the highly influential neoconservative intelligentsia (many of whom have become high-ranking members of the government), a large segment of the media—newspapers, book publishers, television, cinema, even academia—and, not least, the now politically active evangelical Christian churches. In their common effort to achieve the nation, one could say in general that all of these cultural institutions of the post-9/11 occasion are, each in its own way, utilizing in some form or other what, following Nietzsche and Foucault, I have been calling "monumental history" to characterize the principal means by which the dominant culture in America has historically maintained or recuperated the national identity in times of crisis. But if, like Melville, we are attuned to the history of American culture, especially to the origins of the American national identity and the subsequent way in which the dominant culture has responded to historical crises of identity, then we are enabled to be more specific than Nietzsche and Foucault in naming the means by which these post-9/11 ideological state apparatuses are attempting to re-achieve national unity. We are, that is, enabled to say, with Sacvan Bercovitch, that this means is the *American jeremiad*, the Puritan theological rhetorical instrument, appropriated repeatedly in American history, as in the case of Daniel Webster, by the elect (who, like their forebears, always identify themselves as the "saving remnant"), that spoke of "declension and doom," but, like monumental history, was "part of a strategy designed to revitalize the errand [in the wilderness]."[50]

This, in fact, is precisely the strategy adopted by Samuel P. Huntington, one of the most influential neoconservative historian/policy experts, in his recent, aptly named book, *Who Are We?: Challenges to America's National Identity*, written in the wake of 9/11 and the George W. Bush administration's invasion and occupation of Iraq and intended to reunify the American national identity jeopardized by the "deconstructionist" movement and the rise of "subnational cultures" (not least, Hispanic) in the decade of the Vietnam War and to revitalize the exceptionalist "errand"—now, however, in the *global* wilderness. Reminding his readers of the settling of America, Huntington, like Webster, emphasizes the role religion played and singles out the "Puritans, especially of Massachusetts"—and their figural/providential interpretive method—as the primary means of producing the American national identity:

> They took the lead in defining their settlement based on "a Covenant with God" to create "a city on a hill" as a model for all the world.... In the seventeenth and eighteenth centuries, Americans defined their mission in the New World in biblical terms. They were a "chosen people," on an "errand in the wilderness," creating "the new Israel" or the "new Jerusalem" in what was clearly "the promised land." America was the site of a "new Heaven and a new earth" ... God's country. The settlement of America was vested, as Sacvan Bercovitch puts it, "with all the emotional, spiritual, and intellectual appeal of a religious quest." This sense of holy mission was easily expanded into millenarian themes of America as "the redeemer nation" and "the visionary republic." (*WAW*, 64)

Following this "genealogy" of the American national identity, Huntington goes on from his perspective as a member of the saving remnant, to describe—and lament—its disintegration, along with the weakening of its former power to assimilate immigrants, with the rise of "the deconstructionist movement" and "subnational identities"[51] in the 1960s. Then, in the wake of the advent of Osama bin Laden and Al Qaeda, who provided "America" with the "enemy" (and the "adversity"), which its exceptionalist identity has always needed for its rejuvenation, and in the manner of the American jeremiad, he recapitulates the "fault lines" that threaten the American identity, not least the growing Hispanic subculture. Minimizing the power of the "American Creed" (the democratic institutions), in favor of religion, he finally prophecies, if he does not exactly call for, the recuperation of the "Anglo-Protestant core culture":

> People are not likely to find in political principles the deep emotional content and meaning provided by kith and kin, blood and belonging, culture and nationality.... The idea that "We are all liberal democratic believers in the American Creed" seems unlikely to satisfy that need. A nation, Ernest Renan said, may be "a daily plebiscite," but it is a plebiscite on whether or not to maintain an existing inheritance. It is, as Renan also said, "the culmination of a long past of endeavors, sacrifices, and devotion. Without that inheritance, no nation exists, and if the plebiscite rejects that inheritance, the nation ends. America is "a nation with the soul of a church."... So also a nation may, as America does, have a creed, but its soul is defined by the common history, traditions, culture, heroes and villains, victories and defeats, enshrined in its "mystic chords of memory." (*WAW*, 339)

Israel Potter: His Fifty Years of Exile is ostensibly a story about the bizarre adventures of an ordinary American caught in epochal circumstances that made his experience interesting to an ordinary American public, an apparent retreat from the furious pushing across imaginative and moral boundaries that had antagonized the readers and reviewers of *Moby-Dick* and *Pierre* to the safe terrain of the early "realistic" novels of seafaring adventure. As Melville put it to the editors of *Putnam's*, in which he hoped to publish it in serial form: "I engage that the story shall contain nothing of any sort to shock the fastidious. There will be very little reflective writing in it; nothing weighty. It is adventure. As for its interest, I shall try to sustain that as well as I can."[52] If, however, as I have done, one takes Melville's ironic "dedication" of his book "To His Highness, the Bunker-Hill Monument" seriously as a structuring principle (which is to say, his parody of Daniel Webster's filial/canonical commemorations)—and the ironic figural historical analogy between the circular narratives of Israel's life, the history of the American Puritans, and of the Israelites of the Old Testament to which the dedication gives rise—it will be seen that Melville's novel belies his apparently simplistic intent. It will reveal, instead, its complex and "weighty" ontological, aesthetic, historical, ethical, and political significance, specifically, its devastating genealogical (demonumentalizing) critique of the American exceptionalist national identity and the specter that this critique discloses. I mean the specter of another, noncoercive way of being American that has always haunted the filial discourse of the post-Revolutionary American Fathers. This is not to say that *Israel Potter* ranks with *Moby-Dick*, *Pierre*, and *The Confidence-Man*; it is to say, rather, that its neglect as trivial by the Melville Revival and the scant serious attention it has received by contemporary criticism is unwarranted, the result of an anachronistic interpretive problematic that was inadequate to Melville's revolutionary aesthetic/ethical/political vision. Or, to put it positively, it is to say that, like *Moby-Dick*, *Pierre*, "Bartleby, the Scrivener," "Benito Cereno," and *The Confidence-Man*, Melville's *Israel Potter*, in its brilliant de-struction of the American exceptionalist narrative, anticipates the post–Cold War neoconservative version of the (Anglo-Protestant) American national identity and its messianic imperialist democracy—and the New Americanist critical discourse that, under the influence of the revolutionary poststructuralist critique of the truth-discourse of the West, has emerged in recent years to call this undemocratic kind of democracy "directly by its name."

Chapter 4

"Benito Cereno" and "Bartleby, the Scrivener"

Reflections on the American Calling

What made the mistake of political economy possible does indeed affect the *transformation of the object* of its oversight. What political economy does not see is not a pre-existing object which it could have seen but did not see—but an object which it produced itself in its operation of knowledge and which did not pre-exist it; precisely the production itself, which is identical with the object. What political economy does not see is what it *does*.

—Louis Althusser, "From '*Capital*' to Marx's Philosophy"

To enforce its invisibility through silence is to allow the black body a shadowless participation in the dominant cultural body.

—Tony Morrison, *Playing in the Dark*

"Yes. They killed him because he was too innocent to live. . . . He had no more of a notion than any of you what the whole affair's about, and you gave him money and York Harding's books on the East and said, 'Go ahead. Win the East for Democracy,' He never saw anything he hadn't heard in a lecture-hall . . . When he saw a dead body he couldn't even see the wounds. A Red menace, a soldier of democracy."

—Fowler to the American Attaché in Graham Greene, *The Quiet American*

"Benito Cereno": The "Vision" of American Exceptionalism

Herman Melville's small masterpiece "Benito Cereno" (1855) is told by a narrator who rarely departs from the perspective of Amasa Delano, the American (New Englander) captain of a merchant ship, *Bachelor's Delight*, plying the Pacific waters off the coast of Chile, which encounters a Spanish vessel, the *San Dominick*, seemingly in distress, but, as it turns out, is carrying a "cargo" of black slaves who have mutinied and taken over the ship. Indeed, the narrator's "objectivity," his deliberate effort to re-present the story of this encounter from Delano's eyes—he insistently refers to him, after boarding the troubled Spanish vessel, as "the visitor" (from the Latin *videre*: "to see")—is so basic that the reader is compelled from the outset to think of it as a story about visual perception or, more precisely, *American* seeing. The following passage from the beginning of the story is exemplary of this point of view:

> While left alone with them, he [Captain Delano] was not long in observing some things tending to heighten his first impressions; but surprise was lost in pity, both for the Spaniards and blacks, alike evidently reduced from scarcity of water and provisions; while long-continued suffering seemed to have brought out the less good-natured qualities of the negroes, besides, at the same time, impairing the Spaniard's authority over them. But, under the circumstances, precisely this condition of things was to have been anticipated. In armies, navies, cities, or families, in nature herself, nothing more relaxes good order than misery. Still, Captain Delano was not without the idea, that had Benito Cereno been a man of greater energy, misrule would hardly have come to the present pass. But the debility, constitutional or induced by the hardships, bodily and mental, of the Spanish captain, was too obvious to be overlooked. A prey to settled dejection, as if long mocked with hope he would not now indulge it, even when it had ceased to be a mock, the prospect of that day or evening at the furthest, lying at anchor, with plenty of water for his people, and a brother captain to counsel and befriend, seemed in no perceptible degree to encourage him. His mind appeared unstrung, if not still more seriously affected. Shut up in these oaken walls, chained to one dull round of command, whose unconditionality cloyed him, like some hypochondriac abbot he moved slowly about, at times suddenly pausing, starting, or staring, biting his lip, biting his finger-nail, flushing, paling, twitching his beard, with other symptoms of an absent or moody mind. This distempered spirit was lodged, as before hinted, in as distempered a frame. He was rather tall, but seemed never to have been robust, and now with nervous suffering was almost worn to a skeleton. A tendency to some pulmonary complaint appeared to have been lately confirmed. His voice was like that of one with lungs half gone, hoarsely suppressed, a husky whisper. No wonder that, as in this state he tottered about, his private servant apprehensively followed him. Sometimes the negro gave his master his arm, or took his handkerchief out of his pocket for him; performing these

and similar offices with that affectionate zeal which transmutes into something filial or fraternal acts in themselves but menial; and which has gained for the negro the repute of making the most pleasing body servant in the world; one, too, whom a master need be on no stiffly superior terms with, but may treat with familiar trust; less a servant than a devoted companion.

Marking the noisy indocility of the blacks in general, as well as what seemed the sullen inefficiency of the whites, it was not without humane satisfaction that Captain Delano witnessed the steady good conduct of Babo.[1]

What this representative inaugural passage tells us about Captain Delano is that he is not simply acutely conscious of a certain resonant aura of mystery—underscored by the narrator's references to Delano's observations as "seeming" or "appearing"—that is throbbing not too far below the surface of events, but also a keen observer of details—the degraded physical condition of the Spanish ship, the strange lack of order among the blacks and whites, the enervated physical and spiritual condition of the Spanish captain, and the peculiar behavior of the black servant—and, not least, a thoughtful analyst of their significance. There is nothing at this early stage of the encounter, or even later for that matter, to indicate that Delano is a stupid man, as so many commentators on the story have claimed. On the contrary, he is acutely rational, thoughtful, and honest (a "good" man as the narrator insistently reiterates).

At the epistemological level, we are justified by the mysterious conditions of the encounter between the Spanish and American ships and Delano's characteristically American response to them in saying that he sees the way the empirical scientist—the producer of knowledge that Melville's age was coming increasingly to privilege—or, closer to the text, the way the classical detective sees. That is to say, he sees being as a *system* of objects—a differential realm informed by a principle of presence (causality) that renders temporal and spatial differences "clues" that, carefully observed, inevitably reveal their relationality and lead to the solution of a mystery, that is, transforms the contingencies of temporal being into *narrative* totality or spatial form. As such a (metaphysical) system that privileges the transcendent or panoptic eye, the eye that sees from above or from the end (of a temporal process)—time as narrative structure—Delano's is an *optimistic* way of seeing that always already transforms the anxiety and distrust precipitated by the emergence of an anomaly, a contradiction—a mystery, as it were—into a complacent confidence:

> [T]he Western perspective—by which I specifically mean the rational or rather the positivistic structure of consciousness that views spatial and temporal phenomena in the world as "problems" to be

"solved"—expresses itself as a self-deceptive effort to find objects for the dread [which has *no thing* as its object] in order to *domesticate*—to at-home—the threatening realm of Nothingness, the profound not-at-home, into which [human being] is thrown . . . as being-in-the-world. It is, in other words, a rigidified, evasive anthropomorphic . . . consciousness, which obsessively attempts by coercion to fix and stabilize the elusive flux of existence from *meta-ta-physica* (after or beyond things-as-they-are), from the vantage point of a final rational cause. By means of this coercive transformation, this *object*ification of Nothing, the positivistic structure of consciousness is able not only to *man*ipulate, to lay hands on, the irrational world (including man, of course) for the purpose of achieving what one important early spokesman for this perspective (this "inquisition of things") referred to as "man's empire over the universe" "for the benefit and use" of "man's estate." More basically . . . it can also *justify* the absurdity of human existence: it allows man, that is, to perceive the immediate, uncertain, problematic, and thus dreadful psychic or historical present of [humanity] as a necessary part of a linear design, as a causal link between the past and/or future determined from a rational end, a *logos*. The one thing needful to fill the gaps between apparent discontinuities in both the internal and external worlds (that is, memory and history) or, another way of putting it, to apprehend . . . and to exploit this comforting linear design behind the absurd and dislocating or, better, *dis-lodging* appearances, is a "disinterested" or "objective"—and distanced—observer of the uniformity among diverse phenomena, that is, the positivistic scientist or, what is the same thing, the behaviorist psychoanalyst.[2]

But this diagnosis of Captain Delano's mode of perception as an empiricism that objectifies temporality—the un(re)presentable—in the name of causality, though intended by Melville to be registered by the reader, is partial. The cultural allotrope of this generally Western logocentric epistemology is that American way of perception and inquiry—its sense of national selfhood—that had its origins in the Puritans' interpretation of their collective identity as God's "chosen people" and their exodus from the decadent and tyrannical Old World to the New as a divinely ordained "errand in the wilderness" and, accordingly, its matured cultural manifestation in the *myth* of American exceptionalism. Underscored by Melville's insistent identification of Delano as "the American" (from New England) and Benito Cereno as "the Spaniard," this is the inscribed belief that Americans are radically different from and superior to Europeans because they are a *new* people, *innocent* of the debilitating consequences of national old age and a long tradition—cultural decadence, moral corruption, ethical cynicism, practical impotence, and politically tyranny. Americans are instead optimistic, trustful, future-oriented, practically productive, and, not least, benevolent: a messianic people whose providential purpose is to enlighten the benighted everywhere in the world.

This cultural difference pervades the epistemological discourse of the above passage and, increasingly, what follows. Delano, for example, sees Benito Cereno as physically and mentally enervated, despite his awareness of the latter's relative youth (the narrator tells us he is in his late twenties). And though he attributes the cause of this condition and of the disorder on board the Spanish ship in part to the alleged circumstances of the ill-fated voyage, "Still, Captain Delano was not without the idea, that had Benito Cereno been a man of greater energy, misrule would hardly have come to the present pass" (*BC*, 52). This cultural contrast, which persists throughout the novella, Melville surely knew, was a fundamental ideological tenet of the British cultural discourse of empire—"we are not ruthless and exploitative conquerers like those cruel Spanish conquistadors; we bring civilization and its material benefits to the wretched barbarians"—as, for example, in the case of Defoe's *Robinson Crusoe*.[3] It was also and even more fundamental to the cultural discourse of America from the time of the "founding" of the New World, when the Anglo-Americans and the Spanish were locked in struggle over the possession of the continent, to the Mexican War and after.[4] This contrast is further underscored by Delano's interpretation of the Spaniard's enervated demeanor, and above all, of his apparent inability to feel relief, to say nothing about hope, after the rescue of his ship by the optimistic and benevolent American: "A prey to settled dejection, as if long mocked with hope he would not now indulge it, even when it had ceased to be a mock, the prospect of that day or evening at furthest, lying at anchor, with plenty of water for his people, and a brother captain to counsel and befriend, seemed in no perceptible degree to encourage him" (*BC*, 52).

But Delano's American exceptionalist perspective is not limited in this passage to the contrast between his New World optimism and what he feels is Benito Cereno's Old World despair. It also manifests itself in his perception of the blacks on board the ship, particularly one, Babo, who appears to be carefully serving his master. The benevolent and self-congratulating Delano does not attribute the apparent unruliness of the blacks on board the ship to their race; he attributes it, rather, to their "long-continued suffering" on the *San Dominick* and the similarly induced laxity of Benito Cereno's authority. This would suggest that he is not a racist as, his thoughts imply, the Spanish are. His benevolence and humanity toward the slaves become especially manifest in his observations about Babo, who seems anxious about the well-being of his master and performs his offices with care and a kind of "affectionate zeal which transmutes into something filial or fraternal acts in themselves but menial . . ." (*BC*, 52). But as the generalization following this observation makes manifestly clear, this Bostonian's benevolent attitude toward Babo and his race is suspect; indeed, it discloses the underbelly of that "liberal," that is, accommodational, version of the American exceptionalist myth—decisively recorded by Frederick Douglass in his autobiography[5]—that all too pervasively prevailed in Abolitionist New England: "and which has gained for the negro the repute of making the most pleasing body servant in the world; one, too, whom a master need be on no stiffly superior terms with, but may treat with familiar trust; less a servant than a devoted companion" (*BC*, 52).

What is remarkable about Captain Delano's exceptionalist vision here at the beginning and increasingly throughout his experience on board the *San Dominick* is its utter blindless, despite evidence to the contrary, to the possibility that the enigmatic state of affairs on board the Spanish slave ship to which he bears witness is the consequence of the slaves' revolt. This blindness, as I have said, is not a matter of dullness of mind, or failure of observation, or error of judgment. It is, Melville implies, a matter of a frame of mind or, more precisely, a metaphysical mode of vision that sees—and accepts as the truth—only that which it is culturally inscribed to see. That which it cannot see, that which it is blind to, is thus *without being*. Put this way, it will be seen that Melville's representation of Captain Delano's witness to and meditation on the spatial and temporal phenomena on board the Spanish slave ship remarkably anticipates the decisive poststructuralist analysis of the (metaphysical) way modern Western humanity perceives being, particularly Louis Althusser's account of what he calls the "problematic" of the liberal capitalist culture. Since the relationship I am identifying, both in its account of what is *seen* and what is *not seen* by the inquiring subject, is reciprocally illuminating in a remarkable way—and will figure significantly, if antithetically, in my reading of "Bartleby, the Scrivener," a brief summary of Althusser's analysis of the problematic is in order.[6]

As with the exceptionalist frame of reference that determines what Captain Delano sees and does not see on board the Spanish ship, the invisible of the visible field of the problematic, according to Althusser, "is not . . . *anything whatever* outside and foreign to the visible defined by the field. The invisible is defined by the visible as *its* invisible." It is not the "outer darkness of exclusion"; it is "the *inner darkness of exclusion*, inside the visible itself because defined by the structure." The invisible, that is, *belongs to* the visible, is the invisible *of* the visible. We must not be seduced by the spatial *metaphors* (terrain, field, structure, horizon, region) we have been conditioned to use to refer to knowledge production into thinking that the "field" is "a space limited by *another space outside it*." For this "other space is also in the first space which contains it as its own denegation." This first space, in other words, "carries its outside inside it." It is total and totalizing. Its limits are internal to itself. "Hence, if we wish to preserve the spatial metaphor, the paradox of the theoretical field is that it is an *infinite* because *definite* space, i.e. it has no limits, no external frontier separating it from nothing, precisely because it is *defined* and limited within itself, carrying in itself the finitude of its definition, which, by excluding what it is not, makes it what it is."[7]

Because the vision intrinsic to this totalizing operation of the problematic "carries its outside in it," it is not, as the dominant culture of modernity adamantly assumes, the "subject" that determines what is seen. That is to say, it is not the attentiveness of the free individual's vision—I have underscored Captain Delano's—on which the truth depends, in the sense that an attentive subject will see everything that is *there*, whereas an inattentive subject will not. The subject's vision—and its truth—is determined by the visual field of the problematic. What it sees is "the act of its structural conditions." The "sighting" is "the relation of immanent reflection between the field of the problematic and *its* objects and *its* problems," the objects and problems intrinsic to its structural field. The subject, in other words, *is assigned* its sight by the totalizing problematic. The problematic, in short, *sees for* and thus *thinks* and *speaks for* the subject. As Althusser puts it, "It is literally no longer the eye (the mind's eye) of a subject which *sees* what exists in the field defined by a theoretical problematic: it is this field itself which *sees itself* in the objects or problems it defines—sighting being merely the necessary reflection of the field on its objects" (CMP, 25). For this subject every other "object" is not an object; every other "problem" is not a problem. In other words, every thing and every time that is not *of*—that does not properly *belong to*—the problematic has tacitly *no existence*—is not "visible" to—the subject. This subject, whose sight is determined by the problematic is thus a "subjected subject" or, to introduce an Althusserian term to which I will return later, an "interpellated"—a called or hailed—subject."[8]

I

Reconstellated into the Melvillian context I am exploring, Althusser's analysis of the visible intrinsic to the liberal capitalist problematic sheds significant light on the blindness of Captain Delano's American exceptionalist (over)sight. From the inaugural moment he boards the Spanish slave ship to the very end, what he sees—the variations of "The Spaniard's manner," the "noisy indocility of the blacks in general," and "the steady good conduct of Babo" (*BC*, 52)—is determined by his American exceptionalist problematic. Indeed, this is the case, as I will show, *even after the revelation* that everything to which he has borne witness on the *San Dominick* has been a masquerade orchestrated by Babo and intended to conceal the slaves' revolt and takeover of the ship. As I have noted, Captain Delano, acute empiricist that he is, observes many anomalies on board the *San Dominick* in the course of the day—emanating from the erratic behavior of Benito Cereno, the various signs of unruliness among the blacks, the unrelenting shadow-like attentiveness of Babo to his ailing master, and the ambiguous efforts of a couple of white seamen to catch his eye—and thus becomes suspicious of the story of the fate of the *San Dominick* he has been told by its captain. In other words, he is from the beginning, in some intuitive sense, aware of and uneasy over an enigmatic aura that pervades the crippled Spanish ship. But each time a sequence of these observed anomalies precipitates his suspicion, Delano does not explore them; rather, like the classical empiricist (or detective), he objectifies and reduces them to "clues" and then accommodates them to a reconciling narrative structure informed by the American exceptionalist problematic.

Thus, for example, when, early in the narrative, Delano observes a certain disturbance in the demeanor of Benito Cereno that seems incommensurate to the kindness he has shown him, he at first rationalizes this "unfriendly indifference" as the effect of illness: "The Spaniard's manner conveyed a sort of sour and gloomy disdain, which he seemed at no pains to disguise. But this the American *in charity* ascribed to the harassing effects of sickness, since, in former instances, he had noted that there are peculiar natures on whom prolonged physical suffering seems to cancel every social instinct of kindness" (*BC*, 52–53; my emphasis). Shortly after, however, Delano revises his interpretation

> But ere long Captain Delano bethought him that, indulgent as he was at the first, in judging the Spaniard, he might not, after all, have exercised charity enough. At bottom it was Don Benito's reserve, which displeased him; but the same reserve was shown towards all but his faithful personal attendant. . . . His manner upon such occasions was, in its degree, not unlike that which might be supposed to have been his imperial countryman's, Charles V., just previous to the anchoritish retirement of that monarch from the throne. (*BC*, 53)

Here, as the resonant antithesis informing Melville's use of the national metonyms to refer to Benito Cereno and Amasa Delano suggests, the benevolent and democratic American reads the Spaniard's apparent disdainful reserve as a civilizational characteristic, the haughty pride of an aristocratic Old World.

Similarly, Captain Delano interprets Babo's strangely intense care for his master's well-being according to the unerring imperatives of his accommodational exceptionalst problematic. This is exemplified at the time that Benito Cereno recounts the immediate past of the *San Dominick*, when Delano's anxious curiosity about the prior history of the ship has compelled him to ask the Don to "favor him with the whole story" (*BC*, 54). The latter, "like some somnambulist suddenly interfered with, vacantly stared at his visitor, and ended by looking down on the deck." "Equally disconcerted," Delano decides to ask one of the Spanish seamen instead. But when he is about to address him, Don Benito suddenly calls the American back, apologizes for his "absence of mind," and begins to recount the "true" story from its "beginning" with "no one being near but the servant." In the process of narrating the journey " 'from Buenos Ayres bound to Lima,' " Don Benito enumerates the ship's content—" 'several cabin passengers' " as well as the crew and " 'a general *cargo*, hardware, Paraguay tea and the like—and,' pointing forward, 'that parcel of negroes, now no more that a hundred and fifty, as you see, but then numbering over three hundred souls' " (*BC*, 55; my emphasis). As Benito Cereno is "recounting" the gales off Cape Horn that resulted allegedly in the wreck of the ship, the loss of its water supply, and the death of several of his officers and crew, he suddenly collapses, at which point the narrative's focus closes in on Babo's actions, or, rather, Delano's observations of them:

> His servant sustained him, and drawing a cordial from his pocket placed it to his lips. He a little revived. But unwilling to leave him unsupported while yet imperfectly restored, the black with one arm still encircled his master, at the same time keeping his eye fixed on his face, as if to watch for the first sign of complete restoration or relapse, as the event might prove.
> The Spaniard proceeded, but brokenly and obscurely, as one in a dream.
> —"*Oh, my God! rather than pass through what I have, with joy I would have hailed the most terrible gales; but—*"
> His cough returned and with increased violence; this subsiding, with reddened lips and closed eyes he fell heavily against his supporter.
> "His mind wanders. *He was thinking of the plague that followed the gales,*" plaintively sighed the servant; "my poor, poor master!" wringing one hand, and with the other wiping the mouth. "But be patient, Señor," again turning to Captain Delano, "these fits do not last long; master will soon be himself. (*BC*, 55–56; my emphasis)

Having recovered, Don Benito goes on to "recount" the events—the scurvy, the malignant fever, the excessive heat that swept away "whole families of the Africans, and a yet larger number, proportionately, of the Spaniards, including, by a luckless fatality, every remaining officer on board"—that had brought the *San Dominick* to its present plight. His story told, Don Benito brings the episode to its close by returning to Babo and the remaining blacks on the ship:

> "But throughout these calamities," huskily continued Don Benito, painfully turning in the half embrace of his servant, "I have to thank those negroes you see, who, though to your inexperienced eyes appearing unruly, have, indeed, conducted themselves with less of restlessness than ever their owner could have thought possible under such circumstances."
>
> Here he again fell faintly back. Again his mind wandered; but he rallied, and less obscurely proceeded.
>
> "Yes, their owner was quite right in assuring me that no fetters would be needed with his blacks; so that while, as is wont in this transportation, those negroes have always remained upon deck—not thrust below, as in the Guinea-men—they have, also, from the beginning, been freely permitted to range within given bound at their pleasure."
>
> Once more the faintness returned—his mind roved—but recovering, he resumed:
>
> "But it is Babo here to whom, under God, I owe not only my own preservation, but likewise to him, chiefly, the merit is due, of pacifying his more ignorant brethren, when at intervals tempted to murmurings."
>
> "Ah, master," sighed the black, bowing his face, "don't speak of me; Babo is nothing; what Babo has done was but duty." (*BC*, 56–57)

This extended scene of persuasion is replete with anomalous details that seem to contradict the "whole story" Captain Delano has been told, not least, the Don's words and Babo's response I have italicized (which seem to contradict his exceptionalist judgment of Spanish slaveholders) in the previously quoted passage. Nevertheless, the benevolent American responds to it by exclaiming: " 'Faithful fellow! . . . Don Benito, I envy you such a friend; slave I cannot call him;' " and, as he contemplates "master and man," can not help but admire "the beauty of this relationship which could present such a spectacle of fidelity on the one hand and confidence on the other" (*BC*, 57). This liberal democratic "trust" and "confidence," Melville's implies, is not so much Delano's trust and confidence in his fellow man as it is his trust and confidence in the black man's *natural* and childlike propensity to serve the white man or, at any rate, to accept his *natural* higher authority. This is underscored later, after Delano calls the

Don's attention to an attack on a white sailor by two blacks, which brings on a seizure in the latter, when he perceives once more the apparent care Babo takes in ministering to his master. Delano's response unmistakably discloses the racism of his American liberalism:

> His glance thus called away from the spectacle of disorder to the more pleasing one before him, Captain Delano could not avoid again congratulating his host upon possessing such a servant, who though perhaps a little too forward now and then, must upon the whole be invaluable to one in that invalid's situation.
>   'Tell me, Don Benito.' he added, with a smile—'I should like to have your man here myself—what will you take for him? Would fifty doubloons be an object?' (BC, 70)

In the final analysis, Delano's trust and confidence is a blind "American" trust and confidence (like that which Melville will deconstruct in *The Confidence-Man*)—the oversight of the *over*sight of the exceptionalist problematic—that is enabled by his providential view of history, in which everything and every time take their *proper* place in the larger identical and harmonious whole of which America has been chosen by God to be its *logos* or center.

Captain Delano, however, is too observant—too good a detective, as it were, and even, perhaps, too good a man—to entirely accept Benito Cereno's story and to remain fixed on this interpretation of the Don's and Babo's relationship. With every new observation of the hitherto unnoticed details that comprise the vessel, change in the physical appearance of the passengers, blacks or whites; or communicative gestures and words spoken by them that would undermine the authority of his interpretation, Delano revises it, accordingly, thus manifesting his American liberal "open-mindedness" (as opposed to the tyranny of European monologism). But what is remarkable about these revisions of "the good Captain" (Melville repeatedly refers to Delano's "honest" and "progressive" and "benevolent" sociopolitical being to insinuate the point) is that they are *accommodational*: the new and "surprising" observation, like, say, emigrants to the United States, are *assimilated* to the exceptionalist center of his problematic. To put it alternatively—and more bluntly—his exceptionalism renders his vision blind, not to the blacks as such, but to the blacks *as slaves*, to the grim reality that the *San Dominick* is a *slave ship*, and that these human beings, who have been uprooted from their homeland and reduced to "cargo," have suffered inordinately the pain inflicted on their bodies and the degradation of their spirits by the brutality of the white man's abstract racism and, therefore, that their desire for freedom from this pain and degradation is *real*. As Delano's unceasing accommodations testify, however, this reality—this (*non*)*being* of the black men and women on the *San Dominick*, not least, Babo, flickers in the far corner of his eye, as it were. To put this in terms to which I will return, it haunts the very problematic that would annul its being.

This destabilizing contrapuntal relationship between the anomalies Delano experiences on board the *San Dominick* and the rationalizing narratives prescribed by his American exceptionalism constitutes the uncanny force of Melville's transformation of the real Captain Delano's oversimplified and pedestrian account of his encounter with Benito Cereno into a complex symbolic anticanonical masterpiece, one, that is, which bears witness to the inordinate power of the American exceptionalist problematic to produce the truth—and, as we shall see, *its Achilles heel. In fact, Melville increasingly highlights the anomalies that, attended to, would disclose the contradictory reality that lies ever so close below the surface masquerade—the revolt that has reversed the "natural" master/slave relationship—precisely to reveal this nearly indestructible truth-producing power of the American exceptionalist problematic.* To analyze the brilliantly articulated seamlessness of this meticulously ironic contrapuntal structural movement is to risk reducing its aesthetic force, but this will be compensated for by the resonant meaning such an analysis will disclose.

Shortly after he has congratulated Don Benito for his confidence in the goodwill of his servant and his servant's fidelity to his master, Captain Delano, for example, makes a series of observations that seem increasingly to contradict the narrative of his first interpretation of the situation on board the *San Dominick*: the incongruity between the courtly "precision in the Don's attire" and "the unsightly disorder around him" (*BC*, 57); "one of those instances of insubordination previously alluded to," which ends in the knifing of a white boy by a black boy (*BC*, 59); the ambiguous behavior of the black oakum pickers and the hatchet-polishers; the feinting of Don Benito at Delano's subjunctive statement that "were your friend's remains now on board this ship [Alexandro Aranda's, the owner of the slaves, who, the Don has said, had been buried at sea] . . . not thus strangely would the mention of his name affect you" (*BC*, 61); the Don's disturbed silence in the face of Delano's invoking of the key hanging around his neck as the symbol of his absolute authority over the chained and padlocked colossal black man, Atufal, who, at the appointed hour of the day, ritually refuses to ask the Don for pardon; a young Spanish sailor seemingly attempting to catch Delano's eye; and, not least, the apparently rude whispered conversations between the master and the servant and the following questions the Don asks Delano about the American ship. Delano is disturbed by these anomalies; indeed, they compel him to reinterpret the enigmatic situation. But the revised interpretation does not think the enigma as such; it simply accommodates the new and dislocating observations to the binary logic of his American exceptionalist problematic:

> The singular alternations of courtesy and ill-breeding in the Spanish captain were unaccountable, except on one of two suppositions—innocent lunacy, or wicked imposture.
>
> But the first idea, though it might naturally have occurred to an indifferent observer, and, in some respect, had not hitherto been wholly a stranger to Captain Delano's mind, yet, now that . . . he began to regard the stranger's conduct something in the light of an intentional affront, of course the idea of lunacy was virtually vacated. But if not a lunatic, what then? Under the circumstances, would a gentleman, nay, an honest boor, act the part now acted by his host? The man was an imposter. Some low-born adventurer, masquerading as an oceanic grandee; yet so ignorant of the first requisites of mere gentlemanhood as to be betrayed into the present remarkable indecorum. . . . Benito Cereno—Don Benito Cereno—a sounding name. (*BC*, 64)

This retrospective interpretation of the details he has observed seems to counter Delano's "singular guilelessness" (*BC*, 67)—and his American optimism—but, as we learn in the process of his vacillation between the two, it constitutes, in fact, simply a reversal of the earlier one:

> Don Benito's story had been corroborated not only by the wailing ejaculations of the indiscriminate multitude . . . but likewise—what seemed impossible to be counterfeit—by the very expression and play of every human feature. . . . If Don Benito's story was throughout an invention, *then every soul on board, down to the youngest negroes, was his carefully drilled recruit in the plot: an incredible inference.* And yet, if there was ground for mistrusting his veracity, that inference was a legitimate one. (*BC*, 69; my emphasis)

In other words, this interpretation, which sees *all* the details that justified the earlier one as an insidious plot mounted by the Spaniard against the American, does not affect the essence of his exceptionalism. First, in the very process of arriving at this alternative interpretation, Delano reverts to the exceptionalist binary opposition which assumes the corruptness and depravity of the Old World. Second, and more important, in identifying the mechanism of deception (the intricate masquerade) that conceals the reality, he thus paradoxically brings it to the surface. But, like the first, this interpretation literally precludes Delano's *seeing* the situation on board the ship as the consequence of the slaves' revolt and what he sees as having been orchestrated by Babo into a radically different narrative. However "generous" Delano's attitude toward the blacks and Babo in particular, his American exceptionalist problematic makes it impossible for him to *see* what he sees: that the blacks would want to revolt and that Babo is capable of this kind of acute intelligence.

This American exceptionalist assumption of the genetic inferiority of the black race—and its blinding oversight—is underscored on two later significant occasions. The first occurs when Delano, noticing one of the Spanish sailors, marlingspike in hand, seemingly trying to communicate with him, reverts again to the question of the veracity of Benito Cereno's story. Inferring the possibility from his perception of this gesture that the sailor, out of "gratitude for a kind word [Delano's] on first boarding the ship," was attempting to "warn the stranger" that Benito's "recent plea of indisposition, in withdrawing below, was a pretense: that he was engaged there maturing some plot," the "good Captain," recalls his past observations and thinks:

> Was it from foreseeing some possible inference like this, that Don Benito had, beforehand, given such a bad character of his sailors, while praising the negroes . . . ? The whites, too, by nature were the shrewder race. A man with some evil design, would he not be likely to speak *well of that stupidity which was blind to his depravity*, and malign that intelligence from which it might not be hidden? Not unlikely, perhaps. But if the whites had dark secrets concerning Don Benito, could then Don Benito be any way in complicity with the blacks? *But they were too stupid.* Besides, who ever heard of a white so far a renegade as to apostatize from his very species almost, by leaguing in against it with negroes. (*BC*, 75; my emphasis)

The second, and even more repulsive, occurrence of this degrading racist patronization of blacks intrinsic to Delano's American exceptionalist problematic comes in the brilliantly executed episode recounting Babo's shaving of Benito Cereno. Here, Captain Delano, observing the servant's affability, generalizes about the "essential" character of blacks, particularly what he assumes to be the black man's "natural" penchant for serving the white man. As Babo hovers menacingly over the Don, the "good" Captain Delano thinks (in a way the genial nuances of which anticipate an all too familiar "liberal" contemporary discourse of tolerance):

> There is something in the negro which, in a peculiar way, fits him for avocations about one's person. Most negroes are natural valets and hairdressers; taking to the comb and brush congenially as to the castinets, and flourishing them apparently with almost equal satisfaction. There is, too, a smooth tact about them in this employment, with a marvelous, noiseless, gliding briskness, not ungraceful in its way, singularly pleasing to behold, *and still more*

so to be the manipulated subject of. And above all is the great gift of humor. Not the mere grin or laugh is here meant. Those were unsuitable. But a certain easy cheerfulness, harmonious in every glance and gesture; as though God had set the whole negro to some pleasant tune. . . .

When at ease with respect to exterior things, Captain Delano's nature was not only benign, but familiarly and humorously so. At home, he had often taken rare satisfaction in sitting in his door, watching some free man of color at his work or play. If on a voyage he chanced to have a black sailor, invariably he was on chatty, and half-gamesome terms with him. *In fact, like most men of a good, blithe heart, Captain Delano took to negroes, not philosophically, but genially, just as other men to Newfoundland dogs."* (*BC*, 83–84; my emphasis)[9]

Again, Delano's genial blindness to the real Babo is shown to be intrinsic to the racist stereotypes of the benign liberal vision of his exceptionalism. Here, however, the oversight of his oversight—and the tremendous power of the American exceptionalist problematic—is especially marked by the *nearness* of the threatening reality to the surface masquerade.

This invisibility *of* the visibility of Delano's American exceptionalist problematic achieves its most acutely insistent critical force in the devastating ironies that immediately follow this "benignly" tolerant thought. As Babo brandishes the sharpened razor with one hand and lathers his master's neck with the other, Captain Delano, observing "the two postured thus, could [not] resist the vagary, that in the black he saw a headsman, and in the white, a man at the block" (*BC*, 85). Then, after this "antic conceit . . . from which, perhaps, the best regulated mind is not always free," passes away, he notices that the bunting Babo had wrapped around the Don was, in fact, the Spain flag and genially "exclaims": " 'The castle and the lion . . . Why Don Benito, this is the flag of Spain you use here. It's well it's only I, and not the King, that sees this,' he added with a smile, 'but'—turning towards the black,—'it's all one, I suppose, so the colors be gay . . . ' " Delano reduces this observation, which to another would go far to reveal that the ship has been high-jacked—and the slave has become the master—to a vulgar joke that is compounded by the particular stereotype of the black man he is fond of, an irony that, as Melville's comment on Delano's joke makes resonantly clear, "did not fail to tickle the negro."

The irony of Delano's blindness to the diminishing interval between the reality and the masquerade achieves it most acute and sustained expression in his response to the blood Babo's razor "accidentally" draws from Benito's throat. This occurs at the precise moment when Benito starts at Delano's expression of his detective-like incredulity over the chronology he had given him earlier of the *San Dominick*'s voyage from Cape Horn to St. Maria. Holding "up the trickling razor," Babo, "remaining in his professional attitude, back to Captain Delano, and face to Don Benito," says "with a sort of half humorous sorrow, 'See, master,—you shook so—here's Babo's first blood.'" As always, Delano's exceptionalist vision focuses on the white man, leaving the black man at the margins of his sight, despite his enabling centrality:

> No sword drawn before James the First of England, no assassination in that timid King's presence, could have produced a more terrified aspect than was now presented by Don Benito.
> Poor fellow, thought Captain Delano, so nervous he can't even bear the sight of barber's blood; and this unstrung, sick man, is it credible that I should have imagined he means to spill all my blood, who can't endure the sight of one little drop of his own? Surely, Amasa Delano, you have been beside yourself this day. Tell it not when you get home, sappy Amasa. Well, Well. He looks like a murderer, doesn't he? More like as if himself were to be done for. Well, well, this day's experience shall be a good lesson. (*BC*, 86)

Delano reverts to doubt once again when the Don, in rehearsing the voyage from Cape Horn to St. Maria, insistently praises the blacks for "their general good conduct" throughout the difficult time. The American feels "something so hollow in the Spaniard's manner, with apparently some reciprocal hollowness in the servant's dusky comment of silence, that the idea flashed across him, that possibly master and man, for some unknown purpose, were acting out, both in word and deed, nay, to the very tremor of Don Benito's limbs, some juggling play before him. Neither did the suspicion of collusion lack apparent support, from the fact of those whispered conferences before mentioned. But then, what could be the object of enacting this play of the barber before him?" (*BC*, 87) This "revelatory" sequence—the emergence in Delano's consciousness of the possibility that he is caught in the web of the "plot" of a play—culminates when Babo returns from the cabin to which he had brought the Don, holding his hand over a bleeding cheek and wailing, "Ah, when will master get better from his sickness; only the sour heart that sour sickness breeds made him serve Babo so; cutting Babo with the razor, because, only by accident, Babo had given master one little scratch; and for the first time in so many a day, too." To this, Delano, reverting to his American exceptionalist disdain of the decadent tyranny of the Old World, thinks: "Is it possible . . . ; was it to wreak in private his Spanish spite against this poor friend of his, that Don Benito, by his sullen manner, impelled me to withdraw? Ah, this slavery breeds ugly passions in man.—Poor fellow!" (*BC*, 88) Here, in a situation activated by the black man, Delano, for the first time, is driven by the alleged violence the Don perpetrates against Babo, to *see* that the "cargo" on board the *San Dominick* are *slaves* and, therefore, that the issue is *slavery*. But in keeping with his liberal version of American exceptionalism, he is compelled, as his "sympathy" for Babo suggests, to attribute its evil effects primarily to the white man, if not the sadistic Spanish slave owner. Here, in other words, at the very moment when the mysterious events on the *San Dominick* expose the barbarism of Western slavery, it is the white perspective that the good Captain Delano overdetermines at the expense of the black. It seems as if it is impossible, despite the tremors he feels under his feet, for him to be dislodged from his panoptic center. Though the American feels pity for the marginal black man—"Poor fellow!"—everything he thinks, says, and does, suggests that he is incapable of even entertaining the possibility that slavery "breeds ugly passions" in black men as well.

This blindness to the blacks' "passions" continues to prevail, indeed, to become more acute, right up to the moment in the evening of that enigmatic day, when Captain Delano boards the whaler that will bring him back to his ship. Immediately after, Benito Cereno jumps into the boat, an act Delano interprets at first as a gesture intended "to produce the impression among his people that the boat wanted to kidnap him" and then as the prelude to murder by " 'this plotting pirate.' " Then, "in apparent verification of the words," Delano sees the servant, a dagger in hand, "poised, in the act of leaping, as if with desperate fidelity to befriend his master to the last." It is only after he has subdued Babo a second time—as he "was snakily writhing up from the boat's bottom to stab his master" (*BC*, 99)—that Captain Delano comes to *see* that all the events of the day were just the masquerade, mounted by the blacks, he had seen, but not seen, they were. I quote at length to underscore the metaphorics of vision of this (anti)detective-like "retrospective" that relocates all the hitherto misplaced details into their *proper* place in the narrative (plot)—and to prepare for Melville's later deconstruction of this "deconstructive" moment:

> That moment, across the long-benighted mind of Captain Delano, a flash of revelation swept, illuminating in unanticipated clearness his host's whole mysterious demeanor, with every enigmatic event of the day, as well as the entire voyage of the San Dominick. He smote Babo's hand down, but his own heart smote him harder. With infinite pity he withdrew his hold from Don Benito. Not Captain Delano, but Don Benito, the black, in leaping into the boat, had intended to stab.
>
> Both the black's hands were held, as, glancing up toward the San Dominick, Captain Delano, now with the scales dropped from his eyes, saw the negroes, not in misrule but in tumult, not

as if frantically concerned for Don Benito, but with mask torn away, flourishing hatchets and knives, in ferocious piratical revolt. Like delirious black dervishes, the six Ashantees danced on the poop. Prevented by their foes from springing into the water, the Spanish boys were hurrying up to the topmost spars, while such of the few Spanish sailors, not already in the sea, less alert, were descried, helplessly mixed in, on deck, with the blacks.

Meantime Captain Delano hailed his own vessel, ordering the ports up, and the guns run out. But by this time the cable of the San Dominick had been cut; and the fag-end, in lashing out, whipped away the canvas shroud about the beak, suddenly revealing, as the bleached hull swung round toward the open ocean, death for the figure-head, in a human skeleton; chalky comment on the chalked words below, "*Follow your leader.*" (*BC*, 99)

The story recounted by the narrator comes to its "end" with the capture of the *San Dominick* following a ferocious sea battle and, after the two ships and the surviving negroes arrive in Lima, the investigation that disposes of the case. During his brief account of the battle, however, the narrator suggestively refers to the blacks as "fugitives" (*BC*, 101)[10] and describes their hopeless but intense will to escape on the analogy of the doomed Indians futilely fighting the white men and their bullets with ineffectual hatchets. However faintly, this gesture disturbs the finality of the American's victory. And his disturbance is exacerbated by his informing the reader that "midway on the passage, the ill-fated Spaniard, relaxed from constraint, showed some signs of regaining health with free-will; yet, agreeably to his own foreboding, shortly before arriving at Lima, he relapsed, finally becoming so reduced as to be carried ashore in arms. Hearing of his story and plight, one of the many religious institutions of the City of Kings opened an hospitable refuge to him, where both physician and priest were his nurses, and a member of the order volunteered to be his one special guardian and consoler, by night and day" (*BC*, 103).

II

What follows this "termination" of the story is an addendum—the translation of extracts of Benito Cereno's deposition at the trial—that, the narrator writes, "will it is hoped, shed light on the preceding narrative, as well as, in the first place, reveal the true port of departure and the true history of the San Dominick's voyage, down to the time of her touching at the island of St. Maria" (*BC*, 103). Like the "retrospective" of the classical detective story, this addendum—this official Spanish document that "the tribunal, in its final decision, rested its capital sentences"—repeats in minute detail the more general retrospective afforded to the hitherto "benighted" Captain Delano at the epiphanic moment of Babo's attack on Don Benito. Every hitherto anomalous and anxiety-provoking detail in space and event in time, like the pieces of a puzzle, seem to take their *proper* place in the larger conspiratorial design. Nothing seems to remain superfluous. From this *distanced* perspective of "the end," the "American," Captain Delano—and the (American) reader he represents—is reenabled to *see* the *whole* story all at once—retro-spectively—whereas earlier, prior to the epiphany, he, in his immediacy, saw only partially. From this objectifying panoptic perspective, too, his—and the reader's—anxiety in the face of the inexplicable because unquantifiable—the nothing, the aporia, the *differend*—is annulled.

But this "final" recuperation of certainty, this renewed confidence in the benignity of being, enabled by the vision of the American exceptionalist problematic, is, as I have been suggesting by (re)reading the story from the deconstructed perspective precipitated by what I take to be Melville's ironic multiple endings, simply another irony that, in fact, always already defers the conclusive end, that is, discloses the radical absence that haunts the "presence"—the universal truth of American exceptionalism—that enables conclusive endings. But before examining this deconstructive movement in "Benito Cereno," I want, for the sake of clarity, to return briefly to the "second" phase of Althusser's analysis of the liberal capitalist problematic: that which attends to the *invisible* that belongs to the visible. For having thus far overdetermined the latter, we are compelled to ask, "What about the being of the invisible—the "nonexisting objects" and "nonexisting problems"—*of* this problematic? Such an analysis of the invisible *of* the visible will provide a directive for thinking more fully than heretofore the blindness of Captain Delano's exceptionalist vision and Melville's, at least symptomatic, positive purpose in exposing it to view.

Althusser does not offer an adequate answer to the above urgent question, but this "second phase" of his analysis of the problematic prepares the ground for that provocatively unfulfilled possibility. This is especially the case if it is understood in relation to Heidegger's foregrounding of the Nothing that modern science will have nothing to do with (because to this "enlightened" mind "what else can it be . . . but an outrage and a phantasm?"),[11] and to Derrida's rethinking of *différance* in *Specters of Marx* in terms of the *revenant*, the specter that returns to visit the "visitor" (from the Latin *videre*: to see),[12] the epithet Melville uses over and over again to characterize the Delano who boards Don Benito's ship:

> The same connexion that defines the visible also defines the invisible as its shadowy obverse. It is the field of the problematic that defines and structures the invisible as the defined excluded, *excluded* from the field of visibility and *defined* as excluded by the existence and peculiar structure of the field of the problematic;

as what forbids and represses the reflection of the field on its object.... These new objects and problems ... are invisible because they are rejected in principle, repressed from the field of the visible; and that is why their fleeting presence in the field when it does occur (in very peculiar and symptomatic circumstances) *goes unperceived*, and becomes literally an undivulgeable absence—since the whole function of the field is not to see them, to forbid any sighting of them. Here again, the invisible is no more a function of *a subject's sighting* than is the visible: the invisible is the theoretical problematic's non-vision of its non-objects, the invisible is the darkness, the blinded eye of the theoretical problematic's self-reflection when it scans its non-objects, its non-problems without seeing them, *in order not to look at them.* (CMP, 25–26)

Returning to "Benito Cereno," we might say that the Don's deposition retrospectively reveals what Captain Delano's—and the reader's—exceptionalist problematic has made it impossible for him to see, that, in other words, in confirming his epiphany in the story proper, the poststory deposition precipitates its deconstruction, since he comes at last to see everything to which his exceptionalist interpretations of the enigmatic situation on board the *San Dominick* had blinded him. As the narrator puts it—in a language that both recalls the key to Atufal's chains hanging on a cord around the Don's neck and the archetypal metaphor informing the detective story—"If the Deposition have served as the key to fit into the lock of the complication which preceded it, then, as a vault whose door has been flung back, the San Dominick's hull lies open to-day" (*BC*, 114). But this, as the conditional hints, is not the case. For in enabling Delano to see what hitherto he was unable to see, the epiphany and the official deposition that authorizes its "truth" reconfirm the power of the exceptionalist problematic to determine the truth, while at the same time disclosing to the reader "something" different. This difference has to do, not with the explanatory objective facts disclosed by the Don's deposition—that, for example, the good servant, so solicitous of his master, has, in fact, reversed the relationship—but with their moral significance. In the process of his deposition, Benito Cereno not only recounts the facts of the story in its entirety, filling in what hitherto were gaps in Delano's (and the reader's) awareness. In giving his more complete account of the events, he also, whether deliberately or symptomatically—and in keeping with the dissonance of the end of the story I referred to above (the Don's relapse and seclusion in a monastery after the trial)—intensifies certain marginal motifs of the story perceived by Delano that, once *seen*, would undermine the judgment of the tribunal. Put alternatively—in a way that, in fact, Melville's rhetoric demands—in the process of re-telling his story, the Don symptomatically discloses that which *haunts* not only the finality of its "truth," but also the authority of the Spanish tribunal that, "in its final decision, rested its capital sentences upon" his deposition. I am referring particularly to two indissolubly related aspects of this deposition: that which touches on the motives of the black mutineers and that which refers to the intelligence of their leader. The first is epitomized by the following:

> the deponent resolved at the break of day to come up the companion-way, where the negro Babo was, being the ringleader, and Atufal, who assisted him, and ... exhorted them to cease committing such atrocities, asking them, at the same time, what they wanted and intended to do ... ; that, notwithstanding this, they threw, in his presence, three men, alive and tied, overboard; that they told the deponent to come up, and that they would not kill him; which having done, the negro Babo asked him whether there were in those seas any negro countries where they might be carried, and he answered them, No; that the negro Babo afterwards told him to carry them to Senegal, or to the neighboring islands of St. Nicolas; and he answered, that this was impossible, on account of the great distance, the necessity involved of rounding Cape Horn, the bad condition of the vessel, the want of provisions, sails, and water; but that the negro Babo replied to him he must carry them in any way; that they would do and conform themselves to everything the deponent should require as to eating and drinking; that after long conference, being absolutely compelled to please them, for they threatened him to kill all the whites if they were not, at all events, carried to Senegal, he told them that what was most wanting for the voyage was water.... (*BC*, 105)

Read straightforwardly as the tribunal—and Captain Delano—has done, this part of the Don's deposition would seem to confirm the white men's representation of the blacks as having committed a crime against humanity and the black race as unredeemably cruel savages. Read symptomatically, however, attending, in Althusser's terms, to the "fleeting presence" of "these new objects and problems" in the "field of the visible," precipitated by the "very peculiar and symptomatic circumstances" articulated by Melville's text, a "change of terrain,"[13] an estrangement of the familiar—spatialized—surface, occurs that enables the reader now to *see* at least more clearly what the tribunal *and* Captain Delano see, but cannot *see*: that the mutiny of the blacks and the violence they have committed on board the Spanish ship is motivated not by predatory instinct or revenge, but by the passionate desire to be free at all costs of the physical and mental shackles of slavery and to return to the homeland from which they were ruthlessly uprooted to be conveyed as chattel to a distant world.[14]

The second of these marginal motifs of the Don's deposition that achieves "fleeting presence" in the "field of the visible," that which refers to the intelligence of the black's leader, is suggested in the following passage:

> they at last arrived at the island of Santa Maria . . . at about six o'clock in the afternoon, at which hour they cast anchor very near the American ship, Bachelor's Delight, which lay in the same bay, commanded by the generous Captain Amasa Delano; but at six o'clock in the morning, they had already descried the port, and the negroes became uneasy, as soon as at distance they saw the ship, not having expected to see one there; that the negro Babo pacified them, assuring them that no fear need be had; that straightway he ordered the figure on the bow [the skeleton of Alexandro Aranta] to be covered with canvas, as for repairs, and had the decks a little set in order; that for a time the negro Babo and the negro Atufal conferred; that the negro Atufal was for sailing away, but the negro Babo would not, and, by himself, cast about what to do; that at last he came to the deponent, proposing to him to say and do all that the deponent declares to have said and done to the American captain; ****** that the negro Babo warned him that if he varied in the least, or uttered any word, or gave any look that should give the least intimation of the past events or present state, he would instantly kill him, with all his companions, showing a dagger, which he carried hid, saying something which, as he understood it, meant that the dagger would be alert as his eye; that the negro Babo then announced the plan to all his companions, which pleased them; that he then, the better to disguise the truth, devised many expedients, in some of them uniting deceit and defense; that of this sort was the device of the six Ashantees before named, who were his bravoes. . . . (*BC*, 108–109)

Like the previous passage from the Don's deposition, this one too could be read negatively, either as evidence of the blacks' undeviating instinctive malice, as in the case of the tribunal, or, as in the case of Captain Delano prior to his epiphany, as an impossibility. Read against the grain, however, we see in Babo's meticulous organization of deception a quite different possibility. Contrary to the tribunal's interpretation and Captain Delano's undeviating and fundamental assumption that the blacks, however childlike and docile he believed them to be, "were too stupid" as a race (*BC*, 75) to be capable of devising and sustaining the kind of intricate plot he had hypothesized at one point during his visit to the *San Dominick*, we see here, in Don Benito's deposition, the determined and acute intelligence that is capable precisely of what Delano assumed he, as a black, was incapable.

These "sightings" of the "nonobjects" of the "field of vision," which are activated by the "peculiar and symptomatic circumstances" of the deposition, however, are, in Althusser's apt terms, "fleeting presences" that "go unperceived." We might say, in other words, that they haunt the "conclusive" narrative of Don Benito's deposition, but do not affect the judgment of the tribunal nor that of Captain Delano. The full revelation, the awful force of what it discloses to sight, and the imperviousness to these of "the American" comes in the second addendum, another retrospective, though this time in dialogic form: the narrator's recollection of one of the conversations about the recent events on board the *San Dominick* between Don Benito and Captain Delano during the long voyage to Lima prior to the tribunal and before the former's death. In this conversation, which begins with the Don's effort to articulate to the visiting American captain the difficulty of playing the role assigned to him by Babo and the anguish he felt in not being able to communicate the truth of the situation to his suspicious "benefactor." Above all, he apprizes the American of the double bind into which his knowledge of that truth locked him: " 'Do but think how you walked this deck, how you sat in this cabin, every inch of ground mined into honey-combs under you. Had I dropped the least hint, made the least advance toward an understanding between us, death, explosive death—yours and mine—would have ended the scene.' " In response, Delano expresses his gratitude to the Don for saving his life. And when the Don, "courteous even to the point of religion," attributes his benefactor's "safe conduct through all the ambuscades" to "The Prince of Heaven," the American replies:

> Yes, all is owing to Providence, I know; but the temper of my mind that morning was more than commonly pleasant, while the sight of so much suffering . . . , added to my good nature, compassion, and charity happily interweaving the three. Had it been otherwise, doubtless, as you hint, some of my interferences might have ended unhappily enough. Besides that, those feelings, I spoke of enabled me to get the better of momentary distrust, at times when acuteness might have cost me my life, without saving another's; Only at the end did my suspicions get the better of me, and you know how wide of the mark they then proved. (*BC*, 115)

In this remarkable response, Captain Delano gathers together to highlight, privilege, and *rationalize* all the characteristics—ontological, psychological, historical, and moral—that emanate from and constitute his American exceptionalist identity: a metaphysical (or Providential) interpretation of being and an analogous self-present subjectivity that assumes the American's chosenness, that is, centrality, and benevolence; a futural understanding of global history that assumes a benign America to be its real beginning; and thus a moral comportment towards historical experience characterized by optimism and confidence or, to put it negatively, that demonizes a distrust that is activated by acute perception. Indeed, Delano's characteristically American optimistic resistance to distrust in this passage—we might now call it Panglossian—is so determinative that he celebrates his lack of "acuteness"—the blindness of his oversight—as the very agency of his and Don Benito's delivery.

In what follows, the Spaniard (I refer to the Don in this way to underscore his status as a member of the "Old World) attempts, ever so politely, to introduce a darker view of the world than that of his sanguine American benefactor. Recalling the latter's failure of perception as the erring of even the best of men in a world of "malign machinations and deceptions," he adds, "But you were forced to it; and you were in time undeceived. Would that, in both respects, it was so ever, and with all men." But Delano, true to his American optimism, informs him that "the past is passed" and advises him to "Forget it," just as "yon bright sun has forgotten it all, and the blue sea, and the blue sky; these have turned over new leaves." This "dialogue," which is in fact, a monologue—this is one of Melville's most resonant disclosures about American democracy—comes to its devastatingly ironic culmination in a moment the revelatory power of which is only equaled by the climactic moment of Joseph Conrad's *The Heart of Darkness*," when Kurtz exclaims: "the Horror":

> "Because they [the sea and the sky] have no memory," he dejectedly replied; "because they are not human."
>
> "But these mild trades that now fan your cheek, do they not come with a human-like healing to you? Warm friends, steadfast friends are the trades."
>
> "With their steadfastness they but waft me to my tomb, señor," was the foreboding response.
>
> "You are saved," cried Captain Delano, more and more astonished and pained; "you are saved; what has cast such a shadow upon you?
>
> "The negro." (BC, 116)

In the aftermath of Benito Cereno's enunciation of this word, the narrator pointedly tells the reader, "There was silence, while the moody man sat, slowly and unconsciously gathering his mantle about him, as if it were a pall." (*BC*, 116)

What Benito Cereno "sees" as he speaks this simple stunning word is too complicated for any easy discursive answer. But we can get at its existential force indirectly by suggesting that it and the resonant silence surrounding its utterance bring to sudden and intensely ominous—spectral—visibility everything that Captain Delano's discourse (and the "authoritative" document of the tribunal), during that day on the *San Dominick* left necessarily unsaid, everything that, as I have been insisting, was invisible to his vision—the "vision" of his American exceptionalist problematic. I am not simply referring to the takeover of the Spanish ship by the "negroes," the reversal of the master/slave relationship, and the masquerade they enacted, but also—and above all—the entire obscene and shameful history and practices of *slavery*—the forcible uprooting of black people from the African earth they inhabited, the appalling middle passage, the banal reduction of human life to chattel, the degradation of the slave trade, the forced labor, the whippings, the cruel separation of families, the abuse of black women by white masters, and so on—*and*, through this "civilized" white violence, the instigation of a passionate hatred of white men and their "civilization" and a fierce will to revolt in the name of freedom: the e-mergence, in short, of the blackness, or rather, the *specter* of blackness, that will haunt the whites' future.[15]

But this is only one aspect of Melville's intention in introducing this terminal conversation between the representatives of the Old World and the New World as a second addendum to the narrative proper. Equally, if not more important, is that which has to do with Captain Delano's "response" to Don Benito's illuminating dark vision of humanity that culminates in the surface-shattering and dread-provoking annunciation of the name "negro." Before Don Benito speaks the name that identifies it with the "shadow" cast upon him, Delano's speech and behavior is informed by his (American) optimism and his Emersonian disdain for history (memory) in favor of the novel present: "But the past is passed; ... Forget it."—which expresses itself as a bewildered impatience with the Don's bizarre indifference to his having been "saved." After Benito's annunciation, Delano is given nothing to say: "There was," the narrator tell us, "no more conversation that day" (*BC*, 116). The appalling irony Melville is closing in on here is that, despite the Spaniard's revelation of the white man's "Other," which deconstructs every previous narrative effort to accommodate and annul the force of this terrible contradiction, the American remains impervious to it. To return to Althusser's apt language, despite the Spaniard's decisive epiphany and annunciation, which enabled the American to *see* "the true history of the San Dominick's voyage," the latter's vision is incapable of *seeing* what he has been given to see. *It is not, as I have said earlier, his lack of intelligence that has blinded him even to this stark revelation; it is his optimistic exceptionalist problematic.*[16]

It is in part, I submit, the blinding optimism inhering in the naturalized myth of American exceptionalism that Melville underscores and deconstructs in his reconfiguration of the Captain Amasa Delano he encountered in the latter's *Narrative of Voyages and Travels* (1817). In this parodic critique of a totalizing metaphysical vision, which, in its Panglossian confidence in the benignity of being, or, to put it differently, in its distrust of distrust, is blind to its radical contradictions—what theological moralists call evil—we see an affiliative relationship that will be fully developed in *The Confidence-Man*: one between the New World Melville and the Old World Voltaire of *Candide or Optimism*, who, representing the Lisbon earthquake for what it actually was, deconstructed the naturalized myth that insisted, despite this epochal calamity, that the world of the eighteenth-century remained "the best of all possible worlds," or, in Alexander Pope's version, that claimed "whatever is, is right."

But this criticism of the American exceptionalist problematic, as I have been suggesting, is only a part of what Melville intends in overdetermining the blindness of Delanos's (over)sight. The other, indissolubly related to the "change of terrain" the first precipitates, has to do with the invisible *of* the visible: that which, no matter how visible it becomes, the American is blind to, or, to put it otherwise, that which he cannot *see*, precisely because, from this exceptionalist perspective, *"it" has no being*. This phantom is the black man who, in the history of the modern West, not least of white America, as Ralph Ellison's great Melvillian novel, *The Invisible Man*, underscores, has always been "seen" as an indissolubly related sociopolitical continuation of the non-being—the nothing—that the onto-logic of Western modernity "will have nothing to do with." I mean by this last the "white" metaphysical logic that, in the wake of the fulfillment of the potential of Enlightenment modernity, has, paradoxically, precipitated into visibility the continuum of non-beings it and the sociopolitical institutions it has produced are necessarily blind to, now, however, as a relay of *specters* or *revenants*, that have returned to haunt the Being and its institutions that had reduced and relegated them to the oblivion of non-being.

Following the astonishing termination of the conversation between Benito Cereno and Captain Delano, the narrator, attuned to the reverberating "pall"-like silence into which the Spaniard's last words seems to have plunged the practical world of speakers, he brings his "narrative" to its paradoxical deconstructive, that is, opening, close. I quote this extraordinarily powerful—and proleptic—passage at length not only to highlight the system of visual/auditory metaphors through which Melville articulates his story about the blind "vision" of American exceptionalism, but also his recognition of the "innocent New World's" *filiative* relationship with the "corrupt Old World"—and thus its eventual fall:

> But if the Spaniard's melancholy sometimes ended in muteness upon topics like the above, there were others upon which he never spoke at all; on which, indeed, all his old reserves were piled. Pass over the worst, and, only to elucidate, let an item or two of these

be cited. The dress so precise and costly, worn by him on the day whose events have been narrated, had not willingly been put on. And that silver-mounted sword, apparent symbol of despotic command, was not, indeed, a sword, but the ghost of one. The scabbard, artificially stiffened, was empty.

As for the black—whose brain, not body, had schemed and led the revolt, with the plot—his slight frame, inadequate to that which it held, had at once yielded to the superior muscular strength of his captor [Delano], in the boat. Seeing all was over, he uttered no sound, and could not be forced to. His aspect seemed to say, since I cannot [yet] do deeds, I will not speak words. Put in irons in the hold, with the rest, he was carried to Lima. During the passage Don Benito did not visit him. Not then, nor at any time after, would he look at him. Before the tribunal he refused. When pressed by the judges he fainted. On the testimony of the sailors alone rested the legal identity of Babo.

Some months after, dragged to the gibbet at the tail of a mule, the black met his voiceless end. The body was burned to ashes; *but for many days, the head, that hive of subtlety, fixed on a pole in the Plaza, met, unabashed, the gaze of the whites*; and across the Plaza *looked towards* St. Bartholomew's church, in whose vaults slept then, as now, the recovered bones of Aranda; and across the Rimac bridge *looked towards* the monastery, on Mount Agonia without; where, three months after being dismissed by the court, Benito Cereno, borne on the bier, did, indeed, follow his leader. (*BC*, 116–117; my emphasis)

There is at this stage no need to explicate this resonant passage; it speaks powerfully for itself. It will suffice simply to underscore the reversals that the very logic of exceptionalism precipitates in the "end." From the beginning to this "end" of the narrative it is the white American, Captain Delano, whose "look" and "speech" determines the (non)being of the black man (renders him invisible). Here, in the aftermath of the quelled revolt, it is the black man, Babo, or rather, his specter whose silent gaze symbolically prophecies the fate of the white man—and his institution of slavery. As in the case of Bartleby in his relationship to the Wall Street lawyer, as we shall see, the visited has become the visitor; the visitor, the visited. The latter, of course, refers, not to the American, but to the Spaniards, Alexandro Aranda, the owner and master of the slaves, and the irreversibly dislocated Benito Cereno, the representatives of the decadent "Old World," as the pointed reference to the fact that his "silver-mounted sword, apparent symbol of despotic command," was not a real sword makes clear. As the "(anti)logic" of the story inexorably reveals, however, not least its revelation of the blindness of Captain Delano's vision in the face of the stark incarnate truth, this culminating moment of reversal is intended by Melville to underscore the paradoxical similarities between the hierarchical structures of the New ("democratic") World and the Old (feudal) World and to prophecy the fate of an unexceptional exceptionalist America that cannot *see* its own shadow. This, in the end, is what the narrator means when, in recounting the death and burial of Benito Cereno under the silent gaze of Babo's spectral head, he repeats the words chalked by the insurgent blacks below Don Alexandro's skeleton, which becomes the *San Dominck*'s figure-head: "Follow your leader." (*BC*, 99, 117).

III

Melville's "Benito Cereno," like so much of his fiction written in the wake of *Moby-Dick*, is proleptic of America's future in a way that few of the canonical texts of the American literary tradition are. In recreating the character of Captain Amasa Delano as a symbolic figuration of the American national identity, Melville was subverting both the myth of its origins— the Puritans' belief in their election and divinely ordained "errand into the wilderness" of the New World—and its matured secular manifestation—the myth of American exceptionalism that, despite the national traumas precipitated by the Civil War and the Vietnam War, has by and large determined America's national identity and its global role from the beginning. In this, Melville's (anti)narrative not only undermines the authority of this idealized exceptionalist figure as it came down to him in the form of the pioneer or backwoodsman epitomized in American literature by Cooper's Leatherstocking figure. It also anticipates and undermines the authority of its self-conscious, sometimes self-parodic, modern allotropes.

The importance of this assertion is borne witness to by the fact that this innocent, benign, and self-reliant Leatherstocking *figure* pervades the cultural discourse, both popular and elite, of nineteenth-century and modern America. He is ubiquitous in the "dime westerns" of the postbellum period and in the Hollywood westerns of the 1930s through the 1960s and in World War II and Vietnam War films, and, though far more sophisticated and problematic, he appears again and again in modern American literature from Mark Twain's *A Connecticut Yankee in King Arthur's Court* (1889), Owen Wister's *The Virginian* (1902), F. Scott Fitzgerald's *The Great Gatsby* (1925), through William Faulkner's *Absalom, Absalom* (1936) and Ernest Hemingway's *For Whom the Bell Tolls* (1940) to William J. Lederer and Eugene Burdick's *The Ugly American* (1958) and Philip Caputo's *A Rumor of War* (1977).[17] But, I suggest, this American exceptionalist identity is epitomized by the legendary figure, Colonel Edward W. Lansdale, who, as a self-styled modern frontiersman, went, under the auspices of the American government, in the mid-twentieth century, first to the

Philippines and then to Vietnam "to help our Asian friends . . . cope with wars of rebellion and insurgency."[18] As he says in his preface, Lansdale undertook this confident errand in the Asian wilderness—he refers to it as "an American's mission" in the subtitle of his memoir—in the name of the benign American exceptionalist ethos. Characteristically, he combined Jefferson's "secular" oath, " 'I have sworn upon the alter of God eternal hostility against every form of tyranny over the mind of man' " (*IMW*, x), and Paul of Tarsus's religious assertion in *Corinthians*, " 'Where the spirit of the Lord is, there is liberty' " (*IMW*, 104), to wage war not simply against the evil of Communism, but also, as in the case of his mission in Vietnam, the corruptness of French (Old World) colonialism.

The ability of this ideal, that is, mythological, figure of the American exceptionalist imagination to survive the corrosive pressures of historical change—what I have been calling its accommodating power—is, as I have suggested, founded on its deep inscription in the American consciousness. To recall Althusser, its survival reveals the naturalization of the American exceptionalist ideology into a "problematic," in which "it is literally no longer the eye (the mind's eye) of a subject which *sees* what exists in the field defined by [the] problematic: it is this field itself which *sees itself* in the object or problems it defines." This is why Americans, even many of the most thoughtful and critical, have remained historically complicitous with the depredations incumbent on the "benevolent" practices of this American exceptionalist figure. This is also why the perception of the invisible of his exceptionalist vision has been historically largely restricted to the outsider—his victim, a Frederick Douglass, a W. E. B. DuBois, a Martin Luther King, a Malcolm X, or a Toni Morrison, for example—or to the global intellectual exile or nomad—a Frantz Fanon, a C. L. R. James, an Edward Said, a Gayatri Spivak, or, closer to my present purpose, a Graham Greene. For a white American to *see* what the problematic of the American exceptionalist precludes seeing, he or she must, like Herman Melville willfully become a stranger in his or her "homeland"—a-part—as it were.

This concatenation that foregrounds the change of terrain precipitated by refusing to be answerable to the call of America is what enables the reconstellation of the outcast American, Herman Melville, and his novella "Benito Cereno," into an exemplary proleptic relationship with a modern nomadic writer like Greene and his *The Quiet American* (1955).[19] This last is a powerful but, in America, much maligned novel that not only anticipated the United States' initially confident, exceptionalist "errand in the wilderness" of Vietnam and the devastating blindness of its "benevolent" anti-communist and anti-imperial mission to save Vietnam "for the free world," but also, and not incidentally, continues to haunt the (resurgent) American exceptionalist problematic in the aftermath of 9/11/01.[20]

Not accidentally, Edward Lansdale, the historical figure I have invoked as the epitome of the modern cultural manifestations of the American exceptionalist identity that Melville is subverting, was the model for Graham Greene's "quiet American," Alden Pyle. Like Melville's Captain Delano, Greene's Pyle (and his historical prototype) is deeply and inexorably inscribed by the American exceptionalist problematic. A Boston Brahmin, like Captain Delano, with roots in New England Puritanism, he has come to the wilderness of Vietnam ostensibly as a member of an economic mission, but in reality on a mission to clandestinely establish a "Third Force"—a national "democratic" regime ventriloquized by its American "benefactors"—as an alternative to both Soviet and/or Chinese communism and Old World colonialism. In contrast to the narrator, Fowler, a self-exiled British reporter who represents the Old World's complex and dark view of history, Pyle epitomizes the American: innocent, benevolent, self-reliant, optimistic, and confident of the superiority of American democracy over the decadent French colonial regime and, of course, over communism; indeed, he seems to assume that history itself has precipitated American democracy as its perfected and true end.

Like Melville's "Benito Cereno," Greene's *The Quiet American* is fundamentally about seeing from this teleological perspective or, rather, about the oversight—the blindness—of the oversight enabled by it. More specifically, like Delano's, Pyle's vision is determined by the American exceptionalist problematic or, to invoke another less formidable version of this central poststructuralist insight into representation, what Edward Said has called the "textual attitude" (to reality) in his disclosure of the violence informing the discourse of Orientalism:

> It may appear strange to speak about . . . someone as holding a *textual attitude*, but a student of literature will understand the phrase . . . if he will recall the kind of view attacked by Voltaire in *Candide*, or even the attitude to reality satirized by Cervantes in *Don Quixote*. What seems unexceptionably good sense to these writers is that it is a fallacy to assume the . . . problematic mess in which human beings live can be understood on the basis of what books—texts—say; to apply what one learns out of a book literally is to risk folly or ruin.[21]

What both Delano and Pyle see in their respective historical circumstances is what their problematic or textual attitude makes visible. Everything else remains invisible, "non-objects," or "non-problems." The difference is that Pyle's is an American exceptionalism that has accommodated the historical conditions of the Cold War, particularly the "domino theory" to itself. For Delano the determining symbol of his problematic is the highly rarified, but deeply inscribed figure of the self-reliant white Protestant backwoodsman, who is defined against his decadent Old World "Other"; for Pyle, it is this rarified pioneer figure accommodated to the Cold War scenario[22] that informs what he reads as the scriptural texts of the "Orientalist" expert York Harding (*The Advance of Red China, The Challenge to Democracy, The Role of the West*). The following passage from *The Quiet American* epitomizes Greene's satirical representation of Pyle's Cold War allotrope of the American exceptionalist problematic. It is a conversation that takes place in a watchtower guarded by two frightened Vietnamese conscripts, where they have been stranded on the way back to Saigon after Fowler has discovered that Pyle has made contact with the Vietnamese general who will command the "Third Force":

> I said to Pyle, "Do you think they know they are fighting for Democracy? We ought to have York Harding here to explain it to them."
>
> "You always laugh at York," Pyle said.
>
> "I laugh at anyone who spends so much time writing about what doesn't exist—mental concepts." . . .
>
> "No French officer," I said, "would care to spend the night alone with two scared guards in one of these towers. . . . I don't blame them. They don't believe in anything either. You and your like are trying to make a war with the help of people who just aren't interested."
>
> "They don't want Communism."
>
> "They want enough rice," I said. "They don't want to be shot at. They want one day to be much the same as another. They don't want our white skins around telling them what they want."
>
> "If Indo-China goes . . ."
>
> "I know the record. Siam goes. Malaya goes. Indonesia goes. What does "go" mean? If I believed in your God and another life, I'd bet my future harp against your golden crown that in five hundred years there may be no New York or London, but they'll be growing paddy in these fields, they'll be carrying their produce to market on long poles. . . . The small boys will be sitting on the buffaloes. I like the buffaloes, they don't like our smell, the smell of Europeans. And remember—from a buffalo's point of view you are a European too."
>
> "They'll be forced to believe what they are told, they won't be allowed to think for themselves."
>
> "Thought's a luxury. Do you think the peasant sits and thinks of God and Democracy when he gets inside his mud hut at night?"
>
> "You talk as if the whole country were peasant. What about the educated? Are they going to be happy?"

"Oh no," I said, "we've brought them up in *our* ideas. We've taught them dangerous games, and that's why we are waiting here, hoping we don't get our throats cut. We deserve to have them cut. I wish your friend York was here too. I wonder how he'd relish it."

"York Harding's a very courageous man. Why, in Korea . . ."

"He wasn't an enlisted man, was he? He had a return ticket. With a return ticket courage becomes an intellectual exercise, like a monk's flagellation. How much can I stick? Those poor devils can't catch a plane home. Hi," I called to them, "what are your names?" I thought that knowledge somehow would bring them into the circle of our conversation. They didn't answer . . . "They think we are French," I said.

"That's just it," Pyle said. You shouldn't be against York, you should be against the French. Their colonialism."

"Isms and ocracies. Give me facts." . . . (*QA*, 94–95)

Despite the limits of his own discourse—he too speaks for the Vietnamese in some degree—the narrator, as an Old World outsider like the Spaniard, Benito Cereno, sees clearly the differential existential realities of this particular place and time in the history of Vietnam to which Pyle's American Cold War version of the distancing and immunizing exceptionalist problematic or textual attitude blinds him. Like Don Benito, who has come to see the "cargo" of black men and women as brutalized *slaves in revolt*, Fowler sees the Vietnamese as *victims* of imperial scenarios that refer to them as collateral damage.

The full force of Greene's disclosure of the invisible—the terrible unforeseen consequences—of the quiet American's "benign" and unshakably confident exceptionalist vision manifests itself following his Third Force's explosion of bombs, intended to be attributed to the communists, in the heart of Saigon that have killed and maimed many innocent Vietnamese. Having inferred that Pyle had warned Phuong and some European and American women who frequented the square at that time of the day to stay away, Fowler compels Pyle to *look* at the consequence of his "benevolent innocence." I quote at some length to demonstrate the remarkable relationship between Melville's and Greene's texts:

> A woman sat on the ground with what was left of her baby in her lap; with a kind of modesty she had covered it with her straw peasant hat. She was still and silent, and what struck me most in the square was the silence. It was like a church I had once visited during Mass—the only sound came from those who served, except where here and there the Europeans wept and implored and fell silent again as though shamed by the modesty, patience and pro-

priety of the East. The legless torso, at the edge of the garden still twitched, like a chicken which had lost its head. From the man's shirt, he had probably been a trishaw driver.

Pyle said, "It's awful." He looked at the wet on his shoes and said in a sick voice, "What's that?"

"Blood," I said, "Haven't you ever seen it before?"

He said, "I must get them cleaned before I see the Minister." I don't think he knew what he was saying. He was seeing a real war for the first time: he had punted down into Phai Diem in a kind of schoolboy dream, and anyway in his eyes soldiers didn't count.

I forced him, with my hand on his shoulder, to look around. I said, "This is the hour when the place is always full of women and children—it's the shopping hour. Why choose that of all hours?"

He said weakly, "There was to have been a parade."

"And you hoped to catch a few colonels. But the parade was cancelled yesterday, Pyle."

"I didn't know."

"Didn't know!" I pushed him into a patch of blood where a stretcher had lain. "You ought to be better informed."

"I was out of town," he said, looking down at his shoes. "They should have called it off."

"And miss the fun?" I asked him. "Do you expect General Thé to lose his demonstration? This is better than a parade. Women and children are news, and soldiers aren't, in a war. This will hit the world's Press. You've put General Thé on the map all right, Pyle. You've got the Third Force and National Democracy all over your right shoe. Go home to Phuong and tell her about your heroic dead—there are a few dozen less of her people to worry about."

A small fat priest scampered by, carrying something on a dish under a napkin. Pyle had been silent a long while, and I had nothing more to say. Indeed, I had said too much already. He looked white and beaten and ready to faint, and I thought, "What's the good? He'll always be innocent, you can't blame the innocent, they are always guiltless. All you can do is control them or eliminate them. Innocence is a kind of insanity."

He said, "Thé wouldn't have done this. I'm sure he wouldn't. Somebody deceived him. The Communists . . ." (*QA*, 161–163)

Pyle's reaction to the blood on his shoe, which for Fowler is a synecdoche for the carnage wrought in Vietnam by a "benevolent" America, is uncannily similar to Captain Delano's reaction to Don Benito's utterance of the resonantly revelatory word "negro," which, as we have seen, is a synecdoche of the very real ravages of slavery—and the specter of revolt. Like the American in Melville's novella, this quiet American is incapable of *seeing* what he sees because the Vietnamese people are "nonobjects" of his exceptionalist problematic. As in the case of Captain Delano, this invisibility of what is existentially *there* before his eyes is not the consequence of Pyle's lack of intelligence, but of his exceptionalist problematic: "the sighting," we recall, "is . . . no longer the act of an individual subject, endowed with the faculty of vision which he exercises either attentively or distractedly. . . . It is no longer the eye . . . of a subject which s*ees* what exists in the field defined by a theoretical problematic; it is this field itself which *sees itself* in the objects or problems it defines."

Pyle's utter blindness to what he sees, remarkably like Delano's, is the measure of the inordinate power of the American exceptionalist problematic not simply to determine the truth of the way things are, but to render its agents immune to the terrible realities it perpetrates. The "dialogue" in the bombed out square ends with the following observation by a despairing Fowler: "He was impregnably armoured by his good intentions and his ignorance" (*QA*, 163). It is a metaphorical locution that uncannily reminds us not only of Ishmael's ironic identification of Father Mapple's pulpit as "his ["impregnable"] little Quebec," but also, as we shall see more fully in the next chapter, looks forward to Melville's repeated ironic identification of American optimism with siege-fortresses—"Malakoff[s] of confidence."[23]

IV

The excessive violence of the United State's "benevolent" effort to save Vietnam from the evil clutches of both communism and Old World colonialism, coupled with the protestation of the Vietnam War and the civil rights movement in the 1960s undermined in some degree, though temporarily, the perennial authority of the exceptionalist problematic. But during the long aftermath of the humiliating defeat of America in Vietnam, the dominant culture—the political elite, the corporate world, the media, the film industry, a resurgent Protestant evangelical Christianity—mounted a massive cultural and political campaign to "forget" Vietnam or, as it was put in its late phase, to "kick the Vietnam syndrome," which is to say, to recuperate the "healthy" and confidence-inspiring exceptionalist national identity that had been momentarily infected by the virus of doubt in that turbulent decade. This ideological momentum to recover confidence in America culminated in the years between 1990 and 2001. This was the decade that bore witness to the end of the Cold War (the "triumph of liberal capitalist democracy" over communism), the "surgically executed" defeat of Iraq in the first Gulf War, and, above all, the announcement by a neoconservative administration in the wake of the attacks on the World Trade Center and the Pentagon on 9/11/01 of a global "war on terror" (which has authorized the "preemptive" invasions of Afghanistan and then Iraq), and the policy of "regime change": the imposition of capitalist democracies, which means governments ventriloquized by the United States, on those states it considers threats to American interests.

The evidence of this recuperation of the exceptionalist problematic and the rejuvenated missionary zeal it has perennially fostered can be seen and felt in virtually all the contemporary institutions of knowledge production, including higher education.[24] But I will restrict my reference to a representative passage from one post-9/11 neoconservative text which, more than most that are founded on the belief that America is justified in pursuing its errand in the modern world's wilderness, articulates this belief in the traditional terms of its genealogical origins, precisely the Puritan origins that Melville calls into question. I am referring to Samuel P. Huntington's aptly titled *Who Are We?: The Challenges to America's National Identity*,[25] which followed his extraordinarily reductive yet highly influential diagnosis of the contemporary world as the "clash of civilizations."[26] In this book Huntington counters what he takes to be the threat to the unity and global power of the United States posed by the cultural and sociopolitical disintegration of the "Anglo-Protestant core culture" and the proliferation of "subnational cultures" (*WAW*, 141–177, 171–177) in the 1960s under the aegis of what he calls "deconstructionism" (*WAW*, 141–171). He reaffirms this "core culture" and calls for a fifth Protestant "Great Awakening" (*WAW*, 75–80) in behalf of America's war against "militant Islam." Its model would be the Puritan covenant and the providential history on which it was founded:

> Religious intensity was undoubtedly greatest among the Puritans, especially in Massachusetts. They took the lead in defining their settlement based on "a Covenant with God" to create "a city on a hill" as a model for all the world, and people of other Protestant faiths soon also came to see themselves and America in a similar way. In the seventeenth and eighteenth centuries, Americans defined their mission in the new World in biblical terms. They were a "chosen people," on an "errand in the wilderness," creating "the new Israel" or the "new Jerusalem" in what was clearly "the promised land." America was the site of a "new heaven and a new earth, the home of justice," God's country. The settlement of America was vested, as Sacvan Bercovitch put it, "with all the emotional, spiritual, and intellectual appeal of a religious quest." This sense of holy mission was easily expanded into millenarian

themes of America as "the redeemer nation" and "the visionary republic. (*WAW*, 64)[27]

In the blindness of its confident and benevolent global American vision, Huntington's *Who Are We?* brings us back to the spectral witness of Melville's "Benito Cereno," not simply to its proleptic affiliation with demythologizing modern novels like Graham Greene's *The Quiet American* and the decentering theory of poststructuralists like Althusser, Michel Foucault, and Edward Said, but also to the remarkable relevance to the present historical occasion of its exposure of the "invisible" *of*—that *belongs to*—the "visionary" vision of the American exceptionalist problematic

To be American, Melville realized in the wake of the diatribes of those like George Washington Peck, who would "freeze him into silence," he had to become un-American—and, unlike Captain Amasa Delano, to refuse the American *calling*. What "Benito Cereno" tells us by way of its antebellum "protagonist's" blind confidence in America is that more than any other writer in the history of American literature, Melville is our contemporary.

"Bartleby, the Scrivener: A Wall-Street Story": Melville's Politics of Refusal

> The caller is Dasein in its uncanniness [*Unheimlichkeit*]: primordial, thrown Being-in-the-world as the "not-at-home"—the bare "that-it-is" in the "nothing" of the world. The caller is unfamiliar to the everyday they-self [*Das Man*]; it is something like an *alien* voice. What could be more alien to the "they," lost in the manifold "world," than the Self which has been individualized down to itself in uncanniness and been thrown into the "nothing"?
>
> —Martin Heidegger, *Being and Time*

> [E]ven in his catatonic or anorexic state, Bartleby is not the patient but the doctor of a sick America, the *Medicine-Man*, the new Christ or the brother to us all.
>
> —Gilles Deleuze, "Bartleby; or The Formula"

> His refusal is so absolute that Bartleby appears completely blank, a man without qualities or, as Renaissance philosophers would say, homo tantum, mere man. . . .
>
> —Antonio Negro and Michael Hardt, *Empire*

In showing that Captain Amasa Delano is not simply blinded by his American exceptionalist problematic but also complicit with the violence (to its Other) which is intrinsic to its field of vision, I referred to him in

Althusser's language as an "interpellated subject." I want to suggest in the second part of this chapter that Bartleby is Captain Delano's antithesis—in a way, his alter ego, if Babo's invisibility is seen as the specter that haunts his American identity—that, in other words, the two stories belong together in their difference. It will, then, be necessary to briefly explain this much abused Althusserian concept and to justify my appropriation of this French neo-Marxist to write about the American fiction of Herman Melville.

"Ideology interpellates [from the Latin *interpellare*: "to interrupt by speaking") individuals as subjects" (*IIST*, 170). This, in terms of my previous use of Althusser, means that ideology, like the problematic, whether the totalizing system of Christianity or capitalism or democracy or American exceptionalism "hails" or "calls" the individual, and insofar as the individual *responds* or *answers* this calling, he or she becomes a *subject*—an ostensibly "free subjectivity, a center of initiatives, author of and responsible for its actions" (*IIST*, 182)—but also—and invisibly—a "subjected being, who submits to a higher authority and is therefore stripped of all freedom except that of freely accepting his submission" (*IISA*, 182): a *subjected subject* who takes his or her *proper* place in the centered and plenary whole. This process of "ideological recognition" is always reciprocal: "the category of the subject is constitutive of all ideology, but at the same time and immediately I add that *the category of the subject is only constitutive of all ideology insofar as all ideology has the function (which defines it) of 'constituting' concrete individuals as subjects*" (*IISA*, 171). In other words, though the relationship appears to be obviously free—"outside ideology" (*IISA*, 175)—this obviousness—this assumption that what the interpellated subject sees is the way things really are—is "an ideological effect" (*IISA*, 172). With his or her interpellation, the subject, in fact, becomes (unknowingly) *dependent* on the ideology (or problematic) and at the same time the ideology (or problematic) becomes *dependent* on the subject. "What really takes place in ideology seems ... to take place outside it. That is why those who are in ideology believe themselves by definition outside ideology: one of the effects of ideology is the practical *denegation* of the ideological character of ideology: ideology never says 'I am ideological.' ... Which amounts to saying that ideology "*has no outside* (for itself)," but at the same time "it is nothing but outside (for science and reality)" (*IISA*, 175). Like the vision of the problematic, ideology is a totality that accommodates everything/everytime to its center; but this totality contains its own blindness.

What is remarkable about Althusser's analysis of interpellation—and pertinent to both "Benito Cereno" and "Bartleby the Scrivener"—is that the example he proffers to illustrate its operations is the convenient one of the Judeo-Christian tradition, more specifically, the relation between "the Unique, Absolute, and *Other Subject*," i.e., God, and the human subject, Moses, "with the proviso that the same demonstration can be produced for ethical, legal, political, aesthetic ideology, etc." (*IISA*, 177).

"All this," Althusser writes, "is clearly written in what is rightly called the Scriptures. 'And it came to pass at that time that God the Lord (Yahweh) spoke to Moses in the cloud. And the Lord cried to Moses, "Moses!" And Moses replied "It is (really) I! I am Moses thy servant, speak and I shall listen!" And the *Lord spoke to Moses and said to him*, I am that I am.' " God *calls* Moses. Moses *recognizes* and *answers* the *call* (and his *calling*), and, in so doing, he (and the people he represents) becomes a subjected subject:

> God thus defines himself as the Subject *par excellence*.... and he who interpellates his subject, the individual subjected to him by his very interpellation, i.e. the individual named Moses. And Moses, interpellated-called by his Name, having recognized that he is a subject, a subject *of* God, a subject subjected to God, *a subject through the Subject and subjected to the Subject*. The proof: he obeys him, and makes his people obey God's commandments.
>
> God is thus the Subject, and Moses and the innumerable subjects of God's people, the Subject's interlocutors-interpellates: his *mirrors, his reflections*.... As all theological reflection proves, whereas He "could" perfectly well have done without men, God needs them, the Subject needs the subjects, just as men need God, the subjects need the Subject. Better: God needs men, the great Subject needs subjects, even in the terrible inversion of his image in them (when the subjects wallow in debauchery, i.e. sin) (*IISA*, 179; Althusser's emphasis).

Put theoretically, the operation of ideology, like the problematic, comes to be seen as a spatial figure and as *"speculary,* i.e. a mirror-structure, and *doubly speculary,*" which is to say "that ideology is *centered*, that the Absolute Subject occupies the unique place of the Centre, and interpellates around it the infinity of individuals into subjects in a double mirror-connexion such that it *subjects* the subjects to the Subject, while giving them in the Subject in which each subject can contemplate its own image (present and future) the *guarantee* that this really concerns them and Him"—that, in other words, "everything really is so, and that on condition that the subjects recognize what they are and behave accordingly, everything will be all right: Amen—'So be it.' " (*IISA*, 181). To put this in Michel Foucault's somewhat analogous and more familiar secular terms, what Althusser calls the "Subject" of "ideology" is the panoptic gaze, the eye of the dominant culture ("I am that I am") that looks down pyramidally from its privileged height on the errant multitude simultaneously individualizing (calling them by name) and, once answered, disciplining these subjects to take their proper place in its plenary whole by internalizing its "Word."

It is precisely Althusser's invocation of the example of the Judeo-Christian religion as a clear model of the polyvalent workings of interpellation that I find remarkably pertinent to my reading of Captain Delano—and, as we shall see, of Bartleby.[28] As I have suggested in passing, Delano is not only a merchant (i.e., bourgeois) seaman, but also a Bostonian, a geographical/cultural synecdoche that in Melville's time was, as Perry Miller has made clear, automatically identifiable, if not with Puritanism as such, then with the Puritan tradition.[29] Such being the case, it is not an imposition to assume that Delano's American exceptionalist problematic has its origins in, or is informed by, the Puritan doctrine of election or what Max Weber, in tracing the genealogy of "the spirit of capitalism" to the "Puritan work ethic," refers to as the "calling" (German, *Beruf*). As in Althusser's account of interpellation, this Puritan calling is a hailing of the individual by an inscrutable but ever-present God who not only separates him or her from the multitude, individualizes, renders him or her a subject; it is also a calling in the sense of a particular vocation, the fundamental "responsibility" or "duty" or "obligation" of which, as, Benjamin Franklin advocates in *Poor Richard's Alma*nac and his *Autobiography*, is the sharing with one's fellow men, each according to his or her own calling, the methodical or disciplined labor of rationalizing the world, not for gain, but in behalf of the glory of God (*in majorem gloriam Dei*). This, not incidentally, is the disciplinary division of labor, in which everyone takes his or her proper place in the larger totality:

> It seems at first a mystery how the undoubted superiority of Calvinism in social organization can be connected with this tendency to tear the individual away from the close ties with which he is bound to this world. But . . . it follows from the peculiar form which the Christian brotherly love was forced to take under the pressure of the inner isolation of the individual [caused by his or her uncertainty] through the Calvinist faith. In the first place it follows dogmatically. . . . The elected Christian is in the world only to increase this glory of God by fulfilling His commandments to the best of his ability. But God requires social achievement of the Christian because He wills that social life shall be organized with that purpose. The social activity of the Christian in the world is solely activity *in majorem gloriam Dei*. This character is hence shared by labour in a calling which serves the mundane life in the community. . . . Brotherly love, since it may only be practiced for the glory of God . . . is expressed in the first place in the fulfillment of the daily tasks given by the *lex naturae*; and in the process this fulfillment assumes a peculiar objective and impersonal character, that of service in the interest of the rational organization of our social environment.[30]

This is not to imply that Captain Delano is a Puritan in the strict sense of the word; it is say, rather, that he has been interpellated—rendered a subjected subject—by the secularized Word of Puritanism, that is, a Puritan notion of election that had become the more general idea of American exceptionalism in the post-Revolutionary era. As a subject subjected by the call of American exceptionalism, he is not only blind to the invisible ("the negro!") *of* his vision, as we have seen; he is also blind to the subjectedness of his subjectivity. Like the interpellated individual of the capitalist world to which Althusser refers, Captain Delano is imprisoned in the "mirror-structure" of the American exceptionalist problematic. If in the following passage we substitute "American exceptionalism" for "relations of production," it sums up in a more or less precise way the consequence of Delano's interpellation:

> The individual *is interpellated as a (free) subject in order that he shall submit freely to the commandments of the Subject, i.e. in order that he shall (freely) accept his subjection,* i.e. in order that he shall make the gestures and actions of his subjection "all by himself." *There are no subjects except by and for their subjection.* That is why they "work all by themselves."
>
> "So be it! . . ." This phrase which registers the effect to be obtained proves that it is not "naturally" so . . . This phrase proves that it *has* to be so if things are to be what they must be, and let us let the words slip: if the reproduction of the relations of production is to be assured, even in the processes of production and circulation, every day, in the "consciousness," i.e. in the attitudes of the individual-subjects occupying the posts which the socio-technical division of labour assigns to them in production, exploitation, repression, ideologization, scientific practice, etc. Indeed, what is really in question in this mechanism of the mirror recognition of the Subject and of the individuals interpellated as subjects, and of the guarantee given by the Subject to the subjects if they freely accept their subjection to the Subject's "commandments"? The reality in question in this mechanism, the reality which is necessarily *ignored* (*méconnue*) [i.e. remains invisible] in the very forms of recognition (ideology = misrecognition/ignorance) is indeed, in the last resort, the reproduction of the relations of production and of the relations deriving from them. (*IISA*, 182–183)

In answering the call of the Subject, or rather, in being answerable to the Subject's call, Delano becomes caught in a "plenary" and violently repressive discourse he takes to be the truth (hegemonic), in Antonio Gramsci's terms, gives "spontaneous consent" to. He cannot *see* that it is a fabricated discourse that serves the power of a "higher authority." Bartleby, on the other hand, refuses to answer the call or rather to be answerable to the call. This, as we shall see more fully, is why "Benito Cereno" and "Bartleby, the Scrivener" belong together, why Bartleby is Delano's alter-ego or *Other self*.

IV

To come to some understanding of the enigmatic Bartleby—and of Melville's intention—one must go by a complexly indirect itinerary, since *his* "story" is being *told by* a deeply interested or, better, engaged, Wall Street lawyer/narrator (the "ideal" post-Puritan capitalist American) who, despite his intensely sincere and undoubtedly benevolent efforts, has not been able, even in the end, he tells us at the beginning, to make any satisfying sense of him, that is, to reduce his life to a narrative, a biography, that would relieve him of a certain unappeasable anxiety. Bartleby, in Deleuze and Guattari's terms, "wards off" the "apparatuses of capture": "While of other law-copyists I might write the complete life, of Bartleby nothing of that sort can be done. I believe that *no materials* exist for a full and satisfactory biography of this man. . . . Bartleby was one of those beings of whom nothing is ascertainable, *except from the original sources, and in his case those are very small*."[31] Our circuitous itinerary, in other words, must proceed not simply by attending to the narrator's "narrative" and to the stages of its development, but also, and above all, to his very understanding of narrative. This is because the classical idea of biography he implies in the beginning is contradicted by the dislocating inconclusiveness of the "story" he tells. I mean specifically the spectral aura of an unappeasable resistance emanating from the scrivener's dead body—in the fetal position—the narrator "inters" in his response to the grub-man's question—"He's asleep, ain't he?"—with the predictable sentimental quotation—a *deus ex machina*, as it were—from the Book of Job: "With kings and counselors" (*BS*, 43).

The Wall Street lawyer symptomatically draws attention to the crucial importance of his understanding of narrative when, at the outset, he distinguishes Bartleby from all the other scriveners he has employed. He would have no problem writing the latters' biographies ostensibly because he has come to *know* them and thus is certain that the "records" would verify his knowledge. With Bartleby, on the other hand, the lawyer has not come to *know* him, has not been able to penetrate the surface of his bizarre behavior to discover the elusive essence of his being, and the original *sources* are too few to enable him to infer it. Despite the lawyer's genial and tolerant rhetoric (to which I will return), we are at the outset compelled by this distinction to infer that the lawyer, however sincere in his concerns, is not entirely reliable: he *assumes* authorship to be informed by authority and the author's story, therefore, to be conclusive: a temporal representation in which all the parts have their *proper* place in the larger whole. That Melville intends to evoke a certain degree of distrust in the narrator's authority and his understanding of narrative is underscored by the implication that the lawyer's certainty about his ability to write conclusive biographies of all the other scriveners he has encountered derives from the latter's calling: not simply the mindlessly mechanical copying of legal texts, but also the utterly predictable and alienating—useful and docile—identity of the copiers who have been disciplined and rendered "accountable" by this vocation. To use Althusser's language, we might say provisionally that the author understands himself as *S*ubject and the scriveners, whose biographies he could write with little trouble, as interpellated *s*ubjects. It is this tranquillity—this peace, the consequence of an ostensibly "benevolent" democratic capitalist spirit that enables things to *get done* efficiently—biographies—that Bartleby shatters on entering the microcosm of the narrator's law offices.

But before considering this phantom-like intrusion, it will be necessary, following the directive of the structure adopted by the narrator, to establish the metaphysical, cultural, social, and political context that the "advent of Bartleby"[32] (*BS*, 13) disrupts. For, as in the case of Captain Delano, it is obviously Melville's intention to generalize the narrator's identity, to render him a symbolic representative of the dominant culture in antebellum America. This—and the weakness of his authority—is conveyed in his inaugural account of "myself, my *employes*, my business, my chambers, and my general surrounding," which, he says, in an irony of which he is unaware, "is indispensable to an adequate understanding of the chief character about to be *presented*" (my emphasis):

> Imprimis: I am a man who, from his youth upwards, has been filled with a profound conviction that the easiest way of life is the best. Hence, though I belong to a profession proverbially energetic and nervous, even to turbulence, at times, yet nothing of that sort have I ever suffered to invade my peace.... All who know me, consider me an eminently *safe* man. The late John Jacob Astor, a personage little given to poetic enthusiasm, had no hesitation in pronouncing my grand point to be prudence; my next, method. I do not speak it in vanity, but simply record the fact, that I was not unemployed in my profession by the late John Jacob Astor; a name which, I admit, I love to repeat, for it hath a rounded and orbicular sound to it, and rings like unto bullion. I will freely add, that I was not insensible to the late John Jacob Astor's good opinion. (*BS*, 14)

What the narrator emphasizes in both the content and rhetoric of this account of himself is not simply his averageness, but also a certain pride in his conscientious prudence and methodical mental and practical habits that render him prosperous yet "safe," that is, predictable, unmovable, and thus secure—invulnerable to disturbance behind his fortress of confidence[33] and even noteworthy, not simply because he has been noticed by the elite (John Jacob Astor), but also because he sees his optimistic self as a model for those preterites who work for him under his gaze. In short, this self-portrait and his description of his Wall Street "premises"—its gray austerity and its view of the stark and abstract surroundings that were "deficient in what landscape painters call 'life' " (*BS*, 14)—identify him with the emergence—phoenix-like—to defining prominence (election, as it were) of the solid American middle-class out of the ashes of the Puritan work ethic. More precisely, they suggest the lawyer's filial relationship to the Benjamin Franklin of *Israel Potter* (without his sense of humor) or, rather, to the Franklinian American produced by the optimistic sayings of Poor Richard.

But this characterization is only partial. His other defining trait manifests itself inaugurally in his account of his employees, Turkey, Nippers, and Ginger Nut. The first, a man of his own age, works industriously and efficiently in the morning, but in the afternoon grows increasingly "energetic"—"there was a strange, inflamed, flurried, flighty recklessness of activity about him" (*BS*, 15)—and vituperous and belligerent (a condition occasioned by drink), the consequence of which is not simply excessive blotting (inefficiency), but also the rendering of the office a subject of "reproach to me" (*BS*, 17). The second, a "rather piratical-looking young man," works badly in the morning, the consequence of "two evil powers—ambition and indigestion," but productively in the afternoon. The third, a "lad of twelve," has been sent by his father, "ambitious of seeing his son on the bench instead of a cart," to the lawyer's office as "student of law, errand boy, and cleaner and sweeper, at the rate of one dollar a week" (*BS*, 18). The lawyer takes pains before introducing Bartleby to describe these employees, especially the two scriveners, as eccentrics who, each in his own errant way, threaten the stability and efficiency of production and the monetary and social rewards of accomplishment or, to invoke the language that will come to pervade the lawyer's discourse after the advent of Bartleby, getting things done. But he emphasizes their eccentricity, not so much to describe them, as to convey his benevolent *tolerance*. The lawyer is not a tyrant. He knows that tyranny is counterproductive: its overt use of power alienates the person(s) on whom it is applied, indeed, precipitates insurrection. He is, rather, a "good" man, a true American, who *accommodates* the eccentricities of his employees to his stable center, and by so doing renders them productive: "It was fortunate for me," he says of them, "that, owing to its peculiar cause—indigestion—the irritability and consequent nervousness of Nippers, were mainly observable in the morning, while in the afternoon he was comparatively mild. So that Turkey's paroxysms only coming on about twelve o'clock, I never had to do with their eccentricities at one time. Their fits relieved each other like guards. When Nippers' was on, Turkey's was off; and *vice versa*. This was a good natural arrangement under the circumstances" (*BS*, 18). As one who is accommodational in his relations to his employees, in short, the lawyer, like the benevolent Captain Delano, is an exponent of liberal democracy.

But what the lawyer's benevolent democratic ethos conceals is a kind of power that is more invisible (and thus less subject to resistant), though no less repressive, than the power of tyranny: the internalization and normalization of the hierarchical American middle-class value system he represents. (Turkey, for example, prefaces all his responses to his employer's complaints with the phrase "With your permission, sir" [*BS*, 16; 19, 22].) This is what Foucault, echoing Althusser, has called discipline or biopower—the production of "useful and docile bodies" by harnessing knowledge to power—in distinguishing between the ancien régime and the "regime of truth" that emerged in the United States and France in the wake of the American and French Revolutions and achieved hegemony at precisely the time Melville was writing. I will quote this familiar passage from Foucault's *Discipliine and Punish* at some length and, at the risk of digressing, comment on the historical context his genealogy is retrieving to suggest again Melville's uncanny contemporaniety:

> The historical moment of the disciplines was the moment when an art of the human body was born, which was directed not only at the growth of its skills, nor at the intensification of its subjection, but at the formation of a relation that in the mechanism itself makes it more obedient as it becomes more useful, and conversely. What was then being formed was a policy of coercions that act upon the body, a calculated manipulation of its elements, its gestures, its behaviour. The human body was entering a machinery of power that explores it, breaks it down and rearranges it. A "political anatomy," which was also a "mechanics of power," was being born; it defined how one may have a hold over others' bodies, not only so that they may do what one wishes, but so that they may operate as one wishes, with the techniques, the speed and the efficiency that one determines. Thus discipline produces subjects and practiced bodies, "docile" bodies. Discipline increases the forces of the body (in economic terms of utility) and diminishes these same forces (in political terms of obedience). In short, it dissociates power from the body; on the one hand, it turns it into an "aptitude," a "capacity," which it seeks to increases; on the other hand, it reverses the course of the energy, the power that might result form it, and turns it into a relation of strict subjection. If economic, exploitation separates the force and the

product of labour, let us say that disciplinary coercion establishes in the body the constricting link between an increased aptitude and an increased domination.[34]

Foucault's genealogy of the emergent post-Enlightenment "panoptic" institutions—the insane asylum, the medical clinic, the educational classroom, the factory, the penitentiary that, in transforming all manner of de-viants into "useful and docile bodies," gave birth to the modern disciplinary society—draws primarily on European sources, though he does briefly refer to the Walnut Street Prison established by the Quakers in Philadelphia (1790) in the wake of the American Revolution. In drawing the analogy between Jeremy Bentham's ideal prison, The Panopticon, and the emergent factory system, for example, it is the Rousseauean architect and city planner Claude Nicolas Ledoux's "ideal" (circular) factory town Chaux (of which only the salt works of Arc-et-Senans was completed [1775]) to whom he refers. In thus focusing on the European origins of this disciplinary architecture, Foucault overlooked one of the most important—and self-evident—social experiments in disciplinary power (the putting into practice of the knowledge/power nexus in the context of democratic society) in the crucial historical occasion that bore witness to the emergence of America as a republican capitalist industrial society. I am referring to the Lowell, Massachusetts (cotton) factory project inaugurated at the end of the eighteenth century by a group of Bostonian "reformers" under the aegis of Francis Cabot Lowell, a conscious inheritor of the New England Puritan work ethic (what I have been referring to as the American calling), precisely to minimize the possibility of producing an insurrectionary laboring class of the kind that threatened the British factory system represented by the "satanic mills" of Manchester and Birmingham, England. To accomplish this, Lowell and his colleagues designed their factories, very much like Bentham designed his Panopticon (1787–1791), as a mass-producing "total institution," "so that the company might exercise exclusive control over the environment," not simply to enable the constant supervision of the compartmentalized space of the cotton mills but also of the dormitories in which the laborers—they were, unlike in the English mills, a rotating work force of young girls who, it was argued, would be taught the values of "republican morality"—worked. As John Kasson observes:

> Factory work then would not become a lifetime vocation or mark of caste, passed on from parent to child in the omnipresent shadow of the mills. Rather it might form an honorable stage in a young woman's maturation. . . . Her factory experience would be a moral as well as an economic boon, numerous spokesmen for American manufactures maintained, rescuing her from the idleness, and vice, pauperism, possibly even confinement in an almshouse or

penitentiary. Instead, in the cotton mill under the watchful eyes of supervisors, she would receive a republican education, imbibing "habits of order, regularity and industry, which lay a broad foundation of public and private future usefulness." During her term at Lowell the worker would be protected *in loco parentis* by strict corporate scrutiny and compulsory religious services. Such stringent standards of moral scrutiny and company control would serve a treble purpose: to attract young women and overcome the reluctance of their parents, most of them farmers; to provide optimal factory discipline and management control of the operatives; and to maintain an intelligent, honorable, and exemplary republican work force.[35]

My invocation of the Lowell factory project as a (missing) dimension of Foucault's genealogy of the "democratic" disciplinary society to elucidate Bartleby's refusal of the "American calling" is not an arbitrary imposition on Melville's story. This becomes tellingly apparent when it is seen in the light of his diptych "The Paradise of Bachelors and the Tartarus of Maids," published in *Harper's New Monthly* in April 1855, the same year as "Benito Cereno" (in which, not incidentally, Captain Delano's ship is called *Bachelor's Delight*") and less than two years after "Bartleby." In this story, it will be recalled, Melville, through his American narrator, contrasts the luxuriant, easy lives of a male elite in London with the infernal lives of the women working in a newly automated paper factory in the American northeast and in the process subtly but powerfully demonstrates the complicity of the distanced bachelors in the reduction of the immediate women to "blank" dehumanized cogs in the infernal assembly-line machinery. In this allegory about the advent of a technological capitalism in the United States that relied on the Puritan calling, Melville is clearly alluding to the Lowell project and, in so doing, provides further evidence of his uncanny anticipation of Foucault's genealogical critique of the uses to which the triumphant Protestant/bourgeois/capitalist "reformers" of the postrevolutionary period put knowledge in behalf of power.[36]

To return to "Bartleby," in thus reading the Wall Street lawyer's prefatorial biographical remarks, "ere introducing [Bartleby] as he first appeared to me" (*BS*, 13), in the light of the rise of the disciplinary society, I am suggesting provisionally that his perception of being in all its manifestations epitomizes the American exceptionalist problematic as it had come to manifest itself in the antebellum period in the form of the Franklinian "spirit of capitalism." Like Captain Delano, he, too, has been interpellated by the exceptionalist problematic, reduced to a subjected subject by the hailing of a higher (transcendental) Subject, but whereas Melville overdetermines the *effect* of the interpellation of the individual in "Benito Cereno" (the oversight of Captain Delano's calling), in "Bartleby, the Scrivener," he overdetermines the interpellative agent (the operations of the narrator/lawyer's call). In the remarkably appropriate language from Althusser I have adopted to represent the relationship between Bartleby and his employer, the lawyer, insofar as he claims the authority of narrator and is representative of the antebellum American national identity, is the hailing "*Subject*," Cotton Mather's Puritan Moses or, even more particularly, his Nehemiah, John Winthrop.[37]

IV

The lawyer adds Bartleby to his "corps of copyists" after he has been appointed Master of Chancery when his "original business . . . was considerably increased" (*BS*, 19). He assigns the scrivener a desk on his side of the partition that separates him from the other scriveners, and then puts up a green folding screen, "which might entirely isolate Bartleby from my sight, though not remove him from my voice." This arrangement, he writes with a certain satisfaction, was one in which, "in a manner, privacy and society were conjoined" (*BS*, 19). But insofar as it establishes the relationship as that between a caller and the called (the analogy between visitor and visited in "Benito Cereno" should not be overlooked), it also, unbeknownst to the lawyer, betrays this "benign" conjoining of privacy and society to be other than the sanguine one it connotes: a disciplinary mechanism that produces useful and docile bodies. Coupled with a working space that "commanded no view at all" (*BS*, 19), this arrangement—this one way relationship privileging the voice of the American elect over the preterite—is the mise en scène of the transactions of the benevolent Wall Street lawyer and Bartleby, the scrivener—and the arrangement that the "advent" of Bartleby will increasingly disrupt.

The first interruption occurs on the third day of Bartleby's employment, after the lawyer has become convinced that the new scrivener, despite his silent, pale, and mechanical work habits, is reliable. The following passage shows clearly how utterly central the thematic of the calling is to Melville's text:

> It was on the third day, I think, of his being with me, and before any necessity had arisen for having his own writing examined, that, being much hurried to complete a small affair I had in hand, I abruptly called to Bartleby. In my haste and natural expectancy of instant compliance, I sat with my head bent over the original on my desk, and my right hand sideways, and somewhat nervously extended with the copy, so that immediately upon emerging from his retreat, Bartley might snatch it and proceed to business without the least delay.

> In this very attitude did I sit when I called to him, rapidly stating what it was I wanted him to do—namely, to examine a small paper with me. Imagine my surprise, nay, consternation, when without moving from his privacy, Bartleby in a singularly mild, firm voice, replied, "I would prefer not to."
>
> I sat awhile in perfect silence, rallying my stunned faculties. Immediately it occurred to me that my ears had deceived me, or Bartleby had entirely misunderstood my meaning. I repeated my request in the clearest tone I could assume. But in quite as clear a one came the previous reply, "I would prefer not to."
>
> "Prefer not to," echoed I, rising in high excitement, and crossing the room with a stride. "What do you mean? Are you moon-struck? I want you to help me compare this sheet here—take it," and I thrust it towards him.
>
> "I would prefer not to," said he.
>
> I looked at him steadfastly. His face was leaning composed; his gray eye dimly calm. Not a wrinkle of agitation rippled him. Had there been the least uneasiness, anger, impatience or impertinence in his manner; in other words, had there been any thing ordinarily human about him, doubtless I should have violently dismissed him from the premises. But as it was, I should have as soon thought of turning my pale plaster-of-paris bust of Cicero out of doors. I stood gazing at him awhile as he went on with his own writing, and then reseated myself at my desk. This is very strange, thought I. What had one best do? But my business hurried me. I concluded to forget the matter for the present, reserving it for my future leisure. So calling Nippers from the other room, the paper was speedily examined. (*BS*, 20–21)

Read superficially, this passage would seem to suggest that Bartleby's response to the lawyer's call is sheer perversity. Read against its grain, however, the lawyer's words, in the very process of justifying his point of view, turn out to say something quite different. This something else is signaled by the lawyer's inaugural gesture immediately following his call. Expecting "immediate compliance," he holds the copy out with his right hand without looking up from his desk, assuming Bartleby will obediently "snatch it" "and proceed with the business without delay." The source—the genealogy—of this dehumanizing assumption on which the lawyer's seemingly particular and innocuous expectation is founded is not restricted to the protocols of the Wall Street law office. It is, as the context in which Melville has embedded his story suggests, a general antebellum American way of being-in-the-world. It is, more specifically, the totalizing exceptionalist problematic which has accommodated the rise of liberal capitalist democracy—the Franklinian "reality" that "time is money"—to its (transcendental) "center elsewhere,"[38] and whose binary logic is taken spontaneously to be the way things really are: the (hegemonic) truth ("So be it!"), a truth which is blind not simply to its constructedness, but also, as the lawyer's initial unconsciousness of Bartleby's humanity suggests, to the invisible *of* its vision.

This is why the benevolent lawyer is "stunned" by Bartleby's response to his call. There is nothing in his plenary logic that enables him to foresee it. But instead of making the effort to *think* this anxiety-provoking enigma, he inaugurates an anxious process of rationalizing, that is, objectifying "it."[39] I am suggesting that Bartleby is the social allotrope of the nothingness of being that activates anxiety. First, it occurs to him that his ears may have deceived him or that Bartleby had "entirely misunderstood [his] meaning." But when, in the wake of repeating his call, Bartleby responds again in the same way, he is driven to think he is "moon-struck" and, then, after satisfying himself that the scrivener's countenance betrays no "uneasiness, anger, impatience or impertinence," resorts to the possibility that there is nothing "ordinarily human about him"—the "human," of course, defined according to the imperatives of the American exceptionalist problematic. But these rationalizations do not appease his anxiety, partly because they contradict his benevolent democratic ethos and partly because the estranging force of Bartleby's refusal to answer to his call has been too strong. Acknowledging to himself that "this is very strange," and that this dislocating strangeness has denied him the normal means of *doing* something about it, he decides to "forget the matter for the present."

The specter of Bartleby's refusal, however, will not be allayed. A few days later, after Bartleby has copied four lengthy documents, "a week's testimony" in an important suit "taken before [the lawyer] in [his] High Court of Chancery," the lawyer "calls" him to participate, with Turkey, Nippers, and Ginger Nut, in the proofreading of the copies. But again Bartleby responds, " 'I would prefer not to.' " What follows establishes the paradoxical relationship between the caller and the called:

> For a few moments I was turned into a pillar of salt, standing at the head of my seated column of clerks. Recovering myself, I advanced towards the screen, and demanded the reason for such extraordinary conduct.
> "*Why* do you refuse?"
> "I would prefer not to."
> With any other man I should have flown outright into a dreadful passion, scorned all further words, and thrust him ignominiously from my presence. But there was something about Bartleby that not only strangely disarmed me, but in a wonderful manner touched and disconcerted me. I began to reason with him.

> "These are our own copies we are about to examine. It is labor saving to you, because one examination will answer for your four papers. It is common usage. Every copyist is bound to help examine his copy. Is it not so? Will you not speak? Answer!"
>
> "I prefer not to," he replied in a flute-like tone. It seemed to me that while I had been addressing him, he carefully revolved every statement that I made; fully comprehending the meaning; could not gainsay the irresistible conclusion; but, at the same time, some paramount consideration prevailed with him to reply as he did.
>
> "You are decided, then, not to comply with my request—a request made according to common usage and common sense?"
>
> He briefly gave me to understand that on that point my judgment was sound. Yes: his decision was irreversible. (*BS*, 21–22)

What Melville emphasizes here are two contradictory aspects of the narrator's reaction to Bartleby's refusal. One is his impatient bewilderment over what he takes to be the irrationality of Bartleby's refusal to comply with the reasonable dictates of "common usage and common sense," which, from a perspective outside his, would mean the Franklinian problematic. This is markedly enforced immediately following this confrontation, when the exasperated lawyer, beginning "to stagger in his own plainest faith" in the face of being "browbeaten in some unprecedented and violent unreasonable way," calls desperately on the others to vouch for the obvious rationality of his request—that is, for his authority, a call that, given their disciplined status, they all, each in their own way, predictably answer in the affirmative. The other aspect of the lawyer's response, which contradicts the first, is that certain "something about Bartleby that not only disarmed [him], but in a wonderful manner touched and disconcerted [him]." It is this *unnamable* "something" that will henceforth haunt the lawyer, and, in order to resist its disruptive "truth," will compel him to make, in revealing ways, every possible effort to annul "its" estranging force. To put it alternatively, we bear witness here to the inauguration of a corrosive process that threatens not simply to undermine the lawyer's absolute authority, but, more significantly, as reflected in the passive voice he adopts in the first sentence—"I *was turned* into a pillar of salt"—to reverse the relation between the caller and the called.

The lawyer's increasingly excessive efforts to negate the unnamable of Bartleby's "I prefer not to" and to maintain his shaken authority will vacillate between the options of *force* and *accommodation*, his will to the latter always and increasingly, for significant reasons I have alluded to, subduing that of the former. This vacillation manifests itself in an exemplary way soon after the episode referred to above, when, profoundly aggravated by Bartleby's "passive resistance," the lawyer thinks:

If the individual so resisted be of a not inhumane temper, and the resisting one perfectly harmless in his passivity; then, in the better moods of the former, he will endeavor charitably to construe to his imagination what proves impossible to be solved by his judgment. Even so, for the most part, I regarded Bartleby and his ways. Poor fellow! thought I, he means no mischief; it is plain he intends no insolence; his aspect sufficiently evinces that his eccentricities are involuntary. He is useful to me. I can get along with him. If I turn him away, the chances are he will fall in with some less indulgent employer, and then he will be rudely treated, and perhaps driven forth miserably to starve. Yes. Here I can cheaply purchase a delicious self-approval. To befriend Bartleby; to humor him in his strange willfulness, will cost me little or nothing, while I lay up in my soul what will eventually provide a sweet morsel for my conscience. But this mood was not invariable with me. The passiveness of Bartleby sometimes irritated me. I felt strangely goaded on to encounter him in new opposition, to elicit some angry spark from him *answerable to my own*. (*BS*, 23–24; my emphasis)

Overt force, to recall the passage on modern power relations from Foucault I quoted earlier, is the essential mode of relationality in the totalitarian mind (and regime, whether monarchical or fascist); accommodation, on the other hand, is determinative of relationality in the pluralistic mind (and American Wall Street democracy). By this distinction I mean that the totalitarian mind (and regime) indoctrinates or employs force to tether the difference (and the multitude) to its *Logos* or center, whereas the pluralistic mind (and democratic "regime of truth") tolerates difference and incorporates its variety, but, in so doing, *assimilates* it to its center, that is, inscribes the center in its others—renders them simultaneously useful and docile—by means of cultural production. To put it in terms of what Foucault calls "the repressive hypothesis," whereas the totalitarian mind (and regime) effaces names in favor of a collective Name and thus by this overt show of force, becomes vulnerable to insurrection, the mind (and capitalist democracy) *produces* names (subjects) in behalf of aggrandizing the authority and power of a Name (Subject) and minimizing the threat of insurrection.[40]

Finding the hegemonic language of his call utterly useless in the face of Bartleby's passive silence, the lawyer is sometimes driven by the "unaccountable" (*BS*, 27, 37, 42) or "inscrutable" scrivener (*BS*, 27, 35)—his silence—to the point of violence. After Bartleby has become a "fixture in [his] chamber" and the lawyer's "masterly managed" scheme for "getting rid" of him (*BS*, 33)—evicting him from "his premises" (*BS*, 36)—has failed, the lawyer is tempted to murder, that is, to the most extreme form of objectifying the unaccountable:

> I was now in such a state of nervous resentment that I thought it but prudent to check myself at present from further demonstrations. Bartleby and I were alone. I remembered the tragedy of the unfortunate Adams and the still more unfortunate Colt in the solitary office of the latter; and how poor Colt, being dreadfully incensed by Adams, and imprudently permitting himself to get wildly exited, was at unawares hurried into his fatal act—an act which certainly no man could possibly deplore more than the actor himself. (*BS*, 36)

The lawyer is so entirely committed to the truth of his Wall Street discourse—its ontological "premises" as it were—that it is impossible for him to conceive of Bartleby's "I prefer not to"—and his ensuing silence—as anything other than abnormal, either inhuman or the symptom of catatonia. Thus, just as Ahab's metaphysical logic—his ferocious belief in the oneness of being—compels him to monomaniacally reduce the unpresentable (and therefore the unspeakable) white whale—"all that most maddens and torments; all that stirs up the lees of things; all truth with malice in it; all that cracks the sinews and cakes the brain; all the subtle demonisms of life and thought"—to "Moby-Dick" and then, "as if his chest had been a mortar," to "burst his hot heart's shell upon it" (*M-D*, 184), so the deeply inscribed "premises" of the lawyer's American Wall-Street problematic tempt him to reduce the enigma of Bartleby's dread-provokng silence to a seemingly gratuitous and malicious object and, as Ishmael says of Ahab, to make *it* "practically assailable" (*M-D*, 184). Like Captain Ahab's "fiery pursuit" of the white whale, the lawyer's furious impulse to kill Bartleby at this point is the measure of the blindness of his "plenary" truth discourse to the "reality" resonating in Bartleby's silence and thus of his inability to think/say differently and differentially.

But there is, of course, a significant difference between Ahab and the Wall Street lawyer. Ahab's problematic is totalizing and totalitarian and thus, as I have noted, vulnerable to resistance. The lawyer's, on the other hand, is democratic, or, rather, as his easy assimilation of Christian charity and self-interest suggest, that peculiar form of capitalist/democratic being that emerged out of the Puritan quandary over election,[41] which thus enables him, as Ahab's totalizing problematic does not, to resist the temptation to murder:

> But when this old Adam of resentment rose in me and tempted me concerning Bartleby, I grappled him and threw him. How? Why, simply by recalling the divine injunction: "A new commandment give I unto you, that ye love one another." Yes, this it was that saved me. Aside from higher considerations, charity often operates as a vastly wise and prudent principle—a great safeguard to

its possessor. Men have committed murder for jealousy's sake, and anger's sake and hatred's sake, and selfishness' sake, and spiritual pride's sake; but no man that ever I heard of, ever committed a diabolical murder for sweet charity's sake. Mere self-interest, then, if no better motive can be enlisted, should, especially with high-tempered men, prompt all beings to charity and philanthropy. At any rate, upon the occasion in question, I strove to drown my exasperated feelings towards the scrivener by benevolently construing his conduct. Poor fellow, poor fellow! I thought, he don't mean any thing; and besides, he has seen hard times, and ought to be indulged. (*BS*, 36)

What "saves" the lawyer, in other words, is precisely his benevolent American democratic problematic, that Protestant/capitalist way of seeing being that, as I have said, ostensibly acknowledges alterity, not out of radical respect for its nomadic errancy, but in order to accommodate its threatening (non)being to its center, to coax difference into taking its proper—useful and docile—place in the larger identical whole of his exceptionalist problematic, in short, to make the "unaccountable" scrivener *accountable*. This "saving" accommodational perspective is underscored by the lawyer's "looking into '[Jonathan]Edwards on Will,' and 'Priestley on Necessity' "—two versions of the confidence-inducing metaphysical interpretation of being—which, he says, "induced a salutary feeling" as he gradually "slid into the persuasion that these troubles of mine touching the scrivener, had been all predestined from eternity, and Bartleby was billeted upon me for some mysterious purpose of an all-wise Providence, which it was not for a mere mortal like me to fathom" (*BS*, 37). As suggested by the overdetermination of the visual metaphorics, and the emphasis on narrative finality or closure it enables, what follows bears ironic witness to the increasing absurdity—the illegitimacy—of this accommodational American logic: "At last I see, I feel it; I penetrate to the predestined purpose of my life. I am content. Others may have loftier parts to enact; but my mission in this world, Bartleby, is to furnish you with office-space for such period as you may see fit to remain" (*BS*, 37).

This is not to say that the lawyer's invocation of Providential design to account for Bartleby brings him the peace, or the recuperation of the "normal" employer/employee, master/servant, caller/called relationship, for which he so desperately yearns. The impact of the scrivener's astonishing behavior has been too decisive for that. When, for example, his "professional friends" begin to make "unsolicited and uncharitable remarks" about "the strange creature I kept at my office," his exasperation and resentment resurface, as he contemplates an unending future under these impossible conditions and, in the face of his unrelenting and deeply inscribed need to *do something* (*BS*, 38), he decides "decisively" "to gather all my faculties together, and for ever rid me of this intolerable incubus" (*BS*, 38). But even the fulfillment of this decision is pursued according to the imperatives of his liberal accommodational problematic. He will rid himself of Bartleby, but, at the same time, in such a way, typical of the logical economy of the emergent disciplinary institutions, as to both protect and reform him: "Then something severe, something unusual must be done," he says to himself. "What! surely you will not have him collared by a constable, and commit his innocent pallor to the common jail: And upon what ground could you procure such a thing to be done?—a vagrant, is he? What! he a vagrant, a wanderer, who refuses to budge? It is because he will *not* be a vagrant, then, that you seek to count him *as* a vagrant. That is too absurd. No visible means of support: there I have him. Wrong again: for indubitably he *does* support himself, and that is the only unanswerable proof that any man can show of his possessing the means so to do. No more then. Since he will not quit me, I must quit him . . ." (*BS*, 38–39).

Indeed, what is remarkable about the lawyer's story from the time he "quits" Bartleby, is precisely that he relentlessly pursues the logic of his accommodational problematic, which would finally *identify* and *place* the inscrutable and unaccountable scrivener—the "wanderer, who refuses to budge"—within its circumference, until it self-destructs. The more he tries to accommodate the unaccountable Bartleby to his "benevolent" hegemonic narrative, the more the process betrays its inability to do so or, alternatively, the more Bartleby comes to haunt—to visit—him and the American Wall Street reality for which he stands. This "dislocation," as it has been often noted, is symbolized by the paradox that the vagrant who "refuses to budge" drives the lawyer into becoming something like a nomad.[42] But this should not blind us to the fact that the lawyer's vagrancy is always *tethered* to his premises. There is no way he can rid himself of Bartleby. The scrivener who "prefers not to" is, in others words, irremediably a part *of, belongs* to, the lawyer.

This dis-integration of the undeviating logic of the lawyer's accommodational problematic culminates shortly after he is confronted by his agitated former landlord, accompanied by the tenants of the Wall Street building, with the demand that he "must do" something to compel the scrivener to depart the building he "now persists in haunting, sitting upon the banisters of the stairs by day, and sleeping in the entry by night" (*BS*, 40). Unsuccessful in his effort to convince his outraged visitors "that Bartleby was nothing to me" and compelled by his bourgeois fear that he would be "exposed in the papers," he visits Bartleby in one last effort to draw the ec-centric into his orbit:

> "Now one of two things must take place. Either you must do something, or something must be done to you. Now what sort of

business would you like to engage in? Would you like to re-engage in copying for some one?"

"No; I would prefer not to make any change,"

"Would you like a clerkship in a dry-goods store?"

"There is too much confinement about that. No, I would not like a clerkship; but I am not particular."

"Too much confinement," I cried. "Why you keep yourself confined all the time!"

"I would prefer not to take a clerkship," he rejoined, as if to settle that little item at once.

"How would a bar-tender's business suit you? There is not trying of the eyesight in that."

"I would not like it at all; though, as I said before, I am not particular."

His unwonted wordiness inspirited me. I returned to the charge.

"Well then, would you like to travel through the country collecting bills for the merchants? That would improve your health."

"No, I would prefer to be doing something else."

"How then would going as a companion to Europe, to entertain some young gentleman with your conversation,—how would that suit you?"

"Not at all. It does not strike me that there is anything definite about that. I like to be stationary. But I am not particular."

"Stationary you shall be then," I cried, now losing my patience, and for the first time in all my exasperating connection with him fairly flying into a passion. "If you do not go away from these premises before night, I shall feel bound—indeed *am* bound—to—to—to quit the premises myself!" I rather absurdly concluded. . . . Despairing of all further efforts, I was precipitately leaving him, when a final thought occurred to me. . . .

"Bartleby," said I, in the kindest tone I could assume under such exciting circumstances, "will you go home with me now—not to my office, but my dwelling—and remain there till we can conclude upon some convenient arrangement for you at our leisure? Come. Let us start now, right away."

"No: at present I would prefer not to make any change at all." (*BS*, 41)

In this astonishing sequence, the lawyer's effort to domesticate the subversive force of the immovable nomad with his logic of accommodation begins with a certain decisiveness, but as it proceeds, it becomes increasingly frantic—and ludicrous. That is to say, the circumference of his accommodational vision expands and the lines that tether it to his mind's eye (his *Logos*) become increasingly gossamer until they finally break: "the center," to (mis)appropriate a phrase from W. B. Yeats, "will not hold."[43] Or, to put it alternatively, the increasing expansion of the circumference of his accommodational visual horizon is accompanied by the exposure—the coming to "presence" of that to which it is necessarily blind: the "unpresentable"—the contingent or "unnamable" *being* that the lawyer and the Wall Street world he represents "will have nothing to do with." The reversal of the normal power relations that the lawyer had been all along anxious about and had resisted—"that wondrous ascendancy which the inscrutable scrivener had over me, and from which ascendancy, for all my chafing, I could not escape" (*BS*, 35)—has happened. The *caller* has, indeed, become the *called*. But not quite for the author of Bartleby's *"story"—rather, for the reader.*

After Bartleby is "removed" to and imprisoned in the Tombs "as a vagrant" (*BS*, 42) at the instigation of the landlord, the lawyer, compelled by his deep compassion, visits him two more times. On the first, immediately on hearing of Bartleby's confinement, the lawyer attempts to persuade the "right officer" that "Bartleby was a perfectly honest man, and greatly to be compassionated, however unaccountably eccentric" (*BS*, 42), and then, having obtained permission to talk with him, seeks him out in the prison yard, where he has been allowed to wander. He finds Bartleby "standing all alone in the quietest of the yards, his face towards a high wall [a circumstance that underscores the equation between the prison and the Wall Street world], while all around, from the narrow slits of the jail windows, [he] thought [he] saw peering out upon him the eyes of murderers and thieves." Echoing the beginning of the master's dislocating relationship with the servant, he calls him:

> "Bartleby!"
>
> "I know you," he said, without looking round,—"and I want nothing to say to you."
>
> "It was not I that brought you here, Bartleby," said I, keenly pained at his implied suspicion. "And to you, this should not be so vile a place. Nothing reproachful attaches to you by being here. And see, it is not so sad a place as one might think. Look, there is the sky, and there is the grass."
>
> "I know where I am," he replied, but would say nothing. . . .
>
> (*BS*, 43)

In "Benito Cereno," we recall, Delano, even at the revelatory end, betrays the blindness of his optimistic American exceptionalist problematic—and therefore its paradoxical strength—when he tries to persuade the Don that "the past is the past; why moralize upon it? Forget it." Despite the reversal of the caller and the called, the interpellater and the interpellated, so, too, in "Bartleby," the lawyer, with his finally confident Wall Street eyes, not only fails or, rather, refuses in the end to perceive the revelation; he expresses this blindness in optimistic terms remarkably similar to Delano's.

The lawyer's account of his second and last visit manifests a similar rationalization of the destructive element. He is accompanied by a "grub-man," whom he had hired on his previous visit to supplement Bartleby's prison fare, despite his snobbish disdain of the latter's coarseness and his assumption that the lawyer had relations with criminal forgers. After searching the corridors of the prison in vain, the lawyer tells us, he is apprised by a turnkey that the "silent man" lies yonder, "sleeping in the yard." He comments on the "amazing thickness" of the surrounding walls, observing that the "Egyptian character of the masonry weighed upon me with its gloom," but in a typically optimistic gesture, adds that "a soft imprisoned turf grew under foot. The heart of the eternal pyramids, it seemed, wherein, by some strange magic, through the clefts, grass-seed, dropped by birds, had sprung." Then he sees the "wasted" Bartleby, "strangely huddled at the base of the wall, his knees drawn up, and lying on his side, his head touching the cold stones." On closer examination, he sees that Bartleby's "dim eyes were open; otherwise he seemed profoundly sleeping." He touches his hand and a "tingling shiver ran up my arm and down my spine to my feet." As the unintended grotesque mockery of the grub-man's impatience with his new client resonates cacophonously, the lawyer closes Bartleby's eyes, and, in response to his crude companion's question, "Eh!—He's asleep, ain't he?," responds in a murmur with a quotation, no doubt precipitated by Bartleby's fetal position, from the suffering Job's "blasphemous" preference for a death at birth: "With kings and counselors."[44]

These are, indeed, "poignant words" as one critic writes, bent on proving, against the "Bartleby industry," that the lawyer is a "reliable narrator."[45] But as I have shown in pointing to the centrality of the caller/called opposition in the story, they say more about the limitations of the narrator than about Bartleby. Taking this pervasive opposition as a directive, we are compelled to read the dead Bartleby's open eyes as the look of one who, in the beginning, had been the looked-at, on the analogy of the reversed relationship of the caller and the called. And the lawyer's closing of Bartleby's eyes is not simply a humane gesture, but one tainted by the subconscious desire to escape with finality their spectral gaze. Following this directive, we are thus also compelled to interpret the lawyer's quotation from the Book of Job not simply as a sonorous sentimental gesture that is incommensurate with the reality of its referent—the nobody has been apotheosized into the company of kings and counselors—but also as a symptom of precisely the ontological optimism that informs his American exceptionalist problematic.

V

Who, then, is Bartleby?, we are driven to ask, like the lawyer in his epilogue, echoing the bewildered stranger who accosts him immediately after he has "quitted" his old "premises" (" 'In mercy's name, who is he?' " [*BS*, 39]). The lawyer, in a final effort to pin the Protean Bartleby down, divulges "a little item of rumor" that he had heard shortly after the scrivener died: "That Bartleby had been a subordinate clerk in the Dead Letter Office at Washington, from which he had been suddenly removed by a change in the administration." On this basis, he offers an answer to the question of Bartleby's identity on the analogy of the dead letters: "Dead letters! Does it not sound like dead men? Conceive a man by nature and misfortune prone to a pallid hopelessness, can any business seem more fitted to heighten it than that of continually handling these letters, and assorting them for the flames? For by the cart-load they are annually burned." This would suggest that the lawyer is on the verge of condemning an American polity for having reduced its human constituents to disposable reserve.[46] But what he goes on to say annuls this resonant suggestion: "Sometimes from the folded paper the pale clerk takes a ring:—the finger it was meant for, perhaps, moulders in the grave; a bank-note sent in swiftest charity:—he whom it would relieve, nor eats nor hungers any more; pardon for those who died despairing; hope for those who died unhoping; good tidings for those who died stifled by unrelieved calamities. On errands of life, these letters speed to death" (*BS*, 45). As we have seen, the lawyer has been, in some significant degree, drawn (down) into the corrosive existential time of secular American history by Bartleby's dislocating "I prefer not to." Following the directive instigated by Melville's continuous play on the double meaning of the word "premise," we might say that, in quitting his spatial premises, the lawyer has also in some degree quitted the premises of the logic of his American democratic/capitalist problematic and entered into the uncharted realm of the uncanny (*Unheimlichkeit*: not-at-homeness). But instead of addressing the question of the worldly *system* that hails and then domesticates human beings—reduces their singularity to subjected subjectivity and banalizes the suffering it causes—the lawyer (like Captain Delano) willfully withdraws again into a familiar transcendental space.[47] From this recuperated optimistic and domestic vantage point he is enabled to universalize—and sentimentalize—the pain-provoking repressions of the capitalist world—and Bartleby's anxiety-provoking passive act or, rather, *his witness*, into a comforting all-encompassing name: "Ah Bartleby! Ah humanity!" (*BS*, 45). This, too, is a hailing that intends "us," even in its pathos, to confidently affirm the world he represents, to feel that "everything will be all right: Amen—'*So be it.*'"

If the lawyer's suggestion about the identity of Bartleby is incommensurate with the Bartleby of his story, "Who, then, is Bartleby?" we are again compelled to ask. Attuned to Melville's interrogation of identity (the self-present subject) and the imperative of the will, Gilles Deleuze refers to Bartleby as rhizomatic: "the man without references, without possessions, without properties, without qualities, without particularities: he is too smooth for anyone to be able to hang any particularity on him. Without past or future, he is instantaneous. I PREFER NOT is Bartleby's chemical or alchemical formula, but one can read inversely I AM NOT PARTICULAR as its indispensable complement."[48] (74) Similarly, to Giorgio Agamben, Bartleby is "the extreme figure of the Nothing from which all creation derives; and at the same time, he constitutes the most implacable vindication of this Nothing as pure, absolute potentiality. The scrivener has become the writing tablet; he is now nothing other than his white sheet. It is not surprising, therefore, that he dwells so obstinately in the abyss of potentiality and does not seem to have the slightest intentions of leaving it[49] (254). Analogously, though more focused on the worldliness of Bartleby's occasion, by attending to the margins of the lawyer's narrative—to the invisible *of* the visible (or the silence *of* the plenary language) of his American problematic—as I have done, we perceive that he "is" the "non-being" or "no-body" of the Being or Body of the lawyer's empiricist ontological "premises." He is the existent that does not *exist* in the lawyer's American capitalist world.[50] It is no accident, as so many readers have noted, that the baffled, but also anxious lawyer and the citizens of the Wall Street world are driven insistently to use the metaphorics of spectrality—"ghost," "apparition," "incubus," and so on—to characterize the elusiveness of Bartleby's identity and his silence. Nor is it accidental that the lawyer resorts increasingly to hailing Bartleby, to calling him by name in the hope of objectifying his non-being into a (non-being) Being that serves the namer's will to get things done.

But this way of putting the "answer" to the question "Who is Bartleby?" is partial insofar as it overdetermines the negative effects of the interpellating problematic: the reification and annulment of the singularity of the being so called, that is, its subjection of the subject. Melville's intention is also, and above all, to disclose the positive possibilities for resisting this primary "apparatus of capture" of the Wall Street world.[51] And he does so in a way remarkably proleptic of a fundamental theoretical and practical initiative of the postmodern occasion. Like Israel Potter, who, after accidentally boarding an enemy ship, confounds his potential captors by reversing their logic of naming (he becomes, we recall, a nameless "phantom"), Bartley *accepts* the prevailing "premises" of the dominant culture vis-à-vis being (and human being) only to turn them against its truth. As we have seen, the "specter," "the ghost," "the apparition," "the incubus," of Bartleby—the non-being to which he has been reduced—comes to *haunt* the lawyer's "premises"— his "doctrine of assumptions" (*BS*, 35)—and his law offices, the utilitarian world this logic produces: calls them into question by tacitly exploiting their very operations. Interpellation, as we have seen in the case of Captain Delano in "Benito Cereno," reduces the singular individual to a subjected subject, that is, to individuated but passive being. Bartleby, on the other hand, refuses to answer the lawyer's call, no matter how insistently the latter calls him, and this refusal to be interpellated transforms the passivity of the subjected subject into an active "passive resistance" (*BS*, 23).[52] that dislocates the located caller, instigates a "change of terrain." To invoke one of the resonant legal terms the lawyer applies to the scrivener, Bartleby's refusal "unsettles" the lawyer and solicits (unsettles) the very foundations of the infinitely more powerful Wall Street problematic he represents, if it does not entirely compel him to rethink the settling premises of his thinking.

This is by no means to say that Melville intends his readers to understand the lawyer's aborted narrative as a triumph of Wall Street's preterites over the Wall Street elect. His story, like that of Ishmael, of Pierre Gledinning, of Israel Potter, of Babo, is the story of a life damaged by the American problematic. It is to say, rather, that, in perceiving the massive antebellum push to capitalize America—to render democratic capitalism's vision of the world as the truth—Melville not only foresaw its dehumanizing and banalizing effects, but also, if only symptomatically, a way of warding off its insidious life-damaging power, a way that is more appropriate than direct action to the emergent liberal/disciplinary conditions of power relations. Bartleby dies in the end, and Melville means us to mourn his silent passing. But as the lawyer's anxious compulsion to tell his story—and his inability in the end to comprehend and identify his enigmatic protagonist—forcefully suggest, his elusive ghost will continue to *visit* the Wall Street lawyer, who, like the Ancient Mariner of Coleridge's poem, will repeat it over and over again—until he comes to acknowledge Bartleby's singularity—his unpresentability—and to let "it" be.[53]

As Theodor Adorno, Michel Foucault, Louis Althusser, Gilles Deleuze, and a number of other "poststructuralist" thinkers[54] have borne decisive witness, the Enlightenment *episteme* that emerged in the wake of the American and French Revolutions or, perhaps more accurately, after the implosion of the ancien régime, has itself come to its fulfillment in the formation of the "disciplinary" or "administered" society most decisively exemplified by the United States, an end that has precipitated into spectral visibility that differential "reality" its structuralist logic cannot finally accommodate. In this reading of "Bartleby, the Scrivener," I have attempted to show that Melville uncannily anticipates the "advent" of this de-structive thinking over a century before its emergence. It is no accident that Melville's enigmatic Bartleby has produced a host of highly visible "nomadic" or "unsettled"—and "unsettling"—postmodern fictional heirs, such as Franz Kafka's K (*The Castle*), Albert Camus's Mersault (*The Stranger*); Samuel Beckett's Watt (*Watt*); Richard Wright's Cross Damon (*The Outsider*),

Ralph Ellison's Invisible Man (*Invisible Man*); Thomas Pynchon's William Slothrop (*Gravity's Rainbow*); J. M. Coetzee's Michael K (*The Life and Times of Michael K*); Salman Rushdie's Saleem (*Midnight's Children*); and as much, if not more than *Moby-Dick*, has instigated richly provocative philosophical commentary on "Bartleby" by such powerful contemporary critics of Western modernity as Maurice Blanchot, Gilles Deleuze, Giorgio Agamben, and Antonio Negri and Michael Hardt.[55] Equally telling, his strategy of refusal is reflected in significant ways in the work of numerous nomadic modern and contemporary intellectuals, both in the United States and abroad, who have been estranged or exiled from their homelands by the imperial will to repress errancy: E. B. Dubois, C. L. R. James, Frantz Fanon, George Antonius, S. H. Alatas, among the most prominent. But of these representatives of the opposition of refusal, it is above all the work of the late Edward W. Said that Melville's Bartleby most uncannily anticipates, particular his magisterial appropriation in *Culture and Imperialism* of Theodor Adorno's "reflections of a damaged life" in behalf of liberation from the "administered society" ("freedom from exchange") in a time of dearth that has rendered revolution unthinkable:

> "The past life of emigrés is, as we know, annulled," says Adorno in *Minima Moralia*, subtitled *Reflections from a Damaged Life* (*Reflexionen aus dem beschadigten Leben*). Why? "Because anything that is not reified, cannot be counted and measured, ceases to exist" or, as he says later, is consigned to mere "background." . . . Thus the emigré consciousness—a mind of winter, in Wallace Stevens's phrase—discovers that "a gaze averted from the beaten track, a hatred of brutality, a search for fresh concepts not yet encompassed by the general pattern, is the last hope for thought." Adorno's general pattern is what in another places he calls the "administered world" or, insofar as the irresistible dominants in culture are concerned, "the consciousness industry." There is then not just the negative advantage of refuge in the emigré's eccentricity; there is also the positive benefit of challenging the system, describing it in language unavailable to those it has already subdued:
>
>> In an intellectual hierarchy which constantly makes everyone answerable, unanswerability alone can call the hierarchy directly by its name. The circulation sphere, whose stigmata are borne by intellectual outsiders, opens a last refuge to the mind that it barters away, at the very moment when refuge no longer exists. He who offers for sale something unique that no one wants to buy, represents, even against his will, freedom from exchange.

> These are certainly minimal opportunities, although a few pages later Adorno expands the possibility of freedom by prescribing a form of expression whose opacity, obscurity, and deviousness—the absence of "the full transparency of its logical genesis"—move away from the dominant system, enacting in its "inadequacy" a measure of liberation.
>
> > This inadequacy resembles that of life, which describes a wavering, deviating line, disappointing by comparison with its premises, and yet which only in this actual course, always less than it should be, is able under given conditions of existence, to represent an unregimented one.[56]

Adorno's and Said's emigré wards off capture by living a life which "describes a wavering, deviating line." Bartleby, on the other hand, "accomplishes" this by his immovable silence in the face of the Transcendental Subject's call. But these ways of resisting the state apparatuses of capture, as Gilles Deleuze reminds us, are not contradictory: "[T]he nomad," he writes, as if he were deliberately invoking Bartleby, "is not necessarily one who moves; some voyages take place *in situ*, are trips *in intensity*. Even historically, nomads are not necessarily those who move about like migrants. On the contrary, they do not move; nomads, they nevertheless stay in the same place and continually evade the codes of settled people."[57] No less than the orphaned Ishmael's garrulous mobility, as I have argued in *The Errant Art of* Moby-Dick, Bartleby's silent immobility is a rhizomatic mode of erring that not only evades but decodes the American Way.[58] Despite the continuing effort in much American literary criticism to settle with Bartleby by settling him in the disciplinary economy of the liberal democratic household, the vagabond scrivener "who refuses to budge" continues to elude the discourse that would codify and domesticate the spectral force of his mobile passivity. As Melville's great story clearly implies, the positivity of this errancy, of its enabling evasion of the disciplinary codes of the American Way through immobile silence, is, of course, minimal. But insofar as it compels thinking this spectral silence as a nascent form of language that has been paradoxically precipitated by the very fulfillment of the accommodational—read, now, codifying—language of the Wall Street lawyer, it is also a prelude to thinking the errant, the singular, the diverse, the migrant, the preterite—all that the prevailing language of America would encode and settle—different(ial)ly. It is in this sense that the Melville of "Benito Cereno" and "Bartleby" is our (global) contemporary.

Chapter 5

Cavilers and Con Men

The Confidence-Man: His Masquerade

"Yes, sir," said the negro, "it is the custom. We are given one pair of short denim breeches twice a year, and that's all we have to wear. When we're working at the sugar-mill and catch our finger in the grinding-wheel, they cut off our hand. When we try to run away, they cut off a leg. I have been in both these situations. This is the price you pay for the sugar you eat in Europe...."

"O Pangloss!" cried Candide, "this is one abomination you never thought of. That does it, I shall finally have to renounce your Optimism."

"What's Optimism?" asked Cacambo.

"I'm afraid to say," said Candide, "that it's a mania for insisting that all is well when things are going badly."

—Voltaire, *Candide*

Cooper's Leatherstocking is *perfected* in Melville's Indian-hater.... Perfected, he is unmasked—perhaps one day to be undone, no longer necessary even as a figment of our national imagination.

—Roy Harvey Pearse, "The Metaphysics of Indian-Hating"

Way back in 1988, on July 3, the U.S.S. *Vincennes,* a missile cruiser stationed in the Persian Gulf, accidentally shot down an Iranian airliner and killed two hundred and ninety civilian passengers. George Bush the First, who was at the time on his presidential campaign, was asked to comment on the incident. He said quite subtly, "I will never apologize for the United States, I don't care what the facts are."

—Arundhati Roy, *An Ordinary Person's Guide to Empire*

There are no truths outside the gates of Eden.

—Bob Dylan, "The Gates of Eden"

The following passage is the response (in the words of the narrator of Herman Melville's *The Confidence-Man: His Masquerade* [1857]), of "the man with the travelling cap," one of the avatars of the Confidence-Man, to a certain "good merchant's" troubled reaction to a painful story he was told earlier by "a man with the weed on his hat" about an "unfortunate man" and his wife, Goneril, in which the aptly named spouse turns her depravity into moral capital:

> Still, he [the man with the travelling cap] was far from the illiberality of denying that philosophy duly bounded was permissible. Only he deemed it at least desirable that, when such a case as that alleged of the unfortunate man was made the subject of philosophic discussion, it should be so philosophized upon, as not to afford handles to those unblessed with the true light. For, but to grant there was so much as a mystery about such a case, might by those persons be held for a tacit surrender of the question. And as for the apparent license temporarily permitted sometimes, to the bad over the good (as was by implication alleged with regard to Goneril and the unfortunate man), it might be injudicious there to lay too much polemic stress upon the doctrine of future retribution as the vindication of present impunity. For though, indeed, to the right-minded that doctrine was true, and of sufficient solace, yet with the perverse the polemic mention of it might but provoke the shallow, though mischievous conceit, that such a doctrine was but tantamount to the one which should affirm that Providence was not now, but was going to be. In short, with all sorts of cavilers, it was best, both for them and for everybody, that whoever had the true light should stick behind the secure Malakoff of confidence, nor be tempted forth to hazardous skirmishes on the open ground of reason. Therefore, he deemed it unadvisable in the good man, even in the privacy of his own mind, or in communion with a congenial one, to indulge in too much latitude of philosophizing, or, indeed, of compassionating, since this might beget an indiscreet habit of thinking and feeling which might unexpectedly betray him upon unsuitable occasions.[1]

This advice lies at the abyssal heart of Melville's vertiginous, polyvalent, and decisively devastating parody of American optimism, what, as we have seen, he takes, after the publication of *Pierre* (1852), to be the essential characteristic of the American national identity. But equally important, it enables a retrieval of Melville's novel that speaks proleptically and with considerable force to the contemporary, post-9/11 occasion, in which the decision makers in America have become con(fidence)-men, who, by appealing to the deeply backgrounded and inscribed exceptionalist optimism of the American national identity, have been enabled to announce a permanent state of emergency and, in the name of "homeland security," to put into operation a foreign and domestic policy that has not only rendered the American public infinitely more vulnerable to foreign attack, but also brought the world to the edge of a cataclysm.

In the passage, in which the Confidence-Man spells out the vulnerability of optimism to knowledge ("philosophy"), the possessor of "the true light," as the metaphor suggests, is both at the invulnerable fixed, certain, undeviating center of, and at the Archimedean point above, temporal being. This "true light" is, of course, the *Logos*, the transcendental Word of a Providential view of being or the secularized transcendental Word of a Metaphysical view of being, which, in *seeing meta ta physica* (from after or above the be-*ing* of being) enables its finite possessor (which means, above all, his or her limited vision) to sur-vey the infinite temporality of being all at once. It also assures him or her that this temporal being he or she surveys is identical to itself, continuous, directional, end-oriented—a narrative or, to underscore the decisive transformation of time or history into an inclusive and totalized spatial object, a promise-fulfillment *structure*—however contingent, erratic, contradictory, and thus anxiety-provoking this differential being appears to be in his or her immediacy. It thus not only has the negative virtue of setting up a mechanism of protection—"a Malakoff of confidence"—from the corrosive contingencies of finite being; it also has the positive virtue of unerringly instigating an "invulnerable" optimism even in the face of the catastrophic. Every thing and every event that contradicts the "true light" is, no matter how physically and/or psychologically damaging, an illusion—an *appearance* in the discourse and practice of the Western onto-theo-logical tradition. In fact, it has no being: "is not." It is this Western metaphysical interpretation of being *as it has been appropriated by an "exceptionalist"—or "New Adamic"—America from a fallen Europe*—and tellingly epitomized by the Puritan, Mary Rowlandson, in her exemplary captivity narrative, *The Sovereignty and Goodness of* God (1682)[2]—that Melville is parodying in this synecdochical passage of *The Confidence-Man* by way of pushing the American Confidence-Man's spatializing binary logic to its patently absurd and thus self-de-structive "end" or limits—to its "unrealization" as Foucault, following Nietzsche, puts this parodic version of genealogical history: "In short, with all sorts of cavilers, it was best, both for them and for everybody, that whoever had the true light should stick behind the secure Malakoff of confidence, nor be tempted forth to hazardous skirmishes on the open ground of reason."

This irony revealed by the rhetoric of logical excess is enforced by the very metaphor the Confidence-Man uses to emphasize the invulnerability to contradiction of a confidence justified by a metaphysical representation of being at large: "Malakoff" was a fort defended by the Russians against the French in the Crimean War. It was thought to be impregnable, but it fell on September 8, 1855 (while Melville was writing the novel). This is not the only instance of Melville's use of such a hyperbolic optical/military trope to enforce precisely this delegitimizing irony. In the chapter on Father Maple's sermon in *Moby-Dick*, in which, as I have argued in *The Errant Art of Moby-Dick*, Melville prefigures, in synecdochical form, his account of the self-de-struction of America's monomaniacal Adamic mission to redeem humanity of "the intangible malignity which has been from the beginning," Ishmael, having described Father Maple's ascent into the pulpit, pointedly remarks: ". . . I was not prepared to see Father Maple after gaining the height, slowly turn around, and stooping over the pulpit, deliberately drag the ladder step by step, till the whole was deposited within, leaving him impregnable in his little Quebec." Following this allusion to the fall of the Quebec Citadel in the French and Indian Wars, Ishmael, attending to the distanced physical/spiritual perspective this ascent has enabled, comments ironically: "Can it be, then, that by that act of physical isolation, he signifies his spiritual withdrawal for the time, from all outward worldly ties and connexions? Yes, for replenished with the meat and wine of the word, to the faithful man of God, this pulpit, I see, is a self-containing strong-hold—a lofty Ehrenbreitstein, with a perennial well of water within the walls."[3]

Though overdetermined, this negative way of putting Melville's parodic intention is nevertheless partial. He is not simply interrogating the "imperialism"—the will to power over difference—of antebellum American optimist thinking. In rhetorically emphasizing difference's "is not," he is also foregrounding the hitherto repressed fact that the nothingness of being has always, since the Puritans' providentially ordained "errand in the wilderness" and their all too easily justified reduction of its inhabitants to non-being, haunted the truth discourse—the Being—of Adamic (exceptionalist) America and, in so doing, calling his readers' attention to the urgent revolutionary—I am tempted to say poststructuralist—task of thinking positively this nothing *of*—that *belongs to*—America.

This caviling invitation to Americans to return to "the things themselves" is not new in Melville. He had already announced it in *Moby-Dick* when the monomaniacal, panoptic, and self-reliant Captain Ahab proclaimed to the anachronistic (European) cosmic powers that have been: "Serve me? The path to my fixed purpose is laid with iron rails, whereon my soul is grooved to run. Over unsounded gorges, through the rifled hearts of mountains, under torrents' beds, unerringly I rush!" and adds, without the slightest consciousness of the devastating irony, "Naught's an obstacle, naught's an angle to the iron way!" And he returned to it again and again in the fiction immediately preceding *The Confidence-Man*: in *Pierre; or the Ambiguities*" (1852), "Bartleby, the Scrivener" (1853), "Benito Cereno" (1855), and *Israel* Potter (1855). Indeed, I venture to say that this genealogical momentum was instigated by the ferociously self-righteous reaction of the custodians of America's cultural memory, its confidence men—epitomized, as we have seen, by George Washington Peck—to Melville's "latitudinous" "caviling" about the "truth" of postrevolutionary America (Saddle Meadows) in *Pierre*. The man in the traveling hat advises his troubled interlocutor to retreat to the Malakoff of confidence in the face of the dislocating perversities of such an insidious caviler. Peck, on the other hand, would, in behalf of the American reading public, "turn our critical Aegis [read "Medusan eye" or "panoptic gaze"] upon him" and "freeze [Melville] into silence."[4] Both, in the self-parodic excess of their unerring metalogic, expose themselves as confidence men in the double sense of the phrase—and, paradoxically, compel to spectral presence the very nothing—the dread-provoking finitude of the human condition—which their optimism is intended to reify and repress. It is this American Adamic confidence, I want to suggest, this fundamental characteristic of the American national identity, the naturalized consequence of a long cultural process of secularizing and internalizing the inaugural Puritan myth of American exceptionalism, *and* its self-destruction at the moment of the fulfillment of its reifying logic in antebellum America, that Melville's *Confidence-Man* enacts not only in its elusive content, but also in its errant structure.[5] However devastating, Melville's interment—his being "frozen into silence"—by the American custodians of Adamic confidence was what finally enabled him to shed the remaining encumbering philosophical and narrative conventions and the analogous moral and social proprieties demanded by the metaphysics of American optimism (to which he had hitherto paid lip service in order to be published and read). And, insofar as this dis-accommodation of the Adamic mask freed him to think the "naught" or, alternatively, the play of difference that is the shadow of the same, it enabled him to render *The Confidence-Man* the first postmodern American novel.

It will be impossible, in this limited space to undertake an exhaustive reading of *The Confidence-Man*, nor would it be appropriate to do so, given, as we have seen in chapter 2, Melville's deliberate aesthetic errancy, his conscious dismantling of the novel form, especially, as he notes in *Pierre*, as it had been appropriated by an optimistic "young America," which he came to see as the necessary literary analogue of the confidence-inducing metaphysical representation of being:

> Like all youths, Pierre had conned his novel-lessons . . . ; but their false, inverted attempts at systematizing eternally unsystemizable elements; their audacious, intermeddling impotency, in trying to unravel, and spread out, and classify, the more thin than gossamer threads which make up the complex web of life; these things over Pierre had no power now. . . . By infallible presentiment he saw, that not always doth life's beginning gloom conclude in gladness; that wedding-bells peal not ever in the last scene of life's fifth act;

that while the countless tribes of common novels laboriously spin vails of mystery, only to complacently clear them up at last . . . ; yet the profounder emanations of the human mind, intended to illustrate all that can be humanly known of human life; these never unravel their intricacies, and have no proper endings; but in imperfect, unanticipated, and disappointing sequels (as mutilated stumps), hurry to abrupt intermergings with the eternal tides of time and fate.[6]

What I intend in the following, rather, is to proffer a context that will not only render *The Confidence-Man* readable *as a "whole,"* in a way that most commentaries, both critical and favorable, from the time of its publication to the present, have not,[7] primarily because this commentary has attended, not to the directives of Melville's text, but to those of metaphysical optimism. In so doing, I also intend to pursue further the uncanny and urgent relevance of the theme of American confidence to the present post-9/11 occasion. More specifically, I will suggest (1) the provenance of the figure of the Confidence-Man and the way he functions in the novel; (2) the historical, philosophical, and literary tradition that Melville retrieves and reconstellates into the antebellum American occasion; (3) the central polyvalent manifestations of the philosophy of confidence in the novel by way of reference to the most important episodes; and (4) the novel's proleptic insights into the second Bush administration's confident justification and conduct of its "war on terror."

I

It has often been noted, by way of invoking the numerous metaphorical references to the Confidence-Man's reptilian gestures and movements, that Melville derives the many avatars of this enigmatic character from the generalized figure of the *diabolos* in the literature of the Judeo-Christian tradition. According to the imperatives of this narrative, he has been thus invariably identified as unequivocally demonic—the "wily" arch-enemy of Adamic man who, in the form of the serpent, tempts him into one form of damnation or another.[8] I want to suggest a related but different provenance of the Confidence-Man, one that radically reinterprets his function in the novel: Melville derives the Confidence-Man from the figure of Satan in the Book of Job. This source, however muted, is suggested throughout *The Confidence-Man*, as I will show, but its clearest articulations come in chapter 19, "A soldier of fortune," chapter 40, the story of China Aster (to which I will return), and in chapter 24, "A philosopher undertakes to convert a misanthrope, but does not get beyond confuting him," especially in the harlequin-like philanthropist's response to the misanthropic merchant bachelor's exasperated demand (much like the British sailor's to Israel Potter and the lawyer's colleagues to Bartleby) to know "who in thunder are you?," after the former has cavalierly intruded on the latter's brooding privacy. Echoing Satan's nomadic itinerary in the world in his reply to God's question, "Whence have you come?" in the Book of Job, he says: "A cosmopolitan, a catholic man; who, being such, ties himself to no narrow tailor or teacher, *but federates, in heart as in costume, something of the various gallantries of men under various suns. Oh, one roams not over the gallant globe in vain.* Bred by it, is a fraternal and fusing feeling. No man is a stranger. . . . And though, indeed, mine, in this instance, have met with no very hilarious encouragement, yet *the principle of a true citizen of the world* is still to return good for ill.—My dear fellow, tell me how I can serve you" (my emphasis; *C-M*, 132–133).[9]

But the Book of Job that Melville is invoking is not the official Book of Job handed down to the present by the Judeo-Christian tradition—the book in which Job, in the end, admits his folly in questioning God's purposes and "repent[s] in dust and ashes" (Job, 42). It is, rather, the Ur-Job, retrieved, not incidentally, by the existentialist theologians in the 1950s and 1960s, in which the Satanic figure who inaugurates the narrative in the court of God's distanced heaven remains intact. This, to invoke Melville's language, is the "caviling" Satan—the principle of finitude, of the nothingness of being, that always haunts meta-theo-anthropo-logical systems, the reductive narratives of closure, and the optimism they enable ("philosophy" in the inaugural quotation)[10]—who, having come "from going to and fro on the earth, and walking up and down on it," reminds the complacent God that His confidence in the loyalty of his "servant Job" is based on a panoptic perspective—an *oversight* from his remote and impregnable Malakoff, as it were—that enables an optimism which is blind to the corrosive differential realities of temporal/historical existence:

> Now there was a day when the sons of God came to present themselves before the Lord, and Satan also came among them. The Lord said to Satan, "Whence have you come?" Satan answered the Lord, "From going to and fro on the earth, and from walking up and down on it." And the Lord said to Satan, "Have you considered my servant Job . . . a blameless and upright man, who fears God and turns away from evil? Then Satan answered the Lord, "Does Job fear God for nought? Hast thou not put a hedge about him and his house and all that he has, on every side? . . . But put forth thy hand now, and touch all that he has, and he will curse thee to thy face." And the Lord said to Satan, "Behold, all that he has is in your power; only upon himself do not put forth your hand." So Satan went forth from the presence of the Lord. (Job, Prologue, 6–12)

In the process of introducing Job to adversity, that is, in disintegrating the narrativized world—the Malakoff—in which God, the *symbolos* (from the Greek *sym-ballein*: to throw together), has enclosed Job, and thus retrieving the radically differential temporality his distance had enabled him to spatialize, this Ur-Satan provokes Job into "philosophizing," which is to say, *questioning*. To put it alternatively, this *diabolos* (from *dia-ballein*: to throw apart), instigates in Job a distrust, a breakdown of his earlier confidence in God's providential design.[11] Satan's de-struction of Job's former world introduces pain and suffering into his life, but it also humanizes him, renders him *interesse*, an existential being-in-the-world for whom the difference he now encounters makes a difference. Further, in thus subverting the master/servant binary endemic to the transcendental perspective—the "true light"—it brings Job's hitherto distant, inscrutable, and interpellating God into dialogic relationship with him; that is, it demythologizes God, metamorphoses him into the be-*ing* of being. It was this unleashing of the primal "caviler" and the threat "his" suspicion (I am thinking of Nietzsche here) posed to the optimistic worldview—the promise/fulfillment structure of narrative—on which authority relies for its power in the Ur-Job that compelled the later theological confidence men to accommodate the Ur-Satan to God's larger design—the recuperative accommodational strategy epitomized by the four comforters.[12]

But this provenance of the figure of the Confidence-Man in the Ur-Satan of the Book of Job is partial: its most ancient and generalized manifestation. Though Melville was intent on appropriating the figure of the Ur-Satan for *The Confidence-Man*, the historical, especially cultural, conditions in antebellum America precluded the possibility of addressing the American exceptionalist project and its ontological *optimism* in the *sermo gravis* of tragedy. The hostile reception of *Moby-Dick* and especially of *Pierre* by the custodians of American confidence had disabused Melville of any illusion about the greatness or ideality of the American national identity. In keeping with his estrangement from America, he chose, instead, to think the Ur-Satan of the Book of Job in terms of the *sermo humilis* of satire or, more precisely, of a certain unorthodox parody that, as I will momentarily show, uncannily anticipates one of the three modes of genealogical criticism that Michel Foucault was to articulate over a century later in his great poststructuralist essay "Nietzsche, Genealogy, History." What came immediately to hand for this task, as the multiple overt and implicit references to the Lisbon earthquake of November 1, 1755, which killed over 20,000 people, clearly suggests, was Voltaire's *Candide* (1759), appropriately subtitled "*Or Optimism.*" In that *conte philosophique*, it will be recalled, this arch eighteenth century caviler excoriated the vast canonical body of current theological, philosophical, and creative literature that, in the wake of the carnage of the Lisbon earthquake, could be seen retrospectively as having gone to inordinate—indeed, visibly absurd—lengths to justify God's ways to man and to sustain confidence in the benignity of the Creation in the face of the catastrophic, natural and human, in history that always seemed to defy the logic of these narratives of Providence. For Voltaire this philosophy of optimism—and its self-destructive logic of excess—was epitomized by Leibnitz's philosophy of preestablished harmony, by Lord Shaftsbury's *Characteristics*, and, not least, by the certain and authoritative hyperbolic imperatives of Alexander Pope's "Essay on Man":

> Cease then, nor ORDER Imperfection name:
> Our proper bliss depends on what we blame.
> Know thy own point: This kind, this due degree
> Of blindness, weakness, Heaven bestows on thee.
> Submit.—In this, or any other sphere,
> Secure to be as blest as thou canst bear:
> Safe in the hand of one disposing Power,
> Or in the natal, or the mortal hour.
> All Nature is but Art, unknown to thee;
> All Chance, Direction, which thou canst not see;
> All Discord, harmony not understood;
> All partial evil, universal Good:
> And, spite of Pride, in erring Reason's spite,
> One truth is clear, WHATEVER IS, IS RIGHT.[13]

And Voltaire's means of flaying this Philosophy of Optimism was his invention of the parodic figure of the confidence man, Pangloss, the well-read philosophical teacher/adviser and companion of Candide, whose discourse embodies the fulfillment (and, insofar as this fulfillment betrays that which contradicts and haunts it, its demise) of the inexorable binary logic of Leibnitz's, Lord Shaftsbury's, and Pope's Malakoffian metaphysics. I am referring to the perception (seeing) of being from after or above its disseminations (*meta ta physica*) that enables Pangloss to spatialize time or, what is the same thing, to narrativize the unnarrativizable, which is to say, to rationalize or accommodate—and banalize—all manner of horrendous evil he and Candide and Cunegonde encounter in their peregrination though the world—rape, natural disaster, blood-letting, hanging, disemboweling, flaying, torture, theft—to the essentialist—and optimistic—*presupposition* (or *end*) that all is for the best in the best of all possible worlds.

To put this deadly confidence game in a way that is intended to reconstellate Melville's novel and its generic provenance into the postmodern occasion, Pangloss (and Candide), like his immediate predecessor, Don Quixote, who is also a presence in Melville's novel,[14] is possessed by what, following Edward Said's analysis of the Orientalists' representation of the Orient, I earlier called "the textual attitude," a (distanced) perspective on historical reality, *deeply inscribed and naturalized by its institutionalization,* that is determined in advance, not by what is actually encountered, but by what one's prior reading has inscribed in him or her to expect:

> It may appear strange to speak about . . . someone as holding a *textual* attitude, but a student of literature will understand the phrase more easily if he will recall the kind of view attacked by Voltaire in *Candide,* or even the attitude to reality satirized by Cervantes in *Don Quixote.* What seems unexceptionable good sense to these writers is that it is a fallacy to assume that the swarming, unpredictable, and problematic mess in which human beings live can be understood on the basis of what books—texts—say; to apply what one learns out of a book literally to reality is to risk folly or ruin. One would no more think of using *Amadis of Gaul* to understand sixteenth-century (or present-day) Spain than one would use the Bible to understand, say, the House of Commons. But clearly people have tried and do try to use texts in so simple-minded a way, for otherwise *Candide* and *Don Quixote* would not still have the appeal for readers that they do today.[15]

What Melville contributes to this Voltairean and Cervantean version of the confidence-man, I am suggesting, is the figure of the Ur-Satan of the Book of Job. His predecessors, especially Voltaire, create parodic figures whose optimistic representation of being/history they entirely reject; they are, therefore, basically negative figures, figures to whom their creators cannot attribute a positive ontological value. In disclosing Pangloss's optimist philosophy to be an utter mockery of the real world, Voltaire also in the end acknowledges the real world to be irredeemable and is thus compelled to reduce Candide to the deeply dissatisfying recourse of cultivating his own garden. Though the "real" world that Cervantes discloses by way of destructuring Don Quixote's optimistic textual attitude is far less bleak than Voltaire's, it is nevertheless one—as the frenzied effort of Western readers since its publication to accommodate Don Quixote's folly to the metaphysics of optimism the novel is systematically rejecting testifies—that, however attractive its crudity, is also irredeemable. Melville, on the other hand, like the authors of the Ur-Book of Job vis-à-vis Satan—and, not incidentally, like the postmodernists who have appropriated the analogous Greek myth of the Furies (the *Erinyes,* who become the *Eumenides*),[16] understands his Confidence-Man, not as a purely negative figure, but as one in which the negative and positive are in a dialectical relationship: his *mask* of confidence is not simply the means of seducing his American victims into the folly that is endemic to the "textual attitude" (the optimistic metaphysical perspective), but in so doing, insinuates, if it does not disclose, an alternative comportment towards being that lets the nothingness of being be. By his ironic use of the Confidence-Man to disclose the totalizing logic of metaphysical optimism to be an illusion that literally obliterates difference in the name of Identity and the confidence it bestows on the believer, Melville, in fact, calls for a radical secularism—a being-in-the-midst (*interesse*) that acknowledges the absolute contingency of temporal being and the finitude of humanity and, at the same time, the difference that makes a difference in the world.

Melville's target is not Voltaire's—Leibnitzian metaphysics; it is, rather, the deeply backgrounded tradition of American optimism that had its origins in the Puritan's exceptionalist figural/providential view of (American) history that "enabled" Mary Rowlandson's accommodations of her otherwise astonishing, anguish-filled experiences as a captive of the Indians to her belief in the wonder-workings of her Puritan God in America, and its secular fulfillment in the Transcendentalist philosophy of optimism epitomized by Ralph Waldo Emerson in "The American Scholar."[17] And he undertakes his subversion of the optimistic American national identity not by overtly criticizing it, but, by way of the ironies of the Confidence-Man, pushing its inexorably "unerring," frigid (affectless) logic to its end—its limits—at which point it self-de-structs: dis-closes alternative possibilities. In this, and, as we have seen, in so much of his writing after *Moby-Dick*, Melville is remarkably proleptic of that form of genealogy that Michel Foucault, following Nietzsche, calls the parodic, which is "directed against reality, and opposes the theme of history as reminiscence or recognition":

> The [traditional] historian offers this confused and anonymous European, who no longer knows himself or what name he should adopt, the possibility of alternate identities, more individualized and substantial than his own. But the man with historical sense [the genealogist] will see that this substitution is simply a disguise.... The new historian, the genealogist, will know what to make of this masquerade. He will not be too serious to enjoy it; on the contrary, *he will push the masquerade to its limits and prepare the great carnival of time where masks are constantly reappearing*. No longer the identification of our faint individuality with the solid identities of the past, but our "unrealization" through the excessive choice of identities—Frederick of Hohenstaufen, Caesar, Jesus, Dionysus, and possibly Zarathustra. Taking up these masks, revitalizing the buffoonery of history, we adopt an identity whose unreality surpasses that of God who started the whole charade. "Perhaps, we can discover a realm where originality is again possible as parodists of history and buffoons of God." In this, we recognize the parodic double of what the second of the *Untimely Meditations* called "monumental history": a history given to reestablishing the high points of historical development and their maintenance in a perpetual presence, given to the recovery of works, actions, and

creations through the monogram of their personal essence. But in 1874, Nietzsche accuses this history, one totally devoted to veneration, *of barring access to the actual intensities and creations of life*. The parody of his last texts serves to emphasize that "monumental history" is itself a parody. Genealogy is history in the form of a concerted carnival.[18]

In short, through the carnivalesque ironies of the Confidence-Man, Melville retrieves at least the possibility of *interest* and *questioning*—the "actual intensities and creations of life" to which metaphysical optimism, its coldbloodedness, has "barr[ed] access"—as a possibility from the secondary status, if not the oblivion, to which it has been relegated by the naturalization of the American exceptionalist masquerade and the American answerers—the confidence-men—it has spawned to serve its fundamentally misanthropic ends. Melville's Confidence-Man, ironically, is the specter—the nothingness of being—that has haunted the optimistic logic of the American enterprise from the Puritan "errand in the wilderness" to its secularization in the form of Manifest Destiny and American capitalist Progress.

II

Too often, Old Americanist commentaries on Melville's *Confidence-Man* universalized Melville's quite historically specific intentions. They tended to see his Ship of Fools as containing a cross section of *mankind* and the folly of its passengers as the folly of humanity. I want to suggest, to the contrary, that, like the *Pequod*, Melville understands the *Fidele* as the American Ship of State and the folly of it passengers as the folly of the collective American national identity. It is no accident that the mise en scène of the novel is the Mississippi River, which not only flows through the center of the American continent, but, at that time, constituted the nexus of the slavery issue and the frontier between the "civilized" East and the savage West, recently, as Melville reminds us in the chapter entitled "A soldier of fortune" (19), appropriated by the United States from the Spanish in the imperial/racist Mexican War in the name of Manifest Destiny. In other words, the historical time and geographical space in which the action of the novel occurs are intended to foreground the entire history of America or, rather, of the formation of the optimistic American national identity, from the Puritans' divinely ordained exceptionalist "errand in the wilderness," which enabled the "metaphysics of Indian hating" and the imperialist Westward expansion, to the rise of capitalism; a history, that, like Max Weber's analysis of Western modernity, points not simply to the continuity of the Puritan ethic and the predatory Spirit of Capitalism, but also to the accommodational and reductive philosophy of optimism that informs them. I mean the naturalized optimistic notion that nothing in being—in space and time—no matter how apparently contradictory, the fact of slavery or the existence of Indians, for example, can interfere with the fulfillment of America's "destined" *end*. This, in the very process of evoking a different and differential end, I take it, is what Melville is saying in his general description of the passengers on board the *Fidele* at the end of the chapter II:

> As among Chaucer's Canterbury pilgrims, or those oriental ones crossing the Red Sea towards Mecca in the festival month, there was no lack of variety. Natives of all sorts, and foreigners; men of business and men of pleasure; parlor men and backwoodsmen; farm-hunters and fame-hunters; heiress-hunters, gold-hunters, buffalo-hunters; bee-hunters, happiness-hunters, truth-hunters, and still keener hunters after all these hunters. Fine ladies in slippers, and moccasined squaws; Northern speculators and Eastern philosophers; English, Irish, German, Scotch, Danes; Santa Fé traders in striped blankets, and Broadway bucks in cravats of cloth and gold; fine-looking Kentucky boatmen, and Japanese-looking Mississippi cotton-planters; Quakers in full drab, and United States soldiers in full regimentals; slaves, black, mulatto, quadroon; modish young Spanish Creoles, and old-fashioned French Jews; Mormons and Papists; Dives and Lazarus; jesters and mourners, teetotalers and convivialists, deacons and blacklegs; hard-shell Baptists and clay-eaters; grinning negroes, and Sioux chiefs solemn as high-priests. In short, a piebald parliament, an Anacharsis Cloots congress of all kinds of the multiform pilgrim species, man.
>
> As pine, beech, birch, ash, hackmatack, hemlock, spruce, bass-wood, maple, interweave their foliage in the natural wood, so these varieties of mortals blended their varieties of visage and garb. A Tarter-like picturesqueness; a sort of pagan abandonment and assurance. Here reigned the dashing and *all-fusing spirit* of the West, whose type is the Mississippi itself, which, uniting the streams of the most distant and opposite zones, pours them along, helter-skelter, *in one cosmopolitan and confident tide*. (*C-M*, 9; my emphasis)[19]

It is impossible in this limited space to do justice to the brilliantly various ways by which the (anticonfident) Confidence-Man fleeces his victims, that is, undermines the authority of their American optimism. It will suffice to say that they take broadly two forms. In the first part of the novel (chapters 1–24), Melville articulates the function of the Confidence-Man in terms of variations on the parodic strategy, analyzed at the outset of this chapter, that informs the latter's response to the merchant's story about the "unfortunate husband" of Goneril. In these brilliantly intertwined episodes, the Confidence-Man himself inaugurates and relentlessly—and brilliantly—pursues the "con game" to its paradoxical end. In the second part of the novel, beginning with "The Metaphysics of Indian Hating" (chapters 25–44), the Confidence-Man assumes an apparently far more passive role; he becomes the listener to stories (about Colonel Moredock and China Aster) that overdetermine the theme, not of confidence, but one of its antitheses: misanthropy. As the majority of the commentaries on *The Confidence-Man*, which almost invariably treat these stories independently from the whole, bear witness, this part of the novel remains problematic. Either Melville loses control of the figure of the Confidence-Man or he wrings a twist on his parodic intent that has escaped his critics.

Before addressing this question, however, I want to offer an example of the first form of the confidence game, from the beginning of the novel, after his second avatar, the crippled negro, has ostensibly disembarked from the *Fidele*, not without leaving behind an awareness of the existence on board of a "werry nice, good ge'mman wid a weed" (among others) (*C-M*, 13) who would vouch for the cripple's authenticity. The Confidence-Man, now masquerading as this mourning "man with the weed in his hat" (he will later turn out to "be" the "unfortunate" husband of the merchant's story of Goneril in chapter 12), accosts the country merchant who had believed in the crippled negro's integrity and given him alms. His strategy, in this brilliantly articulated scene of persuasion, is exquisitely nuanced, but, like the optimistic (onto)logic underlying confidence, unerring in its end-oriented directionality. First, he introduces himself as if the merchant were an old acquaintance: "How do you do, Mr. Roberts." And then, when the merchant fails to recognize him, he genially accuses him of forgetting his countenance, a move that generates a feint guilt in the merchant, which prompts the latter to recall the crippled negro's invocation of the man with the weed as a reference: "I don't know you—really, really. But stay . . . stay—yes—seems to me, though I have not the pleasure of personally knowing you, yet I am pretty sure I have at least *heard* of you, and recently too, quite recently. A poor negro aboard here referred to you . . . for a character, I think" (*C-M*, 18). Having achieved the merchant's attention, the Confidence-Man goes on relentlessly to tighten his grip by destabilizing the former's sense of identity, the ground of confidence. He "reminds" the merchant in precise detail where and how they had met six years before, and when the latter, bewildered, fails to remember this meeting and his interlocutor's name, John Ringman, the Confidence-Man genially accuses the merchant of possessing a "faithless memory"—a further assault on the merchant's enabling sense of self-presence—and unerringly advises him to "trust in the faithfulness of mine." In what follows, the Confidence-Man, now in complete control of the relationship, gradually but inexorably talks the now de-centered merchant into trusting his, the Confidence-Man's, memory of that time. Then, by way of "recalling" an earlier calamitous personal experience "against which no integrity, no forethought, no energy, no genius, no piety, could guard," and that, therefore, had put him in desperate need of a friend "in whom [he might] confide," he persuades the merchant into believing they were once friends, indeed, "brothers" (members of a Masonic order), and finally into having confidence in him. The inevitable consequence, or end, of this insistent reminding of the merchant of his guilt—the "betrayal" of his confidence in his fellow man—which is to say, of this relentless appeal to the logic of confidence, is a decisive recentering: not simply the merchant's offering the Confidence-Man a sum of money: "At every disclosure, the hearer's commiseration increased. No sentimental pity. As the story went on, he drew from his wallet a bank note, but after a while, at some still more unhappy revelation, changed it for another, probably of a somewhat larger amount; which, when the story was concluded, with an air studiously disclamatory of alms-giving, he put into the stranger's hands; who, on his side, with an air studiously disclamatory of alms-giving, put it into his pocket" (*C-M*, 21). The Confidence-Man's confidence game also "ends" in restoring the merchant's confidence in man—and in setting him up for a future defrauding. As if it had suddenly occurred to him, he informs the merchant that "[T]he president, who is also transfer-agent, of the Black Rapids Coal Company, happen[ed] to be on board" the *Fidele* and that he had heard that the company, in order to frustrate the aim of the alarmists who had instigated a panic and had provoked "some credulous stockholders" to sell their shares, was "ready, but not anxious, to redispose of those shares; and having obtained them at their depressed value, will now sell them at par, though, prior to the panic, they were held at a handsome figure above" (*C-M*, 22).

In representing the typical antebellum American, Melville gives *ontological* priority to confidence over distrust, optimism over pessimism. The merchant's distrust in his fellow man is, from the Confidence-Man's parodic perspective, understood as a falling away from the transcendentally ordained imperative of optimism, that is, from the American *Logos*: the truth of being understood hegemonically as "the best of all possible worlds," in which, therefore, "whatever is, is right." His recentering—his gradual recuperation of trust, both in his self-identical self and in the collective self of his fellow Americans—thus constitutes a metamorphosis of a "caviler" into one who possesses the "true light," a rise from a self-imposed realm of darkness into a paradisiacal state or, rather, a "Malakoff of confidence." But this strategically provoked fulfillment of the logic of optimism brings it to its end understood as demise: the Confidence-Man's con game comes to its end in the "conning" of the merchant. In other words, in the very excessive act of repressing or concealing them, this unerring logic of optimism discloses the contingencies of finiteness that contradict, undermine, and delegitimize its truth.[20] As readers of Melville's text, we are led by the Confidence-Man's undeviating pursuit of the binary logic of American optimism to its *limits*—the logic that gives ontological priority to Identity over difference, the One over the many, Something (*Summun Ens*) over nothing, "Good" over "evil," and so on—not simply to acutely attend to the second, repressed term of the opposition. It also, if only in a symptomatic way (Melville, after all, is writing fiction, not a treatise on ontology), invites, if it does not compel us, to think its positive possibilities.

This parodic genealogical strategy not only informs the episode from the story of Goneril and the unfortunate man I invoked in introducing this chapter, but also, *mutatis mutandis*, all the episodes of the first half of *The Confidence-Man*—as well as the episode, to which I will return, that brings the novel to its ambivalent "close," the one that recounts the Confidence-Man's response to the Old Man who, contemplating the books of the Bible, has been disturbed by the contradictions of "the Apocrypha." All of them, each in their own nuanced way, bear witness, like the ones I have commented on, to the *self-de-struction* of the (onto)logic of American optimism—to its "unrealization," as it were—and, more tentatively, to the releasement of an alternative comportment to being that acknowledges its contingency, its nothingness.

III

In the second part of the novel, beginning with the chapters that relate the story of Colonel Moredock, the Indian hater, a kind of structural reversal seems to occur, as I have noted, that problematizes the consistency of Melville's portrayal of the Confidence-Man. In all the episodes of the first part, the Confidence-Man, in his eight avatars (the lamblike man, Black Guinea, the man with the weed, the man in gray (the agent of the Seminole Widow and Orphan Asylum as well as the provisional treasurer of the World's Charity), the Black Rapids Coal Agent, the herb doctor, and the man from the Philosophical Intelligence Office) unrelentingly steers the logic of the discourse on confidence to its paradoxical self-destructive "end." In these later chapters, in which the Confidence-Man assumes the mask of the philanthropic "Cosmopolitan," on the other hand, it is not simply someone other than he who provides the exemplary story or situation that becomes the point of departure for the excursus on (American) confidence—the Westerner (or Judge Hall) in the case of the story of Colonel Moredock and Egbert, Mark Winsome's practical disciple, in the case of the story of China Aster—while the hitherto loquacious Confidence-Man listens. The stories themselves overdetermine the *misanthropy*, not the confidence (in man) of antebellum Americans. The fact that virtually all the commentaries on these resonantly provocative stories have avoided not only the question of the relationship between the narrator and the story within the story he tells, but also of the structural reversal to which

I am pointing, bears witness to this problem.[21] Does this reversal break the continuity—and thus delegitimize the genealogical/parodic function I have attributed to the various avatars of the Confidence-Man in the first part? Or has Melville deliberately undertaken this reversal to extend the scope of his satire of contemporary American confidence and deepen its historical provenance? I confess to being uncertain as to whether or not Melville has resolved this apparent inconsistency. But given his proleptic postmodern or post*structuralist* insights into the reductive operations of the *Logos* informing the optimism enabled by the American exceptionalism of his time and honoring the acute subtlety of Melville's mind—a subtlety that informs every sentence of this complex, parodic text—my deepest impulse as a reader is to give him the benefit of the doubt. To be specific, I will tentatively suggest (1) that the Confidence-Man in the guise of the philanthropic Cosmopolitan is consonant with his earlier avatars, (2) that he resolves the apparent contradiction between the thematics of confidence in the first part and misanthropy of the second, and (3) that the American confidence (along with American exceptionalism) he is parodying is deeply backgrounded in American history, indeed, has its genealogical origins in the American Puritans' divinely ordained—and therefore optimistic but genocidal—"errand in the wilderness" of the "New World."

The story of Colonel John Moredock is told to the Cosmopolitan by the "bluff" Westerner, who later identifies himself as Charlie Noble. Having overheard an earlier dispute between the Cosmopolitan and the Missourian "misanthrope" and been reminded by the latter's manner of "the late Colonel John Moredock, Indian-hater of Illinois" (*C-M*, 140), he engages the Cosmopolitan in a conversation that eventuates in the latter's (strategic) request to hear the history of this "Indian-hater" as he had heard it from Judge James Hall, the well-known popular historian of Indian affairs.[22] Prior to beginning his story, the Westerner makes it clear that he or, rather, Judge Hall, whose story he will recite verbatim, views Colonel Moredock's ferocious "passion" for killing Indians in a more or less positive light, indeed, that it is grounded in a "philosophical" view of being that is vaguely, but tellingly, associated with the "free-school system," which he associates with "patriotism" (*C-M*, 142), and, later, with Protestant Christianity. The Cosmopolitan, who adopts the persona of a disciple of Rousseau (including the principle of the "noble savage"), suggests that Colonel Moredock—who, as the Westerner puts it, "hated Indians like snakes"—is, in fact, a misanthrope. When he goes on to ask in feigned astonishment, "Was there ever one who so made it his particular mission to hate Indians that, to designate him, a special word has been coined—Indian-hater?," the Missourian answers: "Even so" (*C-M*, 141), thus attesting to the validity of the Cosmopolitan's surmise, which, in emphasizing the reduction of human possibilities to this one identifying name/trait, implies that, from Melville's point of view, Moredock, as he is represented by the

Judge, is an undeviating "fundamentalist" and that his history is informed by an essentialist, that is to say, metaphysical interpretation of being: the same perspective on being—in this case, the being of American/Indian relations—that Cervantes is satirizing in his portrayal of Don Quixote, and Voltaire, in his portrayal of Pangloss. This goes far to explain the otherwise curious title of the following chapter (26), "Containing the metaphysics of Indian-hating, according to the views of one evidently not so prepossessed as Rousseau in favor of savages."

But Melville does not stop here at hinting at the violence of Colonel Moredock's (and the Westerner's) reductive metaphysics. He goes on, by way of the latter's concluding prologomenal remarks, to historicize and generalize Indian-hating, to imply, that is, that his parodic target is, in fact, the American national identity or, rather, that aspect of it, that, in the name of American exceptionalism, endowed heroic status to the Anglo-Saxon pioneer—his errand in the New World's wilderness, as it were—and justified American racism and ethnocentrism, Westward expansion, and genocide:

> Well, I would mostly skip that part [the philosophical basis of Judge Hall's narrative on which the Cosmopolitan implicitly insists in the very act of claiming he "is no rigorist"], only, to begin, some reconnoitering of the ground in a philosophical way the judge always deemed indispensable with strangers. For you must know that Indian-hating was no monopoly of Colonel Moredock's; but a passion, in one form or other . . . largely shared among the class to which he belonged. And Indian-hating still exists; and, no doubt, will continue to exist, so long as Indians do. Indian hating, then, shall be my first theme, and Colonel Moredock, the Indian-hater, my next and last. (*C-M*, 142)

In the following chapter, the Westerner reproduces Judge Hall's generalizations about the historical origins of American Indian hating and its continuing prominence even after " 'Indian rapine [had] ceased through regions where it once prevailed' " (*C-M*, 144) and then his particular history of Colonel Moredock. What characterizes this deceptively attractive discourse, which virtually all commentary on this central episode in the novel has overlooked—it is what I have been calling, after Althusser, the oversight of (metaphysical) oversight[23]—is its tellingly innocent repetition of the rhetorical dynamics of the Confidence-Man's earlier genealogical/parodic discourse: it relentlessly pursues the binary logic—specifically, the opposition that privileges the civilizing American frontiersman over the savage, deceitful, and murderous Indian—of thinking race *meta-ta-physica*, from above or after the dissemination of being, to its fulfillment (end), at which point it self-de-structs.

Hall's/the Westerner's discourse begins with an encomium to the American pioneer, one that, by way of the nation-building texts of early writers like Timothy Dwight, John Filson, John Heckewelder, James Kirk Paulding, James Quinlan, Charles Brockton Brown, James Fenimore Cooper, William Gilmore Simms, Robert Montgomery Bird; the paintings of the Hudson River Valley School (Thomas Cole, David Johnson, George Loring Brown, John Quidor, etc.); the histories of Francis Parkman and George Bancroft; the essays of Ralph Waldo Emerson, Henry David Thoreau, and Theodore Parker; and the speeches of Daniel Webster, among many others (not to say the legion of "scientists" from Charles Caldwell and Josiah Nott to Samuel George Morton [*Crania Americana*, 1839] and Louis Agassiz and the popularizers of their "research"),[24] who had inherited and internalized a secularized version of the divinely ordained Puritan and/or Anglo-Saxon "errand in the wilderness," idealizes the exceptionalist characteristics of the American, not least the self-reliance that distinguished him from the decadent European city-dweller:

> The backwoodsman is a lonely man. He is a thoughtful man. He is a man strong and unsophisticated. Impulsive, he is what some might call unprincipled. At any rate, he is self-willed; being one who less hearkens to what others may say about things, than looks for himself, to see what are things themselves. If in straits, there are few to help; he must depend upon himself; he must continually look to himself. Hence self-reliance, to the degree of standing by his own judgment, though it stand alone. . . . But not merely is the backwoodsman content to be alone, but in no few cases is anxious to be so. The sight of smoke ten miles off is provocation to one more remove from man, one step deeper into nature. . . .
>
> Though held in a sort a barbarian, the backwoodsman would seem to America what Alexander was to Asia—captain in the vanguard of conquering civilization. Whatever the nation's growing opulence or power, does it not lackey his heels? Pathfinder, provider of security to those who come after him, for himself he asks nothing but hardship. Worthy to be compared with Moses in the Exodus, or Emperor Julian in Gaul, who on foot, and barebrowed, at the head of covered or mounted legions, marched so through the elements, day after day. The tide of emigration, let it roll as it will, never overwhelms the backwoodsman into itself; he rides upon advance, as the Polynesian upon the comb of the surf. (*C-M*, 145)

This apparently celebratory passage from the prologue of Hall's/the Westerner's history of Colonel Moredock has often been read as expressing Melville's own sentiments about the America's "errand in the wilderness," the American frontiersman, and the national identity he symbolizes. But such a reading fails to attend to the passage's margins, whose ironies deconstruct its overdetermined tenor. I am not simply referring to the all too obvious allusions to the Leatherstocking figure of Cooper's novel, which, by Melville's time, had become conventional, if not banal. I am also referring to the rhetoric of imperialism that contradicts the "democracy" the backwoodsman represents, and, not least, the tendency, as in the case of the rigorous logic of the Confidence-Man in the first part, toward hyperbolic excess, that culminates in a caricature of the backwoodsman—especially noticeable in the wildly incommensurate image of the Polynesian boat that follows the speaker's identification of the backwoodsman with the prefigurative Moses.

All this signals the decidedly unheroic—self-contradictory—direction this "unerring" binarist discourse will take when, in what follows, Hall/ the Westerner introduces the native American to the backwoodsman's context:

> As the child born to a backwoodsman must in turn lead his father's life—a life which, as related to humanity, is related mainly to Indians—it is thought best not to mince matters, out of delicacy; but to tell the boy pretty plainly *what an Indian is*, and what he *must expect from him*. For however charitable it may be to view Indians as members of the Society of Friends, yet to affirm them such to one ignorant of Indians, whose lonely path lies a long way through their lands, this, in the event, might prove not only injudicious but cruel. At least something of this kind would seem the maxim upon which backwoods' education is based. Accordingly, if in youth the backwoodsman incline to knowledge, as is generally the case, he hears little from his schoolmasters, the old chroniclers of the forest, but histories of Indian lying, Indian theft, Indian double-dealing, Indian fraud and perfidy, Indian want of conscience, Indian blood-thirstiness, Indian diabolism. . . . The instinct of antipathy against an Indian grows in the backwoodsman with the sense of good and bad, right and wrong. In one breath he learns that a brother is to be loved, and an Indian to be hated. (*C-M*, 146; my emphasis)

What is remarkably telling about this genealogy is not simply the reductive violence of its rigorous essentialist logic, which, aided and abetted by the histories of "the old chroniclers of the forest"—which surely include American historians like Francis Parkman[25]—precipitates in the end an absolute racist binary opposition between the divinely guided, virtuous, and noble identity of the backwoodsman and the diabolically guided, treacherous, ruthless, and savage identity of the Indian, an opposition that justified their extermination.

It is also the unrelenting gaze of the white American historian, who *sees* and *freezes* the history of the "clearing," "settlement," and "improvement" of the "New World" according to the inexorable imperatives of this inscribed hierarchical Manichaean logic. In other words, the authorial point of view of this passage obliterates the very obvious fact that the "errand" in the New World wilderness was not only an invasion and occupation of the land inhabited by the Indians, but also one that could be characterized precisely in the popular racist rhetoric Hall/the Westerner uses to damn the Indian and justify the genocidal westward colonial project: "lying," "theft," "double-dealing," "fraud and perfidy," "want of conscience," "blood-thirstiness," "diabolism." Melville, in fact, hints at this repressed (invisible) reality by way of appending the telling clause, " 'whose lonely path lies a long way through *their* lands' " (my emphasis), to the assertion that it "might prove not only injudicious but cruel" to withhold the "truth" about Indians "to one ignorant of their brutal ways." It is a gesture that transforms the alleged Indians' savage violence against the white man, exemplified by Hall's/the Westerner's stories of Mocmohoc's treacherous extermination of "the little colony of Wrights and Weavers" and the massacre of John Moredock's mother and eight of her nine children, into acts of heroic defense of their land and of resistance against brutal aggression. The following paragraph, which at once alludes to the (hypothetical) repression of the Indian's voice and precludes or begs the question of his testimony, bears witness to the deliberateness of Melville's subtly ironic effort to instigate the reader's awareness of this ironic reversal: "The Indians, indeed, protest against the backwoodsman's view of them; and some think that one cause of their returning his antipathy so sincerely as they do, is their moral indignation at being so libeled by him, as they really believe and say. But whether, on this or any point, the Indians should be permitted to testify for themselves, to the exclusion of other testimony, is a question that may be left to the Supreme Court" (*C-M*, 146–47).

Given the relentlessness of the hierarchized binary logic informing Hall's/the Westerner's characterization of the American frontiersman, it should come as no surprise that this prelude to the story of Colonel Moredock should end in the *absolutization* of Indian-hating: a characterization of "the Indian-hater *par excellence*," in which the rhetoric, rhythm, tropes, and thematics not only bring the logic of the "diluted Indian-hater" he has been describing (*M-C*, 150) to its fulfillment, but also, in an irony that escapes the teller (and all too many of Melville's commentators), its self-destruction, as the metamorphosis of the allegedly benign backwoodsman of the beginning into a "Leatherstocking Nemesis," a "Terror," makes chillingly clear:

> The Indian-hater *par excellence* the judge defined to be one "who, having with his mother's milk drank in small love for red men,

in youth or early manhood, ere the sensibilities become osseous, receives at their hand some signal outrage, or . . . some of his kin have, or some friend. Now, nature all around him by her solitudes wooing or bidding him muse upon this matter, he accordingly does so, till the thought develops such attraction, that much as straggling vapors troop from all sides to a storm-cloud, so straggling thoughts of other outrages troop to the nucleus thought, assimilate with it, and swell it. At last, taking counsel with the elements, he comes to his resolution. An intenser Hannibal, he makes a vow, the hate of which is a vortex from whose suction scarce the remotest chip of the guilty race may reasonably feel secure. Next, he declares himself and settles his temporal affairs. With the solemnity of a Spaniard turned monk, he takes leave of his kin; or rather, these leave-takings have something of the still more impressive finality of death-bed adieus. Last, he commits himself to the forest primeval; there, so long as life shall be his, to act upon a calm, cloistered scheme of strategical, implacable, and lonesome vengeance. Ever on the noiseless trail; cool, collected, patient; less seen than felt; snuffing, smelling—a Leather-stocking Nemesis. In the settlements he will not be seen again; in eyes of companions tears may start at some chance thing that speaks of him; but they never look for him, nor call; they know he will not come. Suns and seasons fleet; the tigerlily blows and falls; babes are born and leap in their mothers' arms; the Indian-hater is good as gone to his long home, and 'Terror' is his epitaph." (*C-M*, 149–151)

This polyvalent terrorist teleology, which lies behind the benign rhetoric of official (exceptionalist) America—this necessary and undeviating will to objectify and annihilate that which contradicts, resists, or is an obstacle to, the fulfillment of a preconceived identical, totalized, and monolithic end—a "Talismanic Secret," as he puts the goal of the Western metaphysical thinking that stretches from Plato through the German idealists to the New England philosophers in *Pierre*—is what Melville means by "the metaphysics of Indian-hating." It is also, not incidentally, what he means by Captain Ahab's "monomania" in his earlier, more straightforward indictment of the self-reliant American man in *Moby-Dick*:

The White Whale swam before [Ahab]as the monomaniac incarnation of all those malicious agencies which some deep men feel eating in them, till they are left living on with half a heart and half a lung. That intangible malignity which has been from the beginning . . . Ahab did not fall down and worship it like them [the Christian and the ancient Ophites]; but deliriously transferring its idea to the abhorred white whale, he pitted himself, all mutilated, against it. All that most maddens and torments; all that stirs up the lee of things; all truth with malice in it; all that cracks the sinews and cakes the brain; all the subtle demonisms of life and thought; all evil, to crazy Ahab, were visibly personified, and made practically assailable in Moby Dick. He piled upon the whale's white hump the sum of all the general rage and hate felt by his whole race from Adam down; and then, as if his chest had been a mortar, he burst his hot heart's shell upon it.[26]

The metaphysics of Indian-hating, then, is a reductive ontology that justifies a ruthlessly murderous racial sociopolitics that masquerades as a selflessly ascetic and benign, indeed, divinely or historically ordained practice. As Hall/the Westerner puts this lunatic single-mindedness, after citing Colonel Moredock as an example of the general rule that "nearly all Indian-haters have at bottom loving hearts": "In short, he [Moredock] was not unaware that to be a consistent Indian-hater involves the renunciation of ambition, with its objects—the pomps and glories of the world; and since religion, pronouncing such things vanities, accounts it merit to renounce them, therefore, so far as this goes, Indian-hating, whatever may be thought of it in other respects, may be regarded as not wholly without the efficacy of a devout sentiment" (*C-M*, 155). It is a re-presentation of being (which includes human being) that, in perceiving the be-*ing* of being *meta-ta-physica*—from a transcendental or panoptic perspective—is blind to the *nothingness* that is ontologically prior to the reified and self-identical Being (the *Monos* or One) it constructs as "the real." To put this transcendental American mode of perception—we may now call it "Providential" as well—in terms of the will to power over its "Other" it entails, it is justified in annihilating the differences that time always already dis-seminates in the name of a plenary Identity—*and the confidence* that the peace of the latter enables, a confidence in a being that is otherwise *apparently* indifferent to American man in its erratic and all too often devastating contingent processes. Analogously, it is also a representation of human relations, in this case the American "white man" and the native "red Indian," that, in assuming the former to be the chosen guardian of Being, denies the status of being to the latter or, as in the case of the Indian-hater *par excellence*, justifies the identification of the red man as "diabolic" and thus his annihilation in the name of maintaining an optimistic perspective in a wilderness of conflict. It is this dislocating paradox, I submit, this murderous polyvalent violence latent in the benign optimistic ontology informing the unexceptional exceptionalist American national identity,[27] that is disclosed at the moment that Judge Hall/the Westerner brings his account of the unerring logic of the Indian-hater *par excellence* to its fulfillment in the chilling analogy of a cosmically sanctioned "Leatherstocking Nemesis," from whose vortex-like hate "scarce the remotest chip of the guilty race may reasonably feel secure." It is no accident, then, that Judge Hall/the Westerner ends this prelude to the story of Colonel Moredock by relying on "the diluted Indian-hater, one whose heart proves not so steely as his brain," to describe the otherwise impenetrability of the life of the Indian-hater *par excellence*: "For the diluted Indian-hater, although the vacations he permits himself impair the keeping of the character, yet, it should not be overlooked that this is the man who, by his very infirmity, enables us to form surmises, however inadequate, of what Indian-hating in its perfection is" (*C-M*, 150–151). As Roy Harvey Pearse symptomatically put this paradox of the confident logic of the American errand long ago, "Perfected, he [the Leatherstocking] is unmasked."[28]

It should not be overlooked, furthermore, that, in its escalation toward plenary totality—and the disclosure in the end of what it must repress—the itinerary of the logic of Hall's/the Westerner's discourse is more or less identical to the parodic genealogy of the avatars of the Confidence-Man of the first part of the novel. The difference, of course, is that, unlike the ironic Confidence-Man, Hall/the Westerner is blind to that delegitimating contradiction that its "perfection" discloses.

As I have noted, what is remarkable about this entire episode of *The Confidence-Man* is that, unlike the earlier ones, it is not the Confidence-Man, but his victim who, having overheard the latter's conversation with the Missouri bachelor and been reminded of Colonel Moredock, initiates and dominates the discussion as the former listens in apparent fascination. In response to the story, the Cosmopolitan immediately "challenges" its veracity on the grounds that its parts "don't hang together. If the man of hate, how could John Moredock be also the man of love? Either his lone campaigns are fabulous as Hercules'; or else, those being true, what was thrown in about his geneality is but garnish. In short, if ever there was such a man as Moredock, he, in my way of thinking, was either misanthrope or nothing" (*C-M*, 157). After the Cosmopolitan's "indictment" of Moredock as a misanthrope and, therefore, a "Pagan" (i.e., an "infidel"), Melville invokes the historical occasion of Voltaire's *Candide* and its parody of Pangloss's belief in the Christian God's creation as "the best of all possible worlds" in the following brief dialogue, initiated by the Cosmopolitan, that plays in an inordinately complex way on the opposition between belief and disbelief:

> "As for this Indian-hating in general, I can only say of it what Dr. Johnson said of the alleged Lisbon earthquake: 'Sir, I don't believe it.'"
>
> "Didn't believe it? Why not? Clashed with any little prejudice of his?"
>
> "Doctor Johnson had no prejudices; but, like a certain person," with an ingenuous smile, "he had sensibilities, and those were pained."

"Dr. Johnson was a good Christian, wasn't he?"

"He was."

"Suppose he had been something else."

"Then small incredulity as to the alleged earthquake."

"Suppose he had been also a misanthrope?"

"Then small incredulity as to the robberies and murders alleged to have been perpetrated under the pall of smoke and ashes. The infidels of the time were quick to credit those reports and worse. So true is it that, while religion, contrary to the common notion, implies, in certain cases, a spirit of slow reserve as to assent, infidelity, which claims to despise credulity, is sometimes swift to it."

"You rather jumble together misanthropy and infidelity."

"I do not jumble them; they are coördinates. For misanthropy, springing from the same root with disbelief of religion, is twin with that. It springs from the same root, I say; for, set aside materialism, and what is an atheist, but one who does not, or will not, see in the universe a ruling principle of love; and what a misanthrope, but one who does not, or will not, see in man a ruling principle of kindness? Don't you see? In either case the vice consists in a want of confidence?" (C-M, 157)[29]

In this brief exchange, the Cosmopolitan, it seems, categorically—and defensively—refuses to believe in the existence of Indian-hating on the analogy of Samuel Johnson's disbelief in the actuality of the Lisbon earthquake on the Leibnitzian ground that its truth would delegitimate his Christian theology, undermine his belief in the benignity of God, and subvert his confidence in His creation. Taken at face value, this would seem that Melville is satirizing the Confidence-Man's blind confidence, rather than invoking him as his ironic spokesman against his American interlocutor's confidence in the benign consequences vis-à-vis the nation-building of the backwoodsman's Indian-hating. It would seem, in other words, that Melville has lost control of his essential parodic means of disclosing the violence latent in the relentless forwarding logic of American optimism. But, as I have shown by way of overdetermining the word "metaphysics" in Melville's title and the unerring and totalizing logic it enables—the logic of Hall's/the Westerner's narrative that begins with an encomium to the American pioneer spirit and culminates in the murderous practice of the "Indian-hater *par excellence*"—such a conclusion would be unwarranted. For it would preclude the great force of the apparently paradoxical analogy between the self-destructive metaphysical logic of the American optimism that the Confidence-Man, like Satan of the Ur-Book of Job, teases out of his victims in the first part of the novel and the similar self-destructive metaphysical logic of American "misanthropy" in the chapters on the metaphysics of Indian-hating.

It is, I suggest, this paradoxical analogy, precipitated by the "perfected" logic of Hall's/the Westerner's disquisition on Indian-hating, that the Cosmopolitan ironically discloses without naming it at the very moment he distinguishes decisively—by which I mean excessively or hyperbolically—between the affiliation of fidelity (seeing "in the universe a ruling principle of love,") and optimism, on the one hand, and infidelity or atheism and misanthropy (the refusal or inability "to see in man a ruling principle of kindness"). The neat symmetry of the parallel terms of this distinction, that is, compels us to perceive that *misanthropy is endemic to the American philosophy of optimism* and that the *American philosophy of optimism is endemic to the misanthropy of the Indian-hater.* The chapters on the metaphysics of Indian-hating do not simply expose the terrible absurdity of optimism/confidence and the logocentric ontology that enables them, but also, and more important, the similarity between and *complicity of optimism and misanthropy.* As we have seen—and as Cervantes shows in *Don Quixote* and Voltaire in Candide—a philosophy of optimism, whether onto-logical, theo-logical or anthropo-logical, compels the believer to forcefully deny the existence of—to overlook, accommodate, or annihilate—the contradictions—the differences that temporality always already disseminates—that instigate anxiety and pain in the finite and contingent world. Or, as Melville puts this furious will to annul the nothingness of being in *Moby-Dick*, "all that most maddens and torments; all that stirs up the lee of things; all truth with malice in it; all that cracks the sinews and cakes the brain; all the subtle demonisms of life and thought; all evil, to crazy Ahab, were visibly personified, and made practically assailable in Moby Dick." Similarly, the misanthropy of the American Indian-hater, particularly the Indian hater *par excellence*, is, despite the atheist label, tacitly founded on a metaphysical perspective—an even more "invulnerable," because complex "Malakoff of confidence" than the one to which the Confidence-Man had referred earlier in the day in his exchange with the merchant—that understands the be-*ing* of being as Being, *a Summum Ens* or a Manifest Destiny. It thus enables the representation of the recalcitrant native Indian as a non-being or a spectral agent of the duplicitous *diabolos* that contradicts and threatens the truth of Being or, to put it in terms of the American exceptionalist narrative, impedes the achievement of its plenary totality, and justifies his extermination. The difference between the optimist and the misanthrope, Melville seems to be saying, is merely a matter of perspective. To the confident adherent of the American philosophy of optimism, the violence perpetrated against America's "Other" in its name seems to be benign; to the antimetaphysical observer, like Melville, this violence seems to be a manifestation of a nihilistic misanthropy concealed in the discourse of benignity. In a fundamental way, Hall's/the Westerner's story of the misanthrope, Colonel Moredock—*if* the prelude about the backwoodsman is taken into consideration in the reading of the

Cosmopolitan's response—in fact constitutes the simultaneous fulfillment and self-destruction of the "(onto)logic" of the "optimistic philosophy" that he "espouses."

This apparent paradox becomes tellingly manifest a little later in the conversation between the Westerner, now Charlie Noble, and the Cosmopolitan, when the latter picks up Noble's return to the topic of geneality (which he had earlier, in passing, attributed to Colonel Moredock and the Cosmopolitan to the misanthropic Missourian). In response to Noble's rhetorical question, "it [geniality] is much on the increase in these days, ain't it?" the Cosmopolitan, "hail[ing] the fact," adds that "Nothing better attests the advance of the humanitarian spirit. In former and less humanitarian ages—the ages of amphitheatres and gladiators—geniality was most confined to the fireside and table. But in our age—the age of joint-stock companies and free-and-easies—it is with this precious quality as with precious gold in old Peru, which Pizarro found making up the scullion's sauce-pot as the Inca's crown [another reference to *Candide*]. Yes, we golden boys, the moderns, have geniality everywhere—a bounty broadcast like noonlight" (*C-M*, 175). After thus identifying this "advance" with the rise of the American capitalist spirit, he envisions and predicts the necessary "end" of this "unerringly" progressive logic of optimism: "talking of the advance of geniality, I am not without hopes that it will eventually exert its influence even upon a subject as the misanthrope." To this, Charlie Noble, underscoring the excess and self-destructiveness of the "progressive" itinerary of this logic, responds, "A genial misanthrope! I thought I had stretched the rope pretty hard in talking of the genial hangman. A genial misanthrope is no more conceivable than a surly philanthropist" (*C-M*, 176). The Cosmopolitan's parodic reply brings this logic of optimism to its fulfillment—and demise. Agreeing with Charlie that there is a difference between a "genial misanthrope" and a "surly philanthropist," he says:

> Now, the genial misanthrope, when, in the process of eras, he shall turn up, will be the converse of this; under an affable air, he will hide a misanthropical heart. In short, the genial misanthrope will be a new kind of monster, but still no small improvement upon the original one, since, instead of making faces and throwing stones at people, like the poor old crazy man, Timon [of Athens], he will take steps, fiddle in hand, and set the tickled world a' dancing. In a word, as the progress of Christianization mellows those in manner whom it cannot mend in mind, much the same will it prove with the progress of genialization. And so, thanks to geniality, the misanthrope, reclaimed from his boorish address, will take on refinement and softness—to so genial degree, indeed, that it may possibly fall out that the misanthrope of the coming century will be almost as popular as, I am sincerely sorry to say,

some philanthropists of the present time would seem not to be, as witness my eccentric friend [the Missourian] named before." (*C-M*, 176–177)

This paradoxical itinerary of American optimism—this inexorable "progress," the end of which Melville ironically represent as an analogy with the Roman public's dancing to the tune of the genial misanthropist's fiddle as Rome burns—not only relates the American present to the American colonial past, as it is embodied in the Indian-hater; it also relates it to America's future, as it is banalized and embodied in the duplicitous entrepreneurs of an emergent American capitalism.[30] This genial duplicity—this con-game—becomes, as I will show, the central theme of the following chapters, which include the Cosmopolitan's encounters with the Yankee transcendentalist philosopher, Mark Winsome (Ralph Waldo Emerson), and his practical disciple Egbert (whom scholars identify with Henry David Thoreau, but whose instrumental rationality, is, to me, far more reminiscent of Benjamin Franklin) and the latter's story of China Aster.

IV

To understand Melville's purpose in introducing the story of China Aster after the chapters on the Indian-hater, it is necessary to attend briefly to the Cosmopolitan's "conversation" with Mark Winsome, who, like Charlie Noble vis-à-vis the story of Colonel Moredock, establishes the philosophical and moral context for its telling by his practice-oriented disciple, Egbert. This "genial" conversation is inaugurated by Winsome, a stranger with "a look of plain propriety of a Puritan sort" that made him seem to the Cosmopolitan "a kind of cross between a Yankee peddler and a Tartar priest, though it seemed as if . . . the first would not in all probability play second fiddle to the last," by way of his unsolicited warning to the Cosmopolitan that he should not "see that man [Charlie Noble] again" (*C-M*, 198). This apparently paradoxical description of Winsome, which, not incidentally, reminds us of Melville's demystification of Benjamin Franklin in *Israel Potter* by way of identifying his utilitarian practicality with necromancy,[31] inaugurates a discursive process on the question of the benignity of the Creation. Following Winsome's attribution of a "beautiful soul" to the Cosmopolitan, "one full of all love and truth, for where beauty is; there must those be," the latter replies: "Yes, with you and Schiller, I am pleased to believe that beauty is at bottom incompatible with ill, and therefore am so eccentric as to have confidence in the latent benignity of that beautiful creature, the rattle-snake, whose lithe neck and burnished maze of tawny gold, as he sleekly curls aloft in the sun, who on the prairie can behold without wonder?" Accompanied by the Cosmopolitan's seeming metamorphosis into the object of his discourse, this "sympathetic" assertion, which is articulated in a rhetoric that is unequivocably reminiscent of the (strained) optimistic arguments in favor of God's benign Providence in Puritan accounts of the trials of his chosen people (as well as in both the official Book of Job and the rationalizations of the Lisbon earthquake), evokes the following response from Winsome. It is one that, in signaling the cold-bloodedness of his calculative comportment to the manifestations of discord in being, will eventually self-destruct, that is, disclose the *care*lessness, if not misanthropy, of his "transcendental" philosophy":

> When charmed by the beauty of that viper, did it never occur to you to change personalities with him? to feel what it was to be a snake? . . . to sting, to kill at a touch; your whole beautiful body one iridescent scabbard of death? In short, did the wish never occur to you to feel yourself exempt from knowledge, and conscience, and revel for a while in the care-free, joyous life of a perfectly instinctive, unscrupulous, and irresponsible creature? (*C-M*, 190)

As in the case of the "genial misanthrope," this self-destruction of the "benign" logic of Winsome's transcendentalism, this disclosure of the necessarily dehumanizing imperatives—of the latent inhumanity—of his optimistic philosophy and its "doctrine of labels" (the naming, reification, and domestication of the phenomena of being [*C-M*, 193]), manifests itself when this logic, prompted by the Cosmopolitan, comes to its "fulfillment." Recalling Winsome's earlier encomium to "the joyous life of a perfectly instinctive, unscrupulous, and irresponsible creature," the ironic Cosmopolitan, reinvokes the doctrine of "the best of all possible worlds," and feigns anxiety over the former's rejection of the law of accountability that is assumed to inhere in a self-identical metaphysical universe "suited to breed a proper confidence":

> Now, sir, though, out of a tolerant spirit, as I hope, I try my best never to be frightened at any speculation, so long as it is pursued in honesty, yet, for once, I must acknowledge that you do really, in the point cited, cause me uneasiness; because a proper view of the universe, that view which is suited to breed a proper confidence, teaches, if I err not, that since all things are justly presided over, not very many living agents but must be some way accountable. (*C-M*, 191)

Winsome's response brings the logic of the Cosmopolitan's "optimism" to its chilling "fulfillment": " 'Is a rattle-snake accountable?' asked the stranger with such a preternaturally cold, gemmy glance out of his pellucid blue eye, that he seemed more a metaphysical merman than a feeling man; 'is a rattle-snake accountable?' " The Cosmopolitan underscores this paradoxical "end" when he pushes Winsome's accommodational (teleo)logic vis-à-vis the unaccountability of the rattlesnake to include man: " 'But if now,' " he continues, " 'you consider what capacity for mischief there is in a rattle-snake . . . could you well avoid admitting that that would be no symmetrical view of the universe which should maintain that, while to man it is forbidden to kill, without judicial cause, his fellow, yet the rattle-snake has an implied permit of unaccountability to murder any creature it takes capricious umbrage at—man included' "? (*C-M*, 192). In the undeviating process of this ironic dialogue, Mark Winsome, the transcendental optimist, metamorphoses into the "unaccountable" rattlesnake that the Cosmopolitan had hitherto invoked and embodied. Or, to put this transformation in the terms of its original provenance—the chapters on the metaphysics of Indian-hating—the congenial optimist becomes the philosophical manifestation of the bloodless "congenial misanthrope."

A great deal more could be said about Melville's parodic portrayal of Mark Winsome as the latter pertains to Emerson and his "optimistic" transcendentalism: his satire of the latter's "doctrine of labels" (*C-M*, 193); his implication that the inconsistency Winsome prizes in fact involves the accommodation of the errancy of difference to the stability of Identity (both when the latter identifies himself with the open-mindedness of the Athenian [*C-M*, 192] and when he invokes the lock system of the Erie Canal [*C-M*, 193]); his pointing to the contradiction between Winsome's appeal to lucidity and his mystifying obfuscations (*C-M*, 193); and, not least, his representation of Winsome's refusal of alms to the "crazy beggar" peddling a "rhapsodic tract" written "in the transcendental vein" in terms of a "Yankee cuteness," which, "now replacing his former mystical one, lent added icicles to his aspect" (*C-M*, 195). But enough has been said about Winsome's misanthropic philosophy of optimism to establish the ironic context of Melville's introduction of Egbert, Winsome's practical disciple, "a thriving merchant, a practical poet in the West India [slave?] trade" (*C-M*, 199), and " 'the first among mankind to reduce to practice the principles of Mark Winsome—principles previously accounted as less adapted to life than the closet.' " (*C-M*, 197)—and the story of China Aster he tells the Cosmopolitan to mirror Winsome's transcendentalist "system" (*C-M*, 198).

Melville, in fact, signals the direction this practical application of Winsome's metaphysics will take prior to the establishment of the rules of the hypothetical dialogic game the Cosmopolitan (Frank) and Egbert (Charlie) are about to play by providing the reader with the first impression the latter's clothes and demeanor make on the former: "But, upon the whole, he was, to all appearances, the last person in the world that one would take for the disciple of any transcendental philosophy; though, indeed, something about his sharp nose and shaved chin seemed to hint that if mysticism, as a lesson, ever came in his way, he might, with the characteristic knack of a true New Englander, turn even so profitless a thing to some profitable account" (*C-M*, 200). What I want to suggest provisionally is that Melville intends this first impression and the following "dialogue" on friendship, which, significantly, the Cosmopolitan initiates and Socratically *steers*, to retrieve that history of New England, so brilliantly represented by Max Weber, that bore witness to the secularization of Puritan theology, specifically that inscrutable Calvinist Providential history that predetermined the elect and the preterite (the passed over) and, in the process, privileged the "work ethic" that, in "rationalizing the earth," eventually—in the period in which Emerson and Melville flourished—became the "spirit of capitalism." I mean that materialist "optimism" of the elect—that ruthless faith in economic, cultural, technological, and political "progress"—which not only enabled them to blame their penurious victims (as Winsome blames the victims of the unaccountable rattlesnake and as Egbert will blame China Aster), but also to feel no qualms in doing so. This is the secularized Puritan "calling," that, as I have shown in chapter 4, in subjecting the subject, reduces thinking—in this case, about friendship—to calculation, an ascetic thinking that, in beginning from the end, undeviatingly takes into account in it accounting only those material aspects of being that will in the end confirm that beginning, which is to say, an instrumentalist thinking that denies being to—relegates to preterition—whatever contradicts its "vision."[32]

Melville's ironic representation of this complicity between the optimistic "spirit" of capitalism and the cold blooded indifference to the pain of even a friend—*and the ease with which it can be employed by the con man*—begins when the Cosmopolitan, as "Frank," informs his hypothetical friend Egbert, as "Charlie," of his urgent need for a loan and is turned down on the eminently rational, but self-righteously hypocritical, ground that loaning a friend money, unlike a business transaction, not only "degrades" the *lofty* friendship (brings its purity *down* into the corrupt world), but also breeds enmity: "I give away money, but never loan it; and of course the man who calls himself my friend is *above* receiving alms. The negotiation of a loan is a business transaction. And I will transact no business with a friend. What a friend is, he is socially and intellectually; and I rate social and intellectual friendship *too high* to *degrade* it on either side into a pecuniary make-shift.... In brief, a true friend has nothing to do with loans; he should have a *soul above* loans. Loans are such unfriendly accommodations as are to be had from the soulless corporation of a bank, by giving the regular security and paying the regular discount" (*C-M*, 202–203; my emphasis). This encomium to a *transcendent* friendship is, in fact, a "Yankee" celebration of economic man and an "optimistic" laissez-faire capitalist system, a system the genial "benignity" of which is dependent on the pitiless (misanthropic) suppression of any emotion that would thwart its profit-making end. And it culminates (or self-destructs) at the end of a predictable dialogic process in which the Cosmopolitan has not only incrementally "enabled" his hypothetical friend to name the damaging truth his—and his ventriloquizing master's[33]—hypocrisy hides, but also to glorify in the very act of denying it. To "Frank's" "expression" of horror at hearing "Charlie's" admission, prompted by the "realism"—the "plain-dealing"—his philosophy demands, that the origins of his friendship with him was motivated by a calculative assumption of his friend's initial affluence—"Oh, that I should listen to this cold-blooded disclosure!"—"Charlie," underscoring the earlier identification of Winsome with the "unaccountable" rattlesnake, responds: "A little cold blood in your ardent veins, my dear Frank, wouldn't do you no harm . . . Cold-blooded? You say that, because my disclosure seems to involve a vile prudence on my side. But not so. My reason for choosing you in part for the points I have mentioned, was solely with a view of preserving inviolate the delicacy of the connection" (*C-M*, 205–206). Friendship is thus relegated to a transcendental sphere, while in *this* world human relations become a matter of economic profit and loss: quantity, calculation, and competition.

It is when "Frank" "pleads" with "Charlie" to "speak as you used to" and chidingly tells him that, were the "case reversed, not less freely would I loan you the money than you would ask me to loan it," that "Charlie" invokes the terrible fate of China Aster as a cautionary tale that would warn him against accepting such a loan, "though without asking pressed upon me" (*C-M*, 207). Emerging from this context—one that, to reiterate, has been instigated by the Cosmopolitan—the story of China Aster Egbert goes on to recount, is, in effect, an allegory ostensibly on friendship, but actually, as in the case of the preludial dialogue, about human relations ("friendship") as these are prescribed by the metaphysics (the spirit) of capitalism. More specifically, Egbert's recounting of the inexorable and systematic progress of China Aster's ruin and death is intended as a warning to those, who, like the unfortunate protagonist, put their faith in their fellow men's care (their generosity and sense of justice) and thus threaten to derail the "invisible hand" (Adam Smith)—the "naturally benign" operations of the callously forwarding economic laws—of capital. As in the case of Judge Hall's/the Westerner's story of Colonel Moredock, Melville's intent is to parody Egbert's exemplary allegory by way of allowing its logic to self-destruct, to bear witness, that is, not only to the complicity of Mark Winsome's transcendentalism with the capitalist practice that his overdetermination of the "lofty" ideal of friendship conceals (deflects attention from), but also its illegitimacy.

In keeping with the literary historical provenance of *The Confidence-Man* I have suggested, Melville accomplishes this parodic genealogy, in part, by way of insinuating a reversed version of the archival Book of Job, which not only recalls the theological controversy instigated by the Lisbon earthquake, but also its function as *figura* of the Puritan occasion (including its notion of the calling), into Egbert's narrative about the capitalist worldview. In the received—theo-logical—version, Job's afflictions (as well as the Massachusetts Bay Puritans') are visited on him to test his loyalty to his Lord and his confidence in the goodness of his Creation. And when, following the execution of these devastating social, familial, bodily, and psychic afflictions, the battered Job, defending his righteousness, begins first to question God's Word and the benignity of his Creation and then to accuse him of arbitrary cruelty, he is reprimanded by his (confident) "comforters," Eliphaz, Bildad, Zopha, and, far more decisively, by Elihu, for his distrust and blasphemously hubristic desire to "know the balancing of the clouds/the wondrous works of him who is perfect in knowledge...."[34] In the end, God answered Job out of the whirlwind:

> "Who is this that darkens counsel
>   by words without knowledge?
> Gird up your loins like a man,
>   I will question you, and you shall
>   declare to me.
>
> "Where were you when I laid the
>   foundation of the earth?
> Tell me, if you have
>   understanding.
> Who determined its measurements
>   —surely you know!
>   Or who stretched the line upon it?
> On what were its bases sunk,
>   Or who laid the cornerstone,
> when the morning stars sang
>   together,
> and all the sons of God shouted for joy? . . ." (Job, 38, 1–7)

And Job repents:

> Then Job answered the Lord:
>   "I know that thou canst do all things
>   and that no purpose of thine can
>   be thwarted.
> 'Who is this that hides counsel
>   without knowledge?'
> Therefore, I have uttered what I did
>   not understand,
>   things too wonderful for me, which
>   I did not know.

>   'Hear, and I will speak;
>   I will question you, and you
>   declare to me.'
>   I had heard of thee by the hearing of
>   the ear,
>   but now my eye sees thee;
>   therefore I despise myself,
>   and repent in dust and ashes." (Job, 42, 1–6)

After Job has recuperated his confidence in the benignity of the Creation, God rewards him by "restor[ing] the fortunes of Job.". . . and giving him "twice as much as he had before."

In this official version of Job, the rebellious protagonist eventually attends to the rationalizations of evil by his comforters, just as Mary Rowlandson does to the rationalizations of the Puritan fathers (the "Per Amicus"—possibly Increase Mather—who writes the damage-controlling preface of her memoir), and Candide to the rationalizations of Pangloss. In the version of the Job story Melville adopts in *The Confidence-Man*, China Aster's afflictions are visited on him by a contingent universe, which, however, is represented by Egbert as the ruthless but ultimately benign deterministic laws of capital, the Word of economic Man. This secularized deity, who promises a plenary end in the fullness of time, is, ironically, embodied by China Aster's friend, Orchis, a former shoemaker who, having been "raised from a bench to a sofa" by a "capital prize in a lottery" (*C-M*, 208), nevertheless, takes this accident to be a manifestation of universal law, and, in the name of their friendship and his "bright view of life" (*C-M*, 211) attempts to persuade China Aster to accept a loan to upgrade his unprofitable candle-making business to a more profitable one using spermaceti. Despite his penury and Orchis's insistence that he will never demand payment, China Aster at first resists his friend's offer and the plenary future he promises, a resistance supported by the advice of "two elderly friends," Old Plain Talk and Old Prudence. But Orchis, in a diatribe that invokes the Comforters of the Book of Job, though here they function, not as agents of optimism, but of the interrogative mood—we might say, as "cavilers"—contemptuously and glibly diminishes their advice:

> "Save me from friends, if those old croakers were Old Honesty's [China Aster's father] friends. . . . Why did they let him go in his old age on the town? Why, China Aster, I've often heard from my mother, the chronicler, that those two old fellows, with Old Conscience—as the boys called the crabbed old quaker, that's dead now—they three used to go to the poor house when your father was there, and get round his bed, and talk to him for all the world as Eliphaz, Bildad, and Zophar did to poor old pauper Job. Yes,

Job's comforters were Old Plain Talk, and Old Prudence, and Old Conscience, to your poor father. Friends? I should like to know who you call foes? With their everlasting croaking and reproaching they tormented poor Old Honesty, your father, to death."

At these words, recalling the sad end of his worthy parent, China Aster could not restrain some tears. Upon which Orchis said: "Why, China Aster, you are the dolefulest creature. Why don't you . . . take a bright view of life? . . . It's the ruination of a man to take the dismal one." Then gayly poking at him with his gold-headed cane, "Why don't you then? Why don't you be bright and hopeful, like me? Why don't you have confidence, China Aster?" (*C-M*, 210–211)

Despite his consciousness of the accidental origins of Orchis's wealth and the transformation of his earlier dark view of being to a bright one, and his "Comforter's" arguments, China Aster, abetted by a dream in which an angel named Bright Future comes to him holding a cornucopia in her hand and "pouring down showers of small gold dollars" (*C-M*, 212), eventually succumbs to the seduction of Orchis's glib "optimism," using the loan to buy spermaceti. This "fall" into confidence, coupled with China Aster's careful "honesty" (i.e., innocence and naïveté), which "was no advantage to him" (*C-M*, 215) in a world that (analogous to the distinction between "Chronometricals and Horologicals" in *Pierre*) turns according to the dictates of the callous profit motive of capital, inaugurates a rapid succession of increasingly devastating events: the failure of the spermaceti initiative and the consequent borrowing of more money from a usurer; the return of a much-changed Orchis, who, now married, in poor health, and a member of the sect of "Come-Outers" (an ironic reference to the Transcendentalist's appeal to the inner self)[35] and in financial straits himself (*C-M*, 216), calls in the loan with interest to China Aster; and the consequent loss of the property bequeathed to his wife by an uncle and of his candle-making business. These catastrophic events culminate in the destitution, sickness, and finally death of China Aster. In a devastating irony that, unbeknownst to the "genial" narrator, mockingly betrays his blind, complacent, and facile, assumption that the capitalist world is a benign world, indeed, "the best of all possible worlds"—and, not least, inadvertently recalls God's reassuring restoration of his "servant's" health and wealth in the received Book of Job—Egbert says:

> It is needless to tell of the executions that followed; how that the candlery was sold by the mortgagee; how Orchis never got a penny for his loan; and how, in the case of [China Aster's] poor widow, chastisement was tempered with mercy; for, though she was left penniless, she was not left childless. Yet, unmindful of the

alleviation, a spirit of complaint, at what she impatiently called the bitterness of her lot and the hardness of the world, so preyed upon her, as ere long to hurry her from the obscurity of indigence to the deeper shades of the tomb.

But though the straits in which China Aster had left his family had, besides apparently dimming the world's regard, likewise seemed to dim its sense of the probity of its deceased head, and through this, as some thought, did not speak well for the world, yet it happened in this case . . . that, though the world may for a time seem insensible to the merit which lies under a cloud, yet, sooner or later, it always renders honor where honor is due; for, upon the death of the widow, the freemen of Marietta, as a tribute of respect for China Aster, and an expression of their conviction of his high moral worth, passed a resolution, that, until they attained maturity, his children should be considered the town's guests. No mere verbal compliment, like those of some public bodies; for, on the same day, the orphans were officially installed in the hospitable edifice where their worthy grandfather . . . had breathed his last breath. (*C-M*, 218)

Egbert's (Charlie's) narration of the benighted life of China Aster to the Cosmopolitan (Frank) ends by quoting the epitaph, written by himself but shortened by Plain Talk and Old Prudence, inscribed on his tomb stone: "HERE LIE / THE REMAINS OF / CHINA ASTER THE CANDLE-MAKER, / WHOSE CAREER / WAS AN EXAMPLE OF THE TRUTH OF SCRIPTURE, AS FOUND / IN THE / SOBER PHILOSOPHY / OF / SOLOMON THE WISE; / FOR HE WAS RUINED BY ALLOWING HIMSELF TO BE PERSUADED, / AGAINST HIS BETTER SENSE, / INTO THE FREE INDULGENCE OF CONFIDENCE, / AND / AN ARDENTLY BRIGHT VIEW OF LIFE, / TO THE EXCLUSION / OF / THAT COUNSEL WHICH COMES BY HEEDING / THE / OPPOSITE VIEW." On the surface, this epitaph—especially the postscript that Old Prudence and Plain Talk add, "The root of all was a friendly loan"—epitomizes the warning against too much faith (confidence) in the natural goodness of man. But if, as I have been suggesting, we take into account, as Egbert does not, the fact that, in the end, it is Plain Talk and Old Prudence—China Aster's "caviling" Comforters—who "procure a plain stone" for his memorial and inscribe the edited note they find in China Aster's wallet, a radically different meaning emerges. The confidence to which Egbert is referring is a misplaced confidence: the ruin of China Aster was the result of putting too much faith in friendship (the finite care of the human heart), rather than in the "benign" mechanical operations of the capitalist system. For Plain Talk and Old Prudence (and Melville), on the other hand, the confidence that ruined China Aster was his allowing himself, against his better judgment, to be tempted by the capitalist optimist (Orchis) into "the free indulgence" of precisely the confidence in the dehumanizing operations of the economic market place. This "bright view of life" was the antebellum American version of the "best of all possible worlds," which is to say, the deeply backgrounded "promise" of the emergent American capitalist confidence game.

This fulfillment and self-de-struction of the metaphysical or panoptic logic underlying Egbert's cautionary tale is underscored by the carnivalesque "dialogue" that the Cosmopolitan resumes after Egbert brings his story to its aporetic end in the chapter aptly entitled "Ending with a rupture of the hypothesis." In his parodic response to it, the Cosmopolitan, feigning being offended by its heartlessness, adopts the particular mask of Orchis's "bright view of things" in the telling context of a Franklinian avatar of the "Panglossian" interpretation of being: "A story I can no way approve; for its moral, if accepted, would drain me of all reliance upon my last stay, and, therefore, of my last courage in life. *For, what was that bright view of China Aster but a cheerful trust that, if he but kept up a brave heart, worked hard, and ever hoped for the best, all at last would be well?* If your purpose, Charlie, in telling me this story, was to pain me, and keenly, you have succeeded; but, if it was to destroy my confidence, I praise God you have not." To this, Egbert replies, "Confidence? ... what has confidence to do with the matter? The moral of the story, which I am for commending to you, is this: folly, on both sides, of a friend's helping a friend. For was not that loan of Orchis to China Aster the first step towards their estrangement? And did it not bring about what in effect was the enmity of Orchis? I tell you, Frank, true friendship, like other precious things, is not rashly to be meddled with. And what more meddlesome between friends than a loan? *A regular marplot*" (*C-M*, 221; my emphasis). Always the *Symbolos*, the accommodator of contradictions, even the very ontological principle of inconsistency itself (*C-M*, 222), to his practical version of Winsome's plenary system—in this extremist hermeneutics he recalls "the lunatic single-mindedness" of Don Quixote's invocation of the enchanter as the interpretive principle of last resort[36]—Egbert betrays his adherence to the *meta-physics* of a worldly *laissez-faire* capitalism that understands "self-reliance" as self-interest. In, that is, the very process of apotheosizing "true friendship" against the de-grading and corrupting force of "worldliness," its "mutability" (*C-M*, 222), he discloses his paradoxical commitment to the plenary and self-identical "optimistic" *meta*narrative of the competitive worldly market, a commitment that, indeed, perceives the "meddlesomeness" of "true friendship" (care, in the, Heideggerian sense) to be, like the *diabolos*, a "regular marplot."[37]

As in the case of the Indian-hater, then, Melville, through the ironic mask of the Confidence-Man, discloses the Emersonian optimist to be a "genial misanthrope," who appeals to the deeply inscribed confidence of the American—a frame of mind enabled by the assumption that a principle of presence, in this avatar, the law of supply and demand, informs the differential dynamics of time—in order to ventriloquize him or her. More precisely, he discloses this Emersonian optimist to be a confidence-man, one who appeals to a sedimented American confidence in which belief is ontologically prior to (not the opposite of) disbelief, certainty to uncertainty, complacency to anxiety, trust to distrust, in order to blind his victim to the anxiety-provoking and the painful but enabling contingencies of being or, as Foucault puts it, to "bar access to the actual intensities and creations of life."

V

I have chosen to overdetermine the Westerner's story about Colonel Moredock, the Indian-hater, and Egbert's story about China Aster, the preterited, because, it seems to me, Melville is attempting, at least symptomatically, to establish a thematic and historical relationship between these apparently incompatible symbolic tales about the antebellum American national identity: between, that is, the "*metaphysics*" of American Indian-hating and the *metaphysics* of American capitalism, two indissolubly related plenary problematics that have been perennially justified in the name of optimism (and progress), but whose practice has demanded the preterition and/or annihilation of its "Other," the Indian, on the one hand, and the dispossessed, on the other. This, I think, is why Melville brings his errant novel to its disquieting or exhilarating (non)end (depending on one's point of view) with a brilliant and resonant parody of the Providential exegetical method that, as we have seen throughout this book, produced the "optimistic/exceptionalist" American national identity that Melville is satirizing and justified its violent "genial misanthropy." I am referring, of course, to the unexceptional figural or typological interpretive method the Puritans appropriated from the church fathers of the European Catholic tradition in behalf of their "Exodus" from the "Old World" and their "errand in the wilderness" of the "New World."

    I cannot undertake an extended elaboration of this inaugural and tremendously consequential exegetical method, one, as I have shown at length in *The Errant Art of* Moby Dick, the fanciful but restrictive extremism of which Melville also interrogates in the chapters of *Moby-Dick* devoted to Father Mapple's sermon on the Jonah text,[38] in this limited space. As I have noted, Sacvan Bercovitch has brilliantly analyzed this Puritan hermeneutics in *The Puritan Origins of the American Self* and *The American Jeremiad*, but he fails to indicate that its provenance resides in the prefigurative exegetical system of the Patristic fathers, that the Puritans appropriated its essentials to their historical, nation-building occasion. In overlooking this fundamental *continuity* between the ontologies of the New and the Old Worlds, he fails to see and register this crucial *unexceptional* aspect of American exceptionalism in his otherwise enabling commentaries on the making of the American national identity. For this reason (and for the sake of economy), I will cite Eric Auerbach's lucid definition of figural interpretation in behalf of demonstrating its importance in *The Confidence-Man*.

> Figural interpretation establishes a connection between two events or persons [say, the sacrifice of Isaac in the Old Testament and the sacrifice of Christ in the New Testament, or the Exodus of the Jews from Egypt and the Exodus of the Puritans from Europe], the first of which signifies not only itself but also the second, while the second encompasses or fulfills the first. The two poles of the figure are separate in time, but both, being real events or figures, are within time, within the stream of historical life. Only the understanding of the two persons or events is a spiritual act, but this spiritual act deals with the concrete events, whether past, present, or future, and not with concepts or abstractions [as in the allegorical mode of the Philonian tradition]; these are quite secondary, since promise and fulfillment are real historical events, which have either happened in the incarnation of the Word, or will happen in the second coming. . . . Since in figural interpretation, one thing stands for another, since one thing represents and signifies the other, figural interpretation is "allegorical" in the widest sense. But it differs from most of the allegorical forms known to us by the historicity both of the sign and what it signifies.[39]

In other words, Puritan figural interpretation was grounded in a metaphysical or pro-vidential or theo-logical view of temporality that, though it acknowledged the temporal/finite world in a way that its allegorical allotrope did not, nevertheless privileged the Eternal over the disseminations of history, Identity over difference, the One over the many, the Whole over the parts. This immutable ground, in turn, enabled them to interpret their historical emigration to America—from the "Old" to the "New World"—as a divinely ordained narrative—an "errand in the wilderness"—that fulfilled the promise of an earlier prefiguration, the Exodus of the Israelites from Egypt into the Promised Land. Reading it against its grain, this Puritan exegetical orientation was one that, not unlike Don Quixote's and Dr. Pangloss's, coerced the differential phenomena of reality, no matter how absurdly remote the connection, into its preconceived end. Not least, this ground enabled the Puritan exegetes and their secular descendants to represent the Native Americans as the diabolic "other" of their chosen Being, and thus to justify their extermination. To use the language common to

Voltaire and Melville, it was paradoxically a philosophy of Optimism that, like that of Leibniz, or Shaftsbury, or Pope, in a later period of ontological crisis in Europe, made it easy for the faithful to overlook or repress or disfigure or annul any thing or event or "truth" that threatened to subvert their confidence (and authority).

In this last chapter of *The Confidence-Man*, the Cosmopolitan confronts an old gentleman late at night in the cramped and dimly lighted sleeping quarters of the steamboat who is reading the Bible. He has come to these quarters (they are described by Melville to suggest a symbolic microcosm of the universe) to examine this authoritative text, following his encounter with the *Fidele*'s recalcitrant barber, who had invoked "the son of Sirach in the True Book" (otherwise known as "Ecclesiasticus or the Wisdom of Jesus the Son of Sirach") from the Apocrypha in an unsuccessful effort to outwit his wily interlocutor into paying for his shave (*C-M*, 236). The serene old gentleman, according to the narrator, is "one of those who, at three-score-and-ten, are fresh-hearted as fifteen; to whom seclusion gives a boon more blessed than knowledge, and at last sends them to heaven untainted by the world, because ignorant of it; just as a countryman putting up at a London inn, and never stirring out of it as a sight-seer, will leave London at last without once being lost in its fog, or soiled by its mud" (*C-M*, 241). If, that is, we recall the Confidence-Man's advice near the beginning of the novel to the man who had been disturbed by the story of the "unfortunate man" and Goneril, we might say that the old gentleman was ensconced in his "Malakoff of confidence." Like the Satan figure of the Ur-Book of Job vis-à-vis the complacent Job (he introduces himself to the old gentleman as one who has "moved much about the world, and still keep at it," *C-M*, 250), the Cosmopolitan masquerades as a "dispens[e]r [like Christ] of a sort of morning light through the night" and as the bearer of "good news" (*C-M*, 241), that is, Gospel, but is, in fact, the "caviler" or "marplot," whose excessive "latitude of philosophizing" tempts those "unblessed with the true light" out of their impregnable fortress to "hazardous skirmishes on the open ground of reason." As such, he provokes this complacent old gentleman (who turns out to be a miser, as well) into bewildered anxiety by pointing out what appears to be a scandalous contradiction within the *Logos* of the biblical text: "I love man. I have confidence in man. But what was told me not a half-hour since? I was told that I would find it written—'Believe not this many words—an enemy speaketh sweetly with his lips'—and also I was told that I would find a good deal more to the same effect, and all in this book. I could not think it; and, coming here to look for myself, what do I read? Not only just what was quoted, but also, as was engaged, more to the purpose, such as this: 'With much communication he will tempt thee; he will smile upon thee; and speak thee fair, and say What wantest thou? If thou be for his profit he will use thee; he will make thee bare, and will not be sorry for it. Observe and take good heed. When thou hearest these things, awake in thy sleep' " (*C-M*, 242; *Ecclesiasticus* 13). With this reminder of the Cosmopolitan's dislocating conversations on friendship with Egbert and the barber, the following dialogue, constantly disrupted by a resonant antichoric voice from one of the berths in the cabin of this Ship of Fools, ensues:

"Ah!" cried the old man, brightening up, "now I know. Look," turning the leaves forward and back, till all the Old Testament lay flat on one side, and all the New Testament flat on the other, while in his fingers he supported vertically the portion between, "look, sir, all this to the right is certain truth, and all this to the left is certain truth, but all I hold in my hand here is apocrypha."

"Apocrypha?"

"Yes; and there's the word in black and white," pointing to it. "And what says the word? It says as much as 'not warranted;' for what do college men say of anything of that sort? They say it is apocryphal. The word itself, I've heard from the pulpit, implies something of uncertain credit. So if your disturbance be raised from aught in this apocrypha," again taking up the pages, "in that case, think no more of it, for it's apocrypha."

"What's that about Apocalypse?" here, a third time, came from the berth.

"He's seeing visions now, ain't he?" said the cosmopolitan, once more looking in the direction of the interruption. "But, sir," resuming, "I cannot tell you how thankful I am for your reminding me about the apocrypha here. For the moment, its being such escaped me. Fact is, when all is bound up together, it's sometimes confusing. The uncanonical part should be bound distinct. *And, now that I think of it, how well did those learned doctors who rejected for us this whole book of Sirach. I never read anything so calculated to destroy man's confidence in man.* This Son of Sirach even says—I saw it but just now: 'Take heed of thy friends;' not, observe, thy seeming friends, thy hypocritical friends, thy false friends, but thy *friends*, thy real friends—that is to say, not the truest friend in the world is to be implicitly trusted. Can Rochefoucault equal that? I should not wonder if his view of human nature, like Machiavelli's, was taken from this Son of Sirach. And to call it wisdom—Wisdom of the Son of Sirach! Wisdom, indeed! *What an ugly thing wisdom must be! Give me the folly that dimples the cheek, say I, rather than the wisdom that curdles the blood.; But no, no, it ain't wisdom, it's apocrypha, as you say, sir. For how can that be trustworthy that teaches distrust?*" (*C-M*, 243; my emphasis)

Melville situates his brilliant parody of the biblical canon at the "site" of friendship, which, as I have shown by pushing the rarified logic of Mark Winsome's transcendentalist metaphysics to its self-destructive end in the practice of his disciple Egbert, is disclosed to be a cold-blooded calculative capitalism that de-differentiates and dehumanizes its agents and victims. But this genealogical "unrealization" of the truths of the American national identity is not restricted to this site; it occurs across the continuum of represented being. The parodic or "carnivalesque" thrust of this neglected passage—not least the ludicrous excess of the Cosmopolitan's last remarks—not only discloses the folly of the "Wisdom" of confidence in man's moral relation to man, but also, and more important, of the "sage" ontology and epistemology and even of the secular cultural tradition and sociopolitical institutions that are indissolubly affiliated with this optimistic—Adamic—American morality. The Cosmopolitan's alleged morality of confidence in Man, that is, is informed by an original confidence in the presiding *Logos*—the seminal, patriarchal Word—of metaphysics and an unerring epistemology, a truth discourse, the hermeneutic imperative of which is to "read" (re-present) actual existence—its disseminations—*sub specie aeternitatis*. In other words, it relies for the "certain truth," not on the originative temporal "things themselves," but on a derivative or mediating and regulating common text simultaneously in and above time—what Derrida calls a "Transcendental Signified" or, alternatively, "a center elsewhere," which is "beyond the reach of free-play," that is, of criticism.[40] To read the temporal being of being from a Providential perspective, as the Cosmopolitan "urges" the old gentleman to do, is necessarily—unerringly—to overlook and/or repress the uncanny or anxiety-provoking decentered measure of being-in-the-midst (*interesse*)—the dislocating differences precipitated by time—the contradictions, the *aporias*, the discontinuities, the accidents, the singularity, the differential play, that, as he says, "curdles the blood," that would "destroy man's confidence in man": "So if your disturbances be raised from aught in the apocrypha . . . in that case, think no more of it, for it's apocrypha."

Equally, if not more important, the Cosmopolitan's "confidence" in the patriarchally prescribed Book (or Archive), which was modeled on this speculative epistemology, justifies the coercive and reductive projects of the "learned doctors" to legitimate and reproduce the exceptionalist and optimistic American tradition, to canonize the texts that conform to and confirm the authority of the abiding Adamic center and to reject as "uncanonical part," "apocryphal," "not warranted," "of uncertain credit," those that do not: not least those decentering "caviling" texts, like Melville's, that acknowledge the radical finiteness and contingency of being, the singular difference that makes a difference in the world. Given his acute awareness of the fate of the novels that immediately precede *The Confidence-Man*, it is more than likely that Melville is referring in this culminating passage not only to the seminal, recollective, figural strategies of the Puritan biblical exegetes, from John Winthrop through Increase Mather, Cotton Mather, and Samuel Danforth to Jonathan Edwards. More immediately, he is also referring to those contemporary "learned doctors" who secularized the Puritan faith in Providence and presided over the American literary and cultural scene, those academic critics ("college men") who, in the name of the Emersonian testament of confidence (one of the central targets of this "satanic" or "diabolic" anti-Book, as we have seen), condemned *Moby-Dick* and especially *Pierre* as ec-centric and doubt-instigating—blood-curdling—deviations from the American Adamic tradition and excluded them, as the Cosmopolitan and his old gentleman interlocutor exclude "Ecclesiasticus" from the Bible, from the canon of American literary history. Surely, too, Melville is proleptically anticipating the fate of the decentered and open-ended, indeterminate—dislocatingly heretical—"novel" from which the above passage is taken.

In short, Melville, I am suggesting, invokes this confidence-producing Puritan exegetical method vis-à-vis the Old and New Testaments in this last scene not simply to recall and explain the terror endemic to the optimistic philosophy informing the discourse and practice of the self-reliant pioneering spirit of the American frontiersman. More important, he is also invoking this theological origin of the paradoxical, misanthropic confidence of the contemporary secularized American national identity to point to and explain the terror endemic to the optimistic philosophy informing the *discourse* and practice of the self-reliant or rugged individualist spirit of democratic capitalism that, as the novel testifies, was emerging in America, along with the notion of Manifest Destiny,[41] as the secular allotrope of the Puritan Providential design. What needs to be added to this disclosure is Melville's profound (and, as I will show, proleptic) insight into both the strength and weakness—the Achilles' heel—of this ontology of optimism and power: *its intrinsic need for its anxiety-provoking antithesis*, that is, a "*threatening*" enemy.

Does Melville offer an alternative mode of being-in-the-world to the apparently pessimistic impasse between a bankrupted philosophy of confidence, on the one hand, and an apparently pessimistic nihilism or, as in the case of Voltaire's *Candide*, a stoic—quietist—cultivation of one's garden, on the other, at which he arrives at the "end" of *The Confidence-Man*? If we reconstellate into this context the works he wrote immediately before *The Confidence-Man*, most notably "Bartleby, the Scrivener," *Israel Potter*, and "Benito Cereno"—and his ensuing silence—the answer to this question would seem to be—and most commentary on the matter of Melville's silence draws this conclusion—in the negative. But this, I suggest, would be the consequence of thinking according to the imperatives of the restricted binarist logic of optimistic metaphysics—of being answerable to the call of American exceptionalism—that Melville was committed to discrediting. If, on the other hand, we attend to the *aporias* precipitated by the Confidence-Man's parodic fulfillment of the logic of optimism, we experience a change of terrain that dislocates and reorients our interpretive perspective. If, more specifically, we acknowledge the radical contingency of being that haunts the familiar and confidence-instigating structures of the American world picture fabricated in the name of a secularized Providential view of time—the ontological priority of difference over Identity, to put it in the rhetoric of the poststructuralism he anticipates—then it might be seen that Melville is struggling against what William Carlos Williams called "the American grain" to articulate a comportment toward being in which the metaphysical terms "optimism" and "pessimism," "faith" and "doubt," "confidence" and "distrust," no longer apply, thus disarming the essential ideological weapon in the arsenal of American confidence men.

This, I think, is what we discover by attending to the "end" of *The Confidence-Man*, which depicts the *Fidele*, this American "ship of fools" (or ship of American fools), nearing the end of its voyage through the heart of America at the *limits* of the day (April 1)—between darkness and light—in terms of the symbolism of eschatology. It is a symbolism powerfully reinforced by a spectral voice that explodes suddenly out of the dark, breaking through the "mutually-confirming" conversation of the Cosmopolitan and the old gentleman, precisely at the moment the latter discovers that the disturbing "wisdom of Jesus, the Son of Sirach," is from the "Apocrypha" and, therefore, apocryphal: " 'What's that about Apocalypse?' " If, in other words, we read the voyage of the *Fidele* as the historical journey of America (its national self from its origins to its end, from its *arché* to its *telos*, in the light of the dislocating or decentering *aporia* disclosed at the moment of the fulfillment of its unerring optimistic logic, then we could read the sudden intrusion of the word "Apocalypse" in the dark cabin as signaling two fateful and antithetical possibilities. This, I suggest, is what Melville is referring to in the last enigmatic sentence of the novel: "Something further may follow of this Masquerade" (*C-M*, 251). One would be the catastrophic end of American civilization (which Melville may have foreseen as the coming Civil War); the other, related to the etymology of Apocalypse (*apo*: removal; and *kaluptein*: to cover), the *dis-closure* or *un-concealment*, which is to say, the *releasement* at this terminal, repressive moment of closure of a radically different—and differential—way of comporting oneself toward being. To be specific, this alternative comportment would not simply be one that acknowledges the nothingness *of* being and the analogous identitylessness identity of human being—humanity's ontological orphanage, to use one of Melville's favorite metaphors for the human condition—precipitated by the imploded logic of confidence. It would also be a comportment toward being that, against the optimistic American tradition's demonization of them, thinks this nothing and this identitylessness positively.

I cannot here amplify on this last possibility that I am attributing to Melville's Apocryphal/Apocalyptic (non)conclusion of *The Confidence-Man*. It will suffice to invoke what, in opposition to the traditional understanding of humanist inquiry, I have elsewhere referred to as "post-humanism."[42] The humanism bequeathed to modernity, including American modernity, by the Enlightenment was informed by the *anthropo-logos* (the Word of Man: *zoon logon echon*), a presence that betrayed the transcendental origins of its duplicitous appeal to the world. According to this traditional understanding of the human, Man—as identical to himself and universal—replaced God, the *theo-logos*, as the determining "center elsewhere" of being. He became the measure of all things and events, and thus the *overlord* of being in all its manifestations.[43] In thus pitting Man against being, this traditional humanism, whether in its scientific or poetic form, enabled an *imperial* comportment toward the differential phenomena of being that reduced an originative mode of revealing (knowledge), which acknowledges the nothingness, the differential temporality, of being, to a "challenging forth" that privileges the Answer (and closure) over the question (and openness) as the "end" of inquiry, and that transforms the phenomena of being, including human being, to standing or disposable reserve (*Bestand*).[44] Insofar as this humanism remains metaphysical, its raison d'être has been to instigate optimism: confidence in the face of a temporal world characterized by contingency—natural and human disasters—indifference to suffering, and, not least, a banalized state of mind susceptible to the seductions of confidence-men, who play cold-bloodedly on the deeply inscribed binary relation between confidence and distrust, the benign and the disastrous, hope and despair, certainty and uncertainty, answering and questioning.

The comportment toward being that Melville is symptomatically articulating, on the other hand, might, I am suggesting, be called, after the late Edward Said, a "secular critical" or "critical secular" humanism,[45] by which I take him to mean (1) a humanity that, endowed with consciousness—the ability to ask questions—and language, understands itself as the caretaker, not the master or overlord, of being, and therefore; (2) a comportment toward being that acknowledges its radical temporality, the belongingness of the nothing and something (historical re-presentations) of being; and thus (3) a "worldly" thinking that is radically finite, decentered, nonidentitarian, careful, and differential—that is, "*contrapuntal*." The basis for all humanistic practice, according to Said's Vichian perspective

> is at bottom what I have been calling philological, that is, a detailed, patient scrutiny of and a lifelong attentiveness to the words and rhetorics by which language is used by human beings who exist in history: hence the word "secular," as I use it, as well as the word "worldliness." Both of these notions allow us to take account not of eternally stable or supernaturally informed values, but rather of the

changing bases for humanistic praxis regarding values and human life that are now fully upon us in the new century.... I should like to argue that reading involves the contemporary humanist in two very crucial motions that I shall call reception and resistance. Reception is submitting oneself knowledgeably to texts and treating them provisionally at first as discrete objects . . . ; moving then, by dint of expanding and elucidating the often obscure or invisible frameworks in which they exist, to their historical situations and the way in which certain structures of attitude, feeling, and rhetoric get entangled with some currents, some historical and social formulations of their context.[46]

In disclosing the nothingness that haunts the American philosophies of optimism, the difference that haunts the American national identity, the uncertainty that haunts American confidence, Melville, through the Confidence-Man's parodic genealogy, would transform the war-to-the-end of the binary logic endemic to the transcendental and optimistic perspective of the traditional humanist model into a contrapuntal dialogue or, to appropriate Heidegger's term to my purpose, *Auseinandersetzung*.[47] I mean the unending loving strife between Being and time, Past and present, Representation and the "real," National Identity and cultural multiplicity, which gives ontological priority to the Question over the Answer, errancy over directionality, the nomadic over the sedentary, being-always-on-the-way over arrival. And, in so doing, redeems, without annulling the painful contingencies of humanity's mortal condition.

Chapter 6

American Confidence in the Age of Globalization

Melville's Witness

"And I only am esacaped alone to tell thee."

—Book of Job

The drama's done. Why then here does any one step forth?—Because one did survive the wreck.

—Herman Melville, "Epilogue," *Moby-Dick*

The holes of oblivion do not exit. Nothing human is that perfect, and there are simply too many people in the world to make oblivion possible. One man will always be left to tell the story.

—Hannah Arendt, *Eichmann in Jerusalem*

Melville's *The Confidence-Man* was not simply intended as a scathing carnivalesque indictment of American confidence or, rather, the confidence enabled by the internalization of the founding myth of American exceptionalism in the antebellum period. It was also, as I have been suggesting, intended in some significant degree as an indictment of a collective confidence that enabled the proliferation of confidence-men, who, feeding on the deeply inscribed optimism of the American national identity, were "conning" their gullible fellow country-men in all manner of degrading and dehumanizing ways. This has been well documented by the scholarly custodians of Melville's memory, who trace the origin of the novel back to multiple newspaper reports on such "operators," most notably working the Mississippi River, and to showmen of the type of P. T. Barnum.[1] But, as his establishment of the provenance of this character in a larger historical and/or mythical context and his overdetermination of the sociopolitical stories of Colonel Moredock and China Aster clearly suggest, Melville viewed these "operators" as symbolic of a national cultural symptom (related to the westward expansion of the frontier) that betrayed a fundamental sickness of American democracy: the people's susceptibility, the effect of a deeply backgrounded and inscribed optimism that was also militantly anti-intellectual, to being duped by duplicitous leaders—the elect—whose self-interested sociopolitical agendas were in one way or another remote from theirs. Melville, in *The Confidence-Man*, is clearly more interested in disclosing the *ontological* genealogy of this confidence syndrome—the Puritan figural-providential view of time and history—but there is evidence in his novel to suggest that this metaphysical ontology is applicable, as it is to all the fiction since *Moby-Dick*, to all the sites on the continuum of being, including the site of the sociopolitics of Melville's time.[2]

I am referring above all to the remarkably Voltairean chapter 19, ironically entitled "A soldier of fortune," in which the Confidence-Man, in the guise of the herb doctor, encounters a destitute and badly crippled man, Thomas Fry, "in a grimy old regimental coat," who bitterly claims, at first, that his devastated body is the consequence, not of the Mexican War as the "sympathetic" herb doctor originally thinks, but of being arbitrarily jailed in the notorious New York prison, the Tombs, for a murder that was committed by a "gentleman with friends"—the consequence, that is, of an American judicial system that, despite its claim of equality before the law, automatically favored the privileged class (the elect) over the poor (the preterite). In the black humorous process of what follows, the Confidence-Man, "appeals" to the crippled man's intrinsic but dormant American confidence and patriotism by way, paradoxically, of instigating the crippled man into recounting his gruesome "experience of adversity"—the cause of his mutilated condition, his reduction to the status of a non-entity, and the consequent misery of his alienated existence in a heartless America: "Give me your story." he says, "Ere I undertake a cure, I require a full account of the case" (*C-M*, 94). Predictably, the Confidence-Man gradually, but inexorably dupes the cripple not simply into buying several boxes of his medicinal herbs, but also into forgetting the debilitating damage his government—a "free Ameriky," as the cripple sarcastically calls his country (*C-M*, 98)—has inflicted on him, if not quite into recuperating the patriotism he has lost. In the process, however, the herb doctor's paradoxical "appeal" to this fundamental confidence becomes so hyperbolic that it self-destructs.

In his initial response to the cripple's ghastly story, the herb doctor "gravely" recontextualizes it, as he will the story of Colonel Moredock, into the Leibnizian philosophy of "pre-established harmony": "the herb-doctor was silent for a time, buried in thought. At last, raising his head, he said: 'I have considered your whole story, my friend, and strove to consider it in the light of a commentary on what I believe to be the system of things; but it so jars with all, is so incompatible with all, that you must pardon me, if I honestly tell you, I cannot believe it" (*C-M*, 97). Knowing his story would more likely be believed by those from whom he was begging alms if he impersonated a wounded veteran of the recent Mexican War, the bitterly cynical cripple metamorphoses into a con man: "Happy Tom, who fought at Buena Vista" and was "crippled in both pins at glorious Contreras" (*C-M*, 97). On his return, after "having reaped a pretty good harvest" (*C-M*, 98) by masquerading as a shattered veteran of the Mexican War, he flaunts his cynicism before the herb doctor, who once again invokes the notion of the best of all possible worlds *to accommodate this decimated body*, now, however, escalating the binary logic of optimism that feeds on adversity by representing it in the unmistakable rhetoric of the Panglossian perspective:

> You, my worthy friend, to my concern, have reflected upon the government under which you live and suffer. Where is your patriotism? Where your gratitude? True, the charitable may find something in your case, as you put it, partly to account for such reflections as coming from you. Still, *be the facts how they may*, your reflections are none the less unwarrantable. Grant, for the moment, that your experiences are as you give them; in which case I would admit that government might be thought to have more or less to do with what seems undesirable in them. But it is never to be forgotten that human government, being subordinate to the divine, must needs, therefore, in its degree, partake of the characteristics of the divine. *That is, while in general efficacious to happiness, the world's law may yet, in some cases, have, to the eye of reason, an unequal operation, just as, in the same imperfect view* [the Popean allusion is unmistakable], *some inequalities may appear in the operations of heaven's law; nevertheless, to one who has a right confidence, final benignity is, in every instance, as sure with the one law as the other.* I expound the point at some length, because these are the considerations, my poor fellow, which, weighed as they merit, will enable you to sustain with unimpaired trust *the apparent calamities which are yours.*" (*C-M*, 98; my emphasis)

This deliberate process of logico-rhetorical escalation arrives at its carnivaleque fulfillment—and demise—a moment later, after the cripple expresses his contempt for the herb doctor's "hog-latin," which the narrator refers to as his "most illiterate obduracy," that is, his blindness, no doubt, to the herb doctor's sustained allusion to (a Puritan figural interpretive version of) Voltaire's *Candide*:

> "Charity marvels not that you should be somewhat hard of conviction, my friend, since you, doubtless, believe yourself hardly dealt by; but forget not that those who are loved are chastened."

"Mustn't chasten them too much, though, and too long, because their skin and heart get hard, and feel neither pain nor tickle."

"To mere reason, your case looks something piteous, I grant, But never despond; many things—the choicest—remain. You breathe this bounteous air, are warmed by this gracious sun, and, though poor and friendless, indeed, nor so agile as in your youth, yet, how sweet to roam, day by day, through the groves, plucking the brightest mosses and flowers, till forlornness itself becomes a hilarity, and, in your innocent independence, you skip for joy."

"Fine skipping with these 'ere horse-posts—ha ha!"

"Pardon, I forgot the crutches. My mind, figuring you after receiving the benefit of my art, *overlooked you as you stand before me.*" (*C-M*, 99; my emphasis)[3]

Despite the ludicrousness of the herb doctor's advice—it recalls, not incidentally, Captain Delano's blind response to the "shadow cast" by the "negro" on Benito Cereno's—this damaged American is so susceptible to the paradoxical logic of optimism that he finally succumbs to his interlocutor's seductive con game, accepting his disinherited and alienated lot—his preterition, to use the vocabulary of the Puritans, whose inscrutable God, to invoke Foucault, "started the charade." But as everywhere in Melville's novel, readers cannot help but recognize the absurd—and heartless—Panglossian tenor of this encomium to confidence, even if we don't recognize the allusion:

> Candide had been wounded [during the Lisbon earthquake] by splinters of flying masonry and lay helpless in the road, covered with rubble.
>
> "For heaven's sake," he cried to Pangloss, "fetch me some wine and oil! I'm dying."
>
> "This earthquake is nothing new," replied Pangloss; "the town of Lima in America experienced the same shocks last year. The same causes produce the same effects. There is certainly a vein of sulphur running under the earth from Lima to Lisbon."
>
> "Nothing is more likely," cried Candide; "but the oil and wine, for pity's sake!"
>
> "Likely!," exclaimed the philosopher, "I maintained it's proved!"
>
> Candide lost consciousness, and Pangloss brought him a little water from a fountain close by.[4]

This devastating revelation of the complicity between "free Ameriky" and one kind of optimistic/providential history or other in the "elect's" ideological project of annulling, by accommodating, the potential dissent of those Americans who have been socially and politically exploited—the preterite, as it were—finds, as I have shown, its fullest and most radical expression, as the resonantly dark oxymoron of the title name and its occasion (the American Revolution) suggests, in Melville's *Israel Potter: His Fifty Years of Exile* (1855), especially in his parodic portrait of the political American con man *par excellence*, the venerable Benjamin Franklin. But it is in *The Confidence-Man*, particularly in this episode, which implicates social injustice (the American legal system) with imperialist aggression (the Mexican War), that Melville articulates the essential seductive operations of this American sociopolitical con game—and its genealogy. I mean by the last the deeply backgrounded secret history that the representations of American history by the custodians of the nation's cultural memory have, in various ways, hidden from view in the name of their "Panglossian" confidence in America's domestic (local) and foreign (global) mission: the shameful history that begins with the Puritans' genocidal assault on native Americans in the name of their divinely ordained "optimistic" exceptionalist "errand" and culminates in Melville's time in the emergent capitalists' cold-blooded reduction of the majority of Americans to damaged lives and their arrogantly aggressive imperialist project in the name of the "benign" laws of laissez-faire economics, of History (Manifest Destiny), or both.

If it was Melville's decisive critique of their Puritan morality that provoked the custodians of American culture into inaugurating their "turn[ing] our critical Aegis upon [Melville]" with the aim of "freez[ing] him into silence," it was his decisive exposure of their "genial" optimism as a misanthropic con game—the strategic appropriation of American confidence to accomplish dehumanizing ideological goals—that provoked them into completing this task of interment. Since then, thanks to the recalcitrant spectral force of his post–*Moby-Dick* fiction, Melville has undergone a "revival," but this has, by and large, taken the form of repeatedly accommodating his subversions of optimism to the American exceptionalist vision, as in the case of the Cold War Americanists[5] or, more recently, of criticizing Melville for his supposed complicity with this imperial vision.[6] As a result, Melville's late fiction, not least *The Confidence-Man*, has been denied its "poststructuralist" thrust and thus its prophetic criticism of the recent, post-Vietnam or, more exactly, post-9/11, recuperation with a vengeance of the ontological myth of American exceptionalism—indeed, in its original "Anglo-Protestant" form—and the confidence in its unilateral global errand it enables, which it briefly lost in the period of the Vietnam War. Not least, this nationalist accommodation has domesticated Melville's proleptic exposure of the deadly confidence game the present Bush administration (and the custodians of its nationalist/imperialist policies—I am referring, above all, to "The Project for a New American Century"[7]) has been playing not only with the American public, but with the public of the world at large since the Al Qaeda attacks on the World Trade Center and the Pentagon on 9/11/01.

    I cannot here undertake a full elaboration of Melville's uncanny insight into America's imperial future. But a brief account of the George W. Bush administration's panoptic representation of America's relationship to the Middle East and, beyond that, the world, and the logic informing this representation, in the context I have provided in this book, should suggest heuristically what such an elaboration would entail. I have shown that the Confidence-Man's fundamental "strategy" aboard the *Fidele* is dependent on the American public's deeply backgrounded ontological confidence in the ultimate benignity of being, indeed, in its having been "elected" first by God and then, with the secularization of the Puritan errand, by History, to fulfill His/Its benign Providential/Destinarian design on earth. I have also shown that this confidence derives its positive meaning and its forwarding practical force from its indissoluble relationality with adversity, hardship, and distrust or, rather, with the anxiety precipitated by natural or man-made events that threaten to undermine the legitimacy and authority of the optimistic view. This perennial strategy in fact has its origins in the early American confidence-men's realization that settling, improving, and civilizing—rationalizing—the "New World" wilderness and thus generating collective confidence in America's Westward mission carries with it in the long run the potential for decay and exhaustion, as in the case of their representation of the fate of the Old World and its empires *"sine fine,"* and therefore their insistent, often hysterical, reaffirmation, by way of the ritual of the "American jeremiad,"[8] of the need for a perpetual "frontier" between the sedentary and the nomadic, that is, civilization and savagery—a permanent threat to the unity of the American nation—that would always already mobilize and *renew* the solidarity, the patriotic obligation, and the youthful and optimistic vitality of its people.[9] This paradoxical ideology informs the historiography of Frederick Jackson Turner, the historian who first conceptualized the centrality of the frontier in the making of the American national identity. "The effect of the Indian frontier as a consolidating agent in our history," he wrote, no doubt with Alexis de Tocqueville in mind, "is important. From the close of the seventeenth century various intercolonial congresses have been called to treat with Indians and establish common measures of defense.... This frontier stretched along the western border like a cord of union. The Indian was a common danger, demanding united action.... It is evident that the unifying tendencies of the Revolutionary period were facilitated by the previous cooperation in the regulation of the frontier. In this connection may be mentioned the importance of the frontier, from that day to this, as a military training school, keeping *alive* the power of resistance to aggression, and *developing the stalwart and rugged qualities of the frontiersman.*"[10]

The persistent centrality of this cultural paradigm is borne witness to by the continuity between the westward movement and the gradual decline of the (North)East's status as the defining culture of America in favor of the West. This shift, which replaces the East, now represented on the analogy of the decadent Old World, by the West as the bearer of the American frontier spirit, was exemplified in a dramatically overt way by the presidential election of 2004.

In the con game he is "playing," the Confidence-Man, knowing the depth of his American victims' Panglossian optimism—knowing they, like Candide, are ensconced in their "Malakoff of confidence" no matter what the horrors they experience or what the "caviling" opposition discloses about its origins and operations—actually, if indirectly, *exaggerates the threat* to their passive confidence posed by the apparent contradictions all the more to reactivate it. The aptly called "Red Scare" under the aegis of A. Mitchell Palmer, Woodrow Wilson's Attorney General,[11] after World War I and the "Red Scare" under the aegis of Senator Joseph McCarthy after World War II, both of whom turned out to be con men in precisely the Melvillian sense of the phrase, bear witness to the persistence of this virtually archetypal ploy of the American con-game. The difference between Candide and most of the Confidence-Man's American victims is that the former eventually—by way of the reversal of the logical binary between confidence and distrust precipitated by the excess of violence he experiences—awakens to both the absurdity and cold-blooded inhumanity of Pangloss's "best of all possible worlds." In their gullibility—their ultimate assurance that "whatever is [from the American exceptionalist perspective], is right"—the Confidence-Man's American victims are incapable of perceiving the absolute incommensurability between the optimism of American exceptionalism and the disruptive and "blood-curdling" events that challenge its authority or of acting according to the responsible and humane imperatives of this disclosure.

The analogy between Melville's diagnosis of American national identity of the antebellum period and the revelations of contemporary history, especially since the Vietnam War, is uncanny. Following the long and brutal Vietnam War, during which the perennial myth of American exceptionalism self-destructed when the fulfillment of its "benign" logic manifested itself in the grim spectacle of the ruthless destruction of a Third World culture in the optimistic name of saving it for the "free world,"[12] we have borne witness to a sustained effort on the part of American confidence-men (legislators, military men, corporate executives, the media, and, not least, area experts and government policy makers) to overcome this anxious "Vietnam syndrome"—this "neurotic" collapse of public confidence in America's global mission—to recuperate the healthy optimistic national consensus. This unerringly single-minded effort by the new American Jeremiahs to objectify and forget "Vietnam" was more or less realized when the Cold War came to its end with the internal collapse of the Soviet Union, an event that a prominent American confidence-man euphorically announced, in the typical biblical language of America's elect ("good news"), as "the end of history" and the advent of "the New World Order" under the aegis of the United States.[13] And it was consolidated by the "surgically executed" defeat of Iraq in the first Gulf War. This "kicking of the Vietnam syndrome," as the first President George Bush put it[14]—a recuperation of the national consensus and confidence in America's global errand—rehabilitated the tarnished reputations not simply of the governing elite and the U.S. military command, but also of the media and the cult of the expert, or, in Adorno's phrase, "the consciousness industry." Not least, it spawned a new cadre of governmental policy makers—the aptly named "neocons"—who, responding to the end of the Cold War, and the *demise of the enabling threat of Soviet Communism*, and more acutely aware of the "secret history" of America than most of their predecessors, consciously incorporated, like Melville's Confidence-Man, *the need for a frontier, or an enemy, or a principle of evil* into their national and global confidence game.

Al Qaeda provided these neoconservatives, virtually as a gift, this "enemy," this "threat"—this "new frontier"—as the means of renewing American confidence in it global mission. The euphoria—which is to say, a callous inhumanity matching that of the attackers—with which the attacks on the World Trade Center and the Pentagon—"American soil"—were greeted by the Panglossian, neocon confidence-men is epitomized by Samuel P. Huntington, one of their most prominent members:

> At the end of the twentieth century, numerous nondemocratic regimes still existed, most importantly China, but none of them, including China, was attempting to promote nondemocratic ideologies in other societies. Democracy was left without a significant secular ideological rival, and the United States was left without a peer competitor. *Among American foreign policy elites, the results were euphoria, pride, arrogance—and uncertainty.* The absence of an ideological threat produced an absence of purpose. "Nations need enemies, Charles Krauthammer [a visible neocon pundit] commented as the Cold War ended. "Take away one, and they find another." The ideal enemy for America would be ideologically hostile, racially and culturally different, and militarily strong enough to pose a credible threat to American security. The foreign policy debates were largely over who might be such an enemy....
>
> The cultural gap between Islam and America's Christianity and Anglo-Protestantism reinforced Islam's enemy qualifications. And on September 11, 2001, Osama bin Laden *ended America's*

search. The attacks on New York and Washington . . . makes militant Islam America's first enemy of the twenty-first century.[15]

As it is everywhere evident, the optimistic policy experts of the second Bush administration—Carl Rove, Donald Rumsfeld, Richard Cheney, Paul Wolfowitz, Richard Perle, Richard Haass, and Joseph Bolton, among many others—since 9/11 and the President's declaration of an unending war on terrorism, have deliberately chosen, in a seemingly paradoxical way, to trumpet "homeland security" throughout the land: the formation of a Department of Homeland Security, the passage of the Patriot Act, the intimidation and/or stigmatization of dissent, and, by way of repeated warnings of possible terrorist attacks on the American mainland and heightened security measures at United States borders, airports, and other travel facilities, the tacit rendering permanent of the state of exception and the production of a national environment that resonates with collective anxiety. But, as in the case of the Confidence-Man in Melville's novel, the paradox is only apparent, a masquerade, as it were. Like the duplicitous strategy of the Confidence-Man vis-à-vis natural and man-made disasters, though for an opposite end, this cynical neocon jeremiad, this constant reminder to the American public of the threat that Islamic terrorism poses to its collective well-being and freedom, is based on confidence in the ontological priority of optimism over distrust in the American national identity. In thus activating anxiety—and the normalizing of the state of exception it enables—this strategy is intended to maintain the perpetual support of a unified American public for their reckless imperial foreign policy and for their restriction of the rights of American cavilers who oppose the dangerous hubris informing what these new American con men long ago called their optimistic "Project for a New American Century." In thus overdetermining threat and the anxiety it instigates in behalf of the renewal of faith and confidence in the American calling, these neocon American policy makers, it should not be overlooked, are the legatees of the Massachusetts Bay Puritans, who, massively and strategically overdetermined adversity—exemplified by diabolic, nomadic "salvages" who haunted the forests of "God's country"—in behalf of the rejuvenation of faith in their calling, that is, constructed their covenantal polity on the basis of a permanent state of exception.

Nor should it be overlooked that these arrogant American neocon men like Samuel Huntington have overtly invoked the authority of the Puritan founders of the optimistic American national identity in behalf of this nation-renewing and "missionary" project: precisely in the terms of the ontologico-political ideology that Melville criticizes in his post-*Moby-Dick* fiction. "The Puritans of Massachusetts," he writes, "took the lead in defining their settlement based on 'a Covenant with God' to create 'a city on a hill' as a model for all the world, and people of other Protestant faiths soon also came to see themselves and America in a similar way. In the seventeenth and eighteenth centuries, Americans defined their mission in the New World in biblical terms. They were a 'chosen people,' on an 'errand in the wilderness,' creating 'the new Israel' or the 'new Jerusalem' in what was clearly 'the promised land.' America was the site of a 'new Heaven and a new earth, the home of justice,' God's country." Appropriating Sacvan Bercovitch's critique of the American jeremiad in behalf of his jeremiad, Huntington concludes, "The settlement of America was vested . . . 'with all the emotional and spiritual, and intellectual appeal of a religious quest.' This sense of holy mission was easily expanded into millennarian themes of America as 'the redeemer nation' and 'the visionary republic' " (*WAW*, 64). Identifying themselves, that is, masquerading, as "a saving remnant"—the elect bearers of the Word (or custodians of the original covenant) betrayed by the "evil" forces of "political correctness"—these neocon confidence-men have also demonized the "deconstructionist movement" since the 1960s—as the "learned doctors" demonized the Melville of *Pierre*—as a subversive force that, in encouraging "subnational" identities to assert their subjectivities, has threatened the traditional stabilizing authority of the American calling—the voice of "the Anglo-Protestant core culture"—and the "assimilative" and subjecting process that previously molded and mobilized immigrants into "Americans." Typically, Huntington charges that seditious deconstructionists have undermined the confidence that has perennially distinguished America from the "Old World":

> The deconstructrionists promoted programs to enhance the status and influence of subnational racial, ethnic, and cultural groups. They encouraged immigrants to maintain their birth country cultures, granted them legal privileges denied to native born Americans, and denounced the idea of Americanization. They pushed the rewriting of history syllabi and textbooks so as to refer to the "peoples" of the United States in place of the single people of the Constitution. They urged supplementing or substituting for national history the history of subnational groups. They downgraded the centrality of English in American life and pushed bilingual education and linguistic diversity. They advocated legal recognition of group rights and racial preferences over the individual rights central to the American Creed. They justified their actions by theories of multiculturalism and the idea that diversity rather then unity or community should be America's overriding value. The combined effect of these efforts was to promote the deconstruction of the American identity that had been gradually created over three centuries and the ascendance of subnational identities. (*WAW*, 142)[16]

In representing a healthy, pluralist opposition to an internally repressive and externally aggressive nationalism as "anti-American," indeed, as abetting terrorism, American neoconfidence men like Huntington have not hesitated to enlist the historically resonant authority of the original "Anglo-Protestant core culture" in behalf of their effort to resist this "disintegrative" national momentum allegedly instigated by the "deconstructionists." Taking their cue from the emergence of a powerful Evangelical politics—a fifth "Great [Protestant] Awakening" (*WAW*, 336, 75–78)—this group of policy experts have also invoked it in behalf of reducing the cultural multiplicity of America into a collective religion-oriented, Crusader national identity capable of winning the "war on terror," which really means the war against Islam, or what has come reductively to be called the "clash of civilizations."[17] Invoking the specter of terrorism that "threatens" American confidence, this recuperative project—this neocon con game conducted by what Melville would call a cabal of "metaphysical scamps" (*C-M*, 136)—is intended to galvanize the confidence of the American people or, rather, the "core culture," in behalf of what Melville, at an earlier time of crisis, aptly called the "genial misanthropy" of the philosophy of American optimism.

As Melville's *Confidence-Man* and the other post-*Moby-Dick* fiction I have discussed in this book bear witness, American history has always been directed by confidence men. And this, as we have seen, is because the founding and abiding metanarrative of American exceptionalism necessarily reproduces them. In the past, however, especially in the period following the demise of the Puritan theocracy, the inhumane (teleo)logic of their secular metanarrative of confidence remained obscured by its undeveloped status, its integral relationship with promise and process. It thus remained more or less "benign" in appearance to those marginal Americans who paid the price for its practice. Since Melville's time, culminating in the period between the Vietnam War to the second Bush administration's response to the attack on 9/11/01, the potentiality of this "benign" logic has been fulfilled, that is, come to its end—and, in a theoretical way, to its demise. By this last I mean that its fulfillment has precipitated into visibility not only the anachronism of this optimistic metanarrative (the inexorable thrownness, contingency, and plurality of the human condition), but also its cynical spuriousness: its status as a masquerade, an ideological con game intended to mobilize the American public against internal dissent and to an aggressive and violent imperial global project.[18]

Interrogating the traditional understanding of the nation (in this particular case, John Stuart Mill's), the political scientist William Connolly observes that it is an "imaginary," an entity informed by an absent origin or center that, necessarily, can never become a material reality, must always remain a lack: "Mill," he writes, "invokes the language of commonality, identity, community, same, and collective to imagine nationality, but he does not explain how tight, centered, or close identity must be to *be* identity. It is this constant combination of indispensability and uncertainty within the image of the nation that sets it up to be a condition to be remembered [Connolly is invoking Renan's definition of the nation here] but never known, pursued but never present, absent but never eliminatable as an end. Any regulative ideal, surely, is impossible to realize fully. But the image of the nation seems to be marked by a sense that the *density at its very center* is both always indispensable to it and always insufficiently available." And he concludes, "This constitutive lack at the center of the nation provides a standing temptation for some bellicose constituency to occupy it, doing so by claiming that it [confidently] *embodies* in its ethnicity, faith, loyalty to the past, and/or commitment to the true source of public morality the missing essence of the nation."[19] It is, as I have been suggesting, this flawed and anachronistic, but potently enabling understanding of the nation, nation building, and nation renewal—*this indissoluble relationality of confidence and threat*—that allows a zealous Huntington to identify "Anglo-Protestantism" as the "core culture" of the American nation and as the embodiment of its "missing essence" and thus to call, in the name of confidence, for its occupation of the anxiety-provoking black hole at its center. In calling American optimism into question in the fiction after *Moby-Dick*, Melville, I am suggesting, not only indicates a deep awareness of the violence endemic to the metaphysically ordained American national imaginary, but also of the vulnerability of an intrinsically pluralist society to "some bellicose [read 'confident'] constituency" which the "center elsewhere" of the nation enables.

It is the genius of Herman Melville, no doubt quickened by the damage done to his life by the unerring imperatives of American optimism, to have foreseen this "end" in the middle of the nineteenth century. In *The Confidence-Man*, as well as *Pierre, Israel Potter*, "Bartleby, the Scrivener," and "Benito Cereno," he anticipated the crystallization of the exceptionalist philosophy of optimism into an American con game that conceals a deadly, paranoid will to power over everything, domestic and foreign, that threatens the imperial authority of its call. Nevertheless, in thus rendering the essential source of the power of the American Calling explicit, Melville also exposed its Achilles' heel: its dependency on its polyvalent "Other." That is to say, he created an elusive imaginary figure—the *specter of* American "reality"—whose escalating parodic/genealogical strategy, in mirroring the duplicitous operations of this Panglossian philosophy, exposes its hollowness. In thus enabling us to see the smiling contours of the benign missionary image of American confidence as a metaphysical masquerade—a "genial misanthropy"—Melville also anticipated the most viable means of warding off the machinations of this optimistic exceptionalist apparatus of capture and resisting the American elect's polyvalent imperial agenda in the wake of 9/11/01: a comportment that, like Bartleby, the scrivener's, vis-à-vis his confident Wall Street employer, "prefers not to."

I bring this meditation on Melville's great refusal to be answerable to the American calling to its opening close by returning to the way Theodor Adorno and Edward Said, two of the greatest exilic nay-sayers to the contemporary empire of confidence, put this Melvillian comportment of refusal a century later. Hopefully, by means of this repetition, we will now know them—and Melville—for the first time:

> "The past life of emigrés is, as we know, annulled," says Adorno in *Minima Moralia*, subtitled *Reflection from a Damaged Life*.... Why? "Because anything that is not reified, cannot be counted and measured, ceases to exist" or, as he says later, is consigned to mere "background." Although the disabling aspects of this fate are manifest, its virtues or possibilities are worth exploring. Thus the emigré consciousness—a mind of winter, in Wallace Stevens's phrase—discovers in its marginality that "a gaze averted from the beaten track, a hatred of brutality, a search for fresh concepts not yet encompassed by the general pattern, is the last hope for thought." Adorno's general pattern is what in another place he calls the "administered world" or, insofar as the irresistible dominants in culture are concerned, "the consciousness industry." There is then not just the negative advantage of refuge in the emigré's eccentricity; there is also the positive benefit of challenging the system, describing it in language unavailable to those it has already subdued:
>
>> In an intellectual hierarchy which constantly makes everyone answerable, unanswerability alone can call the hierarchy directly by its name.... He who offers for sale something unique that no one wants to buy, represents, even against his will, freedom from exchange.[20]

In his willingness to "be tempted forth [from "the secure Malakoff of confidence"] to hazardous skirmishes on the open ground of reason," Melville anticipates a secular (post)humanist comportment toward being that, like that of Adorno and Said, acknowledges the nothing that belongs to being—the vulnerability of humanity, the fragility of the apparently solid world humans create—and in so doing, releases the *Question* from the bondage of the confident Answerers. Which is to say, with Nietzsche and Foucault, enables rather than "[bars] access to the actual intensities and creations of life."

In *Billy Budd*, the novella he was working on in 1891, the last year of his exilic life, Melville tells about the hanging of an innocent sailor who had been maliciously charged with fomenting a mutiny aboard the ship into which he had been impressed from a merchantman symbolically named "*Rights of Man.*" The tale is a parable about the ship of state, specifically its response to a threat to its power instigated by an external force. The historical setting of the novella is a British man of war, HMS *Bellipotent*, at the time of "the Great Mutiny" that threatened British dominance of the seas during the French Revolution. But Melville, who is alluding to an analogous case of "mutiny" on board an American ship, the *Somers*, in 1842, makes it ironically clear that this ship of state, like the *Pequod* (and the *Fidele*) is the American exceptionalist ship of state which, following the dictates of the American jeremiad—the deeply inscribed need for a threatening frontier or an anxiety-provoking enemy to rejuvenate itself—renders the state of exception and its arbitrary policing mechanism permanent. In the novella, Melville condemns this exceptionalist ideology of the commanders of the American ship of state, if not the commanders themselves. And in thus "preferring not to" be answerable to the American calling in this last testament, he not only repeats in microcosmic form the entire history of his witness as an exilic American writer, a part of and apart from his homeland, to the will to power inhering in the "benign" ontology and politics of the myth of American exceptionalism—to the brutality of the optimistic exceptionalist perspective in the face of the mystery and ambiguities of—the nothingness that belongs to—being in all its manifestations. He also bears ironic witness to the history of the reception of his writing—the repeated policing of his heresies—by the dominant culture in American that I outlined in the first chapter of this book.

In a resonant coda—the penultimate section of *Billy Budd*—following the narration of the events leading to the hanging of the innocent young sailor and the ambiguous muttering of Billy's executioner, Captain Vere, on his death bed—"Billy Budd, Billy Budd"—Melville ironically juxtaposes against this "inside narration" of actual events an official, retrospective, and decisive "account of the affair"—"doubtless for the most part written in good faith"—published in a "naval chronicle of the time, an authorized weekly publication":

> "On the tenth of the last month a deplorable occurrence took place on board H.M.S. *Bellipotent*. John Claggart, the ship's master-at-arms, discovering that some sort of plot was incipient among an inferior section of the ship's company, and that the ringleader was one William Budd, he, Claggart, in the act of arraigning the man before the captain, was vindictively stabbed to the heart by the suddenly drawn sheath knife of Budd.

> "The deed and the implement employed sufficiently suggest that, though mustered into the service under an English name, the assassin was no Englishman, but one of those aliens adopting the English cognomens whom the present extraordinary necessities of the service have caused to be admitted into it in considerable numbers.
>
> "The enormity of the crime and the extreme depravity of the criminal appear the greater in view of the character of the victim, a middle-aged man respectable and discreet, belonging to the minor official grade, the petty officers, upon whom, as none know better than the commissioned gentleman, the efficiency of His Majesty's navy so largely depends. His function was a responsible one, at once onerous and thankless, and his fidelity in it the greater because of his strong patriotic impulse. In this instance, as in so many other instances in theses days, the character of this unfortunate man signally refutes, if refutation were needed, that peevish saying attributed to the late Dr. Johnson, that patriotism is the last refuge of a scoundrel.
>
> "The criminal paid the penalty of his crime. The promptitude of the punishment had proved salutary. Nothing amiss is now apprehended aboard the H.M.S. *Bellipotent*."[21]

In thus illustrating the crude way the official culture polices the politically revealing aporias inhering in the optimistic logic of American exceptionalism—that is, willfully, though "doubtless . . . in good faith," reduces the contradictions that disclose the violence latent in American-style democracy to its totalizing national Identity in the name of "peace"—Melville, at the end of his life, is surely alluding to the way this official culture of confidence policed the "heresies" he committed in the fiction immediately following *Moby-Dick*. Indeed, I would say that he was in some sense anticipating the continuation of this policing by the custodians of the American national identity beyond his death, when, in the wake of the "revival" in the 1920s, especially after World War II, his irrepressible writing was "rewritten" and harnessed to the imperatives of the Cold War. But if we read the last section of *Billy Budd*, which follows the official narrative and reports this violated lowly seaman's apotheosis as a kind of Christ figure in the hearts and minds of his shipmates, in the light of what I have shown to be the supreme theme of both the content and form of these texts—Melville's refusal to be answerable to the American Calling—we are enabled to infer something more than simply the irresistible power of the hegemonic exceptionalist discourse of America. It enables us to see as well, that, do what it can, the dominant culture has not been able to "freeze [the heretical Melville] into silence." Despite the variously enacted efforts to inter him, from the antebellum period to the present, from the time of the harnessing of the American exceptionalist myth to the capitalist/imperial project to the post-9/11 invasions of Afghanistan and Iraq, Melville has been a specter that has haunted the exceptionalist ethos ever since his novel about the drowned sailor who returns as an orphan to tell us the inside story of the *Pequod*'s "fiery pursuit" of the white whale and of its terrible fate. Let me put this negative disclosure precipitated by reconstellating the fiction after *Moby-Dick* into the contest of his last unfinished work in a positive, if only tentative way. Precisely by refusing to answer the American Calling, by "preferring not to" answer its covenantal summons, Melville enables us to imagine an alternative America, one aware of the brutality of the exceptionalist Answerer, that acknowledges the ontological priority of the question—and the dignity, not simply of humanity at large but of all the phenomena on the continuum of being: the groundless ground, of any political formation that would claim the name of democracy.

Notes

Chapter 1. Melville's Specter

1. William V. Spanos, *The Errant Art of Moby-Dick: The Canon, the Cold War and the Struggle for American Studies* (Durham, NC: Duke University Press, 1995), pp. 277–278.
2. See David Halberstam, *The Best and the Brightest* (New York: Random House, 1972). These included Robert McNamara, McGeorge Bundy, Dean Rusk, and Walt Rostow, all managerial types, who planned and executed the murderous war in Vietnam in terms of a preconceived end (a "scenario") that could be accomplished statistically.
3. Ron Suskind, "Without a Doubt," *New York Times Magazine* (October 17, 2004).
4. Herman Melville, *Moby-Dick; Or The Whale*, ed. Harrison Hayford, Hershel Parker, and G. Thomas Tanselle (Evanston. Ill.: Northwestern University Press, 1988), p. 184.
5. Bill Ayers, *Fugitive Days: A Memoir*, new ed. (New York: Penguin Books, 2003), pp. 120–121; first published by Beacon Press, 2001.
6. Perry Miller, *The Raven and the Whale: The War of Words and Wits in the Era of Poe and Melville* (New York: Harvest Books, 1956).
7. See Martin Heidegger, "What Is Metaphysics?," in *Basic Writings*, rev. and expanded ed., ed. David Farrell Krell (New York: HarperCollins, 1993), p. 101.
8. Evert Duykinck, "Melville's *Moby-Dick*, or, *The Whale*," in *Literary World*, 9 November 22, 1851, pp. 403–404.
9. Review of *Pierre*, *New York Herald*, September 18, 1852, in *Herman Melville: The Contemporary Reviews*, ed. Brian Higgins and Hershel Parker (Cambridge, UK: Cambridge University Press, 1995), p. 438.
10. Perry Miller, *The Raven and the Whale*. Miller notes that even Melville's *Omoo* "outraged [Peck] to the point of hysteria" in " 'stimulat[ing] curiosity and excit[ing] unchaste desires' " and in libeling missionaries, pp. 216–217. Peck's review of *Omoo* appeared in *American Whig Review* (July 6, 1847); *Herman Melville: The Contemporary* Reviews, pp. 131–142.
11. Peck, *The American Whig Review*, 16 (November 1852), 446–454; *Herman Melville: The Contemporary Reviews*, pp. 413, 443–445.
12. The essential validity of my generalization of Peck's perspective is amply borne out by Perry Miller's historical account in *The Raven and the Whale* of

American literary culture as it was reflected by American intellectuals in the era of Melville and Poe.

13. Letter, June 7, 1854; quoted in "Historical Note" to *Israel Potter: His Fifty-Years of Exile*, ed. Harrison Hayford, Hershel Parker, G. Thomas Tanselle (Evanston, Ill.: Northwestern University Press, 1982), p. 182.

14. By the word "problematic" I mean, with Louis Althusser, that culturally inscribed perspective or frame of reference that mediates and represents the truth of being. It is, as Althusser puts this in "Ideology and Ideological State Apparatuses (Notes towards an Investigation)," in *Lenin and Philosophy and Other Essays* (London: Monthly Review Press, 1971), that "Ideology" which is "a 'Representation' of the Imaginary Relationship of Individuals to their Real Conditions of Existence," p. 162. I will amplify considerably on this important poststructuralist concept in my commentaries on "Benito Cereno" and "Bartleby the Scrivener" in chapter 4.

15. See Carol Gruber, *Mars and Minerva: World War I and the Uses of the Higher Learning in America* (Baton Rouge: Louisiana State University Press, 1975). Tracing the origins of the famous Contemporary Civilization Course established at Columbia University in 1919 to the War Issues Course that was mandated and made universally compulsory by the state during World War I, Gruber writes: "The introduction of the required course in contemporary civilization at Columbia University illustrates the relationship between the War Issues Course and curricular reform. . . . A required course in contemporary civilization, offered by members of the departments of history, economics, government, and philosophy was introduced at Columbia in the fall of 1919. Its purpose was to survey the historical background of Western civilization and to acquaint the students with current world problems. Its promotion as a bulwark against radicalism [Bolshevism] betrayed its origins in the patriotic War Issues Course. . . ." pp. 243-244. See also Spanos, "The Violence of Disinterestedness: A Genealogy of the Educational 'Reform' Initiative in the 1980s," in *The End of Education: Toward Posthumanism* (Minneapolis: University of Minnesota Press, 1993), pp. 118-161.

16. William V. Spanos, *The Errant Art of* Moby-Dick, pp. 16-17.

17. See especially Donald E. Pease, "Visionary Compacts and the Cold War Consensus," in *Visionary Compacts: American Renaissance Writings in Cultural Context* (Madison: University of Wisconsin Press, 1987), pp. 3-48; and "New Americanists: Revisionist Interventions into the Canons," in *New Americanists: Revisionist Interventions into the Canon*, 1, a special issue of *boundary* 2, vol. 17 (Spring 1990), 1-37.

18. Martin Heidegger, "What Is Metaphysics?," in *Basic Writings*, ed. David Farrell Krell (New York: HarperSanFransciso, 1993), p. 96.

19. Jacques Derrida, "Structure, Sign, and Play in the Discourse of the Human Sciences," in *Writing and Difference*, trans. Alan Bass (Chicago: University of Chicago Press, 1978), p. 279.

20. Giorgio Agamben, "Bartleby, or On Contingency," in *Potentialities: Collected Essays in Philosophy*, trans. Daniel Heller-Roazin (Stanford: Stanford University Press, 1999), pp. 253-256. Agamben goes on to insist that this pure potentiality is not a willful refusal. But his unwillingness to identify Bartleby's "I prefer not to" with the political will does not preclude the attribution of a "politics" to it. As I will argue, the raison d'être of the "I prefer not to" is *not* to enable a kind of thinking that is not political, but rather that is not accountable to the meaning of the political that the Western metaphysical tradition has bequeathed to modernity.

21. Michel Foucault, *Language, Counter-Memory, Practice: Selected Essays and Interviews*, trans. Donald F. Bouchard and Sherry Simon, and ed. Bouchard (Ithaca, N.Y.: Cornell University Press, 1977), p. 111.

22. See Maurice Blanchot, *The Writing of the Disaster*, trans. Ann Smock (Lincoln: University of Nebraska Press, 1896), pp. 115–187; Jacques Derrida, "Donner la mort," in *L'Éthique du don*, ed. Jean-Michel Rabate and Michael Wetzel (Paris: Metailie-Transition, 1992); Gilles Deleuze, "Bartleby; or the Formula," in *Essays Critical and Clinical*, trans. Daniel W. Smith and Michael A. Greco (Minneapolis: University of Minnesota Press, 1997), pp. 68–90; and Giorgio Agamben, "Bartleby, or On Contingency."

23. Michel Foucault, "What Is an Author?" in *Language, Counter-Memory, Practice: Selected Essays and Interviews*, trans. Donald Bouchard and Sherry Simon, and ed. Bouchard (Ithaca, N.Y.: Cornell University Press, 1977), p. 131.

24. Samuel Huntington, *Who Are We?: The Challenges to America's National Identity* (New York: Simon and Schuster, 2004).

25. For exemplary instances of the ubiquity of this term, coined during the J. F. Kennedy administration, in the early years of the United States' intervention in Vietnam, see especially John Hellman, *American Myth and the Legacy of Vietnam* (New York: Columbia University Press, 1986), and William V. Spanos, *America's Shadow: An Anatomy of Empire* (Minneapolis: University of Minnesota Press, 2000), and *American Exceptionalism in the Age of Globalization: The Specter of Vietnam* (Albany: SUNY Press, 2008).

26. Herman Melville, *White Jacket; or, the World in a Man-of-War*, eds. Harrison Hayford, Hershel Parker, and G. Thomas Tanselle (Evanston, Ill. and Chicago: Northwestern University Press and The Newberry Library, 1970), pp. 150–151.

27. Herman Melville, "Hawthorne and His Mosses," in *Piazza Tales, and Other Prose Pieces, 1839–1860*, ed. Harrison Hayford, Alma A. MacDougall, G. Thomas Tanselle et al. (Evanston, Ill. and Chicago: Northwestern University Press and the Newberry Library, 1987), p. 246.

28. Sacvan Bercovitch, *The American Jeremiad* (Madison: University of Wisconsin Press, 1978), p. 176.

29. See Sacvan Bercovitch, *The Puritan Origins of the American Self* (New Haven: Yale University Press, 1975). Despite his failure to make explicit that which the figural interpretation must ruthlessly accommodate to authenticate its truth, this great work of scholarship, in my mind, remains indispensable to anyone engaged in the issue of the origins and nature of the American national identity. See especially his sustained analysis of Cotton Mather's biography of John Winthrop, "*Nehemias Americanus*," pp. 1–8, 35–49, 55–58, 64–73, 106–109, 126–131, 216–219.

30. See Bercovitch, *The American Jeremiad*.

31. Herman Melville to Nathaniel Hawthorne, April 16, 1851. *The Letters of Herman Melville*, pp. 124–125.

32. Gilles Deleuze, "Bartleby; or, the Formula," in *Essays Critical and Clinical*, trans. Daniel W. Smith and Michael A. Greco (Minneapolis: University of Minnesota Press: 1997), p. 86.

33. Giorgio Agamben, "Bartleby, or On Contingency," pp. 253–254. Antonio Negri and Michael Hardt also refer to Bartleby as "homo tantum, *mere man, and nothing more*," in *Empire* (Cambridge: Harvard University Press, 2000).

34. Deleuze, "Bartleby; or the Formula," pp. 86–87.

35. Herman Melville to Nathaniel Hawthorne, April 16, 1851. *The Letters of Herman Melville*, ed. Merrill R. Davis and William Gilman (New Haven: Yale University Press, 1960), pp. 24–125. For my reading of Melville's letter, see *The Errant Art of* Moby-Dick, pp. 109–112.

36. Nick Selby, ed. Herman Melville: *Moby-Dick* (New York: Columbia University Press, 1998), p. 165. This text is one in the series of "Columbia Critical Guides."

Chapter 2. Pierre's Extraordinary Emergency

1. Donald Pease, "New Americanists: Revisionist Interventions into the Canon," in *New Americans: Revisionist Interventions into the Canon*, a special issue of *boundary* 2, vol. 17 (Spring 1990): "By the term field-imaginary I mean to designate a location for the disciplinary unconscious mentioned earlier. Here abides the field's fundamental syntax—its tacit assumptions, convictions, primal words, and the charged relations binding them together. A field specialist depends upon this field-imaginary for the construction of her primal identity within the field. Once constructed out of this syntax, the primal identity can neither reflect upon its terms nor subject them to critical scrutiny. The syntactic elements of the field-imaginary subsist as self-evident principles" (pp. 11–12).

2. The virtual absence of reference to contemporary theory in the bibliographies and indexes of the new *Cambridge History of American Literature*, vols. 1 and 2, ed. Sacvan Bercovitch (Cambridge University Press, 1992, 1995) bears witness to this inability to get outside of the American exceptionalist problematic. This absence does not square with a history that claims it is elaborating a momentum of the past three decades in which "Americanist literary criticism has expanded from a border province into a center of humanist studies," according to the directives of a variety of conflicting perspectives (p. 1). This is not to say that the "New Americanists" involved in this project have not benefited from contemporary theory. It is to suggest that whatever use has been made of this theory has involved its appropriation to and disfigurement by an exceptionalist based version of liberal humanist pluralism. What I am suggesting is epitomized by the overdetermination of the consensus/dissensus binary in the "Introduction"—specifically, the privileging of dissensus over a previously privileged consensus. In this reversal the "difference" that is retrieved from traditionalist American Studies is not *differential*.

3. William V. Spanos, *The Errant Art of* Moby-Dick: *The Canon, the Cold War, and the Struggle for American Studies* (Durham, N.C.: Duke University Press, 1995). (My emphasis.) I have amplified this argument implicating metaphysical thinking and imperialism in *America's Shadow: An Anatomy of Empire* (Minneapolis: University of Minnesota Press, 2000) and in *American Exceptionalism in the Age of Globalization: The Specter of Vietnam* (Albany, N.Y.: SUNY Press, 2008).

4. Herman Melville, *Moby-Dick or The Whale*, ed. Harrison Hayford, Hershel Parker, and G. Thomas Tanselle (Evanston, Ill.: Northwestern University Press, 1988), p. 184.

5. Frederick Jackson Turner, "The Significance of the Frontier in American History" (New York: Henry Holt, 1953).

6. See, for example, Emory Eliot, "Art, Religion, and the Problem of Authority in *Pierre*," in *Ideology and Classic American Literature*, ed. Sacvan Bercovitch and Myra Jehlen (Cambridge: Cambridge University Press, 1987), 337–348; Sacvan Bercovich, "*Pierre* and the Ambiguities of American Literary History," *The Rites of Assent: Transformations in the Symbolic Construction of America* (New York: Routledge, 1993, pp. 246–306; John Carlos Rowe: "A Critique of Ideology: Herman Melville's *Pierre*," *At Emerson's Tomb: The Politics of Classic American Literature* (New York: Columbia University Press, 1997), pp. 63–95. Most recently, this tendency to universalize Melville's worldly fiction can be seen in the essays included in Giles Gunn, *A Historical Guide to Herman Melville* (Oxford: Oxford University Press, 2005).

7. Martin Heidegger, "What Is Metaphysics?" in *Basic Writings* ed. David Farrell Krell (New York: Harper & Row, 1977), p. 96.

8. Herman Melville, *Pierre; or the Ambiguities*, ed. Harrison Hayford, Hershel Parker, and G. Thomas Tanselle (Evanston, Ill.: Northwestern University Press), p. 89. Hereafter, this work is cited parenthetically as *P*.

9. Louis Althusser, "From 'Capital' to Marx's Philosophy," in *Reading Capital*, ed. Althusser and Étienne Balibar (London: Verso, 1970), p. 24.

10. Heidegger, "What Is Metaphysics?" in *Basic Writings*, p. 101. See also Heidegger, *Being and Time*, trans. John Macquarrie and Edward Robinson (New York: Harper & Row, 1962), pp. 228–235; 392–396.

11. Wei-chee Dimock, *Empire for Liberty: Melville and the Poetics of Individualism* (Princeton, N.J.: Princeton University Press, 1989). Dimock identifies Melville's "orphan" or "foundling" trope with the "Lockean model of selfhood" that, in spatializing identity and thus reducing it to " 'property,' " "is perhaps inevitably a territorial [and imperial] one" (p. 148). This identification constitutes the basis of her reading of *Pierre* (as well as *Moby-Dick*). I agree with Dimock's critique of the Lockean concept of self, with her recognition that this self-identical self had become fundamentally American in antebellum America, and with her appropriation of Michel Foucault's and Jacques Donzelot's demonstration of the complicity between the "individual" and the disciplinary society in pursuing that critique. But I also think that her attribution of this imperial Lockean concept of the self-present self, this "orphanlike individual" (p. 142) to Pierre (and Melville) constitutes a willful misreading of Melville's characterization of Pierre and of the essential *élan* of the novel. It is an attribution, for example, that astonishingly renders Pierre's subtly authoritarian mother, Mrs. Glendinning, the "victim" of his manifest destinarian individualist will to knowledge: "Mrs. Glendinning is . . . as doomed as Ahab. . . . [Pierre] has effectively reduced his mother from a parent to a product" (153). Dimock's criticism of Pierre's treatment of his mother is no doubt grounded in a certain feminist solidarity with Mrs. Glendinning. But the fact is that she simply is not the complex and differential being that Dimock would make her. On the contrary, as I will show, she is the post-Revolutionary hegemonic voice of America, whose elected authority is dependent on reducing the force of historicity to monument and its difference to "docility." It is testimony to the willfulness of her reading of *Pierre* that Dimock never once mentions the word "ambiguities," which Melville ironically juxtaposes against "Pierre" (French: "rock") in the title. Nor, even more tellingly, does she refer to the crucial passages (quoted

below) on the *absence*—"the appalling vacancy"—at the core of Pierre's being, in which Melville clearly and decisively deconstructs the "Lockean"/"imperial"—and Emersonian—representation of the American self. As in her reading of *Moby-Dick*, Dimock's "demonstration" of Pierre's (and Melville's) complicity with the American "empire for liberty" nexus is an instance of the very spatializing imperial practice she attributes to Pierre. Dimock, in other words, "victimizes" Melville's *Pierre* in precisely the way she claims Pierre (and Melville) victimizes Mrs. Glendinning (as well as Lucy and Isabel). See Spanos, *The Errant Art of* Moby-Dick, pp. 229–230. For my quite different interpretation of what the metaphor of orphanage means in Melville, see *The Errant Art of Moby-Dick*, pp. 151–156.

12. Louis Althusser, "Ideology and Ideological State Apparatuses (Notes towards an Investigation)," in *Lenin and Philosophy and Other Essays*, trans. Ben Brewster (New York: Monthly Review Press, 1971), p. 181. I will amplify on the Althusserian concept of interpellation (hailing) in my readings of "Benito Cereno" and "Bartleby, the Scrivener" in chapter 4 to show its remarkable relationship to the Puritan "calling."

13. Even for F. O. Matthiessen, whose social consciousness should have prompted him otherwise, *Pierre* is an "American *Hamlet*," albeit imperfectly realized, which has "very little to do with political and social values," *American Renaissance: Art and Expression in the Age of Emerson and Whitman* (London: Oxford University Press, 1941), p. 469.

14. Emory Eliot. "Art, Religion, and the Problem of Authority in *Pierre*," p. 346.

15. George Washington Peck, in a review of *Pierre* in *American Whig Review*, vol. 16, (November 1852), 446–454; reprinted in *Herman Melville: The Contemporary Reviews*, ed. Brian Higgins and Hershel Parker (Cambridge: Cambridge University Press, 1995), p. 443.

16. Peck, *Herman Melville, The Contemporary Reviews*, p. 443.

17. Antonio Gramsci. *Selections from the Prison Notebooks*, ed. and trans. Quintin Hoare and Geoffrey Nowell Smith (New York: International Publishers. 1971), p. 12; Michel Foucault, *Discipline and Punish: The Birth of the Prison*, trans. Alan Sheridan (New York: Pantheon, 1977). See especially the chapter entitled "Docile Bodies," pp. 135–170; Althusser, "Ideology and Ideological State Apparatuses (Notes towards an Investigation)," pp. 127–188, and "From *Capital* to Marx's Philosophy"; Raymond Williams, "Hegemony," in *Marxism and Literature* (Oxford: Oxford University Press, 1977), pp. 108–114.

18. Ernest Renan, "What Is a Nation?," trans. Martin Thom, in *Nation and Narration*, ed. Homi K. Bhaba (London: Routledge, 1990), pp. 11, 19.

19. Renan, "What Is a Nation?," p. 11.

20. This latter conjunction, as I have suggested in *The Errant Art of* Moby-Dick, is at the core of *Moby-Dick*. See especially, pp. 101 ff., 206–215. John Carlos Rowe has thought the economic motif in a brilliant Marxist reading of *Pierre* in *At Emerson's Tomb*. But, like other New Americanists, he focuses on Pierre's failure to transcend the limits of the Emersonian self. As a result, he fails to penetrate beyond the ideology imbedded in capitalist economy to the metaphysical ideology that, as I am suggesting, for Melville constitutes the ground of the former. As a result, he also fails to respond to Melville's directive to rethink American thinking, not least, the positive content of Pierre's silence.

21. Jacques Derrida. "Structure, Sign, and Play in the Discourse of the Human Sciences," in *Writing and Difference*, trans. Alan Bass (Chicago: University of Chicago Pres, 1978), p. 279.

22. Raymond Williams, *Marxism and Literature*, pp. 109–110. My emphasis. I have underscored the constraints incumbent on the total naturalization of an ideological program that Williams puts in terms of the metaphor of movement to signal a more literal consequence: the reduction of voice to silence, that is, interdiction (Latin, *inter+dicere:* "to forbid to say." Williams and many of those following him allow for saying/resistance by pointing to the exploitable fissures that are endemic to the hegemony. What I will suggest is that, since this potential resistance must be carried out in the terms of the thought permitted by the discourse of hegemony, it is a saying/resistance that, as in the case of Pierre's, is necessarily doomed to fail. In an ultimate sense then it is not saying/resistance in any real sense of these words.

23. In identifying Scots and Yankees in this passage, Melville, I think, is referring to the significant influence of Thomas Carlyle's "natural supernaturalism" on Ralph Waldo Emerson's Transcendentalism.

24. Hannah Arendt, *The Life of the Mind*, ed. Mary McCarthy (New York: Harcourt Brace, 1978), p. 153.

25. Martin Heidegger, *Parmenides*, trans. André Schuwer and Richard Rojcewicz (Bloomington: University of Indiana Press, 1992), pp. 39–45.

26. As far as I know, only John Carlos Rowe has noted the pervasiveness of the metaphorics of monumentality in *Pierre*. But his interpretation of this trope, following Marx, emphasizes its affiliation with the "arbitrary powers" of ancient despots, not with the ontologically grounded remembrance that, as Renan makes clear and as Melville intends to suggest, constitutes one the essential agencies of modern nation building, that is, the achievement of consensus by the dominant culture: "In particular, Marx calls attention to the 'colossal works' of this coordinated slave labor in terms designed clearly to gloss his theory of surplus value. The monumental projects undertaken by such coordinated labor forces are generally made possible by large state surpluses often generated by military conquests. These monuments are thus testaments to the surplus value on which the ancient despot based his political power—the capital of domination.... In addition the monuments built by such despots often serve no other purpose than to represent that arbitrary power in the form of such purely ceremonial structures as tombs, pyramids, obelisks.... As such, these ancient monuments—so often dedicated to death and/or a religious or military ideal—are testaments to social waste as well as dramatic illustrations of the kind of reification that will be the ultimate product of capitalism. *At Emerson's Tomb*, p. 80.

27. Michel Foucault, "Nietzsche, Genealogy, History," in *Language, Counter-Memory, Practice: Selected Essays and Interviews*, ed. Donald F. Bouchard, trans. Bouchard and Sherry Simon (Oxford: Basil Blackwell, 1977) (p. 143). See also Nietzsche's decisive dismantling of monumental history in "On the Uses and Disadvantages of History for Life," in *Untimely Meditations*, trans. R. J. Hollingdale (Cambridge: Cambridge University Press, 1983), 59–123.

28. Althusser, "Ideology and Ideological State Apparatuses," in *Lenin and Philosophy and Other Essays*, pp. 179–183.

29. Ralph Waldo Emerson, "Young America," in *Nature, Addresses, and Lectures*, vol. 1 of *The Collected Works of Ralph Waldo Emerson*, eds. Robert E. Spiller

and Alfred R. Ferguson (Cambridge, Mass.: Harvard University Press, 1971), pp. 211–230. (My emphasis.)

30. Jean-Paul Sartre, *Nausea*, trans. Lloyd Alexander (New York: New Directions, 1964), pp. 39–40.

31. See Edgar Dryden, "The Entangled Text: Melville's *Pierre* and the Problem of Reading," *boundary* 2, vol. 7 (Spring 1979), 45–73. See also Joseph N. Riddel, "Decentering the Image: The 'Project' of 'American Poetics?" in *The Problems of Reading in Contemporary American Criticism,* a special issue of *boundary* 2, vol. 8 (Fall 1979), 164–166; reprinted in *The Question of Textuality: Strategies of Reading in Contemporary American Criticism* (Bloomington: University of Indiana Press, 1982).

32. Louis Althusser, " 'On the Young Marx': Theoretical Questions," in *For Marx*, trans. Ben Brewster (London: New Left Books, 1977), p. 54.

33. Edward Said, *Beginnings: Intention and Method* (NewYork: Basic Books, 1975), pp. 4–6; 174–175.

34. Michel Foucault, "Nietzsche, Genealogy, History," p. 143.

35. Melville does not focalize slavery in *Pierre*. As I have noted, he limits reference to this violent American practice to his genealogical account of Pierre's "noble" heritage (if we do not take Dates, the "servitor" in the Glendinning household to be a black man, which may not be the case), more specifically, to his satirical account of "grand old Pierre," Pierre's grandfather and namesake, who owned slaves in "those fine old robust times" (*P*, 29). But it is a marginal reference that, coming as it does at the beginning of the novel, where Melville is establishing Saddle Meadows as a synecdoche of antebellum American culture, infuses its marginality with a spectral resonance that carries over into and haunts the rest of the story. I am referring to that juncture of this genealogy where Melville is speaking of "grand old Pierre's" inordinately love for his horses—they are his "intimate friends"—in the context of his slaves, whose responsibility is to care for them: "This grand old Pierre always rose at sunrise; washed his face and chest in the open air; and then, returning to his closet, and being completely arrayed at last, stepped forth to make a ceremonious call at his stables, to bid his very honorable friends there a very good and joyful morning. Woe to Cranz, Kit, Douw, or any other of his stable slaves, if grand old Pierre found one horse unblanketed, or one weed among the hay that filled their rack. Not that he ever had Cranz, Kit, Douw, or any of them flogged—a thing unknown in that patriarchal time and country—but he would refuse to say his wonted pleasant word to them; and that was very bitter to them, for Cranz, Kit, Douw, and all of them, loved grand old Pierre, as his shepherds loved old Abraham" (*P*, 30). If this marginal satirical reference to slavery is seen in the context of the pervasiveness of Melville's use of the metaphorics of darkness and shadow to render the spectral resonance of the silence of those bereft of language by the American discourse of hegemony, the black African will also be seen to be a link in the indissoluble chain of absent presences that haunts this imperial discourse. In this, Melville's *Pierre*, in fact, anticipates Toni Morrison's resonant disclosures about the rhetoric of the *canonical* texts of the American literary canon in *Playing in the Dark: Whiteness and the Literary Imagination* (New York: Vintage Books, 1993): "Explicit or implicit, the African presence informs in compelling and inescapable ways the texture of American literature. It is a dark and abiding presence, there for the literary imagination as both a visible

and an invisible mediating force. Even, and especially, when American texts are not 'about' Africanist presences or character or narrative or idiom, the shadow hovers in implication, in sign, in line of demarcation," pp. 46–47.

36. Heidegger, "What Is Metaphysics?," p. 95.

37. See Spanos, *The Errant Art of Moby-Dick*, pp. 124–127; 127–131; 169–172; 197–201; 269–270.

38. Derrida, "Differance," in *Speech and Phenomena and Other Essays on Husserl's Theory of Signs*, trans. David B. Allison (Evanston, Ill.: Northwestern University Press, 1973), 129–160.

39. The image Pierre invokes to visualize the kind of book he would write is the atoll: "the primitive coral islets which, raising themselves in the depths of profoundest seas, rise funnel-like to the surface, and present there a hoop of white rock, which though on the outside everywhere lashed by the ocean, yet excludes all tempests from the quiet lagoon within" (*P*, 283). Pierre invokes this image because it ostensibly refers to the primordial nature at which he thinks he has arrived. But his description of this natural phenomenon is remarkably like the description of a man-made monument intended to resist the ravages of time. Indeed, it is, as Joseph Riddel, following the lead of Edgar Dryden, has brilliantly shown, quite like the pyramid that Melville invokes on the next page to deconstruct the scriptural Book that Pierre, in his "unprecedented situation," envisions. See Riddel, "Decentering the Image," pp. 165–166; and Dryden, "The Entangled Text," pp. 162–163. The pyramid, it needs to be emphasized, is that fundamental spatial structure projected by civilized man not simply to transcend the ephemeral state of mortality but also, by way of its panoptic allotrope, to facilitate a dominant culture's domination of the "Other." Not too far behind the atoll/pyramid trope, as I am suggesting by way of invoking the metaphor of the microcosm, is the trope of the map.

40. As I have pointed out elsewhere, the word "comprehend," which is intrinsic to the discourse of knowledge production in the West, derives from the Latin *com*, an archaic form of *cum* ("with") used in compounds and meaning "together, in combination or union," "altogether, completely," and *prehendere* "to seize," "to take hold of," that is to say, from two complicitous *metaphorical* systems—seeing and grasping—that belie the originality of the truth of being. This etymology thus discloses the pursuit of knowledge in the West to be a process informed by the will to power over the be-ing of being. I mean the willful reduction of temporality to spatial form (a microcosm mirroring the macrocosm) or, what is the same thing, the reification of an essentially unreifiable being for the purpose of dominating it. Western epistemology, in other words, serves the function of annulling the anxiety of being-in-the-world and/or of transforming the difference that time disseminates to "standing reserve" (Heidegger) or "useful and docile body" (Foucault). "Comprehend," not incidentally, is one of the key philosophical words in the discourse of Hegel's metaphysical dialectics. See Spanos, *Heidegger and Criticism: Retrieving the Cultural Politics of Destruction* (Minneapolis: University of Minnesota Press, 1993), 141–144. See also the chapter entitled "Heidegger and Foucault: The Politics of the Commanding Gaze," pp. 132–180.

41. Martin Heidegger, "What Is Metaphysics?," 100–101; Jean-François Lyotard, *The Postmodern Condition: A Report on Knowledge*, trans. Geoff Bennington and Brian Massumi (Minneapolis: University of Minnesota Press, 1984), pp. 79–82.

42. As Dominique Arnaud-Marçais observes in "The Presence and Significance of France and the French Language in *Moby-Dick; or, The Whale*," in *Melville "Among the Nations": Proceedings of an International Conference, Volos, Greece, July 2–6, 1997*, eds. Sanford E. Marovitz and A. C. Christodoulou (Kent, Ohio: Kent State University Press, 2001), p. 506, Melville is consciously eliding the meaning of the French word *blanc* ("white") with the English word *blank* ("the absence of presence") in the following passage from the chapter "The Whiteness of the Whale" in *Moby-Dick*: "Is it that by its indefiniteness it shadows forth the heartless voids and immensities of the universe, and thus stabs us from behind with the thought of annihilation, when beholding the white depths of the milky way? Or is it, that as in essence whiteness is not so much a color as the visible absence of color, and at the same time the concrete of all colors; is it for these reasons that there is such a dumb blankness, full of meaning, in a wide landscape of snow—a colorless, all-color of atheism from which we shrink?," (p. 195).

43. Martin Heidegger, "The End of Philosophy and the Task of Thinking," in *Time and Being*, trans. Joan Stambaugh (New York: Harper & Row, 1972), pp. 55–73.

44. Martin Heidegger, "The Age of the World Picture," in *The Question Concerning Technology and Other Essays*, trans. William Lovitt (New York: Harper and Row, 1977), pp. 115–154.

45. Martin Heidegger, "Language in the Poem: A Discussion of Georg Trakl's Poetic Work," trans. Joan Stambaugh, *On the Way to Language* (New York: Harper & Row, 1971), pp. 177–179.

46. Derrida, *Of Spirit*, trans. Geoffrey Bennington and Rachel Bowlby (Chicago: University of Chicago Press, 1989).

47. Heidegger, *Being and Time*, 102–107; 164–166.

48. Louis Althusser, "From *Capital* to Marx's Philosophy," p. 24.

49. Giorgio Agamben, "Bartleby, or On contingency," in *Potentialities: Collected Essays in Philosophy*, ed. and trans. Daniel Heller-Roazen (Stanford: Stanford University Press, 1999), pp. 243–271.

50. Martin Heidegger, "On the Essence of Truth," trans. John Sallis, in *Basic Writings*, pp. 132–135.

51. See Spanos, *The Errant Art of* Moby-Dick, especially, pp. 191–203.

52. For an amplification of this etymology, see Spanos, *America's Shadow: An Anatomy of Empire* (Minneapolis: University of Minnesota Press, 2000), pp. 96–99. Wei-chee Dimock makes explicit the pervasiveness of the metaphorics of empire in *Pierre*, a "domestic" novel, and shows convincingly that the domestic *topos* which the novel overdetermines is utterly continuous with the geopolitical: "C. B. Macpherson, commenting on Hobbe's model of selfhood, makes just this point. A society of 'possessive individualism . . . permits and requires the continual invasion of every man by every other.' The self that inhabits such a society must be an 'imperial' self then: in its defensive pose no less than in its appropriative venture, it must act like an imperial polity. From this perspective, there is nothing fortuitous about the presence of Manifest Destiny in *Pierre*, and nothing decorative about its allusions to empire. [She is referring to "the frontier images in *Pierre's* domestic landscape" (p. 146).] Those allusions describe, on the contrary, both the structure of its 'untrammelled' self and the structure of the environment that dictates to the self its particular shape. The imperial trappings of Love, especially, have everything to do with the 'internalization' of Manifest Destiny, with the constitution of the

self as a 'dominion,' a terrain subject to sovereignty and expropriation both" (pp. 148–149). But see my reservations about Dimock's use of this continuum in her reading of *Pierre* in footnote 6.

53. "Region" (of knowledge), for example, derives from the Latin *regere*, "to command"; "province," from *vincere*," to conquer"; "domain," from *dominus*, "master." See Michel Foucault, "Questions Concerning Geography," in *Power/Knowledge: Selected Interviews and Other Writings 1972–77*, ed. Colin Gordon (New York: Pantheon Books, 1980), p. 69. As Heidegger suggests, "territory" derives from the Latin *terra*, "earth," understood, not, like the Greeks' *gaia* or *ge*, as the in-between in which *aletheia* ("un-concealment") happens, but as *territorium*, which, means "land of settlement as realm of command" and in which "can be heard an imperial accent," *Parmenides*, p. 60.

54. In a provocative "New Americanist" reading of *Pierre*, Patricia Wald interprets Pierre's declaration to "gospelize the world anew!" in the following way: "His use of 'gospelize' suggests that he *cannot* reject the basic tenets he thinks he has overthrown. Pierre *wants* to be the instrument through which an absolute eternal truth is filtered; he wants to transcribe rather than write." In this, Pierre is to Wald, following Donald Pease, "not only Ahab's heir . . . but Ishmael's as well." She thus reads Melville's attitude towards Pierre's declaration as one of mockery: "Pierre's text, which also features an author-hero, mirrors both Pierre and *Pierre*; the former is, again, not conscious of the full implications of reflection, whereas the latter exploits it. Melville ridicules Pierre, whose manuscript betrays not the darkness of his vision that horrified his publishers, but the ludicrousness that undermines his tragedy." (My emphasis.) "Hearing Narrative Voices in *Pierre*," in *New Americanists: Revisionist Interventions into the Canon*, p. 126. Wald, I think, is right in saying that Pierre "cannot reject the basic tenets he thinks he has overthrown." But I would take issue with her subtle restatement of this negative in positive terms: as *wanting* "to be the instrument through which an absolute eternal truth is filtered." Melville is not ridiculing Pierre's juvenile obtuseness. He is pointing, rather—as he is in his portrayal of Captain Amasa Delano in "Benito Cereno," to the depth to which Pierre is inscribed by the triumphant hegemonic discourse of America, that is, to the global scope and power of the discourse he would overthrow. He *cannot* reject it because no other language but that of the dominant imperial culture is available to him. For my reservations about Donald Pease's reading of Ishmael's narrative as an internalization of Ahab's monomaniacal "acts of interpretation," which Wald appropriates for her reading of Pierre's abortive effort to "gospelize the world anew," see *The Errant Art of Moby-Dick*, pp. 224–225, 243–245, 274–275.

55. These pistol shots constitute a reversal of the binary logic that justifies the world's violence against the unaccommodatable "Other." As such, of course, it leaves this binary logic in tact. I am not saying that Melville endorses such a reversal. I am suggesting, rather, that he is disclosing to his self-righteous and complacent—self-confident—American audience that such a retributive or revolutionary response of the silenced "Other" is endemic to its "truth." More fundamentally, I am also suggesting that the only way of transceding the violence of binarist logic is to think the silence that lies behind it.

56. See Fredric Jameson, *Postmodernism; or, The Logic of Late Capitalism* (Durham, N.C.: Duke University Press, 1991). See also Antonio Negri and Michael Hardt, *Empire* (Cambridge, Mass.: Harvard University Press, 2000), pp. 137–156.

57. Derrida, *Specters of Marx: The State of the Debt, the Work of Mourning, and the New International*, trans. Peggy Kamuf (New York: Routledge, 1994), 99–102.

58. Bercovitch, *Rites of Assent*, p. 296. The phrase he quotes is from *Pierre*, p. 17.

59. My interrogation of Bercovitch's dissociation of Isabel and Pierre applies as well to John Carlos Rowe, who invokes Bercovitch's reference to Isabel's haunting shadow to claim that "Isabel is . . . a key to Melville's social theory of the American family," especially as it relates the issue of labor. *At Emerson's Tomb*, p. 73. Rowe's overdetermination of the labor characterizing the antebellum American family (as this motif is embodied in the figure of Isabel) at the expense of the ontological ground of this family structure (the ground that Pierre, above all, is attempting to think), deflects his attention away from the substantiality of the shadow—its affiliative relationship to the "light" of the world of Saddle Meadows. It thus precludes his attending to the question of silence—or, rather, the question of "the voice of silence—which I take to be Melville's supreme theme in *Pierre*.

60. See Spanos, *The Errant Art of* Moby-Dick, pp. 271–274.

61. Hannah Arendt, "Antisemitism," Part I of *The Origins of Totalitarianism* (New York: Meridian, 1958) and *Men in Dark Times* (New York: Harcourt, Brace, and World, 1968).

62. Jean-François Lyotard, *Differend: Phrases in Dispute*, trans. Georges Van Den Abbele (Minneapolis: University of Minnesota Press, 1988); and *Heidegger and "the jews,"* trans. Andreas Michel and Mark Roberts (Minneapolis: University of Minnesota Press, 1990).

63. Gayatri Chakravorty Spivak, "Marginality in the Teaching Machine," in *Outside in the Teaching Machine* (New York: Routledge, 1993), pp. 53–76.

64. Michel Foucault, "Theatrum Philosophicum" in *Language, Counter-Memory, Practice: Selected Essays and Interviews*, ed. Donald Bouchard, trans. Bouchard and Sherry Simon (Ithaca, N.Y.: Cornell University Press, 1977), pp. 165–196. This essay is a review of Gilles Deleuze's *Différence et repetition* (1969) and *Logique du sens* (1969), which inaugurate Deleuze's sustained effort to think the "phantasmic" excess of the Western philosophical tradition that culminates in the rhizomatic thinking of the nomad in his and Guattari's *A Thousand Plateaus*. See below.

65. Jacques Derrida, *Specters of Marx: The State of the Debt, the Work of Mourning, and the New International*.

66. Gilles Deleuze and Félix Guatarri, *A Thousand Plateaus: Capitalism and Schizophrenia*, trans. Brian Massumi (New York: Routledge, 1987).

67. Negri and Hardt, *Empire*, p. 203.

68. Giorgio Agamben, *The Coming Community*, trans. Michael Hardt (Minneapolis: University of Minnesota Pres, 1993), p. 1.

69. Priscilla Wald verges on thematizing this momentous, but still to be adequately thought, postmetaphysical legacy: "Insofar as we come to see the narrators' perspective as an alternate narrative (as, that is, *an* other, not *the* other narrative, then perhaps Silence can indeed speak to the attuned reader. The narrative unravelling that follows undermines narrative authority and alerts the reader to the possibility of an alternative discourse. Silence (and its counterpart, meaningless noise) emerges in resistance to narrative and meaningful language, not as an absence but as an alternative presence, the *embodiment*, perhaps of possibility."

"Hearing Narrative Voices in Melville's *Pierre*, p. 120. But because her insight is occluded by her vestigially American exceptionalism, she is compelled to refer to Pierre's predicament as a problem more or less of authorial identity and to contain Melville's *Pierre* within "the scene of writing." She thus fails to perceive the global scope of Melville's domestic "drama" and, above all, of the "possibility" vis-à-vis thinking inhering in his evocation of the Silence to which the American "world" reduces those who refuse their spontaneous consent to its truth.

70. Deleuze and Guattari, *A Thousand Plateaus*, pp. 351–423.

71. Hannah Arendt, *Imperialism*, Part II of *The Origins of Totalitarianism*.

72. Said, *Culture and Imperialism* (New York: Alfred A. Knopf, 1993), p. 332. See also, the chapter entitled " 'Theory' and the End of History," in Spanos, *America's Shadow: An Anatomy of Empire* (Minneapolis: University of Minnesota Press, 2000).

73. Paul Bové, "Notes toward a Politics of 'American' Criticism, in *In the Wake of Theory* (Hanover, N.H.: Wesleyan University Press, 1992), p. 63. See also, Gayatri Spivak, *The Post-colonial Subject: Interviews, Strategies, Dialogues*, ed. Sarah Harasym (New York: Routledge, 1990), and *Outside in the Teaching Machine* (New York: Routledge, 1993).

Chapter 3. Herman Melville's *Israel Potter*

1. Herman Melville, *Israel Potter: His Fifty Years of Exile*, ed. Harrison Hayford, Hershel Parker, and G. Thomas Tanselle (Evanston, Ill.: Northwestern University Press, 1982), pp. vii–viii. Further citations will be abbreviated to *IP* and incorporated in the text in parentheses.

2. See, for example, the historical essay by Walter Bezanson appended to the Northwestern and Newberry Library edition of *Israel Potter*. See also Arnold Rampersad, *Melville's* Israel Potter: *A Pilgrimage and Progress* (Bowling Green: Bowling Green University Popular Press, 1969).

3. Michel Foucault, "Nietzsche, Genealogy, History," in *Language, Counter-Memory, Practice: Selected Essays and Interviews*, trans. Donald F. Bouchard and Sherry Simon and ed. Bouchard (Ithaca, N.Y.: Cornell University Press, 1977), p. 161. See also Friedrich Nietzsche, "The Use and Abuse of History" trans. Adrian Collins (Indianapolis: Bobb-Merrill, 1978, rev. ed.), pp. 12–17.

4. Edward W. Said, *Culture and Imperialism* (New York: Alfred A. Knopf, 1993): "In practical terms, 'contrapuntal reading'. . . means reading a text with an understanding of what is involved when an author shows, for instance, that a colonial sugar plantation is seen as important to the process of maintaining a particular style of life in England. Moreover, like all literary texts, these are not bounded by their formal historic beginnings and endings. References to Australia in *David Copperfield* or India in *Jane Eyre* are made because they *can be*, because British power (and not just the novelist's fancy) made passing references to these massive appropriations possible; but the further lessons are no less true: that these colonies were subsequently liberated from direct and indirect rule. . . . The point is that contrapuntal reading must take account of both processes, that of imperialism and that of resistance to it, which can be done by extending our reading of the texts to include what was once forcibly excluded. . . . " pp. 66–67.

5. Michel Foucault, "Truth and Power" in *Foucault Reader*, ed. Paul Rabinow (New York: Panthon Books, 1984), p. 73.

6. Sacvan Bercovitch, *The American Jeremiad* (Madison: University of Wisconsin Press, 1978).

7. Jared Sparks was editor of *The North American Review*, a noted historian of the American Revolution, and the editor of the writings of George Washington and Benjamin Franklin. For Melville, as the reference to him in the dedication makes clear, he was a monumentalist historian.

8. Melville found the original in a bookstall in London in the fall of 1849, though he did not start writing until 1854. See Walter Bezanson, "Historical Note" in *Israel Potter*, p. 174. The Bunker Hill Monument, we are told in the editor's introduction to Webster's first speech, was, not incidentally, sponsored by the "King Solomon's Lodge" (a Masonic Order) of Charlestown, Massachusetts. This Masonic Order invited Webster, who was the president of the monument association, to dedicate the monument. He was accompanied by General Lafayette. Daniel Webster, *Memoir: Speeches on Various Occasions, vol. I, The Writings and Speeches of Daniel Webster* (Boston: Little, Brown, and Co. 1903), p. 234. Further citations will be abbreviated to *M* and incorporated in my text in parentheses.

9. In his very long "Historical Note" to the standard Northwestern/Newberry Library edition of *Israel Potter*, Walter Bezanson invokes the laying of the cornerstone of the monument and Webster's part in the ceremonies in a footnote expanding on his account of Trumbull's strategy to exploit, in behalf of gaining a government pension for Israel Potter, an occasion in which "a country already [was] aquiver with semicentennial celebration plans, including a huge monument to celebrate Bunker Hill." The footnote reads: "The cornerstone was laid June 17, 1825, by Lafayette, and Daniel Webster's oration was a school classic for a century. The Monument, completed in 1843, was dedicated by President Tyler and his cabinet before a massive crowd. '*His Highness*' (Melville's dedicatory phrase) is 39 feet square at the base, 221 feet high" (p. 186). With such a detailed documentary knowledge of the events, statistics, personages, literary antecedents, and so on, associated with the occasion of Melville's writing and publication of *Israel Potter*, it comes as a surprise that this erudite commentator, like so many other earlier Melvilleans, should not let his reader know that Webster also delivered a second dedicatory address at the time of the completion of the Bunker Hill Monument in 1843. Michael Paul Rogin is, as far as I know, the only critic who has invoked Webster's orations in his commentary on *Israel Potter*, but his comments on this connection are minimal. See *Subversive Genealogy: The Politics and Art of Herman Melville* (New York: Alfred Knopf, 1983), p. 225

10. Jay Leyda, *The Melville Log: A Documentary Life of Herman Melville, 1819–1891*, vol. 1 (New York: Harcourt, Brace, 1951), pp. 488–489.

11. See also Webster's equally classic speech "First Settlement of New England," in *The Writings and Speeches of Daniel Webster*, vol. 1, delivered at Plymouth, Massachusetts on the two-hundredth anniversary of the Pilgrims' landing in 1620, in which the nationalistic metaphorics of "filiation"—and the will to power over alterity intrinsic to them—I have been emphasizing are even more pronounced: "We have come to this Rock, to record here our homage for our Pilgrim Fathers; our sympathy in their sufferings; our gratitude for their labors; our admiration of their virtues; our veneration of their piety; and our attachment to those principles of civil and religious liberty, which they encountered the dangers of the ocean,

the storms of heaven, the violence of savages, disease, exile, and famine, to enjoy and to establish. And we would leave here, also, for generations which are rising up rapidly to fill our places, some proof that we have endeavored to transmit the great inheritance unimpaired; that in our estimate of public principles and private virtue, in our veneration of religion and piety, in our devotion to civil and religious liberty, in our regard for whatever advances human knowledge or improves human happiness, we are not altogether unworthy of our origin," p. 183. In invoking the term "filiation," I am indebted to Edward Said's theorization of its relationship with and difference from "affiliation" in the essays of *The World, the Text, and the Critic* (Cambridge, Mass.: Harvard University Press, 1983).

12. See Eduardo Cadava, *Emerson and the Climates of History* (Stanford, Ca.: Stanford University Press. 1997), pp. 106–114. Cadava invokes Webster's first oration of 1825 and its jeremiadic structure and intent in the context of his effort to show "that Emerson's admiration for Webster [whom he had referred to as 'Nature's own child'] was not as unqualified in the 1830s as we have been taught to believe," p. 107. His critical account of Webster's address is admirable in its disclosure of the complicity of his encomium to the revolutionary Fathers and the contemporary rise of capitalism. But I have found Cadava's defense of Emerson against the charge, epitomized by Donald Pease, that his refusal of the founding Fathers was not radical enough, unconvincing. See Pease, *Visionary Compacts: American Renaissance Writings in Cultural Context* (Madison: University of Wisconsin Press, 1997), p. 222.

13. Like so many of the intellectual deputies of the dominant culture in America in the eighteenth and nineteenth centuries, Webster identified the American spirit of liberty with the Anglo-Saxon race. Here, this racism is revealed in Webster's appeal to Alfred the Great. In the second oration it is more clearly seen in his tracing of the origins of Americans' love of liberty not simply to the Protestant Reformation's "spirit of commercial and foreign adventure" and its "love of religious liberty," but also, and above all, to the Anglo-Saxon race's love of civil liberty. These "were the powerful influences under which character was formed and men trained, for the great work of introducing English civilization, English law, and what is more than all, Anglo-Saxon blood, into the wilderness of North America (W, 270). For a persuasive history of the role race theory played in the formation of the American national identity and political practice, see Reginald Horsman, *Race and Manifest Destiny: The Origins of American Racial Anglo-Saxonism* (Cambridge, Mass.: Harvard University Press, 1981).

14. I am appropriating the distinction that Antonio Negro and Michael Hardt make in *Empire* (Cambridge, Mass.: Harvard University Press, 2000) between "the people" and "the multitude": "The multitude is a multiplicity, a plane of singularities, an open set of relations, which is not homogeneous or identical with itself and bears an indistinct, inclusive relation to those outside of it. The people, in contrast, tends toward identity and homogeneity internally while posing its difference from and excluding what remains outside of it. . . . The people provides a single will and action that is independent of and often in conflict with the various wills and actions of the multitude. Every nation must make the multitude into people," pp. 102–103.

15. See William V. Spanos, *The Errant Art of Moby-Dick: The Canon, the Cold War, and the Struggle for American Literary Studies* (Durham, N.C.: Duke University Press, 1995), pp. 105–106.

16. Ernest Renan, "What Is a Nation?," trans. Martin Thom in Homi Bhabha, ed. *Nation and Narration* (London: Routledge), p. 19. Further citations will be abbreviated to *WN* and incorporated in the text in parentheses.

17. Herman Melville, *The Confidence-Man: His Masquerade*, ed. Harrison Hayford, Hershel Parker, and G. Thomas Tanselle (Evanston, Ill.: Northwestern University Press, 1984), p. 66. Malakoff was a theoretically impregnable fort held by the Russians in the Crimean War; it fell to the French forces on September 8, 1855.

18. Figural exegesis, as Eric Auerbach has defined the means by which the Patristic Fathers reconciled the apparent historical contradictions between the Old Testament and the New, is based on a promise/fulfillment structure that is believed to inhere in history. It "establishes a connection between two events or persons, the first of which signifies not only itself but also the second, while the second encompasses or fulfills the first. The two poles of the figure are separated in time, but both, being real events or figures, are within time, within the stream of historical life." "Figura," in *Scenes from the Drama of European Literature: Six Essays* (New York: Meridian Books, 1959), pp. 53–54. As Sacvan Bercovitch has shown, the Puritans appropriated this figural method of interpretation for their particular historical purposes. See *The Puritan Origins of the American Self* (New Haven: Yale University Press, 1975); and *The American Jeremiad* (Madison: University of Wisconsin Press, 1978), pp. 12–13. I invoke the European provenance of Auerbach's definition to underscore the unexceptional nature of the Puritans' exceptionalism, a point that Bercovitch leaves unsaid. For an extended discussion of Melville's critique of this Puritan exegetical strategy, see my reading of Father Mapple's sermon in, *The Errant Art of* Moby-Dick, pp. 96–114.

19. Bezanson, "Historical Note," *Israel Potter*, pp. 188–189.

20. Herman Melville, *Pierre; or the Ambiguities*, eds. Harrison Hayford, Hershel Parker, and G. Thomas Tanselle (Evanston, Ill.: Northwestern University Press, 1971), p. 89.

21. Michelle Foucault, "Nietzsche, Genealogy, History," p. 161

22. Benjamin Franklin, *Autobiography*, eds. J. A. Leo Lemay and P. M. Zall (New York: Norton Critical Edition (1986), pp. 16, 27, 34, 36, 40, 56.

23. In *Don Quixote*, the Don betrays the insanity of the unerring mono-logic of his interpretive frame of reference when he is compelled by singular events that cannot be accommodated rationally to his preconceived narrative to invoke the "enchanter" as a principle of last resort. Like Cervantes vis-à-vis Don Quixote, Melville, I suggest, is satirizing Franklin's empirical will to force the smallest detail in being into its *proper* place in the larger whole. Melville makes what I am suggesting remarkably clear in *The Confidence-Man*, when, in justifying the structural errancy of his *mimesis*, he writes: "If reason be judge, no writer has produced such inconsistent characters as nature herself has. It must call for no small sagacity in a reader unerringly to discriminate in a novel between inconsistencies of conception and those of life. As elsewhere, experience is the only guide here; but as no one man's experience can be coextensive with *what is*, it may be unwise in every case to rest upon it. When the duck-billed beaver of Australia was first brought stuffed to England, the naturalists, appealing to their classifications, maintained that there was, in reality, no such creature; the bill in the specimen must needs be, in some way, artificially stuck on," p. 70. (Melville's emphasis.)

24. In one of these, Melville specifies the nature of Franklin's gravity by identifying it, as I do, with practical reason: " 'Pears to me you have rather high heels to your boots,' said the grave man of utility, looking sharply down through his spectacles; 'don't you know that it's both wasting leather and endangering your limbs, to wear such high heels? I have thought at my first leisure, to write a little pamphlet against that very abuse,' " p. 40.

25. The satire against the economy of gravity (of mind, demeanor, and of style) in the name of play (waste, errancy) pervades Laurence Sterne's, *The Life and Opinions of Tristram Shandy, Gentleman*, ed. Ian Watt (Boston: Houghton Mifflin, 1965). I quote briefly one of innumerable examples: "I need not tell your worships, that this [raising of 'a hue and cry' against the play of wit by 'your graver gentry'] was done with so much cunning and artifice,—that the great *Locke*, who was seldom outwitted by false sounds,—was nevertheless bubbled here. The cry, it seems, was so deep and solemn a one, and what with the help of great wigs grave faces, and other implements of deceit, was rendered so general a one against the *poor wits* in this matter, that the philosopher himself was deceived by it, . . . so that instead of sitting down cooly, as such a philosopher should have done, to have examined the matter of fact before he philosophized upon it;—on the contrary, he took the fact for granted, and so joined in with the cry, and halloo'd it as boisterously as the rest. This has been made the *Magna Charta* of stupidity ever since,—but your reverences plainly see, it has been obtained in such a manner, that the title to it is not worth a groat;—which by the bye is one of the many and vile impositions which gravity and grave folks have to answer for hereafter," pp. 149–150.

26. For an account of the pervasiveness of this American penchant in the nineteenth century to equate science, particularly technological inventions, with magic, see Alan Trachtenberg, *The Incorporation of America: Society in the Gilded Age* (New York: Hill and Wang, 1982).

27. Melville's uncanny anticipation of Joseph Conrad's similar image in *Heart of Darkness*, ed. Robert Kimbrough (New York: Norton Critical Editon, 1988), should not be overlooked: "Now when I was a little chap I had a passion for maps. . . . At that time there were many blank spaces on the earth and when I saw one that looked particularly inviting on a map . . . I would put my finger on it and say: When I grow up I will go there. . . . But there was one yet—the biggest—the most blank, so to speak—that I had a hankering after," p. 11. As Ivy Wilson has suggested in an unpublished essay on *Israel Potter* he kindly allowed me to read, " 'the vast spaces in the middle' most likely refer to the Northwest Territory and trans-Allegheny West that he negotiated for the U.S. with John Jay and John Adams." He goes on to say that "Franklin's abode becomes the site where home and nation meet; the map signals both the demarcation of the nation and the movement of westward expansion which Melville's post-Jacksonian reading audience would have recognized. This particular map, then, shows the inchoate nation, as it were, under construction. But its representation depends upon the figurative erasure of the native indigenous population, already understood to be unassimilable to the national landscape, demarcated by the word DESERT." "On Native Ground: Transiency and Affiliation in *Israel Potter*."

28. Raymond Williams, *Marxism and Literature* (Oxford: Oxford University Press, 1977), p. 110.

29. See Max Weber, *The Protestant Ethic and the Spirit of Capitalism*, trans. Talcott Parson (New York: Charles Scribner's Sons 1958), pp. 48–55. For a commentary on the spirit of capitalism informing Webster's speech, see Cadava, *Emerson and the Climates of History*, pp. 106–112.

30. Melville's several references in *Redburn* (pp. 181, 293) to John Howard (b. 1726, d. 1790), the English prison reformer who, along with Blackstone, was, according to Foucault, instrumental in establishing the principles of penal reform in England and the United States that would transform prisons into "reformatories," clearly indicate that he was aware of the debates over penal reform that were raging in the period between 1800–1840.

31. Michel Foucault, *Discipline and Punish*, pp. 137–138.

32. Jacques Derrida, "Structure, Sign, and Play in the Discourse of the Human Sciences," in *Writing and Difference* (Chicago: University of Chicago Press, 1978), p. 279.

33. Franklin, as representative of the exceptionalist American character, privileged a plain over a decorative style on the analogy of the New World's innocent purity over the Old World's corrupt flamboyance.

34. Herman Melville, *The Confidence-Man*, p. 150.

35. Søren Kierkegaard, *The Concept of Irony, with Constant Reference to Socrates*, trans. Lee M. Capel (London: Collins, 1966), p. 308.

36. See also chapter 20, "The Shuttle."

37. Arnold Rampersad, *Melville's* Israel Potter: *A Pilgrimage and Progress* (Bowling Green: Bowling Green University Popular Press, 1969).

38. Walter Bezanson, "Historical Note," *IP*, 202. Though Bezanson characterizes Allen's speeches as "harangue" or "rant" and refers to Melville's appropriation of this language (probably) from *A Narrative of Colonel Ethan Allen's Captivity* (Philadelphia: Robert Bell, 1779), he is silent about Melville's intention in doing so.

39. In using this word, I am referring to Heidegger's interpretation of the "hermeneutic circle." All interpretation is necessarily circular in the sense that asking a question about being implies knowing beforehand what one is searching for. But, according to Heidegger, interpretation in the Western tradition, including the empiricism of the Enlightenment, which claims to be objective, is, in fact, metaphysical: it perceives being *meta ta physica* (after or about temporality) and is thus viciously circular. It is a *method*, that is, that compels the difference that time always disseminates into Identity from a transcendent standpoint: it ends up confirming the presupposition with which the inquirer begins. Though Repetition begins with a presupposition, the latter is put at risk in the face of the temporal/historical process of inquiry; in this *process* the presupposition of the beginning is always already de-structured by the inquirer's existential encounter with the differential dynamic of temporality. At the point of the circular return to the beginning, a difference is precipitated. See Heidegger, *Being and Time*, trans. John Macquarrie and Edward Robinson (New York: Harper and Row, 1962), pp. 362–363 and 437–438.

40. Gilles Deleuze and Félix Guattari, *A Thousand Plateaus*, trans. Brian Massumi (Minneapolis: University of Minnesota Press, 1987), pp. 424–473.

41. Edward W. Said, *Culture and Imperialism* (New York: Alfred A. Knopf, 1993), p. 333. The quotation from Adorno is from *Minima Moralia: Reflections from a Damaged Life* trans. E. F. N. Jephcott (London: Verso, 1974), p. 68.

42. *Life and Remarkable Adventures of Israel Potter* (Providence, R.I.: Henry Trumbull, 1824), p. 106 (in *IP*, 93).

43. Jay Leyde notes that Melville dates his dedication of Israel Potter on June 17, 1854, the anniversary of the Battle of Bunker Hill, in *The Melville Log*, vol. 1, p. 489. But he does not indicate that this anniversary was also that of Webster's orations, the first of which "had obtained the widest circulation throughout the country; passages from it had been passed into household word throughout the Union." "Introductory Note" to Webster, "The Completion of the Bunker Hill Monument" (June 17, 1843) in *The Writings an Speeches of Daniel Webster*, vol. I, p. 257.

44. I am indebted to my colleague Susan Strehle for referring me to this poem by Emily Dickinson.

45. Jacques Derrida, *Specters of Marx: The State of the Debt, the Work of Mourning, and the New International*, trans. Peggy Kamuf (New York: Routledge, 1994), pp. 100–102.

46. Derrida, "Structure, Sign, and Play in the Discourse of the Human Sciences," p. 279.

47. William E. Connolly, *Why I Am Not a Secularist* (Minneapolis: University of Minnesota Press, 1999), p. 81. The coalition of the neoconservative right and Evangelical Christianity in the post-9/11/01 era is testimony to this momentum. It is, as I will show below, also "theorized" by Samuel P. Huntington in *Who Are We?: The Challenges to America's National Identity* (New York: Simon and Schuster, 2004; further citations will be abbreviate to *WAW* and incorporated in the text in parentheses), in which he identifies the "Anglo-Protestant" culture as the "core culture of America" (pp. 59–80) and, on the basis of the opportunity offered by the attacks on the World Trade Center and the Pentagon by Al Qaeda, calls for a "Great Awakening" modeled on the four Great Awakenings in the history of American Protestantism, "each of which was associated with and immediately followed by major efforts at political reform," p. 76.

48. The target of Melville's criticism is not only Webster, but many other nineteenth-century "historians" of the United States, not least those who were persuaded, ironically, by the foreigner Alexis de Tocqueville's announcement of its exceptionalist status and his interpretation of its peculiar "nationhood." William Connolly's commentary on de Tocqueville's understanding of the American nation, clearly with Renan's in mind, is a propos:

> In the Tocquevillian imagination the mores of a *nation* are burned into the imagination and reason of the *individual*:
>
> > "What keeps a great number of citizens under the same government is much less a reasoned desire to remain united than the instinctive and, in a sense, involuntary accord which springs from the feelings and similar opinions . . . ; only when certain men consider a great many questions from the same point of view and have the same opinions on a great many subjects and when the same events give rise to like thoughts and impressions is there a society. . . . Although there are many sects among the Anglo-Americans, they all look at religion from the same point of view."

"Involuntary accord," "like feelings," "similar opinions," "same point if view," "like thoughts and impressions," and (elsewhere on the same pages) "a single nation." While some variations across localities and individuals are possible and even admirable, each member of the nation is to be inhabited by the same general mores and to draw upon the same basic god.

The higher accord upon which Tocquevillian civilization rests involves a common commitment to Christianity . . . and an agricultural way of life (as opposed to nomadic ways of being). Tocqueville concedes that the quest for the civilizational wholeness he admires necessarily engenders violence against "wandering nomads" who occupied America before Europeans arrived. For they lack the Christian faith and mastery over nature essential to a democratic civilization. (*Why I Am Not a Secularist*, p. 142).

49. Edward Said, *Culture and Imperialism*, p. 332. The quotation within the cited passage is from T. S. Eliot's "Little Gidding" in "Four *Quartets*," *The Complete Poems and Plays, 1909–1950* (New York: Harcourt Brace, 1958), p. 144.

50. Sacvan Bercovitch, *The American Jeremiad*, p. xiv.

51. Huntington devotes an entire chapter, "Deconstructing America: The Rise of Subnational Identities," 141–178, to this thematics.

52. Bezanson, "Historical Note," in *Israel Potter*, p. 182.

Chapter 4. "Benito Cereno" and "Bartleby, the Scrivener"

1. Herman Melville, "Benito Cereno," in *The Piazza Tales and Other Prose Pieces, 1839–1860*, eds. Harrison Hayford, Alma A. MacDougall, G. Thomas Tanselle, and others (Evanston, Ill.: Northwestern University Press, 1987), pp. 51–52. Further citations will be abbreviated to *BC* and incorporated in the text in parentheses.

2. William V. Spanos, "The Detective and the Boundary: Some Notes on the Postmodern Literary Imagination," in *Early Postmodernism: Foundational Essays*, ed. Paul A. Bové (Durham, N.C.: Duke University Press, 1995), p. 20. The quotation is from Francis Bacon.

3. Meditating on the "cannibals" he has observed, Crusoe contrasts his English comportment to them with that of the Spanish:

> That this would justify the Conduct of the *Spaniards* in all their Barbarities practic'd in *America*, where they destroy'd Millions of these People, who however they were Idolaters and Barbarians, and had several bloody and barbarous rites in their Customs, such as sacrificing human Bodies to their idols, were yet, as to the *Spaniards*, very innocent People; and that the rooting them out of the Country, is spoken of with the utmost Abhorrence and Detestation, by even the *Spaniards* themselves, at this Time, and by all other Christian Nations of *Europe*, as a meer Butchery, a bloody and unnatural Piece of Cruelty, unjustifiable either to God or man; and such, as for which the very Name of a *Spaniard* is reckon'd to be frightful and terrible to all People of Humanity, or of Christian Compassion: As if the Kingdom of *Spain* were particularly Eminent for

the Product of a Race of Men, who were without Principles of Tenderness, or the common Bowels of Pity to the Miserable, which is reckon'd to be a Mark of generous Temper in the Mind. (Daniel Defoe, *Robinson Crusoe*, 2nd ed., ed. Michael Shinagel [New York: Norton, 1994], pp. 124–125).

The continuous authority of this eighteenth century rationalization of British imperialism is borne witness to by the distinction Joseph Conrad makes between the Belgians (and Romans) and the British in *Heart of Darkness*, 3rd ed., ed. Robert Kimbrough (New York: Norton, 1988): "They [the Romans and the Belgians] grabbed what they could get for the sake of what was to be got. It was robbery with violence, aggravated murder on a great scale, and men going at it blind. . . . The conquest of the earth, which mostly means the taking it away from those who have a different complexion or slightly flatter noses than ourselves, is not a pretty thing when you look into it too much. What redeems it is the idea only. An idea at the back of it, not a sentimental pretense but an idea; and an unselfish belief in the idea—something you can set up, and bow down before, and offer a sacrifice to," p. 10. See also the similar distinction to which Said points in *Orientalism* (New York: Vintage Books, 1979) between Napoleon's comportment toward Egypt and that articulated by the Spanish Conquistadors toward the Amerindians: "Napoleon tried everywhere to prove that he was fighting *for* Islam. . . . (Compare, in this regard, Napoleon's tactics in Egypt with the tactics of the *Requerimiento*, a document drawn up in 1513—in Spanish—by the Spaniards to be read aloud to the Indians: 'We shall take you and your wives and your children, and shall make slaves of them, and as such sell and dispose of them as their Highnesses . . . may command; and we shall take away your goods, and shall do you all the mischief and damage that we can, as to vasssals who do not obey.' " p. 82.

4. See, for example, William Gilmore Simms, *The Yemassee: A Romance of Carolina* (New Haven, Conn.: College and University Press, 1964): "The Carolinians still pressed on, their numbers greatly increased by the presence of several slaves, who, volunteering even against the will of their masters, had armed themselves with knives or clubs, and, by their greater numbers, held forth a prospect of ultimately hemming in the smaller force of the enemy. . . . [The Spanish] had no idea of that gentler form of treatment which, with the Carolinians, won the affections of their serviles; and, knowing no other principle in their own domestic government than that of fear, and assured of the instability of any confidence built upon such a relationship between the ruler and the serf, they had miscalculated greatly when they addressed their bribes and promises to the negroes, as well as to the Indians of Carolina," p. 383. This invidious and false distinction was not limited to American fiction. It also pervaded the narratives of the American historians Francis Parkman, George Bancroft, and, not least, William H. Prescott (*Conquest of Mexico*, 1843), and, as Richard Slotkins observes, the Jacksonian Democrat journalists of the antebellum period. As, for example, one writing for the influential *Democratic Review*, puts it in the context of the Mexican War: "While the colonists of other European nations sought, in the wilds of the American continent, only a secure home, in which their industry might meet its rewards and their religious scruples be unmolested, the Spanish colonists sought empire by conquests . . . and imposed a regime of oppression and religious bigotry." Quoted in Slotkin, *The Fatal Environ-*

ment: *The Myth of the Frontier in the Age of Industrialization, 1800–1890* (Norman: University of Oklahoma Press, 1994), p. 177.

5. Frederick Douglass, *Narrative of the Life of Frederick Douglass, An American Slave*, ed. William L. Andrews and William S. McFeely (New York: Norton, 1997).

6. For a fuller analysis of Althusser's problematic, see the chapter entitled "Althusser's Problematic: Vision and the Vietnam War," in Spanos, *American Exceptionalism in the Age of Globalization: The Specter of Vietnam* (Albany: SUNY Press, 2008); originally published as "Althusser's 'Problematic' in the Context of the Vietnam War: Toward a Spectral Politics," in *Rethinking Marxism*, vol. 10, 3 (Fall 1998), 1–21. For this analysis of Melville's "criticism" of Captain Delano's way of perceiving and representing the world, I could have invoked Antonio Gramsci's concept of hegemony; Raymond Williams's understanding of "culture" (in *Marxism and Literature* [Oxford: Oxford University Press, 1977], pp. 108–114); or, not least, Michel Foucault's understanding of the "episteme" or the "archive" or "archival knowledge: "What I shall call an *archive* is neither the totality of texts which a civilization has preserved, nor the ensemble of traces which have been saved . . . after its disasters, but the play of rules which in a culture determine the appearance and the disappearance of utterances, their paradoxical existence as *events* and as things. To analyze facts of discourse in the general element of the archive is not to consider them as documents (which have a hidden meaning, or . . . a rule of construction), but as *monuments*; and this without reference to any geological metaphor, without assigning them any origin, without the least gesture towards a beginning, an *arché*—not these things, but to do instead what, according to the playful prerogatives of etymology, would be something like an archeology." Michel Foucault, "Réponse au Cercle d'épistémologie," *Cahiers pour l'Analyse* 9 (summer 1869), quoted in Edward Said, *Beginnings: Intention and Method* (New York: Basic Books, 1975), p. 292. I have chosen Althusser's notion of the problematic because, more clearly than the others, it overdetermines vision just as Melville's "Benito Cereno" does.

7. Louis Althusser, "From *Capital* to Marx's Philosophy," in Althusser and Étienne Balibar *Reading* Capital (London: Verso, 1979), pp. 26–27. Further citations will be abbreviated to CMP, and incorporated in the text in parentheses.

8. Louis Althusser, "Ideology and Ideological States Apparatuses (Notes towards an Investigation)," in *Lenin and Philosophy and Other Essays*, trans. Ben Brewster (New York: Monthly Review Press, 1971), pp. 170–183).

9. Another significant manifestation of the racism of Delano's *liberal comportment* toward the blacks occurs shortly after the scene, when, while vacillating between his two interpretations of the mysterious situation on board the *San Dominick*, he sees a black woman suckling her child: "There's naked nature, now; pure tenderness and love, thought Captain Delano, well-pleased. This incident prompted him to remark the other negresses more particularly than before. He was gratified with their manners; like most uncivilized women, they seemed at once tender of heart and tough of constitution; equally ready to die for their infants or fight for them. Unsophisticated as leopardesses; loving as doves. Ah! thought Captain Delano, these perhaps are some of the very women whom Mungo Park saw in Africa, and gave such noble account of" (*BC*, 73). Mungo Park, not incidentally,

traveled to the Niger in the latter part of the eighteenth century in behalf of the British Association for Promoting the Discovery of the Interior Parts of Africa, an "alliance of aristocrats and wealthy business men," who "were economic expansionists, interested in 'legitimate commerce,' that is, not colonialism or settlement, and above all not the slave trade," Mary Louise Pratt, *Imperial Eyes: Travel Writing and Transculturation* (New York: Routledge, 1992), p. 70. In invoking Park's inordinately popular, *Travels in the Interior of Africa*, first published in 1799, Melville is tacitly referring to Park's liberal sentimentality, what Pratt calls his "anticonquest" orientation, that concealed its ultimately racist/imperial function.

10. One wonders if Melville is ironically invoking here the Fugitive Slave Law of 1851.

11. Martin Heidegger, "What Is Metaphysics?," in *Basic Writings*, ed. David Farrell Krell (New York: Harper Collins, 1993), p. 96.

12. Jacques Derrida, *Specters of Marx: The State of the Debt, the Work of Mourning, and the New Internationalism*, trans. Peggy Kamuf (New York: Routledge, 1994), 6–13, 99–102. The word "visit," also derives from *videre*, which, besides meaning "to see," also means "deal severely with, assail, afflict; punish."

13. In producing the object it sees, the "political economy" of capitalism, according to Althusser's reading of Marx's *Capital*, "produced a new latent question [that of the invisible *of* its visible].... Far from knowing it, it remained convinced that it was still on the terrain of the old problem, whereas it has " '*unwittingly changed terrain*' " (*CMP*, 24). This blindness constitutes the point of departure of Althusser's *lecteur symptomale*, a symptomatic reading which, "insofar as it divulges the undivulged event in the text it reads, and in the same movement relates it to *a different text*, present as a necessary absence in the first" (*CMP*, 28). This *lecteur symptomale*, not incidentally, is similar to the "contrapuntal reading" Edward Said brings to canonical texts like Jane Austen's *Mansfield Park*.

14. Benito Cereno's references in his deposition to the black women, so radically different from Captain Delano's, is equally, if not more revelatory of this deeper and more sympathetic understanding of the blacks' revolt: "the negresses, of age, were knowing to the revolt, and testified themselves *satisfied at the death of their master, Don Alexandro; that, had the negroes not restrained them, they would have tortured to death, instead of simply killing, the Spaniard slain by command of the negro Babo*; that the negresses used their utmost influence to have the deponent made away with; that, in the various acts of murder, they sang songs and danced—not gaily, but solemnly; and before the engagement with the boats, as well as during the action, they sang melancholy songs to the negroes, and that this melancholy tone was more inflaming than a different one would have been, and was intended so...." (*BC*, 112; my emphasis). This does, indeed, imply a ferocious desire for revenge, but it also resonates with its appalling cause: a slavery that also included the white master's common violation of black women slaves.

15. See Toni Morrison, *Playing in the Dark: Whiteness and the Literary Imagination* (Cambridge: Harvard University Press, 1992). As Michael Paul Rogin obverses, "When Melville changed *The Tryal's* name [in the original text] to the *San Dominick*, he was calling attention to the slave seizure of power on Santo Domingo, in the wake of the French Revolution. That slave uprising spread terror throughout the American South," *Subversive Genealogy*, p. 213. For a powerful

account of this revolution that haunted the American slave owners, see C. L. R. James's magisterial history, *The Black Jacobins: Toussaint: L'Ouverture and the San Domingo Revolution*, 2nd ed. (New York: Vintage, 1989). James was the author of *Mariners, Renegades, Castaways: The Story of Melville and the World We Live In* (1953), the book on *Moby-Dick* he wrote on Ellis Island awaiting deportation under the notorious McCarran Act. For a brilliant analysis of James's Melville book, which attests to James's attunement to the proleptic significance of *Moby-Dick* for the McCarthy era, see Donald Pease "C. L. R. James's *Mariners, Renegades, and Castaways* and the World We Live In," in James, *Mariners, Renegades, Castaways*, ed. Pease (Hanover, N.H.: University Press of New England, 2001), vii–xxxiii.

16. In his intelligent reading of "Benito Cereno," Edgar Dryden invokes "the narrator's ironic query as to whether or not Delano's "undistrustful good nature" implies "along with a benevolent heart, more than ordinary quickness and accuracy of intellectual perception" to conclude that "the American captain is not a man a gifted with profound insight," by which I take him to mean that he is not very intelligent. *Melville's Thematics of Form: The Great Art of Telling the Truth* (Baltimore: The Johns Hopkins University Press, 1968) p. 201. This is also Myra Jehlen's judgment in "Melville and Class," in *A Historical Guide to Herman Melville*, ed. Giles Gunn (Oxford: Oxford University Press, 2005), p. 95. Both, I think, miss the point Melville is making about Delano's national identity in that they render the thematics of American exceptionalism invisible.

17. See John Hellmann, *American Myth and the Legacy of Vietnam.* (New York: Columbia University Press, 1896), pp. 4–41.

18. Edward Geary Lansdale, *In the Midst of Wars: An American's Mission to Southeast Asia* (New York: Harper & Row, 1972), p. ix. Further references will be abbreviated to *IMW* and incorporated in the text in parentheses.

19. For an amplified reading of *The Quiet American* from the perspective of the "problematic," see the chapter entitled "Who Killed Alden Pyle?: The Oversight of Oversight in Graham Greene's *The Quiet American*" in Spanos, *American Exceptionalism in the Age of Globalization: The Specter of Vietnam*.

20. That the specter of Greene's novel continues to haunt the American "elect" in the wake of 9/11 is borne dramatic witness to by President George W. Bush's speech to the Veterans of Foreign Wars in Kansas City, August 22, 2007, when he invokes *The Quiet American* to inaugurate an incredible revision of the history of that war in behalf of persuading the American public to "stay the course" in Iraq: "The argument that America's presence in Indochina was dangerous had a long pedigree. In 1955, long before the United States had entered the war, Graham Greene wrote a novel called, "The Quiet American." It was set in Saigon, and the main character was a young government agent named Alden Pyle. He was a symbol of American purpose and patriotism—and dangerous naivete. Another character describes Alden this way: "I never knew a man who had better motives for all the trouble he causes."

After America entered the Vietnam War, the Graham Greene argument gathered some steam. As a matter of fact, many argued that if we pulled out there would be no consequences for the Vietnamese people. . . . The world would learn just how costly these misimpressions would be. In Cambodia, the Khmer Rouge began a murderous rule in which hundred of thousands of Cambodians died by starvation and torture and execution. In Vietnam, former allies of the United States and government workers and intellectuals and business men were sent off to prison camps, where tens of thousands perished. Hundreds of thousands more fled the country on rickety boats, many of them going to their graves in the South China Sea. . . ."

I am indebted to Adam Spanos's unpublished honors thesis, "Innocence and Imperialism: American Exceptionalism from the Frontier to Abu Ghraib" (Binghamton University, 2005), for pointing out the remarkable similarities between Melville's Captain Amasa Delano in "Benito Cereno" and Greene's Alden Pyle.

21. Edward W. Said, *Orientalism* (New York: Alfred A. Knopf, 1977), pp. 92–93.

22. Tracing the heritage of the type of Lansdale/Pyle back to "the proto-Gringos who found the New England woods too raw and empty for their peace and filled them up with their own imported devils," Michael Herr calls the attitude of these early enthusiasts "the romance of spooking" both to suggest its origins in the likes of Cooper's Leatherstocking romances and the folly of their practice in a war that had become high tech slaughter: "History's heavy attrition, tic and toc with teeth, the smarter ones saw it winding down for them on the day that [Ambassador Henry Cabot] Lodge first arrived in Saigon and commandeered the villa of the current CIA chief . . . Officially, the complexion of the problem had changed (too many people were getting killed, for one thing), and the romance of spooking started to fall away like dead meat from a bone. As sure as heat rises, their time was over. The war passed along, this time into the hard hands of firepower freaks out to eat the country whole, and with no fine touches either, leaving the spooks on the beach," *Dispatches* (New York: Vintage, 1977), p. 51.

23. For my reading of Melville's use of this fortress metaphorics in *Moby-Dick*, see *The Errant Art of Moby-Dick*, pp. 99 ff.

24. One of the most recent—and telling—post-9/11 manifestations of this recuperation of the myth of American exceptionalism in the wake of its self-destruction during the Vietnam War can be found in the volume of essays written by eleven prestigious political scientists and professors of law from major American universities entitled *American Exceptionalism and Human Rights*, edited by Michael Ignatieff (Princeton, N.J.: Princeton University Press, 2005). In taking up the question of American exceptionalism in the context of "the war on terror," including the issue of torture (Abu Graib), these eminent scholars, astonishingly, make no reference to the United States' brutal conduct of the Vietnam War in the name of its exceptionalist "errand in the wilderness [of Vietnam]." As in the case of Francis Fukuyama, who, over a decade before, dismissed the witness of the Vietnam War in announcing exceptionalist America as "the end of history" (*The End of History and the Last Man* [New York: Free Press, 1992]), they write about America's global role after 9/11 as if the singular history of this war of attrition bordering on genocide, which decisively delegitimized the American exceptionalist ethos, never happened.

25. Samuel P. Huntington, *Who Are We?: The Challenges to America's National Identity* (New York: Simon & Schuster, 2004). Further citations will be abbreviated to *WAW* and incorporated in the text in parentheses.

26. Samuel P. Huntington, *The Clash of Civilizations and the Remaking of World Order* (New York: Simon and Schuster, 1996), which expands his essay

"The Clash of Civilizations" published in *Foreign Affairs* in the summer of 1993. For major critiques of Huntington's thesis, see Edward W. Said, "The Clash of Definitions," in *Reflections on Exile and Other Essays* (Cambridge, Mass.: Harvard University Press, 2000), pp. 569–590; and "The Uses of Culture," in *The End of the Peace Process: Oslo and After* (New York: Vintage, 2001), pp. 139–143.

27. It should not be overlooked that Huntington invokes Sacvan Bercovitch's *The American Jeremiad* (Madison: University of Wisconsin Press, 1978), a severe criticism of the repressive uses to which the Puritan Jeremiad has been perennially put by the dominant culture in American, in behalf of his recuperative project.

28. Althusser is clearly thinking of French Catholicism, but what he says about the relation between man and God is more pertinent to Congregationalist Puritanism.

29. Perry Miller, *The Raven and the Whale: The War of Words and Wits in the Era of Poe and Melville* (New York: Harvest Books, 1956).

30. Max Weber, *The Protestant Ethic and the Spirit of Capitalism*, trans. Talcott Parsons (New York: Charles Scribner's Sons, 1950), pp. 108–109.

31. Herman Melville, "Bartleby, the Scrivener: A Story of Wall-Street," in *The Piazza Tales and Other Prose Pieces, 1839–1860*, p. 13; my emphasis. Further references will be abbreviated to BS and incorporated in the text in parentheses.

32. To speak of a beginning as "advent" is to assume a temporal process that contains and therefore moves in a promissory way inexorably toward its End. Melville, in other words, highlights "the beginning" of the lawyer's narrative in order to call attention to Bartleby as disruptive or, to invoke his name for subversiveness in *Moby-Dick*, a dia-bolic agent: one who "throws apart" or "disperses (*dia*: apart; *ballein*: to throw). See Spanos *The Errant Art of* Moby-Dick, pp. 223–245.

33. As we shall see, Melville, will refer to this unwillingness of the elect—those who possess the "true light"—to "be tempted forth to hazardous skirmishes on the open ground of reason," the "secure Malakoff of confidence," in *The Confidence-Man*.

34. Michel Foucault, *Discipline and Punish: The Birth of the Prison*, trans. Alan Sheridan (New York: Pantheon, 1977), pp. 137–138.

35. John F. Kasson, *Civilizing the Machine: Technology and Republican Values in America, 1776–1900*, 2nd ed. (New York: Hill and Wang, 1999), pp. 69–70. See also, pp. 30, 88, and 229. First published in 1976, Kasson's book precedes Foucault's *Discipline and Punish*, and though its analysis of the Lowell project lacks the scope, depth, and critical force of the genealogical perspective Foucault brings to similar contexts, it does, seen through Foucault's lens, point more precisely than Foucault's book as such to the operations of the panoptic gaze and its disciplinary function in its postrevolutionary American setting. This is, above all, because Kasson's reading of the Lowell project bears symptomatic witness to the role that the American exceptionalist ethos, particularly the founders' appeal to the New England Puritan calling as it was secularized in Benjamin's Franklin's *Way to Wealth* and promoted by New England intellectuals such as Edward Everett and Daniel Webster, and to their acute awareness of the need to always rejuvenate American civilization to avoid the fall into luxury, decadence, and tyranny, which was the fate of Britain and the "Old World."

36. Melville pursues this severe criticism of the emergent techno-capitalist factory economy in his short-story "The Bell-Tower" (also published in 1855),

which, probably alluding to the bell towers used in the Lowell factory system to discipline the work habits of the workers, projects the disastrous consequences of the reduction of human temporality on the analogy of the technology of the assembly line. For a similar analysis of the "incorporation" of time, which begins with the addition of "cupolas and stark brick bell towers of mills and factories" to the emergent structures of the corporate economy of American industry and culture in the latter half of the nineteenth century, see Alan Trachtenberg, *The Incorporation of American: Culture and Society in the Gilded Age* (New York: Hill and Wang, 1982), pp. 52–60. See also Ivy Wilson, "Hieroglyphs of Leisure and Labor: Melville, Inverted Similitudes, and a Hermeneutics of Materiality" (forthcoming), a brilliant reading of Melville's "The Paradise of Bachelors and the Tartarus of Maids," which refers to the Lowell project—and in the end invokes Bartleby's "I prefer not to" as Melville's alternative to the "maids' " answerability to the American calling, but addresses the diptych from a neo-Marxist rather than Foucauldian perspective. I am indebted to my student James Martin for bringing John Kasson's *Civilizing the Machine* to my attention. See his dissertation "The Spirit of Utility's Connection to Republican Virtue: Engaging the Transatlantic Origins of the American Enlightenment (Binghamton University, 2007).

37. Cotton Mather, "*Nehemiahs Americanus: The Life of John Winthrop Esq.* Governor of the Massachusetts Colony," reprinted from Mather, *Magnalia Christi Americana* in Bercovitch, *The Puritan Origins of the American Self*, pp. 187–205.

38. Jacques Derrida, "Structure, Sign, and Play in the Discourse of the Human Sciences," in *Writing and Difference*, trans. Alan Bass (Chicago: University of Chicago Press, 1978), p. 279.

39. See Martin Heidegger, "What Is Metaphysics?," in *Basic Writing*, revised ed., ed. David Farrell Krell (New York: HarperSanFranscisco, 1993): "Anxiety," according to Heidegger, unlike fear, has no thing as its object. It "rob us of speech," p. 101.

40. Michel Foucault, *The History of Sexuality, Vol. 1: An Introduction*, trans. Robert Hurley (New York: Pantheon, 1978), pp. 15–49.

41. See Weber, *The Protestant Ethic and the Spirit of Capitalism*: "It was impossible, at least so far as the question of a man's own state of grace arose, to be satisfied with Calvin's trust in the testimony of the expectant faith resulting from grace, even though the orthodox doctrine had never formally abandoned that criterion. Above all, practical pastoral work, which had immediately to deal with all the suffering caused by the doctrine, could not be satisfied. It met these difficulties in various ways. So far as predestination was not reinterpreted, toned down, or fundamentally abandoned, two principal, mutually connected, types of pastoral advice appear. On the one hand it is held to be an absolute duty to consider oneself chosen, and to combat all doubts as temptations of the devil, since lack of self-confidence is the result of insufficient faith, hence imperfect grace. The exhortation of the apostle to make fast one's own call is here interpreted as a duty to attain certainty of one's own election and justification in the daily struggle of life. In the place of the humble sinners to whom Luther promises grace if they trust themselves to God in penitent faith are bred those self-confident saints whom we can rediscover in the hard Puritan merchants of the heroic age of capitalism and in isolated instances down to the present. On the other hand, in order to attain

that self-confidence intense worldly activity is recommended as the most suitable means. It and it alone disperses religious doubts and gives the certainty of grace" (pp. 111–112). For an American example of this kind of "pastoral advice," see John Cotton, "Christian Calling," in *The American Puritans: Their Prose and Poetry*, ed. Perry Miller (New York: Anchor Books, 1956), pp. 172–182. See also, Perry Miller, "The Marrow of Puritan Divinity," in *Errand into the Wilderness* (Cambridge, Mass.: Harvard University Press, 1956), pp. 48–98.

42. As J. Hillis Miller puts this observation, "It is then [when "Bartleby's presence in his offices is scandalizing his professional reputation"] that the narrator, who is nothing if not logical, conceives his strangest way of dealing with Bartleby. Since Bartleby will not budge he himself will leave. The immobility of Bartleby turns the narrator into a nomad," p. 169.

43. William Butler Yeats, "The Second Coming," in the *Collected Poems* (New York: Macmillan 1956), p. 184.

44. Job 3, in which Job "curse[s] the day of his birth": " 'Why did I not die at birth, / come forth from the womb and expire? / Why did the knees receive me? / Or why the breasts, that I should suck? / For then I should have lain down and been quiet; / I should have slept; then I should have been at rest,' / with kings and counselors of the earth / who rebuilt ruins for themselves."

45. Dan McCall, *The Silence of Bartleby* (Ithaca, N.Y.: Cornell University Press, 1989), p. 129.

46. Martin Heidegger, "The Question Concerning Technology," in *The Question Concerning Technology and Other Essays*, trans. William Lovitt (New York: Harper, 1977): "What kind of unconcealment is it, then, that is peculiar to that which comes to stand forth through this setting-upon that challenges [technology]? Everywhere everything is ordered to stand by . . . , indeed to stand there just so that it may be *on call* for a further ordering. Whatever is ordered about in this way has its own stranding. We call it the standing-reserve [*Bestand*]. The word expresses here something more, and something more essential, than mere 'stock,' " p. 17 (my emphasis).

47. For deconstructionists reading of "Bartleby" that invoke and identify the scrivener with the "uncanny" (*Unheimliche*), see John Carlos Rowe, "Ecliptic Voyaging: Orbits of the Sign in Melville's 'Bartleby the Scrivener,' " in *Through the Custom-House: Nineteenth-Century American Fiction and Modern Theory* (Baltimore: The Johns Hopkins University Press, 1982), 111–138; J. Hillis Miller, "Who Is He? Melville's 'Bartleby the Scrivener,' " *Versions of Pygmalion* (Cambridge: Harvard University Press, 1990); and Jeffrey A. Weinstock. "Doing Justice to Bartleby," *American Transcendental Quarterly*, vol. 17 (March 200). I am sympathetic with this deconstructionist type of commentary for its calling attention to Melville's proleptic attunement to the relationship between textuality and undecidability. But insofar as it draws on Freud's version of the uncanny, it tends to restrict Melville's insight to the relations between language and psyche, a limit that seems to orient a reading of the story that stresses the tragic inability of the narrator to communicate—to take "responsibility" for—and thus to do "justice" to Bartleby: "If the narrator can encompass Bartleby with words, if he can do justice to him, he may simultaneously have accounted for him, naturalized him after all, and freed himself from his unfulfilled obligation. He will have made an adequate response to the demand Bartleby has made on him. The narrator, that is, may have justified

himself while doing justice to Bartleby. This is impossible because Bartleby cannot be identified. His story cannot be told." Miller, "Who Is He?," p. 73. In my view, on the other hand, the uncanny to which Melville is attuned in "Bartleby" is closer to Heidegger's *ontological* version, which, insofar as it discloses the nothingness on which the *world* (humanity's at-home) is constructed, enables perceiving the lawyer's dis-location into the *Unheimliche*—and his concern with Bartleby—not simply as psycho-textual, but also cultural and political: "This state-of-mind brings Dasein, more or less explicitly and authentically, face to face with the fact 'that it is, and that it has to be something with a potentiality-for-Being as the entity which it is.' For the most part, however, its mood is such that its thrownness [*Geworfenheit*] gets *closed off*. In the face of its thrownness Dasein flees to the relief which comes with the supposed freedom of the they-self [*Das Man*]. This fleeing has been described as a fleeing in the face of the uncanninness [*Unheimlichkeit*] which is basically determinative for individualized Being-in-the world. Uncanniness reveals itself authentically in the basic state-of mind of anxiety [*Angst*]; and, as the most elemental way in which thrown Dasein is disclosed, it puts Dasein's Being-in-the-world face to face with the 'nothing' of the world'; in the face of this 'nothing,' Dasein is anxious with anxiety about its ownmost potentiality-for-Being. *What if this Dasein, which finds itself* [sich befindet] *in the very depths of its uncanniness, should be the caller of the call of conscience?*" *Being and Time*, trans. John Macquarrie and Edward Robinson (New York: Harper & Row, 1962), p. 321.

48. Gilles Deleuze, "Bartleby; or, the Formula," in *Essays Critical and Clinical*, trans. Daniel W. Smith and Michael A. Greco (Minneapolis, University of Minnesota Press, 1997), p. 74.

49. Georgio Agamben, "Bartleby, or On Contingency," in *Potentialities: Collected Essays in Philosophy*, trans. Daniel Heller-Roazen (Stanford: Stanford University Press, 1999), pp. 253–254.

50. In answer to the question "Why does Bartleby's expression . . . function so well to bring things to a stop," J. Hillis Miller writes: "One answer is purely logical. As opposed to positive statements or negative statements . . . what Bartleby says resist dialectical sublation. The phrase is neither black nor white. There is nothing you can do with it. It is like an endless loop in a process of reasoning. The disruptive energy of this extraordinary group of everyday words is limitless. A shorthand way of describing that power is to say that Bartleby's sentence cannot be assimilated to any dialectical or oppositional way of thinking. You can neither deny it not accept it. It is neither constative nor performative, or perhaps it might be better to say that it is an exceedingly disquieting form of performative. It is a use of words to make something happened, but what it makes happened is to bring about the impossibly of making anything happened with words. It performs the blockage of all those forms of performative language by which the narrator lives and makes his living. It neutralizes his power of narration." "Who Is He?: Melville's 'Bartleby the Scrivener'," p. 156. If one emphasizes Miller's qualification of his definition of "performative," this reading of Bartleby coincides with mine. But early in his essay, Miller says that "It will be seen already that 'Bartleby the Scrivener' is not so much the story of Bartleby as it is the story of the narrator's ethical relation, or failure of ethical relation, to Bartleby," p. 142. What this marginalization of the marginalized Bartleby who is being given center stage by Melville suggest to me is that Miller intends to emphasize the notion of undecideability as

such, rather than Melville's invocation of undecidability as a sociopolitical weapon against the dominant American culture.

51. Gilles Deleuze and Félix Guattari, *A Thousand Plateaus*, trans. Brian Massumi (Minneapolis: University of Minnesota Press, 1987), pp. 424–473.

52. The question as to whether or not Melville's passive resistance can be equated with Thoreau's or Ghandi's or Martin Luther King's is a topic worthy of pursuing. I would tentatively distinguish Melville's from the others' on the grounds that, in basing it on ontological nothingness, it is far more radical in its political implications.

53. See, also, James S. Hans, "Emptiness and Plentitude in 'Bartleby the Scrivener' and *The Crying of Lot 49*," *Essays in Literature*, vol. 22 (Fall 1995). Hans's reads "Bartleby" as a proto-existentialist text, thus, in my mind, overlooking its political dimension.

54. Here, and throughout this book, I use the term "post-structuralism," not in the technical, but in its general sense: as a mode of thinking that has its raison d'être in de-structuring the onto-logic of the West that has perennially spatialized, that is, structured, the dissemination of temporal being.

55. Maurice Blanchot, *The Writing of Disaster*, trans. Ann Smock (Lincoln: University of Nebraska Press, 1986), pp. 17 ff, 145; Gilles Deleuze, "Bartleby or the Formula"; Giorgio Agamben, "Bartleby, or Contingency," pp. 243–271; and *The Coming Community*, trans. Michael Hardt (Minneapolis: University of Minnesota Press, 1993), pp. 33–36; Antonio Negri and Michael Hardt, *Empire* (Cambridge: Harvard University Press, 2000), pp. 203–204.

56. Edward W. Said, *Culture and Imperialism* (New York: Alfred A. Knopf, 1993), p. 333.

57. Gilles Deleuze, "Nomadic Thought," in *The New Nietzsche: Contemporary Styles of Interpretation*, ed. David B. Allison (New York: Delta Books, 1977), p. 149.

58. William Spanos, *The Errant Art of* Moby-Dick, pp. 270–272.

Chapter 5. Cavilers and Con Men

1. Herman Melville, *The Confidence-Man: His Masquerade* (Evanston, Ill. and Chicago: Northwestern University Press and The Newberry Library, 1984), p. 66; further references will cited in the text in parentheses.

2. I invoke Rowlandson's text in this context not simply because it is exemplary of Puritan exegesis, but also because it is what I call a threshold text. I mean by this a text in which the effort to accommodate—and be protected from—contradictions to the Puritan figural/providential view of history—is so extreme that it calls itself into question, manifests itself as a paranoia. Thus for example, Rowlandson writes in awe of one of the "remarkable passages of providence, which I took special notice of in my afflicted time": "Which also I have hinted before, when the English Army with new supplies were sent forth to pursue after the enemy, and they understanding it, fled before them till they came to Baquaug River, where they forthwith went over safely: that River should be impassable to the English. I can admire to see the wonderful providence of God in preserving the heathen for farther affliction to our poor Countrey. They could go in great

numbers over but the English must stop: God had an over-ruling hand in all those things." *The Sovereignty and Goodness of God*, ed. Neal Salisbury (Boston: Bedford Books, 1997), p. 105.

3. Herman Melville, *Moby-Dick or The Whale*, ed. Harrison Hayford, Hershel Parker, and G. Thomas Tanselle (Evanston, Ill. and Chicago: Northwestern University Press and Newberry Library), p. 39. Ehrenbreitstein is a fortress on a cliff overlooking the Rhine River at Coblenz. It was first built by the Romans and then rebuilt many times until it became a famous tourist attraction. It was always celebrated for its impregnability, but, like Quebec and Malakoff, it fell. For my reading of Father Mapple's pulpit and the exegesis of the Jonah text he delivers to the congregation of errant sailors, see *The Errant Art of Moby-Dick: The Canon, the Cold War, and the Struggle for American Studies* (Durham, N.C.: Duke University Press, 1995), pp. 93–114.

4. George Washington Peck, Review of *Pierre* in *American Whig Review* 16 (November 1852): 446–454; reprinted in *Herman Melville: The Contemporary Reviews*, ed. Brian Higgins and Hershel Parker (Cambridge: Cambridge University Press, 1995), p. 443.

5. In stressing the deeply backgrounded and inscribed nature of American optimism, I am taking exception to Gary Lindbergh's "exceptionalist" representation of the passengers on board the *Fidele* as an America without a tradition and thus more fluid and youthful than nations in which the authority of tradition guides social behavior: "The problem . . . is to establish a workable relationship between principle and experience, to square stated beliefs with immediate conduct. In a community informed by a vital religious belief, dogma can serve as a guide to conduct and as a means of understanding it. Even when religious fervor has decayed, communal habits, traditions, and manners may provide the authoritative ground on which the immediate situation is related to the large principle. But on the *Fidele* neither approach works. The captain never appears; . . . and this is a manifestations of the more general and thorough absence of authority in the narrative world. Familiar hereditary patterns have been broken; class lines dissolve; "society" is not characterized by communal patterns but by the extreme fluidity of human encounters. . . . As the *Fidele* accumulates and discharges a remarkable range of passengers, it provides a collective image of social life in "a new country," ("Melville's *The Confidence-Man: Duplicity and Identity in a New Country*," in *The Confidence Man in American Literature* [New York: Oxford University Press, 1982], p. 24).

6. Herman Melville, *Pierre; or the Ambiguities* (Evanston, Ill. and Chicago: Northwestern University Press and Newberry Library), p. 141. Melville also writes about narrative art in more or less the same vein in *The Confidence-Man*. See especially pp. 69–71. I invoke this passage from *Pierre* because it constitutes a clearer and more amplified articulation of his revolutionary understanding of the art of the novel.

7. Much of the early scholarship and criticism of *The Confidence-Man* consists of biographical readings or readings that focus on particular episodes such as the chapters on Goneril, Indian-hating, and China Aster. More recent commentary under the influence of "theory" all too often treats the novel as if it were a philosophical treatise rather than a work of fiction. For example, in *Empire for Liberty: Melville and the Poetics of Individualism* (Princeton, N.J.: Princeton University Press, 1989), Wei-chee Dimock writes about the chapters on the metaphysics of Indian-hating

as if the sentiments expressed by the narrator(s) were Melville's. In her chapter on *The Confidence-Man* in *Ugly Feelings* (Stanford, Calif.: Stanford University Press, 2005), Sienne Ngai, despite her preoccupation with aesthetics (and her valuable insights into the ideological function of "tone"), disregards the complex novelistic features of Melville's novel in favor of plundering it in behalf of an aesthetics of "ugly feelings." This is not to say that Dimock, Ngai, and others who have addressed *The Confidence-Man* in this abstract way have contributed nothing to our understanding of it. It is to say, rather, they are not *reading* Melville's *fiction*.

8. See especially, John W. Schroeder, "Sources and Symbols for Melville's *Confidence-Man*," *PMLA*, vol. 26 (June 1951), 364–380.

9. Melville invokes the Book of Job explicitly in the "Story of China Aster," which Egbert tells the Cosmopolitan, specifically in the episode, to which I will return, that refers to Job's Comforters, that is, precisely the occasion that deals with the question of confidence, p. 210.

10. In that passage, Melville is using the word "philosophy," not in the technical sense—as an equivalent for metaphysics—but in the sense given to it by the French *philosophes*, of the eighteenth century—Voltaire, for example: as the love of knowledge, or more precisely, as a mode of thinking being freely in all its manifestations, independent of the authority of systematic thought, whether, metaphysical, theological, or political.

11. For an analysis of this opposition between the *diabolos* and the *symbolos*, see Spanos, *The Errant Art of Moby-Dick*, pp. 232–244.

12. See Søren Kierkegaard, *Repetition: An Essay in Experimental Psychology*, trans. Walter Lowrie (New York: Harper & Row, 1964), 101–127. For a convenient summary of the textual history of the Book of Job, see Ralph E. Hone, ed. *The Voice Out of the Whirlwind: The Book of Job* (San Franscisco: Chandler Publishing Company), 1960.

13. Alexander Pope, *Selected Poetry and Prose*, ed. William K. Wimsatt, Jr. (New York: Rinehart, 1951), p. 137.

14. There are at least two direct references to Cervantes' novel in *The Confidence-Man*, one on page 231, which refers to "the pleasant barbers in romances" and the other on page 238, which, in a chapter on the art of fiction, refers to Don Quixote (along with Hamlet and Milton's Satan) as "quite an original." It is also possible that Melville derived the fortress metaphor for a secure confidence from the following passage in the "Tale of Inappropriate Curiosity" in *Don Quixote*: "The moment arrived when [Lotario] decided that he must intensify his siege of this fortress [Camilla's virtue] while the opportunity provided by Anselmo's absence lasted; so he attacked her pride by praising her beauty, because there's nothing that can demolish the fortified towers of a beautiful woman's vanity sooner than that vanity itself when deployed by flattery. And he mined away at the fort of Camilla's integrity with such charges that even if she'd been made of bronze she'd have come toppling down." *Don Quixote*, trans. John Rutherford (New York: Penguin Books, 2000), p. 313.

15. Edward W. Said, *Orientalism* (New York: Alfred Knopf, 1979), pp. 92–93.

16. See, for example, the use to which proto-postmodernist writers such as Fedor Dostoyevsky (*Notes from Underground*), Leo Tolstoy (*The Death of Ivan Ilych*), Joseph Conrad (*Victory*), Franz Kafka (*The Trial*), Alfred Camus (*The Fall*),

Archibald MacLeish (*J.B.*), Graham Greene (*Brighton Rock*), and postmodernists such as Jean-Paul Sartre (*The Flies*), Eugene Ionesco (*Victims of Duty*), Harold Pinter (*The Birthday Party*), Samuel Beckett (*Watt*), Iris Murdoch (*A Severed Head*), and many others put the Aeschylean Furies (the Greek analogue of the Ur-Satan) in their work. For an amplification of this "mythic" nexus, see Spanos, "The Detective and the Boundary: Some Notes on the Postmodern Literary Imagination, *boundary 2*, vol. 1 (Fall 1972); repr. in *Early Postmodernism: Foundational Essays*, ed. Paul Bové (Durham, N.C.: Duke University Press, 1995), 17–39.

17. On the continuity between the Puritan prefiguralism and Emersonian Transcendentalism, see Sacvan Bercovitch, *The Puritan Origins of the American Self* (New Haven: Yale University Press, 1975), pp. 163–174

18. Michel Foucault, "Nietzsche, Genealogy, History," in *Language, Counter-Memory, Practice: Selected Essays and Interviews*, ed. Donald F. Bouchard and trans. Bouchard and Sherry Simon (Ithaca, N.Y.: Cornell University Press, 1977), pp. 160–161 (my emphasis.)

19. Melville uses the Anarchasis Cloot metaphor in the same way in *Moby-Dick*, p. 121.

20. My emphasis on this rhetoric of hyberbolic excess is not arbitrary. It is fundamental to the Confidence-Man's "logic." Thus, for example, in the episode in which the Confidence-Man, in the guise of the man in a gray coat, encounters the young clergyman who had previously distrusted the crippled black man, the former, responding to the latter's question as to how to fortify his weak confidence, answers: " 'By strangling the least symptom of distrust, of any sort, which hereafter upon whatever provocation, may arise in you' " (*C-M*, 33). Thus, also, in the episode in which the man in gray encounters the "gentleman with gold sleeve buttons," the former, representing himself as a philanthropist/financier "projecter," describes his philanthropic purpose in such a way that it builds toward "the World's Charity" (modeled on the Crystal Palace Exposition in London), whose "mission" would be "quickened with the Wall Street spirit," that is, which culminates in a self-destructive hyperbole, one that, significantly, constitutes a comedic mirror of Ahab's ferocious monomania ("Swerve me? ye cannot swerve me . . . The path to my fixed purpose is laid with iron rails, whereupon my soul is grooved to run. Over unsounded gorges, through the rifled hearts of mountains, under torrents' beds, unerringly I rush! Naught's an obstacle, naught's an angle to the iron way!" (*M-D*, 168). To the gentleman's "doubts" as to the feasibility of this lunatic project (" 'But think of the obstacles!' ") the projector replies: "Obstacles? I have confidence to remove obstacles, though mountains. Yes, confidence in the World's Charity to that degree, that, as no better person offers to supply the place, I have nominated myself provisional treasurer" (*C-M*, 41–42).

21. See Roy Harvey Pearse, "The Metaphysics of Indian-Hating: Leatherstocking Unmasked," in *Historicism Once More; Problems and Occasion for the American Scholar* (Princeton, N.J.: Princeton University Press, 1969), pp. 109–136; Hershel Parker, "The Metaphysics of Indian-hating," *Nineteenth-Century Fiction* (September 1963), 165–173.

22. See James Hall, *Sketches of History, Life, and Manners in the West* (Philadelphia: Harrison Hall, 1835).

23. Louis Althusser, "From *Capital* to Marx's Philosophy," in Althusser and Étienne Balibar, *Reading* Capital (London: Verso, 1979), p. 21.

24. For amplified accounts of the "scientific racialism" of these American scientists, see Reginald Horsman, *Race and Manifest Destiny: the Origins of American Racial Anglo-Saxonism* (Cambridge, Mass.: Harvard University Press, 1981). As Horsman observes, many of these men of letters, historians, and scientists attributed the origins of the vigorous "love of freedom" of the American pioneers with the Germanic, particularly Anglo-Saxon people or, at any rate, with Tacitus's representation of them in *Germania*, p. 12.

25. Francis Parkman, *The Oregon Trail and The Conspiracy of Pontiac* (New York: The Library of America, 1991): "Nature has stamped the Indian with a hard, and stern physiognomy. Ambition, revenge, envy, jealousy, are his ruling passions; and his cold temperament is little exposed to those effeminate vices which are the bane of milder races. With him revenge is an overpowering instinct; nay, more, it is a point of honor and duty. His pride sets all language at defiance. He loathes the thought of coercion; and few of his race have ever stooped to discharge a menial office. A wild love of liberty, an utter intolerance of control, lie at the basis of his character, and fire his whole existence.... These generous traits are overcast by much that is dark, cold, and sinister, by sleepless distrust, and rankling jealousy. Treacherous himself, he is always suspicious of treachery in others. Brave as he is—and few of mankind are braver,—he will vent his passion by a secret stab rather than an open blow. His warfare is full of ambuscade and strategem; and he never rushes into battle with that joyous self-abandonment, with which the warriors of the Gothic races flung themselves into the ranks of their enemies. In his feasts and his drinking bouts we find none of the robust and full-toned mirth, which reigned at the rude carousals of our barbaric ancestry. He is never jovial in his cups, and maudlin sorrow or maniacal rage is the sole result of his potations," pp. 387–388. Parkman's reference to "Gothic races" is a racist allusion to Tacitus's representation of the Germanic tribes who, for Parkman, are the ancestors of the Anglo-Saxon white man.

26. Herman Melville, *Moby-Dick; or The Whale*, p. 184. See also, Spanos, *The Errant Art of Moby-Dick: The Canon, the Cold War, and the Struggle for American Studies*, pp. 123–127.

27. As I have argued in *America's Shadow: An Anatomy of Empire* (Minneapolis: University of Minnesota Press, 2000), the founding and collective acknowledgment of the metaphysical interpretation of being was simultaneous with the founding of the Occident as a cultural space different from the Orient.

28. Pearse, "The Metaphysics of Indian-hating," p. 136.

29. In referring to "the robberies and murders alleged to have been perpetrated under the pall of smoke and ashes after the Lisbon earthquake," Melville may be referring to the episode in *Candide*, in which, as Pangloss searches for "a sufficient reason" for this phenomenon [the earthquake] and Candide cries out that "the Day of Judgment has come," the sailor (who had been rescued from certain death by the Anabaptist at the expense of his own life), goes looting in the devastated city: "[He] rushed straight into the midst of the debris and risked his life searching for money. Having found some, he ran off with it to get drunk; and after sleeping off the effect of the wine, he bought the favours of the first girl of easy virtue he met amongst the ruined houses with the dead and dying all around." When Pangloss reprimands him—"This will never do, my friend; you

are not obeying the universal rule of Reason . . . ," the sailor replies: "Bloody hell . . . I am a sailor and was born in Batavia. I have had to trample on the crucifix four times in various trips to Japan, I'm not the man for your Universal Reason!" *Candide*, p. 34.

30. As David Bosworth has shown in an essay entitled "Two Sides of a Tortoise: Melville, Dickens, and the Eclipse of the West's Moral Imagination," *The Georgia Review* vol. LVII, 4 (Winter, 2004), Melville introduces the theme of the "genial misanthrope" in his great short story, "Bartleby, the Scrivener." In this essay Bosworth identifies the lawyer narrator as a "genial misanthrope": "In Bartleby, Melville has fashioned the *ultimate irritant* to the moral duplicity of the new money economy, a character who quickly becomes both a mocking mirror of and a provocative prod to the dubious presumptions which justify that economy's practices. Those presumptions are embodied, with equally exquisite authorial care, in Bartleby's turn-a-blind-eye, 'make nice boss'—who is also the story's nameless narrator, Melville capturing through his disingenuous voice a new species of American identity. In *The Confidence-Man*, he dubs this newly evolving moral character 'the genial misanthrope,' predicting a time when 'the whole world will be genialized' and when even the most hateful schemes shall be hidden beneath 'an affable air.' As an early version of this 'new kind of monster,' the story's narrator is portrayed not as an overtly ruthless robber baron but as a faux humanitarian. . . .

"Nameless, he has been crafted by Melville as a comic incarnation of the age's new managerial class: a figure whose purblind mind has evolved to hide the darker side of an industrial economy which is rapidly co-opting the American experiment. As someone who vaguely accepts the new rational materialist optimism . . . can somehow solve the perpetual problem of human unhappiness, Bartleby's boss can't quite accept the obvious fact of his scrivener's melancholy, with its uncongenial endorsement of the tragic sense of life. More important . . . the narrator (as someone whose own social and financial standing depends on the new economy's rank inequalities) can't admit that the very system which enriches him is itself a primary source of Bartleby's manifest misery" (pp. 859–860).

My reservation about this otherwise brilliant insight into Melville's fiction is that it interprets the rise of capitalism as a "coopting [of] the American experiment," whereas I am suggesting that in *The Confidence-Man* (as well as in "Bartleby"), Melville, like Max Weber, at least symptomatically, understands the rise of the capitalist spirit—and the banalization of its misanthropy—as the *fulfillment* of "the American experiment."

31. Herman Melville, *Israel Potter: His Fifty Years of Exile* (Evanston, Ill. and Chicago: Northwestern University Press and Newberry Library, 1982), p. 38.

32. See chapter 4 for a fuller discussion of the relationship between the Puritan Calling and Althusser's analysis of "interpellation."

33. "Oh, this, all along, is not you, Charlie, but some ventriloquist who usurps your larynx. It is Mark Winsome that speaks, not Charlie." (*C-M*, 206)

34. The speech of Elihu is thought by recent Biblical scholarship to have been written and included at a much later date. The main reason for this is that it preempts the power of the speech delivered by God to Job out of the whirlwind. It has also been hypothesized that the speech of Elihu was added to neutralize the ambiguities vis-a-vis the original poet's attitude toward Job's rebellion in favor

of a representation of Job that decisively affirmed repentance, his loyalty, and his now proverbial patience.

35. See Hershel Parker, "The Story of China Aster: A Tentative Explication," in *The Confidence-Man: His Masquerade*, ed. Parker (New York: Norton Critical Edition, 1971): "[The] story is also rather obviously satiric of the Transcendental respect for private impulses, best epitomized in 'Self-Reliance,' where Emerson replies to the suggestion that 'these impulses may be from below' by declaring: 'They do not seem to me to be such; but if I am the Devil's child, I will live then from the Devil.' Orchis joins the Transcendentalist-like Come-Outers, whose distinctive practice is to bring their hidden thoughts and emotions out into the open and to indulge in a 'free development'of their inmost natures," p. 356.

36. Michael Seidel, *Satirical Inheritance: Rabelais to Sterne* (Princeton, N.J.: Princeton University Press, 1879), p. 130. I am referring to that genealogical form of parody used by Cervantes to mock Don Quixote's figural hermeneutics—his monomaniacal reading of worldly phenomena as signatures of a Sacred Book. When the differential force of these cannot finally be accommodated to the logic of his metanarrative, he is compelled to invoke "the enchanter," who like the *diabolos*—the "marplot"—of the Christian narrative, is the ultimate Other of the *Logos*, and thus the principle of last resort that legitimates, but also delegitimates, all logocentric and totalizing ontologies. The most striking example of Cervantes's parodic use of this pervasive figure occurs in the second book of *Don Quixote* when the Don, preceded by Sancho, who by this time is familiar with the bizarre operations of his master's mind and can thus manipulate his visionary expectations, finally "meets" his beloved Dulcinea at the outskirts of El Toboso, only to find that she is a plain-faced village girl who rides an ass astride and stinks of raw garlic: "Sancho, what is your opinion about this grudge that the enchanters bear me? You can see how far their malice and hatred extend, for they have deprived me of the joy that I could have experienced on beholding my lady in her true being. I was indeed born to be a mirror of misfortune, the eternal target for the arrows of adversity. And you should also note, Sancho, that those traitors were not content just to transform my Dulcinea, but had transformed her into a figure as wretched and ugly as that peasant wench, and at the same time they took away from her what is so characteristic of fine ladies, the sweet smell that they derived from living among ambergris and flowers. Because I would have you know, Sancho, that when I went to replace Dulcinea on her palfrey (as you call it, although I thought it was a donkey), I was half suffocated by a blast of raw garlic that poisoned my soul." *Don Quixote*, trans. John Rutherford (New York: Penguin Books, 2000), p. 550.

37. Melville, I suggest, is using this figure of the "marplot" (*dia-bolos*) in precisely the same revisionary way he will uses it in *Billy Budd* (c. 1891; first published, 1924) : "[There] was just one thing amiss in him [Billy Budd]. No visible blemish indeed . . . ; no, but an occasional liability to a vocal defect. Though in the hour of elemental uproar or peril he was everything that a sailor should be, yet under sudden provocation of strong heart-feeling his voice . . . was apt to develop an organic hesitancy, in fact, more or less of a stutter or even worse. In this particular Billy was a striking instances that the *arch interferer, the envious marplot of Eden*, still has more or less to do with every human consignment to this planet of Earth" (p. 53). For amplified readings of this metaphorics in Melville's *Billy Budd*, see Barbara Johnson, "Melville's Fist: The Execution of *Billy Budd*," in *The*

Critical Difference: Essays in the Contemporary Rhetoric of Reading (Baltimore: Johns Hopkins University Press, 1980), 79–109; and Spanos, *The Errant Art of Moby-Dick*, pp. 234–236, 339–341.

38. Spanos, *The Errant Art of* Moby-Dick, pp. 87–113. In this reading of Father Mapple's jeremiad, my intention is to show that his reductive exegetical method, which in the end justifies violence against those who deviate from God's Word (" 'Delight is to him, who gives no quarter in the truth, and kills, burns, and destroys all sin though he pluck it out from under the robes of Senators and Judges. Delight—top-gallant delight is to him, who acknowledges no law or lord, but the Lord his God, and is only a patriot of heaven.' ") is replicated in secular terms by Captain Ahab's ontological interpretation of being, which justifies his "fiery pursuit" of the white whale. See chapter III for a discussion of the relevance of Mapple's jeremiad to the theme of nation-building (monumental history) in *Israel Potter*.

39. Erich Auerbach, "Figura," in *Scenes from the Drama of European Literature: Six Essays*, trans. Ralph Manheim (New York: Meridian Books, 1959), 53–54. See also Sacvan Bercovitch, *The Puritan Origins of the American Self* (New Haven: Yale University Press, 1975), and *The American Jeremiad* (Madison: University of Wisconsin Press, 1978).

40. Jacques Derrida, "Structure, Sign, and Play in the Discourse of the Human Sciences," in *Writing and Difference*, trans. Alan Bass (Chicago: University of Chicago Press, 1978), p. 279.

41. There are multiple references to the recent Mexican War, undertaken in the name of Manifest Destiny, in *The Confidence-Man*. And they are treated in a way that is analogous to Melville's treatment of the sites on the continuum of being he overdetermines: the ontological, the subjective, the cultural, and economic. Melville shows that, like the violence against difference or singularity perpetrated at these sites, the violence against the Spanish in the South West was "justified" by American exceptionalism and its racist/imperialist philosophy of optimism. See, for example, *C-M*, 14, 86, 98. Indeed, it might even be said that Melville's references to the imperialist Mexican War are continuous with his interpretation of Indian-hating.

42. See Spanos, *The End of Education: Toward Posthumanism* (Minneapolis: University of Minnesota Press, 1993), especially chapter 6, "The Intellectual and the Posthumanist Occasion: Toward a Decentered *Paideia*," pp. 187–222.

43. Though there is little indication in *The Confidence-Man* that Melville is thinking about Defoe's *Robinson Crusoe*, his clear parodic allusions to Benjamin Franklin, a living American counterpart of the fictional Crusoe, in this novel and in *Israel Potter*, warrant invoking his protagonist as another exemplary lunatic "optimist," like Don Quixote and Pangloss. Just as the latters' idealist hermeneutics manifest themselves in the end in hyperbolic images of confidence that self-destruct, so Crusoe's empirical metaphysical interpretative perspective "unrealizes" itself in the end in its brutally banal reduction of a human being to a frightened animal desperately seeking domestication: "I beckoned to him again to come to me, and gave him all the Signs of Encouragement that I could think of, and he came nearer and nearer, kneeling down every Ten or Twelve steps in token of acknowledgement for my saving his Life: I smil'd at him, and look'd pleasantly, and beckon'd to him to come still nearer; at length he came close to me, and then he kneel'd down

again, kiss'd the Ground, and laid his Head upon the Ground, and taking me by the Foot, set my Foot upon his Head; this it seems was in token of swearing to be my Slave for ever." Daniel Defoe, *Robinson Crusoe*, ed. Michael Shinagel (New York: Norton Critical Edition, 1994), p. 147

44. Martin Heidegger, "The Question Concerning Technology," in *The Question Concerning Technology and Other Essays*, trans. William Lovitt (New York: Harper and Row, 1977), 16–17. Gilles Deleuze and Félix Guattari's refer to this epochal turn to capitalism "stockpiling." See *A Thousand Plateaus: Capitalism and Schizophrenia*, trans. Brian Massumio (Minneqapolis: University of Minnesota Press, 1987), pp. 440ff.

45. See Edward W. Said, *Humanism and Democratic Criticism* (New York: Columbia University Press, 2004); Amir Mufti, "Critical Secularism: A Reintroduction for a Perilous Times," in "Critical Secularism," a special issue of *boundary 2*, 9, vol. 31, 2 (Summer 2004), 1–9; and Spanos "Humanism and the *Studia Humanitatis* After 9/11," in *Symploke* vol. 13, 1–2 (2005), 220–262.

46. Said, *Humanism and Democratic Criticism*, p. 61.

47. Martin Heidegger, *An Introduction to Metaphysics*, trans. Ralph Manheim (New Haven: Yale University Press, 1959): "The *polemos* named here is a conflict that prevailed prior to everything divine and human, not a war in the human sense. The conflict, as Heraclitus thought it, first caused the realm of being to separate into opposites . . . In such separation cleavages, intervals, distances, and joints opened. In the conflict (*Aus-einandersetzung*, setting-apart) a world come into being. Conflict does not split, much less destroy unity. It constitutes unity, it is a binding-together, *logos*. *Polemos* and *logos* are the same," p. 62.

Chapter 6. American Confidence in the Age of Globalization

1. See the appended supplementary materials of Melville, *The Confidence-Man: His Masquerade*, ed. Hershel Parker (New York: Norton Critical Edition, 1971).

2. In his parodic genealogy of American confidence, Melville overdetermines the indissoluble relationality of the ontological (the philosophy of optimism), the racial (Indian-hating), and the economic (the spirit of capitalism). But to leave it at that would be to miss what is crucial about his profound insight into the antebellum American national identity: that the philosophy of optimism is polyvalent and manifests itself as a representational continuum that ranges from being as such through the subject, race, ethnicity, gender, economics, and cultural production (not least the media—recall the parodic encomium to the "voice of the people" (*C-M*, 163–166) and the "poetical eulogy of the Press" (chapter 30, pp. 167–178)—articulated by "the boon companions," Charlie Noble and Frank Goodman—historiography, science, and literature, to the nation and to the relations between nations. Beside those sites on this continuum I have emphasized, two of the most important are natural science and realistic fiction (the kind of "productive" science that was emerging, under the influence of Linnaeus, Cuvier, Buffon, in antebellum America and the kind of writing that Melville's optimist critics demanded of him after *Mardi* and *Moby-Dick*, but which he preferred not to provide). In *The Confidence-Man*, Melville intentionally represents these modes of knowledge production as complicitous with the coercions of the Quixotic hermeneutics of optimism. This can be conveniently summarized by the following

carnivalesque quotation (so reminiscent, not incidentally, of the style and thematics of *The Education of Henry Adams*, that other exposure of the American confidence game in the nineteenth century), from one of the chapters Melville devotes to the art of fiction, specifically his carnivalesque defense of character inconsistency against his harsh confidence-driven critics: "If reason be judge no writer has produced such inconsistent characters as nature herself has. It must call for no small sagacity in a reader unerringly to discriminate in a novel between the inconsistencies of conception and those of life. As elsewhere, experience is the only guide here; but as no one man's experience can be coextensive with *what is*, it may be unwise in every case to rest upon it. When the duck-billed beaver of Australia was first brought stuffed to England, the naturalists, appealing to their classifications, maintained that there was, in reality, no such creature; the bill in the specimen must needs be, in some way, artificially stuck on" (*C-M*, 70).

3. The Confidence-Man's "appeal" to trial and chastening by the divine to account for extraordinary suffering in this world, was, a I have been suggesting, a standard rationalization in the discourse of the American Puritans. It is, for example, at the heart of Mary Rowlandson's captivity narrative, *The Sovereignty and Goodness of God*, not least in "The Preface to the Reader," in which the theological explanation of Rowlandson's "trials" are strikingly similar to Pangloss's reasoning about the Lisbon earthquake: "That God is indeed the supream Lord of the world, ruling the most unruly, weakening the most cruel and salvage, granting his People mercy in the sight of the unmercifull, curbing the lusts of the most filthy, holding the hands of the violent, delivering the prey from the mighty, *and gathering together the out casts of* Israel. Once and again you have heard, but here you may see, *that power belongeth unto God*; that our God is the God of Salvation, and him belong the issues from Death. That our God is in the heavens, and doth whatever pleases him. Here you have *Sampson's* Riddle exemplified, and the great promise, *Rom.* 8.28 verified, Out of the Eater comes forth meat, and sweetness out of the strong; The worst of evils working together for the best. How evident is it that the Lord hath made this Gentlewoman a gainer by all this affliction, that she can say, *'tis good for her, yea better that she hath been, than that she should not have been thus afflicted. Oh how doth God shine forth in such things as these!*" p. 67.

4. Voltaire, *Candide or Optimism*, trans. John Butt (London: Penguin Books, 1947), p. 34.

5. On the emergence of the "New Americanist" critique of the (Cold War) founders of the "field imaginary" of American studies, see especially Donald Pease, ed. *New Americanists: Revisionist Interventions into the Canon*, a special issue of *boundary 2*, vol. 17, 1 (Spring 1990).

6. Wei-chee Dimock, *Empire for Liberty*. There is, however, as I have been suggesting throughout this book, a marginal but growing momentum, especially among European intellectuals, if not European Americanists—Maurice Blanchot, Gilles Deleuze, Giorgio Agamben, Antonio Negri, among others—to focus precisely on that subversive aspect of Melville's fiction that I am calling attention to: what, for short, I having been calling the *spectral*, those aspects of being that metaphysical interpretation will, confidently, have nothing to do with, yet that always haunt its confident affirmations.

7. This extremely influential neoconservative think tank and its "defense" strategy document, *Rebuilding America's Defenses,* predate 9/11/01, but its global "project" has been clearly the model for the domestic and foreign practice of the

Bush administration's "war on terror" in its aftermath. Reminiscent of the deadly, dehumanized, short-hand rhetoric and style of the memoranda of *The Pentagon Papers* written by the Washington bureaucrats who conducted the War in Vietnam—and of the cruel banalities of confidence-men like Egbert in *The Confidence-Man*—it calls for the establishment and "preservation of Pax Americana" and a "unipolar 21st century" by way of "securing" and "expanding zones of democratic peace, deterring a rise of new great-power competition, defending key regions (Europe, East Asia, Middle East) and exploring transformations of war." Many of the members of this astonishingly confident collective have held and now hold high-level positions in the George W. Bush administration. They include Donald Rumsfeld, Richard Cheney, Paul Wolfowitz, Richard Perle, Francis Fukuyama, Donald Kagan, and William Bennett, among other prominent neoconservatives. For a devastating critique of the collective mind of the American confidence-men who planned and executed the Vietnam War, see Richard Ohmann, *English in America: A Radical View of the Profession* (New York: Oxford University Press, 1976), 190–208; see also Spanos *The End of Education*, pp. 171–174, 177–178.

8. See Sacvan Bercovitch, *The American Jeremiad* (Madison: University of Wisconsin Press, 1978): "No doubt these threats [that God would "withdraw their (the Puritan settlers') 'special appointment,' weed them out, pluck them up, and cast them irrevocably out of His sight," should they stray from their obligation to Him] were prompted in part by anxiety; their stridency speaks of hardships to come in settling an unknown land. But more significant . . . is how closely they foreshadow the major themes of the colonial pulpit. False dealing with God, betrayal of covenant promises, the degeneracy of the young, the lure of profits and pleasures, the prospect of God's just, swift, and total revenge—it reads like an index of favorite sermon topics of seventeenth-century New England. In particular of course, I refer to the political sermon—what might be called the state-of-the-covenant address, tendered at every public occasion (on days of fasting and prayer, humiliation and thanksgiving, at covenant-renewal and artillery-company ceremonies, and, most elaborately and solemnly, at election-day gatherings)—which has been designated as the jeremiad," p. 4.

9. See Spanos, "American Exceptionalism, the Jeremiad, and the the Frontier, Before and After 9/11/01: The Puritan and the Neo-Con Man," in *American Exceptionalism in th Age of Globalization: The Specter of Vietnam* (Albany: SUNY Press, 2008). See also Richard Slotkin, *Regeneration through Violence* (Hanover, N.H.: Wesleyan University Press, 1973) and *The Fatal Environment* (New York: Athenaeum Press, 1975).

10. Frederick Jackson Turner, "The Significance of the Frontier in American History," in *The Frontier in American History* (New York: Dover, 1996), p. 15; originally published by Henry Holt, 1920. (My emphasis.)

11. The scare tactics that always accompanies American optimism is self-parodically put by Palmer in his essay "The Case Against the Reds." There, he charges that "tongues of revolutionary heat were licking the altars of the churches, leaping into the belfry of the school bell, crawling into the sacred corners of American homes, seeking to replace marriage vows with libertine laws, burning up the foundations of society."

12. As one American military officer put this "fulfillment" of the promissary logic of America's "errand in the wilderness" of Southeast Asia, "We had to destroy

Ben Tre [read Vietnam] in order to save it." See Michael Herr, *Dispatches* (New York: Vintage Books, 1991), p. 71.

13. Francis Fukuyama, *The End of History and the Last Man* (New York: The Free Press, 1992). For a critique of Fukuyama's euphoric announcement of the end of history that rightly overdetermine the ontological grounds of his euphoric "confidence," see Jacques Derrida, *Specters of Marx: The State of the Debt, the Work of Mourning, and the New International*, trans. Peggy Kamuf (New York: Routledge, 1994), pp. 56–75. See also William Spanos, *America's Shadow*, pp. xvi–xviii, 115–120, and the chapter entitled "History and the Specter: Rethinking Thinking in the Post-Cold War Age," in *American Exeptionalism in the Age of Globalization*, 1–34.

14. George Bush, reported in *Newsweek*, No. 117, March 11, 1991.

15. Samuel P. Huntington, *Who Are We?: The Challenges to America's National Identity* (New York: Simon and Schuster, 2004), pp. 263–264; my emphasis. Further references will be abbreviated to *WAW* and incorporated in the text in parentheses.

16. Huntington devotes and entire chapter to this effort to demonize "deconstruction," but nowhere, despite the many complaints of its theoreticians, does he indicate that he has read any of the major articulations of this discourse or understood its essential tenets. See "Deconstructing America: The Rise of Subnational Identities" (*WAW*, 141–177).

17. As Edward Said has pointed out in demonstrating the superficiality of Huntington's scholarship, the phrase had its origins in the Orientalist, Bernard Lewis's essay "The Roots of Muslim Rage," *The Atlantic Monthly* (September 1990). See "The Clash of Definitions," in *Reflections on Exile and Other Essays* (Cambridge, Mass.: Harvard University Press, 2000). p. 572.

18. Michael Moore's parodic documentary *Farenheit 9/11* (2004) goes far to pushing the underlying optimistic logic of the Bush administration's "war on terror" to the point where is discloses itself as a con game.

19. William E. Connolly in *Why I Am Not a Secularist* (Minneapolis: University of Minnesota Press, 1999), p. 81–82. See also Ernest Renan, "What Is a Nation?," trans. Martin Thom, in *Nation and Narration*, ed. Homi Bhabha (London: Routledge, 1990), pp. 8–22. I am indebted to R. Radhakrishnan for pointing me to Connolly's provocative critique of nationalism.

20. Edward W. Said, *Culture and Imperialism* (New York: Alfred A. Knopf, 1993), p. 333. See also Theodor Adorno, *Minima Moralia: Reflections from a Damaged Life*, trans. E. F. N. Jephcott (London: New Left Books, 1974), p. 68.

21. Herman Melville, *Billy Budd, Sailor (An Inside Narrative)*, ed. Harrison Hayford and Merton M. Sealts Jr. (Chicago: University of Chicago Press, 1962), pp. 130–131.

Index

Adams, Henry, 54; *The Education of Henry Adam*, 267n
Adams, John, 245n
Adorno, Theodor, 99; and the administered society, 163, 164–166; *Minima Moralia: Reflections from a Damaged Life*, 91–92, 165–166, 225, 246n
Agamben, Giorgio, 10, 12, 15, 165, 267n; *The Coming Community*, 54; "Bartleby, or On Contingency," 230–231n; on Bartleby, 44, 163, 230–231n, 258n
Agassiz, Louis, 185
Althusser, Louis, vii, 25, 29, 37, 44, 164; "From Capital to Marx's Philosophy," 105, 250n; "Ideology and Ideological State Apparatuses," 141–145, 230n; and interpellation, 23, 34, 79–80, 111, 141–146, 234n; and *lecteur symptomale*, 251n; " 'On the Young Marx': Theoretical Questions," 236n; and the "problematic," 110–111, 123–124, 133, 141–146, 230n
Allen, Ethan, *A Narrative of Colonel Ethan Allen's Captivity*, 246n
Alatas, S. L., 165
Al Qaeda, 2, 12, 100, 102, 218, 220, 247n
America, and Adamic myth, 170–172, 208–209; as administered society, 163, 164–166; Anglo-Protestant core culture of; 12–13, 139–140, 222–223; and Ahabism, 4, 188–189, 261n; and confidence, 11, 107–108, 138, 224–225, 266–267n; and con men, 223; and the frontier, 218–219; and imperialism, 218; and Manifest Destiny, 14, 20, 178, 192, 209, 217, 238–239n; the New World Order, 1, 55; and optimism, 78–79, 107–108, 138, 168, 171, 175–177, 181–182, 200–209, 259n, 265n, 266–267n; and Puritan tradition 6, 8, 13–14, 20, 42, 45–46, 49, 62; 69–70, 87, 92–96, 101–103, 139–140, 143–145, 150–151, 171, 178, 208–209, 218, 242–243n, 244n, 255–256n, 267n; and September 11, 2001, 2–4, 34, 55, 217–218; and the Vietnam War, 100; its "war on terror," 3, 17, 100–101, 268; *See also* American exceptionalism; and American Calling; American jeremiad; *Pax Americana*
American Calling, 7, 10, 14, 78–80, 140, 140–145, 150–151, 224, 227–228; *See also* Althusser, and interpellation
American exceptionalism, 1, 11, 17, 20, 35, 53–54, 62–67, 80, 144, 169–170, 171, 253n, 265n
Americanists, New, 9–10, 19–20, 24, 34, 46, 52–53, 55, 103, 267n
Americanists, Old, 19, 34; on *The Confidence-Man*, 178–179; field imaginary of, 52, 232n
American jeremiad, 59–67, 101–103, 218, 219–225, 267n, 268n

271

American Renaissance, 42
Anderson, Benedict, 27
Anderson, Quentin, 9
Antonius, George, 165
Appadurai, Arjun, *Modernity at Large*, 54
Arendt, Hannah, 2, 50, 51; *Life of the Mind*, 235n; *The Origins of Totalitarianism*, 240n
Arnaud-Marcais, Dominique, on *Moby-Dick*, 238n
Auerbach, "Figura," 244n, 265n; figural interpretation in, 244n
Austen, Jane, *Mansfield Park*, 251n
Ayers, Bill, *Fugitive Days: A Memoir*, 229n; on Melville's *Moby-Dick*, 3–4
Auld, Jedediah B., 4

Bancroft, George, 70, 249n
Barnum, P. T., 213
"Bartleby, the Scrivener," Bartleby in: his refusal of the call, 144–145, 151–154, 158–61; his identity (question of), 162–166, 256–258n; his spectrality, 162–166; the narrator in: his accommodations, 154–156, 157–161; his benevolence, 145–146; his deconstruction, 158–161; his Franklinian character, 147, 152; his unreliability, 145–46; his similarity to Captain Delano; as Subject (Caller), 146–148; his Wall-Street truth, 156–157; and the calling (interpellation), 144–145
Beckett, Samuel, *Watt*, 12, 164, 261n
"Benito Cereno," Alexandro Arandas in, 116, 132, 251n; Amasa Delano in: as Alden Pyle figure, 134–138; his American exceptionalism, 109–110, 120–121, 134–138; his vision (blindness of), 106–110, 114–115, 117–118, 127–130; his confidence, 107–108, 114–115; his Puritan origins, 108; his racism, 118–120, 250–251n; Babo in: his "servitude," 112–113; his masquerade, 109–110, 113–115; as specter, 123–127, 130–132; Benito Cereno in: his Old World demeanor, 109, 112, 130–131; his silence, 128–129, 130–132; as detective story, 111–112, 115, 122–123; retrospective deposition in, 122–127; and the nothing, 123–124; and vision, 110–111
Bentham, Jeremy, and the Panopticon, 149
Bennett, William, 268n
Bercovitch, Sacvan, xii, 9, 139, 222; *The American Jeremiad*, 59, 101, 204, 244n, 254n, 268n; *Cambridge History of American Literature* (ed), 231n; on *Pierre*, 48–49, 240n; *The Puritan Origins of the American Self*, 204, 231n, 244n; *The Rites of Assent: Transformations in the Symbolic Construction of America*, 233n
Bezanson, Walter, 9, 67–68, 242n, 246n
Bhabha, Homi, *The Location of Culture*, 51; *Nation and Narration* (ed.), 234n
Billy Budd, and the *diabolos*, 264–265n; and spectrality, 226–228. See also Melville, Herman
Bin Laden, Osama, 3, 102, 220
Bird, Robert Montgomery, 185
Blackstone, Sir William, 246n
Blanchot, Maurice, 12, 165, 267; *The Writing of Disaster*, l23n, 258n
Bolton, Ambassador John, 221
Bosworth, David, on Bartleby, 263n
Bove, Paul, 52–53; *In the Wake of Theory*, 241n
Brooks, Van Wyck, 8
Brown, Charles Brockton, 185
Brown, George Loring, 185
Buffon, 266n
Bundy, McGeorge, 229n
Bush, President George, 220
Bush, President George W., 2, 101; and Puritan tradition, 218; on *The Quiet American*, 252n; and the war on terror, 3, 17, 100–101, 221–225, 268n

Cadava, Eduardo, *Emerson and the Climates of History*, 246n; on Webster, Daniel, 243n
Caldwell, Charles, 185
Camus, Alfred, *The Fall*, 260; *The Stranger*, 164
Caputo, Philip, *A Rumor of War*, 132
Cervantes, Miguel, *Don Quixote*, 134, 205, 260n, 265n; and the enchanter figure, 76, 203, 244n, 264n; and textual attitude, 176
Chakrabarty, Dipesh, *Provincializing Europe*, 54
Chase, Richard, 9
Chaucer, Geoffrey, 179
Chatterjee, Partha, *The Nation and Its Fragments*, 54
Cheney, Richard, 221, 268n
Cheyfiz, Eric, 9
Clark, Louis Gaylord, 5
Coetzee, J. M., *The Life and Times of Michael K*, 165
Cole, Thomas, 185
Coleridge, Samuel Taylor, 164
Confidence-Man, The: His Masquerade, as aesthetic whole, 259–260n; and *Candide*, 174–178, 190–193, 214–217; and confidence (Malakoff of) in, 168–172, 219–220; Confidence-Man in: his avatars, 182; as *dia-bo-los*, 172–178, 203–204, 260n, 264n; his function, 172–178, 179–182; his methods, 180–183; his relation to Satan in the Book of Job, 173–176; Fidele in, 178–180, 210; and *Don Quixote*, 175–176, 184, 192, 203, 260n; Egbert (Thoreau?) in, 194, 196–204; figural interpretation in, 204–212; "Metaphysics of Indian-Hating" in: metaphysics of, 182–184, 189–190; Col. Moredock in: Ahabism of, 188–189; as backwoodsman, 185–188; as Leatherstocking Nemesis, 187, 189; racism of, 187; "genial misanthropy" in, 192–194; Marl Winsome (Emerson, Ralph Waldo), in, 194–197; metaphysical vision in,

169–170; a "Soldier of Fortune" in, 214–217; "Story of China Aster" in: and Book of Job, 197–204; as critique of optimism, 181–182, 200–204, 206; positive implication of, 209–212
Connolly, William, on nation building, 98–99, 223–224, 247–248n; *Why I Am Not a Secularist*, 247n
Conrad, Joseph, *Heart of Darkness*, 83, 128, 245n, 249n; *Victory*, 2660n
Cooper, James Feninore, 185; the Leatherstocking figure in, 72, 81, 132, 186
Coover, Robert, 12
Cotton, John, vii; "Christian Calling," 256
Cuvier, George, 266n

Danforth, John, 209
Defoe, Daniel, *Robinson Crusoe*, 109, 265–266n; and imperialism, 248–249n
Delano, Amasa, *Narrative of Voyages and Travels*, 130
Deleuze, Gilles, 12, 14, 164, 165, 267n; and apparatuses of capture, 163, 166; on Bartleby, 163, 258n; "Bartleby; or the Formula," 15–16, 140; *Différence et repetition*, 240n; *Logique du sens*, 240n
Deleuze and Guattari, Felix, 50, 91; and nomadology, 51; *A Thoussnd Plateaus: Capitalism and Schizophrenia*, 54, 240n
DeLillo, Don, 12
Derrida, Jacques, 12, 22, 44, 50, 208; and deconstruction, 37; "Differance," 40–41, 123, 237n; "Donner la mort," 231n; on Fukuyama, Francis, 269n; and the revenant, 47, 97; *Specters of Marx; The State of the Debt, the Work of Mourning, and the New International*, 51, 54, 123–124, 240n; *Of Spirit*, 238n; "Structure, Sign, and Play in the Discourse of the Human Sciences," 235n; and visiting, 251n

Diabolos, 172–178, 203–204, 260n, 264n
Dickinson, Emily, 96
Dimock, Wei-chee, 14, 22; on *The Confidence-Man*, 259–260n; *Empire for Liberty: Melville and the Poetics of Individualism*, 233–234n; on *Pierre*, 233–234n, 238–239n
Donzelot, Jacques, 233n
Dostoyesvky, Feodor, *Notes from Underground*, 260n
Douglass, Frederick, 110, 133; *Narrative of the Life of Frederick Douglass*, 250n
Drinnon, Richard, 9
Dryden, Edgar, on "Benito Cereno," 252n; "The Entangled Text: Melville's *Pierre* and the Problem of Reading," 236n, 237n; *Melville's Thematics of Form: The Great Art of Telling the Truth*, 252n
Dubois, W. E. B., 165
Duyckinck, Evert, 4, 5
Dwight, Timothy, 185
Dylan Bob, 167

Edwards, Jonathan, 157, 209
Eliot, Emory, 24, 233n
Eliot, T. S., 99; *Four Quartets*, 248n
Ellison, Ralph, *Invisible Man*, 130, 165
Emerson, Ralph Waldo, 70, 185, 243; "The American Scholar," 177; and imperialism, 35; as Mark Winsome in *The Confidence-Man*; 194–197; and optimism, 177, 203–204; "The Young American," 35, 38
Everett, Edward, 254n

Faulkner, William, *Absalom, Absalom*, 132
Fanon, Frantz, 133, 165
Figural interpretation, 204–205, 244n, 268n. See also America, Puritan tradition; *The Confidence-Man*; *Israel Potter*
Filson, John, 185

Fitzgerald, F. Scott, *The Great Gatsby*, 132
Foucault, Michel, 1, 11, 12, 23, 25, 50, 164, 233n; and the archive, 250n; *Discipline and Punish*, 148–149, 2343n; and genealogy, 33, 37–38, 57, 58–59, 61, 101, 169, 177–178, 225; on knowledge/power, 78, 148–151; *Language, Counter-Memory, Practice*, 231n; "Nietzsche, Genealogy, History," 235n; "Questions Concerning Geography," 239n; "Reponse au Cercle d'epistemologie," 259n; "Theatricum Philosophicum," 19, 240n; and the repressive hypothesis, 155–156; "What Is an Author?," 231n. See also Nietzsche, Friedrich
Franklin, Benjamin, 20, 194, 217, 265n; *Autobiography*, 143; and philosophy of optimism, *Poor Richard's Almanac*, 77, 79–80, 143; *Way of Wealth*, 254n. See also *Israel Potter* and Melville, Herman
Freeman, John, 8
Freud, Sigmund, 12; and the uncanny, 256–257n
Fukuyama, Francis, 253n, 268n; *The End of History and the Last Man*, 232n, 269n
Furies (*Erinyes*); and Satan (Book of Job), 176

Genealogy, 33, 37–38, 57, 58–59, 61, 101, 111, 169, 177–178, 225. See also Foucault, Michel, and Nietzsche, Friedrich
George III, 74
Goethe, Wolfgang, 42
Gramsci, Antonio, 23, 25, 144; on hegemony, 27–28, 77, 250n; *Selections from the Prison Notebooks*, 234n
Greene, Graham, *Brighton Rock*, 261n; *The Quiet American*, 105, 133–140, 252n
Gruber, Carol, *Mars and Minerva: World War I and the Uses of the*

Higher Learning in American, 230n
Guha, Ranajit, *Elementary Aspects of Peasant Insurgency in Colonial India*, 54
Gunn, Giles, *A Historical Guide to Herman Melville* (ed.), 233n

Haass, Richard, 221
Halberstam, David, *The Best and the Brightest*, 229n
Hall, James, Judge, 183–190; *Sketches of History, Life, and Manners in the West*, 261n
Hans, James S., on Bartleby, 258n
Hawthorne, Nathaniel, 14
Heckewelder, John, 185
Hegel, Friedrich, 37
Heidegger, Martin, xi–xii, 5; "Age of the World Picture," 43, 50, 238n; and *Auseinandersetzung*, 212, 266n; and *die Abgeschiedene*, 43–46, 50; *Being and Time*, 44, 140, 246n; "The End of Philosophy and the Task of Thinking," 238n; *An Introduction to Metaphysics*, 19, 266n; and destruction, 30; and the hermeneutic circle, 246n; "Language in the Poem: A Discussion of Georg Trakl's Poetic Works," 238n; and the ontotheological tradition, 54; and the nothing (*das Nichts*), 38–39, 4, 123; and silence, 21, 47; and the uncanny *Unheimlichkeit*, 257n; "What Is Metaphysics?," 38–39; *Parmenides*, 31, 239n; "The Question Concerning Technology," 256n; and repetition (*Wiederholung*), 41, 246n
Hellman, John, *Americna Myth and the Legacy of Vietnam*, 231n, 252n
Hemingway, Ernest, *For Whom The Bells Toll*, 132
Herr, Michael, on Lansdale, Edward, 253n; *Dispatches*, 253n, 268–269n
Hobbes, Thomas, 77
Homer, *The Odyssey*, 82

Hone, Ralph, ed. *The Voice Out of the Whirlwind: The Book of Job*, 260n
Horsman, Reginald, *Race and Manifest Destiny: The Origins of American Racial Anglo-Saxonism*, 243n, 262n
Howard, John, 246n
Hudson River Valley School (painters), 185
Huntington, Samuel, P., and Anglo-Protestant core culture, 139, 222–223, 247n; *The Clash of Civilizations and the Remaking of World Order*, 253–254n; and "clash of civilizations," 139; and "deconstructionists;" 222–223, 269n; and "great awakening," 139, 223, 247n; as Jeremiah figure, 101–102, 220–224; neoconservativism of; 220–224; and Puritan tradition, 221–222; *Who are We? Challenges to American's National Identity?*, 101–102, 139–140, 247n. *See also* American jeremiad
Hussein, Saddam, 3

Ionesco, Eugene, *Victims of Duty*, 261
Ignatieff, Michael, *American Exceptionalism and Human Rights* (ed.), 253n
Israel Potter; Allen, Ethan, in, 61, 80, 85–87; and American jeremiad, 59–67; and Bartleby, 90–91; Benjamin Franklin in, 61, 71, 75–81, 245n; as confidence-man, 78–81; and con men, 71; as deconstructive novel, 92; and exile, 75; The Bunker Hill Monument, 59–67; and figural interpretation, 69–70, 74–75, 87, 92–95; George III in, 74; and identity, 87–91; John Paul Jones in, 61, 80–85; Millet, Sir John, in, 72–73, 99; and monumentalism, 31–32, 57–67, 71, 95–99; and *Life and Remarkable Adventures of Israel R. Potter*; and preterition, 68; and Puritan tradition, 69–70, 87; and singularity, 73–75, 80, 98–99; and

Israel Potter (continued)
   September 11, 2001, 99–103; and spectrality, 88–91, 97–98. *See also* figural interpretation; Melville, Herman; America, Puritan tradition

Jackson, Andrew, 249n
James. C. L. R., 133, 165; *Black Jacobins: Toussaint L'Ouverture and the San Domingo Revolution*; *Mariners*, 252n; *Renegades, Castaways: The Story of Melville and the World We Live In*, 252n
Jameson, Fredric, 11; *Postmodernism; or, The Logic of Late Capitalism*, 239n
Jefferson, Thomas, 133
Jehlen, Myra, on "Benito Cereno," 252n
Job, Book of, 213; in "Bartleby, the Scrivener," 145, 162, 256n; in *The Confidence-Man*, 172–174, 195, 199–203, 263–264n; existentialist interpretation of, 173–174
Johnson, Barbara, on *Billy Budd*, 264–265n; *The Critical Difference: Essays in the Contemporary Rhetoric of Reading*, 265n
Johnson, David, 185
Johnson, Samuel, 190–191
Jones, William Alfred, 4
Joyce, James, *Ulysses*, 12

Kant, Immanuel, 31
Kafka, Franz, *The Castle*, 12, 164; *The Trial*, 260
Kagan, Donald, 268n
Kaplan, Amy, 9
Kasson, John, *Civilizing the Machine: Technology and Republican Values in America*, 254n; and Lowell factory system, 149–150
Kennedy, John F., and the "New Frontier," 231n
Kierkegaard, Søren, 12, 82; *The Concept of Irony, with Constant Reference to Socrates*, 246n; *Repetition: An Essay in Experimental Psychology*, 260n
King, Martin Luther, 133
Knickerbocker Set, 5
Krauthammer, Charles, 220

Lansdale, Col. Edward W., 132–133, 253n; *In the Midst of Wars: An American's Mission to Southeast Asia*, 252n
Layda, Jay, *The Melville Log: A Documentary Life of Herman Melville*, 242n, 247n
Lederer, William J., and Burdick, Eugene, *The Ugly American*, 132
Ledoux, Claude Nicholas, and the circular city, 149
Leibnitz, Gottfried 78, 175, 177, 191, 206, 214
Lewis, Bernard, 269n
Levin, Harry, 9
Linnaeus, 266n
Lindbergh, Gary, on *The Confidence-Man*, 259n
Locke, John, 245n
Lowell factory system, 149–151, 254–255n
Lowell, Francis Cabot, 149
Lyotard, Jean-Francois, 50; *The Differend: Phrases in Dispute*, 54, 123, 240n; *The Postmodern Condition: A Report on Knowledge*, 237n; and the unpresentable, 41

Machiavelli, 77
MacLeish, Archibald, *J. B.*, 261n
Malcolm X, 133
Marovitz, Sanford and A. C. Christodoulou, eds., *Melvile Among the Nations: Proceedings of an International Conference, Volos, Greece, July 2–6, 1997*, 238n
Martin, James, "The Spirit of Utility's Connections to Republican Virtue: Engaging the Transatlantic Origins of the American Enlightenment," unpublished Ph.D. dissertation, 255n

Marx, Karl, 12
Marx, Leo, 9
Mather, Cotton, 151, 209; *Magnalia Christi Americana*, 12, 255n; *Nehemiahs Americanus: The Life of John Winthrop*, 231n, 255n
Mather, Increase, 209
Mathiessen, F. O., 9; *American Renaissance: Art and Expression in the Age of Emerson and Whitman*, 234n
Matthews, Cornelius, 4
McCarthy, Senator Joseph, 252n; as con man, 219
McCall, Dan, *The Silence of Bartleby*, 256n
McNamara, Robert, 229n
Melville, Herman, and American exceptionalisman (critique of), 130; anti-racism of, 129–130; "Bartleby, the Scrivener," 10, 16, 49, 103; "The Bell Tower," 254–255n; "Benito Cereno," 49, 59, 103, 150; *Billy Budd*, 49, 50, 59; his contemporaniety, 2–4, 12–13, 99–103, 132–141, 164–166, 217–228; and con men (American), 214, 223–224; *Confidence-Man, The*, 49, 59, 65, 75, 81, 103, 115; and enchanter principle, 244; and errancy, 171–172; and the exilic consciousness, 53–54; and Foucault, 59; "Hawthorne and his Mosses," 231n; *Israel Potter*, 7, 16, 20, 27, 31, 45, 50, 67, 103, 147; *Mardi*, 5, 266n; *Moby-Dick*, 2, 10, 16–17, 20, 34, 40, 49, 50, 64, 103, 165, 188–189, 213; Father Mapple in, 64–65, 138, 170, 204, 259n; and the nothing, 11; and the novel, 35–37, 40–41, 259n; *Omoo*, 25, 229n; "The Paradise of Bachelors and the Tartarus of Maids," 150, 254–255n; *Pierre*, 5–6, 16, 58, 98, 103, 171–172; reception of after *Moby-Dick*, 4–13; *Redburn*, 25, 232n, 246n; resistance, 54–54; and slavery, 236–237n, 251n; as specter, 5–13, 217–218, 226–228; and textural attitude, 134–138; and thinking, 54–55; *Typee*, 25; *White-Jacket*, 13–14, 25, 59; the worldliness of his fiction, 17, 20; *See also* America, "Bartleby, the Scrivener," "Benito Cereno," *Billy Budd*, *The Confidence-Man*, *Israel Potter*
Melville Revival, in the 1920s, 3, 7–8, 103; during Cold War, 9–10
Mill, John Stewart, 223–224
Miller, J. Hillis, 9; on Bartleby, 256–257n, 257–258n
Miller, Perry, 143; *Errand in the Wilderness*, 256n; *The Raven and the Whale*, 4, 229n
Moore, Michael, *Farrenheit 9/11*, 269
Morrison, Toni, 12, 133; *Playing in the Dark: Whiteness and the Literary Imagination*, 105, 236–237n, 251n
Morton, Samuel George, *Crania Americana*, 185
Mudimbe, V. Y., *The Ideas of Africa*, 54
Mufti, Aamir, 266n
Mumford, Lewis, 8
Murdoch, Iris, *A Severed Head*, 261
Musil, Robert, *The Man Without Qualities*, 12

Napoleon, 249n
Negri, Antonio, and Michael Hardt, 50, 165, 267n; on Bartleby, 140, 231n; *Empire*, 51, 54, 234n; *Multitude*, 51, 54, 243n
Ngai, Sienne, *Ugly Feelings*, 260n
Nietzsche, Friedrich, 12; and genealogy, 33, 37–39, 58, 101, 169, 225; *Untimely Meditations*, 235n
Nott, Josiah, 185

Ohmann, Richard, *English in America: A Radical View of the Profession*, 268n
Olson, Charles, 12

Palmer, A. Mitchell, "The Case Agaisnt the Reds," 268n; as con-man, 219

Park, Mungo, *Travels in the Interior of Africa*, 251n
Parker, Hershel, on the story of China Aster, 264n
Parker, Theodore, 70, 185
Parkman, Francis, 70, 185, 186, 249; *The Conspiracy of Pontiac*, 262n; racism of, 262n
Paulding, James Kirk, 185
Pax Americana, 12, 55
Pax Metaphysica, 31, 54, 55
Pax Romana, 31
Pearse, Roy Harvey, 167, 190; "The Metaphysics of Indian-Hating: Leatherstocking Unmasked," 261n
Pease, Donald, E., xiii, 9, 19, 232n, 239n, 267n; on C. L. R. James, 252n; "New Americanist Revisionist Interventions into the Canon," 230n; *Visionary Compacts: American Renaissance Writing in Cultural Context*, 230n, 243n
Peck, George Washington, 5–7, 25, 50, 140, 229n
Perle, Richard, 221, 268n
Pentagon Papers, 268
Pierre; or the Ambiguities, 5–6; blacks in, 27; "Chronometricals & Horologicals" in, 24; deconstructionist reading of, 37–38; deferral (of presence) in, 40–41; errancy in, 44–45; and hegemony, 21–24, 28–29; and genealogy (of Saddle Meadows), 26, 37–39; and imperialism, 45–46; Isabel in: as phantom, 21, 48–49; and *Moby-Dick*, 50–51; Pierre in: as exilic figure (*die Abgeshciedene*), 43–44, 51, 53–55; his extraordinary emergency (de-centering), 35, 39–45; as preterite, 50–51; his spectrality, 39–44, 47–52; Plinlimmon in, 24, 30; and metaphysics ('the talismanic secret"), 22, 29–30, 31, 35, 41–42, 48; and monumentalism, 26–27, 31–34, 39, 45; and the nothing, 41–44; and the novel, 35–37, 39, 40; and silence (voice of), 39–40, 42–44, 47–52; and "young America," 35

Pinter, Harold, *The Birthday Party*, 262n
Plato, 42
Pope, Alexander, 78, 130, 206; "Essay on Man," 175
Poststructuralism, 29; meaning of, 258n
Pratt, Mary Louise, *Imperial Eyes: Travel Writing and Transculturation*, 251n
Prescott, William H., *Conquest of Mexico*, 249n
Priestley, Joseph, 157
Project for a New American Century, 217, 221; *Rebuilding America's Defenses*, 267–268
Pynchon Thomas, 12, 49, 54; *Gravity's Rainbow*, 165

Quidor, George, 185
Quinlan, James, 185

Radhakrishan, R., 269n
Rampersad, Arnold, on *Israel Potter*; *Melville's* Israel Potter: *A Pilgrimage and Progress*, 241n, 246n
Renan, Ernest, 102; on nation building, 26, 32, 34, 65–66, 98, 224, 247n; "Qu'est ce qu'une nation?," 65–66, 234n
Riddel, Joseph, "Decentering the Image: The Project of American Poetics?," 236n, 237n
Rogin, Michael Paul, 9; on "Benito Cereno," 251–252n; *Subversive Genealogy: The Politics and Art of Herman Melville*, 242n, 252n
Rostow, Walt, 229n
Rove, Carl, 221
Rowe, John Carlos, 9; *At Emerson's Tomb: The Politics of Classic American Literature*, 233n; on Bartleby, 256n; on *Pierre*, 234n, 235n, 240n; *Through the Custom-House: Nineteenth-Century American Fiction and Modern Theory*, 256n
Rowlandson, Mary, 177; "Preface" by Per Amicus quoted, 267n; and Providence, 258–259n; *The Sovereignty and Goodness of God*, 259n

Rumsfeld, Donald, 221, 268n
Rusk, Dean, 229n
Rushdie, *Midnight's Children*, 165

Said, Edward W., xi–xii, 11, 15, 133, 269n; *Beginnings: Intention and Method*, 236n, 250n; "The Clash of Definitions," 254n; on contrapuntal reading, 99, 211–212, 241n, 251n; *Culture and Imperialism*, 51, 54, 91–92, 165–166; and exilic consciousness, 51, 165–166, 225; and filiation, 242–243n; *Humanism and Democratic Criticism*, 266n; *Orientalism*, 249n; and secular criticism, 211–212; and the textual attitude, 134–135, 175–176; "The Uses of Culture," 254n; and worldliness, 17, 20; *The World, The Text, and the Critic*, 243n
Sartre, Jean Paul, *The Flies*, 261n; *Nausea*, 36–37, 236n
Schroeder, John W., 260n
Selby, Nick, *Herman Melville: Moby-Dick*, 16–17, 232n
Shaftsbury, Lord, *Characteristics*, 175, 206
Shelley, Percy, "Ozymandias," 64
Seidel, Michael, *Satirical Inheritance: Rebelais to Sterne*, 264n
Simms, William Gilmore, 185; and imperialism, 249–250; *The Yemassee: A Romance of Carolina*, 249n
Slotkin, Richard, 9; *Fatal Environment: The Myth of the Frontier in the Age of Industrialization, 1800–1890*, 249–250n, 268n; *Regeneration through Violence*, 268n
Smith Adam, 31
Smith, Henry Nash, 9
Spanos, Adam, 253
Spanos, William, *American Exceptionalism in the Age of Globalization: The Specter of Vietnam*; 231n, 232n, 250n, 252n, 268n; *America's Shadow: An Anatomy of Empire*, 231n, 238n, 241n; "The Detective and the Boundary: Some Notes on the Postmodern Literary Imagination," 261n; The *End of Education: Toward Posthumanism*, 230n, 265n *The Errant Art of* Moby-Dick, 1, 5, 8–9, 20, 166, 170, 204, 234n, 239n, 254n, 259n, 265n; *Heidegger and Criticism: Retrieving the Cultural Politics of Destruction*, 237n

Sparks, Jared, 59, 70, 242
Spinoza, Benedictus, 42
Spivak, Gayatri, 59, 133; *Outside in the Teaching Machine*, 54, 240n; *The Postcolonial Subject*, 51, 53
Sterne, Laurence, *Life and Opinions of Tristram Shandy, Gentleman*, 76, 245n
Strehle, Susan, 247n
Suskind, Ron, 229n

Thoreau, Henry David, 185, 194, 196–294; *See also The Confidence-Man*
de Tocqueville, Alexis, 218, 247–248n
Tolstoy, Leo, "The Death of Ivan Ilych," 260
Trachtenberg, Alan, *The Incorporation of America: Society in the Gilded Age*, 245n, 255n
Trakl, Georg, 43–46, 50, 238n
Transcendentalists, 177, 197
Trilling, Lionel, 9
Trumbull, Henry, *Life and Remarkable Adventures of Israel R. Potter*, 58, 60, 66–67, 69, 94–95
Turner, Frederick Jackson, 20, 46, 218; "The Significance of the Frontier in American History," 232n
Twain, Mark, *A Connecticut Yankee in King Arthur's Court*, 132

Vietnam syndrome, 219–220
Vietnam War, 13, 133–138, 212, 223, 250n, 252–253n, 268n
Virgil, *The Aeneid*, 37
Vico, Giambattista, 15
Victor of St. Hugo, vii
Voltaire, *Candide*, 48, 76, 79, 94, 130, 134, 167, 184, 205, 209, 217, 219, 224, 260n, 262–263n, 265n

Wald, Priscilla, on *Pierre*, 239n, 240–241n

Weaver, Raymond, 8
Weber, Max, 27; *The Protestant Ethic and the Spirit of Capitalism*, and the Puritan ethic, 178–179, 246n; and capitalism, 77–78, 263n; the Puritan Calling (*Beruf*), 143–144, 255–256n
Webster, Daniel, his Bunker Hill Monument orations, 32, 60–67, 75, 77, 96–99, 185, 242n, 247n 243n, 254n; and capitalism, 62; and the jeremiad, 62–67, 91, 242–243; racism of, 243n; *Writings and Speeches*, 247n
Weinstock, Jeffrey, on Bartleby, 256n
Wiegman, Robyn, 9

William, Raymond, 25; on culture, 250n; on hegemony, 28–29, 77, 235n; *Marxism and Literature*, 234n
Williams, William Carlos, 210
Wilson, Ivy, xiii, 245n, 255n
Wilson, Woodrow, 219
Winthrop John, 62; and figural interpretation, 209; as Nehemiah, 151, 231n. *See also* America, Puritan tradition and figural interpretation
Wister, Owen, *The Virginian*, 132
Wolfowitz, Paul, 221, 268n
Wright, Richard, *The Outsider*, 164

Yeats, William Butler, "The Second Coming," 256n

www.ingramcontent.com/pod-product-compliance
Lightning Source LLC
Chambersburg PA
CBHW020640230426

43665CB00008B/250